Keith W Wade

22nd Apr

(date of publication)

# Control Self Assessment

# Control Self Assessment

## For risk management and other practical applications

Edited by Keith Wade and Andy Wynne

Bentley Jennison

JOHN WILEY & SONS, LTD
Chichester • New York • Weinheim • Brisbane • Singapore • Toronto

*National* 01243 779777
*International* (+44) 1243 779777
e-mail (for orders and customer service enquiries):
cs-books@wiley.co.uk
Visit our Home Page on http://www.wiley.co.uk
or http://www.wiley.com



*Other Wiley Editorial Offices*

John Wiley & Sons, Inc., 605 Third Avenue,
New York, NY 10158-0012, USA

WILEY-VCH Verlag GmbH, Pappelallee 3,
D-69469 Weinheim, Germany

Jacaranda Wiley Ltd, 33 Park Road, Milton,
Queensland 4064, Australia

John Wiley & Sons (Asia) Pte Ltd, 2 Clementi Loop #02-01,
Jin Xing Distripark, Singapore 129809

John Wiley & Sons (Canada) Ltd, 22 Worcester Road,
Rexdale, Ontario M9W 1L1, Canada

*British Library Cataloguing in Publication Data*

A catalogue record for this book is available from the British Library

ISBN 0-471-98619-4

Typeset in 10/12 Goudy by MHL Typesetting Limited
Project management by Macfarlane Production Services, Markyate
Printed and bound in Great Britain by Biddles Ltd, Guildford and King's Lynn.
This book is printed on acid-free paper responsibly manufactured from sustainable forestry in which at least two trees are planted for each one used for paper production.

# Contents

# Preface

There are many enthusiastic champions of CSA; many powerful speakers, persuasive consultants, convinced practitioners who exhort their colleagues to rise to the challenges faced by internal auditors, managers and their organisations through adopting a revolutionary substitute for 'traditional' audit methods. We have compiled this book neither to praise CSA, nor to bury it. Rather we aim to provide an objective consideration of the benefits and limitations of control self assessment, and 'warts and all' descriptions of the practical implementation of CSA in its various forms. We are not evangelists for CSA. We leave our readers to form their own judgements based on the experience of others and the issues we highlight.

Various labels have been attached to the process of management appraisal of control systems, control self assessment and control risk self assessment being the most common. Branding has been strong and claims made to proprietary rights to such terms and related acronyms. For ease of understanding, except where individual contributors employ their own nomenclature, the term 'Control Self Assessment' (CSA) is used in this book to refer to the idea and its application in its various guises.

Through the contributors to this book, we consider the general history of CSA, examine current practices in more than 20 organisations and ponder upon its future development. We explore the four phases organisations must go through in introducing the technique: adoption, implementation, sustainment and improvement. We also consider why some organisations have abandoned it.

Keith Wade
Andy Wynne

# Notes on Contributors

**Keith Wade**, MA, CPFA, FIIA, is Director and owner of CATS International, Chairman of CATS International (Asia), and Chief Executive of Internal Audit Worldwide. He also holds the post of Director of Audit Studies at Henley Management College. He founded CATS as Consultancy & Audit Training Services in 1986 as an independent company specialising in training in internal audit, business control and corporate governance. It is now recognised as one of the foremost international audit training consultancies. CATS International has five divisions. Through The Centre for Integrated Auditing, the research and public course division, CATS organises numerous public courses and seminars. The in-house training division provides tailored courses for a wide variety of organisations, large and small, in the public, private and voluntary sectors in the UK and abroad. Through its consultancy arm, CATS advises organisations and governments on the establishment and operation of a modern audit service and provides guidance on all aspects of audit work. The Academic and Professional Division works in many capacities with universities, business schools and professional bodies such as CIPFA and IIA. Activities outside the UK are organised through the International Division, which works with organisations such as Crown Agents, DFID and British Council, and co-ordinates its work with Internal Audit Worldwide, the newly established consortium of internal audit consultants initiated by CATS.

Keith is a qualified accountant and has over 20 years' experience in internal audit as practitioner, academic, professional adviser, lecturer, consultant and trainer, and has organised several top level conferences in addition to running courses on virtually every aspect of the subject.

His consultancy work includes advising organisations, internal audit units and State Audit Institutions on developing the function, analysing training needs, introducing standards, improving audit practices; and working with both auditors and managers to help establish appropriate frameworks of control.

Keith has been involved in control self assessment in many ways. He has presented many conference papers on the subject, frequently invited because of his independent stance and honest opinions. (Unlike other consultants, he has no 'own-brand' CSA to sell and is in a position to assess the relative merits of the various methodologies and products, and to comment on them 'warts and all'). He has devised his own training courses on the topic and associated matters such as risk assessment, workshop management and developing facilitation skills, and has organised many in-house events for clients, as well as advising individual organisations on the implementation of the techniques. In 1996 he presented the key-note address at five Controls Assurance workshops around the country by the NHS Executive. He has also lectured extensively on the subject overseas.

Keith can be contacted on telephone: 01732 (international code: +44-1732) 746010, 451223 or 452126; fax 01732 741482; email: train@catsint.co.uk; web: www.catsint.co.uk; or by writing to Pond House, 105 Chevening Road, Chipstead, Sevenoaks, Kent, UK TN13 2SA.

**Tim J. Leech**, FCA, MBA, CFE, is the co-founder and Managing Director of MCS Control Training and Design based in Mississauga, Ontario, Canada. Prior to setting up MCS, Tim was the Managing Director of the Canadian subsidiary of Network Security Management Ltd., part of the Hambros Bank group of companies headquartered in London, England. He also served as Director – Control and Risk Management Services with The Coopers and Lybrand Consulting Group in Toronto after a varied career with Gulf Canada in Toronto and Calgary. He holds a Master in Business Administration degree majored in human resources and accounting and is Fellow of the Ontario Institute of Chartered Accountants.

**Bruce McCuaig**, B.Comm, CA, joined MCS Control Training and Design in 1995. Prior to joining MCS Bruce held senior executive positions with Gulf Canada in Calgary and Toronto and Gulf Oil Corporation in Houston, Texas. While General Auditor of Gulf Canada Resources in 1987, Bruce, with the assistance of Tim Leech, conceived and implemented the original work team self-assessment concepts, including development of officer and board level presentations outlining the benefits of this new approach. He directed the first series of CSA pilots conducted during the summer of 1987 presented by Tim Leech and Paul Makosz.

**Phil Tarling** is the Head of Internal Audit at Burnett Swayne and a Director of the Institute of Internal Auditors, UK. He is a qualified fellow of the IIA and a Certified Fraud Examiner. Burnett Swayne's Internal Audit Division has a number of public-sector internal audit clients including the NHS local and central government as well as United Nations Agencies based outside the UK. Phil has also provided assistance on internal audit techniques to former Soviet bloc countries of Eastern Europe under a number of Phare projects.

Although CSA has had a major impetus in the NHS the participative organisation-wide internal audit techniques based upon a high degree of understanding of business risk, developed by Phil and employed for the NHS client base, has meant that to date none of these clients has sought to introduce CSA.

**Jeffrey Ridley** is an independent consultant and a Visiting Professor of Auditing at South Bank University, London. His auditing experience spans both the public and private sectors, in government, local government and the manufacturing industries. He was the manager of internal auditing at Kodak Limited, England and is a Past President of the Institute of Internal Auditors, UK. He is a Fellow of the Institute of Chartered Secretaries and Administrators, a Fellow of the Institute of Internal Auditors and a Certified Internal Auditor.

**John Rowson** has worked in a number of roles within the Guardian Royal Exchange Group. This included a long spell in internal audit which he left in 1992. As Manager, Special Projects in Guardian Financial Services, one of the projects for which he was responsible was to introduce CSA within the business. This he undertook both in Financial Services and the IT areas of the overall UK Division of the Group.

**Darryl Clark**, ACIS, MSc, MA, PIIA, CFE, is Director of Finance and IT with Folgate Insurance Company. He joined Folgate in 1996 from the Independent Order of Foresters – a Canadian Life Assurance organisation recognised as one of the world's pioneers in the CSA technique. As Head of Audit and Compliance he Anglicised the technique into the IOF's UK operations. His internal audit experience spans 15 years over a broad range of industries.

Between 1995–7 Darryl completed academic research into the technique, and in 1996 founded and still Chairs the UK CSA User Group. Despite his new role at Folgate he maintains a keen interest in internal audit and CSA by speaking at conferences (including the 1997 European CSA Summit), and as an occasional lecturer at Kingston University teaching internal audit and risk management to post-graduate students.

**Martin Reinecke**, M.Comm, CA(SA), currently practices as an independent business risk management and control consultant in South Africa. He was previously a senior manager in the Corporate Governance Services Division of Deloitte and Touch where his main responsibility was the national co-ordination of Enterprise Risk Management services. This included risk management and control self-assessment methodologies, tools and techniques and control consulting services.

Martin received his control self-assessment and risk management training with Deloitte and Touche in the USA. He has facilitated various projects to design, implement, assess or effectively apply control frameworks and control self-assessment at clients such as Standard Bank of South Africa, Eskom and the Namibia Development Corporation. These projects also included training on topics such as internal control, control self-assessment and risk management. He recently sommences a project to lead the implementation of control self-assessment at the African Development Bank in Abidjan, Côte d'Ivoire.

**Dave Gammon** is an independent consultant. He was formerly a Senior Manager with Ernst and Young's Business Risk Consulting practice. He works with a wide range of private and public sector organisations designing and delivering risk management strategies.

He has ten years of Internal Auditing experience in the Consumer Products and Retail sectors. During this time he was involved in the design and implementation of control and risk self assessment strategies in two FTSE100 companies. Dave is a Fellow of the Institute of Internal Auditors and regularly address risk management and control assessment conferences in the UK and abroad.

**Gus Cottell** is a member of the Institute of Internal Auditors and is a Certified Information Systems Auditor. He also holds an MBA from Bristol Business School.

Gus commenced his career with Bath City Council and spent a number of years in the Council's internal audit section. He then moved to the Research Councils' Internal Audit Service where he was introduced to a unique form of control self assessment implemented in one of the Research Councils. Confident of the value it could provide he soon became a CSA convert. He was subsequently a pioneer in its use throughout the other Research Councils.

Gus has since moved on from the Research Councils and is currently a manager with the Information Risk Management (IRM) practice of KPMG in Bristol.

**Glyn Rodgers** was a senior manager with Price Waterhouse Internal Audit Services. He joined Price Waterhouse in 1994 after 14 years of internal audit experience including the role of internal audit manager with Rowntree PLC and then Nestlé SA.

Glyn has co-authored the internal audit methodology that Price Waterhouse adopted worldwide and he is heavily involved in the development of software to support the methodology. He has been involved with a number of key international internal audit clients both as the manager of outsourced internal audit services and as a consultant to the in-house team.

Glyn is a member of the Chartered Institute of Management Accountants, the British Computer Society and the Institute of Internal Auditors, UK.

**Arnie Skelton** is Managing Director at Effective Training and Development Ltd. Arnie took his first degree (MA) at Cambridge University and later gained an MSc in Management Sciences at Birmingham University. He worked for Cheshire County Council as a Policy Planner before joining Manchester Metropolitan University as a Senior Lecturer in Public Sector Management.

In 1990 Arnie left the University to form his own training and development company. For the last ten years he has designed and delivered a wide range of courses for public- and private-sector clients throughout the UK.

**David Nowell-Withers** is a Chartered Accountant and qualified IIA member who has more than fifteen years experience of developing internal audit functions in large international companies such as Merck & Co. Inc., The Wellcome Foundation Ltd and Securicor plc. He has an IOD Diploma in Company Direction and is currently a member of the ICAEW Audit Faculty Internal Audit Committee.

**Jane Shipway**, is an Executive Auditor at British Telecommunications plc. She joined BT some 20 years ago after a short period working for a high street banking institution. Her career in BT has been very varied and has included working in the debt recovery group where she spent many hours knocking on doors trying to obtain money against unpaid telephone debts. She has held several training and development roles and when the company embarked on the TQM journey she was fortunate enough to undergo eight weeks intensive facilitator training. More recently her work with the Internal Audit Department, reporting directly to the Group Chief Internal Auditor, has allowed her to explore and develop new audit techniques – CSA being the most innovative.

**Raj K. Pradhan**, FCA, PIIA, currently heads up the internal audit department of the BOC Group plc. His previous experience includes some four years as General Auditor and Corporate Officer of Burroughs Corporation (now Unisys), some eight years with Price Waterhouse and five years with Litton Industries Inc.

Raj has been with BOC since 1985 when he started as Audit Manager for the UK and Europe and progressed to his current position which he has held for the past five years. The Internal Audit Department is a global function with Offices in Windlesham, UK and Murray Hill, New Jersey, USA. The Department holds a global accreditation for BS EN ISO 9001: 1994.

**Duncan Stephenson** is a senior manager in the Business Risk Consulting and Assurance division of Arthur Andersen. Duncan transferred to Arthur Andersen when the internal audit department of ASDA Group plc was outsourced. He had worked for ASDA for nearly ten years prior to transferring.

Duncan's career as a chartered accountant started with Coopers & Lybrand in Leeds where he qualified. During his time at Coopers & Lybrand he specialised in insolvency and in computer audit. He later moved to Touche Ross in Spain, and from there to an internal audit position with Bass plc. He spent a year in the internal audit department of SG Warburg prior to moving to ASDA.

Duncan's specialisms are internal audit and CSA as drivers of improvement in operations and ownership of risk and control. Applied psychology and effective communication are crucial to the success of CSA and these are Duncan's particular spheres of interest.

**Vicky Kubitscheck**, BSc, MIIA, FIIA, has over 13 years experience in the auditing profession in the financial services industry. Since December 1996, she is the Chairperson of the Insurance Internal Audit Group (IIAG) in the UK, a dedicated group for heads of audit, that consists of some 100 companies in the financial services industry. Vicky is also a Committee Member of the IIA Scottish District Society, having served on other IIA District Society Committees in the past.

Over the last 5 years, she has devoted much of her time developing techniques that raise the profile of internal audit and management's awareness of controls and corporate governance. She has spoken at conferences and seminars on these matters. Developing and implementing CSA techniques coincide with the initiatives she advocates as part of promoting the audit profession.

Vicky is currently the Group Chief Internal Auditor at AEGON UK, which is part of the international AEGON group and is the holding company of the Scottish Equitable group of companies. Since joining AEGON UK in December 1997, Vicky was given yet another opportunity to develop and adapt her approach to CSA in an increasingly competitive business environment. Her first formal opportunity to develop CSA was when she was Head of Internal Audit at AXA Equity & Law, where interest at an international group level was encouraging as well as enriching.

**Mike Haselip** was in the Civil Service from 1958 until his retirement in 1998. He served in the Admiralty, Foreign Office, Department of Trade and Industry, Department of Transport and Department of the Environment (DOE). He was Head of Internal Audit for DOE from 1988 to 1997 and subsequently became Head of Internal Audit for the newly created Department of the Environment, Transport and the Regions (DETR). He was responsible for advising the Department's Chief Executive (Accounting Officer) on internal control in DETR including its sponsorship of a range of Agencies, Non-Departmental Public Bodies (NDPBs) and Nationalised Industries (e.g. Highways Agency, Health and Safety Executive, Environment Agency, Drivers and Vehicles Licensing Agency, etc.).

Mike's extensive experience prior to joining internal audit and his spell as an organisational analyst convinced him that internal audit was too focused on systems and procedures and not enough on people and their cultural environment.

**Neil Cowan** is Director of Control and Audit Projects and Director General of the European Confederation of Institutes of Internal Auditing (ECIIA). Neil has had ten years' line management experience in the international car rental industry followed by five years' financial experience in the retail sector. He then spent eighteen years in local government.

He has spoken at numerous conferences and seminars on subjects as diverse as public-sector competitive tendering, marketing services, control and risk assessment and corporate governance. He is the author of *Business Control, Accountability and Corporate Governance* (Stanley Thorne Publishers) and is a contributor to *The Corporate Governance Handbook* (Gee and Co).

Neil is a Chartered Secretary and a qualified internal auditor. He is a Past President of the Institute of Internal Auditors, UK and is Vice President of the European Confederation of Institutes of Internal Auditing.

As Assistant Director of Finance (Operational Review), with Fife Regional Council, Neil Cowan was a key member of the management team of a department of some three hundred employees and directly controlled a Division of over twenty audit and IT professionals. The Council itself employed upwards of fourteen thousand (full-time equivalent) employees, had a revenue spend of £400 million and capital expenditure of £25 million annually. On the run up to a unitary authority coming into being in Fife, Neil Cowan was appointed interim treasurer of the new authority and held this post until reorganisation in April 1995.

**David King** has worked for 31 years in local government, almost 23 at chief internal auditor level. He works for Ashford Borough Council in Kent where, following 16 years as the authority's Chief Internal Auditor he was promoted in 1996 to Assistant Director of Finance (Audit and Revenues).

In the same year David completed his MBA. His dissertation addressed the subject of control self assessment and his research endeavoured to establish to what extent the technique could improve the management of his local authority's business objectives, risk and controls and therefore contribute significantly to its governance.

Following his research work, David has addressed both the 1997 CIPFA Audit Conference in Cardiff and the Scottish Audit Conference in Glasgow on the subject of control self assessment, given many presentations to audit groups and local authorities and has conducted a series of pilot schemes at Ashford to gain first-hand experience of the technique.

**Mike Dudding** is a freelance consultant with Cornwell Associates. Mike began his career with the Greater London Council where he trained as an accountant. He moved to Kent County Council as Assistant County Treasurer (Audit) where he developed a risk assessment-based approach to audit and established the Authority's value for money process. Mike then moved on to a more senior role in the Finance Department. Here he was responsible for designing and leading the major remodelling and devolution of the finance function.

Mike subsequently took on the role of Head of Corporate Review to support the Chief Executive in the development and Kent's performance review process. In this latter role he helped to develop the risk management approach described in this chapter.

After nearly 30 years in local government Mike became a freelance consultant in 1998. He is also a member of CIPFA's Education and Training Committee and a CIPFA nominated member of the AAT Council.

**Tim Crowley** is Chief Internal Auditor at Mersey Internal Audit Agency. His NHS career commenced in 1981 as a Regional Finance Trainee. After gaining senior audit management experience at a number of south east health authorities Tim was appointed to head up MIAA in 1990. MIAA has a client base of 26 NHS organisations encompassing North Wales, Cheshire, Lancashire and Merseyside. MIAA were the first public-sector team to acquire ISO 9000 (1992), were awarded Investors in People status in 1994, and were the winners of the North West Quality Award in 1995.

In 1994 Tim was seconded to work with the NHS Executive on the Internal Audit Development Initiative and continues to be involved in providing professional advice on internal audit and assurance issues. He is a member of CIPFA's Audit Panel, the HFMA Audit and Corporate Governance Committee and the NHS Executive's Corporate Governance Group. He also is chairman of CIPFA's Anti Fraud and Corruption Panel.

**Caroline Greenwood** is Head of Group Audit and Risk Management at Anglia Housing Group. Caroline came to internal audit in the mid-1980s via the Civil Service and building societies. This experience in the 'real' world of operational management has been a key element in her achievements as an auditor.

As an auditor within a financial services group it became apparent that common control weaknesses existed across different functions. Consequently she designed and presented 'control awareness' sessions for inclusion in standard in-house management courses. This approach grew into requirements for managers to perform self assessment as part of audit reviews.

When CSA became a recognised management function she was working as a freelance auditor in the public sector. She developed a workshop approach designed to prepare managers and their teams for self assessment and trained audit colleagues in presentation of the material. This workshop approach has been the basis of the move towards risk management education and self assessment within the Anglia Group. It has been consolidated in the action to be taken to fulfil the Housing Corporation's requirement for formal risk mapping by registered social landlords.

**Steven Barlow** is Director of Contract Audit Services at Arthur Andersen. He is involved in a wide range of internal audit and business risk management consultancy projects utilising leading-edge techniques. His clients include IMS Health, Ministry of Defence, British Standards Institution, Adecco Alfred Marks, Tektronix, Worldspan and ITT Industries.

Prior to joining Arthur Andersen, Steven had extensive internal audit experience as head of internal audit at the Department of Energy and with the Pearson Group (the £2 billion turnover media group) where he established the internal audit function. He was also the Operations Director responsible for IT and systems, distribution and customer service, and property and facilities management of a significant operating company in the Pearson Group. In addition he set up and ran a corporate finance and venture capital function at the Royal Trust Bank where he was an investment banking director.

Steven qualified as a Chartered Accountant with Coopers & Lybrand.

**Andy Wynne**, BSc, PGCE, FCCA, moved into public finance at a small district council after teaching for several years in England and Sudan.

His internal audit career started at Leicester City Council where he obtained a sound introduction to systems auditing. Andy then obtained a second tier post in an NHS internal audit consortium in London. He was responsible for staff management with an emphasis on computer audit and value for money work.

Now with Bentley Jennison, Andy is the firm's National Technical Manager and is responsible for co-ordinating the development and adherence to the firm's internal audit standards. He has recently rewritten the firm's internal audit manual. He is also the Senior Manager at the Nottingham office which undertakes a wide range of client-based work including appointments at district councils, NHS trusts, housing associations, further education colleges, a university and an NDPB.

Andy is a member of the ACCA's Auditing Committee and the ACCA's representative on the Auditing Practices Board's working party on internal audit. He initiated the formation of the ACCA's Internal Audit Sub-committee. His book reviews and articles are regularly published in the professional press. He has been a member of two CIPFA Audit Panel projects. The first was a guide to internal audit for chief executives and committee members of small public-sector organisations. The second was a guide to internal audit's role in risk management. Andy is also Chair of the editorial board of CIPFA's volume on internal audit in their Financial Information Series.

Andy regularly undertakes internal audit training. He is an associate lecturer with the City Business School on their MSc internal audit course. He recently led workshops at the National Housing Federation's Finance Conference and at the CIPFA Audit Conference. Andy is currently researching the scope and objectives of internal audit in African central government departments.

Andy can be contacted on telephone: 0116 (international code +44-116) 2858794; email at: andy.wynne@btinternet.com; or by writing to: 8 Vincent Close, Leicester, UK, LE3 6ED.

# Part 1

## The Development of CSA

# 1

# The Rise and Rise of Control Self Assessment

*Keith Wade*

## INTRODUCTION

This opening chapter provides a summary of the nature and development of control self assessment (CSA). Specifically it examines:

- the claims made for CSA
- the issue of who 'owns' the process
- its history
- the broader concept of 'control self management and assessment'
- the current state of the art.

It goes on to explain in detail the main reasons for its introduction:

- as a new audit tool
- to satisfy corporate governance and regulatory requirements
- as a management tool and duty.

The chapter describes the six main approaches to CSA and concludes by considering:

- the implications for internal audit
- factors to take into account when implementing CSA
- practical matters arising.

Readers who want an immediate account of the introduction of CSA in practice should turn to Part 2.

## SO WHAT'S NEW

Like it or not, CSA – in one form or another – is here to stay. No matter how much you may be irritated by the hype, envious of CSA consultants' earnings, or despairing of the unthinking acceptance of claims that this is something original and life-saving, the momentum is so strong, its broad acceptance so widespread, and the reasons for its adoption in some cases so compelling that no internal auditor, line manager, senior executive, audit committee member or company director can afford to ignore its merits and impact.

When it burst on the international scene in its present form some seven or so years ago, many were sceptical. 'It's a JAF (Just Another Fad)', was the cry, 'a successor to TQM, BPR, VFM and the like – a novelty dreamt up by consultants and academics with a short life-span and hidden limitations'.

Certainly some of the claims and sales methods ('If CSA is not adopted, internal audit will not survive') warranted some scepticism. Some auditors believed, bought and benefitted – CSA was a route to salvation and success, But initially, many internal auditors feared the opposite – that implementation of CSA would be professional suicide. 'Allow managers to assess their own controls? The very idea! And where would that leave us?'

Some of us, looking in from the outside, could see the reasons for its advocation and acknowledged its potential value. But equally at times it appeared to be a solution in search of a problem; a re-cycled but sophisticated re-packaging of old ideas and previously tried practices. The pictures painted were too black and white, too stark. Dogmatically, it was asserted that CSA would replace traditional audit work; we would be wrong in continuing to use 'out-moded' audit methods. Many of the arguments put forward in support of CSA still tell me more about the nature and faults of the advocates' understanding and previous practice of internal audit, than the inherent advantages of control self assessment.

Inevitably, the compilation which follows, based in the main on practitioners' experience of the technique, stresses the benefits and successes. But it is vital not just to trot behind the pack. Like any other important decision, a business case must be made. The blind must not follow the bland.

It does depend where you (as an audit function or organisation) are coming from and going to. For an under-developed internal audit unit, the apparently radical and revolutionary step of introducing CSA could mean that the intervening stages of evolution are bypassed – with all the consequences, beneficial or otherwise. If your audit staff are in a rut or ineffective, if all other methods of getting managers to discharge their control responsibilities have failed, or if your directors are obliged to report publicly on the organisation's controls and audit cannot cope on its own, then CSA may well be the answer.

So – CSA may be regarded as a threat or an opportunity; a consultant's meal-ticket or the perfect answer to corporate-governance requirements, audit success and management control. For some it represents a key element of the control framework, management philosophy and corporate culture. For others it is merely another audit tool, for use as time and circumstances warrant. As the examples in this book show, its introduction has transformed some audit units; managers regard auditors as useful at last and partnerships are forged which result in the open discussion of risks and joint development of solutions. Other auditors worry about losing their independence (and perhaps ultimately their job). Deep down they do not trust managers and rationalise this by asserting that managers do not possess the objectivity, time, skills or knowledge to examine their own arrangements. And how can a four-hour session by amateurs produce the same results as an in-depth, thorough, professional and independent examination by properly trained specialist staff? For those in a competitive audit environment (such as the UK National Health Service and the commercial firms selling internal audit services) who believe in its merits or are at least prepared to try it, the crucial question is 'will our clients buy?'.

As virtually all our contributors stress, introducing and operating CSA consumes an unexpected amount of time and the effort involved must not be underestimated. A handful of large organisations have been able to experiment with CSA but few enterprises can afford that luxury – especially if the experiment fails. Organisations need to move into CSA with their eyes wide open. Is it right for us in principle? And are we capable of introducing it successfully in practice?

## 'OWNERSHIP' OF CONTROL SELF ASSESSMENT

In plain English, who is responsible for initiating, driving, running, managing, monitoring and evaluating CSA? Up till now, I would guess that in 99 per cent of cases it was internal auditors who first heard of and subsequently sought to introduce (and then manage) CSA programmes. They may have come across it in attending conferences, reading professional magazines or talking to colleagues. World-wide, there can be only a handful of internal auditors in the most remote corners of the world who have not come across the idea and considered its application. Many, of course, have been introduced to the concept and its 'advantages' through contact with consultants and professional firms providing internal and external audit and related services.

But internal audit must not own CSA. It is a management tool and a manager's responsibility. If involved in its introduction and operation, internal auditors must plan for their disengagement and the smooth transfer of responsibility (for more details on CSA stakeholders see Chapter 5).

## THE NATURE AND DEVELOPMENT OF CSA

There are as many definitions of CSA as there are approaches to it, and many are contained in this book. Some equate it with programmes designed to identify, assess and control risks, and define it in management terms. Others are 'audit-centric'. BT, for example, use CSA as 'an innovative approach to internal auditing which enlists the support of all people in the business both to review existing controls for effectiveness and in implementing improvements' – see Chapter 13. Very crudely it is self-audit. From an internal-audit perspective, it can be seen as teaching managers and their staff how to perform systems-based audits without the normal time, experience, training or skills. See Appendix 1.1 on page 30 for other definitions.

The Institute of Internal Auditors – UK claim that 'a CSA programme is a process which allows individual line managers and staff to participate in reviewing existing controls for adequacy, and recommending, agreeing and implementing improvements to existing controls.'[1] But the world does not revolve around internal audit. Rather, the other way round. We must not be condescending, allowing others to join in our ball-game but in accordance with our rules and reserving the right to take our ball home when we choose to. We, as internal auditors, are the privileged interlopers, despite our authority and independence. Managers have knowledge, rights and power. They 'own' control and the management of control including, where appropriate, CSA and its operation.

My own (1993) definition of CSA, adopted I note by CIPFA, is:

> A formalised, documented and committed approach to the regular, fundamental and open review by managers and staff of the strength of control systems designed and operated to achieve business objectives and guard against risks within their sphere of influence.

Within CSA, there are three underpinning concepts and practices, which are by no means new in themselves, but might be novel to some in combination.

1. *Systems thinking*: this focuses the mind on business processes, objectives, risk, environment and control.
2. *Control evaluation*: the systematic appraisal of the adequacy, application and effectiveness of the management control framework and systems designed to achieve business objectives, contain risks, exploit opportunities, make best use of resources, and cope with the business environment. Including 'soft' as well as 'hard' controls.
3. *Group involvement*: the use of facilitated teams to address issues and solve problems within their remit in a frank, but where necessary protected, manner by use of techniques such as brainstorming, business-process analysis, and local knowledge.

The use of workshops, more often than not with audit involvement, is only one approach to CSA, but it tends to be the method most frequently discussed if not necessarily adopted. Indeed, the IIA Research Foundation publication *Control Self Assessment: Experience, Current Thinking and Best Practices*[2] discusses only this technique.

Many of the characteristics of the various approaches are similar to other

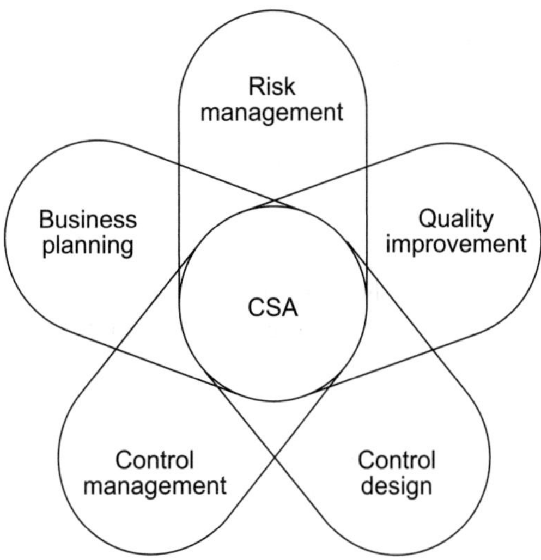


**Figure 1.1** Integration of CSA with other business processes.

management techniques in the field of quality management, business process re-engineering, management by objectives, and the like.

CSA is also directly related to, and where necessary should be integrated with, other organisational processes such as business planning, risk management, quality improvement, control management, and control design (often using standard control models such as COSO[3]) – see Figure 1.1.

In most organisations, managers are beset with change, and are suffering from initiative overload. CSA must be needed, seen to be necessary, sold – not imposed, appropriate to the culture, and developed within existing mechanisms and projects. It must not be – or appear to be – yet another fad.

## CONTROL SELF MANAGEMENT

It is a truism to say that managers are responsible for control. Most would acknowledge that control is inextricably linked with planning and setting goals, and that a control is any action taken by a manager to increase the chance of meeting objectives, achieving set standards of performance and guarding against risk. So why do we have to keep repeating this? Once controls have been put in place, it is only common sense periodically to make sure they are still adequate, appropriate and effective. Controls are never perfect, people are human and circumstances change.

Review and appraisal mechanisms should be part of any control system, and monitoring (including the periodic re-appraisal of controls) is a key element of the COSO framework. But the assessment of controls by managers needs to be set in the broader context of the management of the whole of the control process, i.e., Control Self Management and Assessment (CSMA). This recognises the broader control duties of managers and uses as a framework the life cycle of control development, implementation and review.

My own standard, bi-partite approach to business process analysis, separating strategic matters from operational practices, can be used to describe the control management cycle in broad terms:

1. *Overall arrangements*: establishing the control environment, including the corporate commitment to control, attitudes, responsibilities, standards, systems and structures.
2. *The control process*:
    - determination and specification of the need for control; overall, in particular operations and for specific issues (including an assessment of risk)
    - design of an appropriate control framework, systems and mechanisms
    - establishment of the control procedures
    - operation of controls on a day-to-day basis
    - maintaining control; to ensure continuing appropriateness and adequacy, proper application in practice, and effectiveness in achieving its purpose
    - reviewing the control system; periodic management appraisal (CSA) complemented by independent assurance and professional assistance
    - re-designing controls; to strengthen or otherwise modify where necessary
    - demonstrating control; internal and, where required, external reporting, with validation where necessary.

See Appendix 1.2 on page 31 for details.

## THE STATE OF THE ART

This book does not pretend to provide a definitive guide to the current position or best practice world-wide. It serves to provide a broad range of examples of the practical application of CSA, primarily in the UK. It assumes that by now most readers are broadly familiar with the concept and are seeking guidance on its practical implementation.

Broadly there are 12 phases of maturity in understanding and, where relevant, applying CSA.

1. Never heard of it (there can now be few such innocent souls).
2. Vague idea (awareness that it's a 'hot' topic and used by some auditors).
3. Greater understanding (through discussions with others, attending conferences, etc.).
4. Enlightenment (perhaps with a hint of cynicism!).
5. Purposeful research (the desire to find out more; asking and shopping around).
6. Experimentation (if this can be afforded).
7. Decision (making the business case; acceptance, rejection or dithering, given other events and priorities).
8. Introduction (often phased, in carefully selected areas and with further pilot studies).
9. Adaptation and extension (up, down, across the organisation; addressing a broader range of issues and operations; learning lessons).
10. Refinement and consolidation (improving, tailoring).
11. Assured use (greater confidence and sophistication in implementation; all responsibilities properly assigned, and management and audit arrangements in place; teaching others, becoming a consultant).
12. And then ...? (Why have some, apparently successful users, abandoned it? Why do we rarely hear of the failures ...?).

So ... just like any project. And many of the problems are caused by poor project management, rather than any innate flaws in CSA.

## REASONS FOR ITS INTRODUCTION

There are numerous reasons why CSA is being considered and introduced, but the driving forces (and related perceptions of the nature of the techniques) can be grouped into three categories, which will be briefly examined in turn.

1. As a new audit tool.
2. To satisfy corporate governance and regulatory requirements.
3. As a management tool and a means to reinforce managers' control responsibilities.

## A NEW AUDIT TOOL

> 'Control self assessment represents a quantum leap forward in the internal auditing process.'
>
> Arthur Andersen, for IIA Research Foundation

> 'Rubbish – unless internal audit has been in the dark ages for the past 25 years.'
>
> Keith Wade, for auditors everywhere

Internal audit reactions to CSA have been mixed. At a professional level, the IIA-UK responded strongly in its Professional Briefing Note to the perceived threat to internal audit, arguing that CSA should not be seen 'superficially as an attractive cost savings exercise' and a replacement for the internal audit function. Whilst admitting to the possible benefits, and giving guidance on setting up and running a CSA programme, the Institute frets about the validity of some of the claims made, the benefits from a truly independent assessment by internal audit which may be lost if CSA is used as a substitute, and the dangers of audit objectivity being compromised through too close an involvement, for example as project managers or workshop facilitators.

Nevertheless the UK Institute has a CSA Users Group under its auspices and in the USA IIA Inc established in January 1997 a Control Self-Assessment Centre 'to offer guidance, training and communication opportunities to individuals engaged in the practice of Control Self Assessment'. Enthusing about the technique, the IIA grandly claim that

> CSA is a powerful tool of corporate governance that can be used by internal audit, management, and other functions to examine and assess business process and control effectiveness within the organisation. CSA helps auditors evaluate informal or subjective controls that could not be reviewed in the past in areas such as ethics, management philosophy, and human resource practices. By encouraging employee involvement, CSA solicits open communication, teamwork, and continuous improvement. CSA assures the Board of Directors and senior management that the organisation is meeting its objectives.

The IIA CSA Centre will provide its participants with

- a forum for sharing new information, innovative techniques and successful practices
- The *CSA Sentinel*, an exclusive tri-annual newsletter
  - Professional guidance on CSA implementation
  - A series of CSA conferences, seminars and workshops, and upon satisfactory completion, a CSA Qualification.

> The CSA Centre aims also to foster development of the body of knowledge surrounding implementation of control models (COSO, CoCo, Cadbury, and others) that use control self-assessment workshops and techniques.

At the practitioner level, some auditors regard CSA as of no or marginal interest. For others it represents a fundamental change in approach. Within organisations, there are many apparent benefits to audit in introducing CSA: it could be used:

- where audit resources are stretched, to ensure a broader 'audit' coverage of the organisation's operations
- to help extend audit scope into operational matters, significant business risks, strategic operations and 'soft' issues such as ethical conduct, informal controls and human behaviour
- to demonstrate the value audit can add by working with managers to improve their controls, at the same time enhancing audit's image, relevance and contribution
- to focus audit work on high-priority issues
- to ensure audit keeps in touch with operations at 'grass-roots' level and the day-to-day concerns of staff, adding balance and understanding to the audit process
- to boost audit morale and inject new life into a flagging section
- to help discharge any audit responsibilities to provide an annual assurance on the state of control.

Many organisations, such as the UK Inland Revenue internal audit service (see Appendix E), latched on to CSA as a means of improving audit productivity – covering more ground with the same or even fewer resources. In the well-documented case of MAPCO Inc, it is claimed that the audit cycle time was reduced from five to three years without an increase in staff.

One UK government department introduced CSA on a selective basis for both audit and managerial reasons:

- as an alternative way of confronting resource and other obstacles to the implementation of audit action points, and
- to provide increased risk awareness across the organisation. As delegated powers were extended through the department, there was a greater shift to making managers more accountable for the resources they consumed, the systems they were responsible for, and the results achieved. Consequently there was a pressing need for line managers and operational staff to be more acutely aware of the risks to the business.

Others have linked CSA to related developments. Several audit functions, for example, use it as a means of responding efficiently to the COSO requirement to examine the full range of control elements and issues. But there may be other, more appropriate solutions to the audit problems and challenges implied above.

Less objectively, CSA may be introduced because audit might be seen to be out of date and out of touch if it is not doing it. Or, as some powerful 'gurus' claim, CSA is the answer because traditional audit methods have failed: they are inefficient, ineffective, inappropriate and add little corporate or local value. Not only this, but times have changed and external expectations demand reform. Sweeping changes in business, an 'empowerment' culture and a dynamic environment require a more participative, 'hands-on', user-friendly audit approach and the transfer of responsibilities and techniques.

Some of this is no doubt true. But let us not ignore the options nor the interests and background of the advocates. Internal audit must indeed 'add value' (whatever that awful buzz-phrase means) and keep up with the times. But CSA is just one option for change. And if adopted, it can be used in many ways:

- to replace internal audit, in whole or in part
- to complement and supplement, but not supplant
- to cover activities and issues which otherwise would not have been subject to audit
- as part of a 'conventional' audit; as a preceding phase, an extension of planning, an alternative means of control evaluation, or a 'bolt-on' addition.

Its application may be selective or comprehensive; it may be used to revolutionise or merely refine and extend the audit methodology. Let us be wary of generalisation and exaggeration, of inappropriate use in the wrong circumstances and culture. As in all purchasing decisions, *caveat emptor*.

To be fair, some of the early proponents of CSA recognise that their early claims were overstated. For example, Bruce McCuaig of MCS Control Training and Design Inc. in Ontario (and formerly of Gulf Canada, acknowledged as the birthplace of modern approaches to CSA) writes in the June 1998 edition of *Internal Auditor*:

> Many of us who pioneered the control self-assessment (CSA) concept in the later 1980s and early '90s, myself included, held the view that control self-assessment would one day completely replace the traditional audit as the primary assurance tool in the auditor's tool kit. We were wrong.
>
> Nonetheless, control and risk self-assessment has become a highly effective assurance tool with a diverse range of applications extending far beyond what we ever imagined when a co-author and I wrote 'Ripe for a Renaissance', an *Internal Auditor* article published in December 1990. In describing CSA

> approaches we had developed at Gulf Canada, we suggested that the process could be narrowly defined and that one basic CSA process would fit all the assurance requirements of any organisation. We believed that if the choice had to be made between traditional direct report audits and CSA, then CSA would win hands down every time. We vastly underestimated the strategies that would emerge and where each would work.

There is a risk that CSA is over-sold and its adoption is inappropriate or unnecessary. But let us also re-examine the essential role of internal audit and recognise the flaws, limitations and needs of some audit functions.

Conceptually, the essential role of internal audit has not changed in 25 years. Nor does it need to. Internal audit is the independent appraisal of the adequacy, application and effectiveness of management systems of internal control designed and operated to promote the achievement of business objectives and required standards of performance. This is – and always will be – internal audit's core business.

> The overall aim is to help strengthen the framework of control by whatever means are appropriate. The challenge is to promote effective control for an acceptable cost. Internal audit's task is to provide both independent assurance and practical assistance whilst reconciling the two.

So audit is no longer simply a matter of performing audits. The use of CSA may indeed be an appropriate means of strengthening control and helping managers to discharge their control and risk management responsibilities.

In some of its forms, CSA is little more than an extension or refinement of conventional systems-based audits. At a recent NHS controls assurance seminar, one consultant from a well-known firm was privately embarrassed to admit as much. That's fine, as long as we do not pretend. If it achieves its purpose and we all benefit and are satisfied with the results, so be it. But it has to be admitted that for far too many auditors the concepts of business systems, objectives and risks are new. If not new, for some the application of systems (or 'business process') audit methods is not advanced, or is confined to financial, administrative or low-level activities.

A stated aim of the NHS Executive's Controls Assurance project (incorporating the introduction of CSA in a series of pilots), was (yet again) to encourage internal auditors in health trusts and authorities to stick their heads over the parapet separating financial systems from the real business of hospitals, and work with managers and clinical staff in examining operational issues. Some success can be claimed, but is it solely due to CSA? Perhaps it is the maturer audit functions which see limited use for the technique.

The presumptions that underpin many CSA approaches are the principles which underpin the most sophisticated forms of systems audit:

- that modern internal audit is less a verification and policing function than a catalyst promoting the formal allocation and effective discharge of managerial responsibilities
- that the role of the internal auditor is to negotiate with management in order to agree a level of residual risk that is as acceptable as it can be to all interested parties
- that 'auditees' are 'clients' who should be encouraged to use their experience and local knowledge to participate in the audit process, speak freely about the issues and problems that concern them, and put forward ideas for improvement
- that audit needs to be set in the context of ambivalent attitudes to empowerment and self-regulation of all kinds: on the one hand senior management depend on decentralised units and need to place trust in the integrity, competence and knowledge of local management and staff; on the other hand, a reluctance to lose power, and the risk of error, neglect or even malpractice engender distrust.

## CSA AS A RESPONSE TO GOVERNANCE AND REGULATORY REQUIREMENTS

Undoubtedly in many countries a major driving force behind the introduction of CSA has been regulatory pressure on organisations, particularly the requirement to report publicly on controls. Back in 1977 in the USA, the Foreign Corrupt Practices Act was the precursor to further legislation (such as the Federal Deposit Insurance Corporation Improvement Act of 1991) demanding that organisations provide assurance to third parties on the state of their controls.

Just as the United States had its Lockheed scandals and Savings and Loans disaster, so the UK had Maxwell, Polly Peck, BCCI, Barings, and the like, with the saga continuing with tales of 'fat cat' directors, pensions mis-selling, more rogue traders, 'black-holes' in the accounts and other causes of regulatory, public and government concern. Section 4.5 of the 1992 Code of Best Practice of the Cadbury Report[4] recommended that directors should report on the effectiveness of internal control. This was watered down in the subsequent Rutteman Report (*Internal Control and Financial Reporting*[5]) which stated that, unless directors chose otherwise, the reporting requirement could be limited to confirming that the directors (or a board committee) have *reviewed* the effectiveness of the system of internal *financial* control. The guidance became standard for accounting periods beginning on or after 1 January 1995.

In November 1995 the Hampel Committee was established. The Committee's recommendations were incorporated into The Combined Code[6] that consolidates all corporate governance requirements for companies listed on the London Stock Exchange.

The relevant Section of the Combined Code states that:

> D2 Internal Control Principle
> The board should maintain a sound system of internal control to safeguard shareholders' investment and the company's assets.
>
> Code Provisions
>
> D.2.1 The directors should, at least annually, conduct a review of the effectiveness of the group's system of internal controls and should report to shareholders that they have done so. The review should cover all controls, including financial, operational and compliance controls and risk management.
>
> D.2.2 Companies that do not have an internal audit function should from time to time review the need for one.

Hampel and the Combined Code therefore modify Cadbury and Rutteman in that they recommend that directors should review the effectiveness of the internal control system, i.e.

1. They should not be required to report on the effectiveness of the control system.
2. The reporting requirements should cover the whole system of control, not just internal financial control.
3. Auditors should report privately to directors on the controls.

The guidance contained in the Code became standard from 1 January 1999. A committee chaired by Nigel Turnbull (Director of Finance at Rank plc) has been established to develop a framework for effective internal control. The committee is expected to report in June 1999.

In the regulated sectors in the UK, especially financial services, there are increasing requirements on directors to disclose their control arrangements, and for external auditors to report on those arrangements to the regulators.

Many parts of the public sector have adopted the Cadbury and other principles of corporate governance, as a reflection of good practice, to improve standards of public accountability, in reaction to the occasional public scandal and as a response to the various reports such as those of the Nolan Committee[7] (see Appendix 4.4).

From where might directors, audit committee members and senior managers obtain their information and gain their assurance about the adequacy and effectiveness of controls? Internal audit is one obvious source, but although internal audit functions are increasingly being required to provide an annual assurance on the overall control framework, the scope of their work, and therefore their assurance, will inevitably be limited. Other review activities (such as quality assurance and health, safety and environmental auditors where they exist), *ad hoc* reviews and regular sources of information may provide a further degree of assurance. (Note that specialist functions such as those just listed will provide data and opinions to support any public statements on controls in particular areas, such as an Environmental Statement. In the public sector, certain specific control assurances are sought by The Treasury (central government) and Audit Commission (local government and health) relating to such matters as value for money, fraud and corporate governance.)

The obvious answer is to turn to divisional and line managers and require them formally and honestly to assess the strength of control in areas of their responsibility. The results of this process are collected, consolidated, verified as appropriate and used for both accountability and control improvement purposes.

External auditors may also of course be a source. However, in the private sector currently they are reluctant to go beyond the minimum reporting requirements on the directors' own report. Nevertheless the Management Letter may be a valuable source of information in so far as it notes control issues as a by-product of the audit. Given the different circumstances and wider duties of external auditors in the public sector, there may be greater scope to make use of their work to add to or confirm assurance gained internally. And it is open to any organisation to commission external consultants to perform an internal control review.

Regulatory pressure was a major factor in the development of CSA in Canada, and is becoming so in many other countries around the world. Obviously the particular regulatory requirements will have a significant influence on the nature and form of CSA within the organisation. As we state so often in this book, for the successful implementation of CSA it is essential that the reasons and objectives be clear and a commitment made. Even if the organisation is not required to publish its opinion on the state of its controls, it obviously makes good business sense periodically to review the adequacy, application and effectiveness of the control systems overall, in particular areas and relating to particular business issues, and to arrive 'privately' at an informed view, for example, through an audit committee.

## CSA AS A MANAGEMENT TOOL

Although outside pressures may provide the strongest stimulus, the main driving force behind CSA ought always to be the perceived and carefully

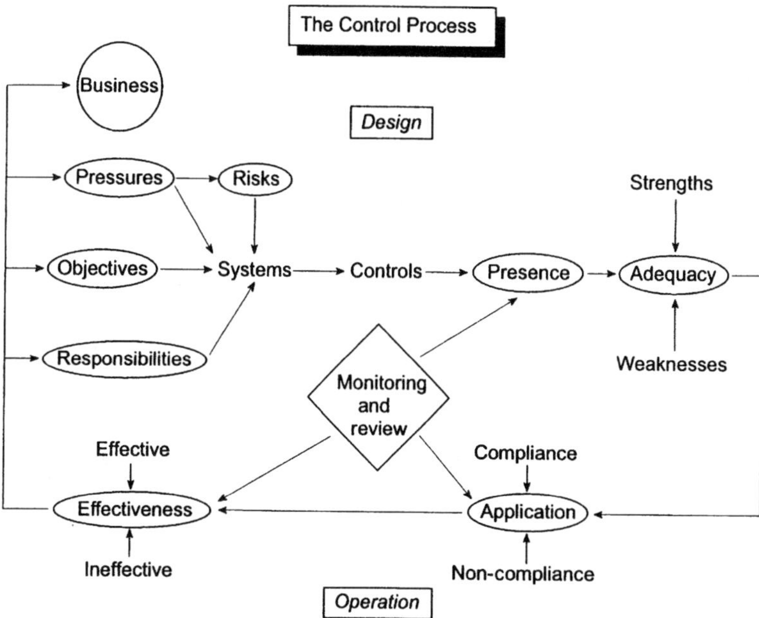


**Figure 1.2**

evaluated business need. CSA can be an appropriate, opportune and powerful way of helping managers to recognise and discharge their responsibilities for control as summarised in Figure 1.2. CSA can serve to reinforce the control message and clarify management's responsibilities. It may well be a suitable technique if the organisation is seeking to devolve power to line managers, strengthen accountability or achieve a sense of common purpose and a set of common values. Conversely it may be used as a catalyst for changing the culture of the organisation, although many will warn that CSA can fail or back-fire if the environment is not right. It may be opportune to employ CSA during times of organisational re-structuring, acquisition or merger. New procedures for business planning, quality assurance and other initiatives can also provide opportunities to integrate CSA in management arrangements.

Although more and more commentators recognise CSA as a management tool, sightings are few in the pages of management texts or course material. The authors of the IIA Research Foundation's publication give fulsome praise to the Control Self-Assessment Concept as a vital tool for any organisation seeking a new understanding of its business processes, better methods for employee empowerment, or simply a different approach to internal auditing. But the focus of the research is still on the implications for internal auditors.

If CSA is to be introduced, by internal auditors or whoever, its benefits to management – at all levels – must be sold. The most commonly claimed benefits are

1. Directors and senior managers derive information and assurance about control across the organisation.
2. An annual CSA cycle will normally provide a greater frequency of review than equivalent internal audit coverage.
3. Line managers obtain a better understanding of risk, and are put in a position of being able to develop their own approaches to dealing with the obstacles which get in the way of achieving business objectives.
4. The participative approach facilitates consensus at all stages of the process and between all parties.
5. 'Ownership' and 'buy-in' to action plans improve timely and effective implementation of corrective measures.
6. CSA helps managers to discover the root-cause of problems.
7. It can be used as a generic management tool: its application can be widened beyond risk and control to address other issues such as process efficiency, customer satisfaction, staff morale, quality improvement, etc.
8. A common language, set of values and control models (such as COSO) can be introduced throughout the organisation.
9. Open participation brings out the best in staff, improving morale, releasing information, generating ideas and creating better working relationships and communications.
10. It transfers responsibility for risk and control from auditors to managers and employees.

Many others are described in the following pages. The benefits depend of course on the methods adopted. Many stem from group workshop techniques which are not peculiar to CSA, or from simply finding the time to look afresh at current arrangements.

Finally, in considering CSA as a management tool, it should be noted that many externally set standards for particular management systems, for example, relating to quality (ISO 9001 series), environment (ISO 14001 and EMAS – the European Eco-Audit and Management Scheme), health and safety (e.g., the Standards of BSI and the Health and Safety Executive) and workers' rights (Social Accountability 8000, the standard issued in December 1997 by CEPAA, the Accreditation Agency of the Council on Economic Priorities) require some form of management 'review', 'audit' or 'self-assessment' as a key element of the overall arrangements. Evaluating their own controls is by no means new to many people. What may be new is the development of a common methodology and its systematic application, together with active participation of staff. Such approaches, however, may not be appropriate for all organisations.

## APPROACHES TO CSA

There are many forms of CSA, involving internal audit to a greater or lesser extent. They can be grouped as follows:

1. An enhanced form of normal internal audit practice (e.g., through adopting a more participative approach in audit assignments – see Chapter 9).
2. Audit-initiated control awareness seminars (perhaps open to managers and staff from several parts of the organisation – see Chapter 22).
3. The use of management letters of representation concerning
   (a) financial controls, or
   (b) all controls, addressing the broad range of control and performance issues
   (i.e., 'self-certification', normally annually).
4. Management use of risk and control assessment techniques and forms, including control questionnaires (to ensure that their assessment is structured, comprehensive, documented and as objective as possible – see Chapter 15).
5. Practical control assurance workshops – a systematic, open-minded approach to the assessment of control and risk using group methods; currently the workshops are usually facilitated by internal audit but they should be regarded as an integral part of the management control process and framework. The workshop approach itself takes various forms – see Chapter 6.
6. Management and staff assume total responsibility for control design, implementation, review and reporting, with independent examination and practical specialist assistance when necessary but on an exception basis.

It is in the fifth sense in which CSA is now most widely understood, if not practised. Several of these methods could be used in conjunction.

The various approaches and attitudes to CSA can be seen as a continuum, ranging from management indifference to control and review, presuming that the responsibility lies elsewhere, perhaps with audit (increasingly rare, we hope!), to total management acceptance and commitment, with minimal or no audit involvement. After all, to the quality experts, audit is a 'cost of failure'. It could be argued that the ultimate goal of internal audit is to ensure the abolition of the function or at least reduce dependence upon it. The message from audit to management is 'Don't rely on us'. These six CSA methods are now briefly detailed.

## 1 An Enhanced Conventional Audit Approach

This builds on standard audit practices, using a more participative style. Throughout the audit process, auditors, managers and staff work closely together in planning the assignment, analysing the business processes, identifying, evaluating and where necessary testing the critical controls, forming the opinion, considering means of improvement, and agreeing and implementing the action plan.

For many this is no more than a statement and marginal refinement of good audit practice. Others may quail at the thought of reduced audit independence – of rolling up the shirt-sleeves, addressing the important business issues, talking to real people and coming up with practical answers, not anodyne advice. This may simply reflect the age-old dilemma, how best to reconcile the often conflicting demands of independent examination and practical assistance. Or it may indicate a reluctance by some auditors to enter the real world – or a lack of understanding of how to do so.

As an example of this 'enhanced' approach, an article in the December 1997 *Internal Auditor*[8] described how auditors assist managers and staff to assess their risks and control using the COSO[9] framework as a model. This audit approach is based on three premises:

1. People know best: the staff of an organisation are best placed to provide insights into the strengths and weaknesses of their processes.
2. Internal auditors should work 'in a collegial spirit' to identify control problems and solutions.
3. The use of focus groups and 'affinity processes' provides one of the most efficient and effective means of gathering substantial amounts of highly relevant and useful data.

These methods are supported by self-completed control question checklists and individual interviews. Agreement is sought on levels of inherent, residual and acceptable risk, and corroborative evidence obtained before the final audit assessment is made.

## 2 Spreading the Gospel through Control Awareness Seminars

This is hardly a form of CSA. But remember, audit is much more than simply performing audits. Raising levels of awareness and giving practical guidance to managers and staff from across the organisation can be a cost-effective way of gaining information and strengthening control.

Many auditors have found that time is normally needed during a CSA project (preferably before a workshop if circumstances permit) to explain the essential concepts and practices of control, control assessment, and control design.

## 3 Management Letters of Representation

This is a tried and tested method used by many external auditors to obtain reassurance from Chief Executives and Financial Directors, who in turn seek assurances from relevant line managers about the adequacy of the relevant financial controls in the accounting period. This approach can be extended to be forward-looking and constructive, covering operational issues related to key business objectives for corporate and local benefit.

Making self-certification an annual requirement can act as a powerful incentive, especially if coupled with known validation and appropriate action if returns are discovered to be carelessly or even falsely completed. The risk is that the exercise is seen as a chore and the response may not be entirely reliable, especially if the task is given to the wrong person. Attitudes and practices (corporate and local) will depend on the culture but a positive, participative approach, perhaps facilitated by internal audit, should help reduce any problems.

## 4 Questionnaires and Surveys

Internal control questionnaires, risk identification and prioritisation, and other survey techniques can be used across the board or for individual business units and processes. Any auditor knows both the advantages and pitfalls of questionnaires, and their use within audit functions is declining. They can serve as useful checklists to help managers assess their own controls and they can be used to gather comparative data relatively efficiently. However, once more guidance needs to be given in their use and the interpretation of the data, and they may not be appropriate for the culture of the organisation.

Some 'gurus' look down on questionnaires, excluding them from 'true' CSA approaches, arguing that form filling cannot beat teamworking, but as a relatively cheap and efficient way of introducing CSA they may have their place, as contributions in this book try to show. They may be used in their own right, or in conjunction with workshops; before, to gather advance data, or during, instead of voting technology. Some questionnaire-based approaches, such as ASDA's SAS methodology, are sophisticated software-based packages incorporating self-help checklists, control databases, scoring systems and automated action plans, far removed from traditional paper-based audit ICQs. Others simply use modified ICQs.

## 5 Workshops

It is the workshop format using group processes and the frank and broad-ranging exchange of views which has received most attention and herein, many claim, lies the essence of CSA and the secret of success. There are in fact various formats. Workshops may:

- be one-off or part of a series
- involve solely managers or include their staff
- be self-run or facilitated by others, such as internal audit or outside consultants
- be 'low tech' or heavily dependent on computers to enable anonymous expression of views and rapid data capture and analysis
- focus on business control, risk, processes, objectives, constraints or performance (in practice, workshops must include all six elements)
- address hard or soft controls (or both)
- be single or multi-issue; a particular topic or business area may be selected, or the whole of the activities of the operation may be examined
- operate at high or low level examining control issues ranging from clerical activities to board perspectives
- function as a stand-alone exercise or as just one element of a CSA programme
- be horizontal (covering inter-departmental issues), vertical (specific to a business unit), or both.

The contributions in this book describe all the various approaches. The pioneers of CSA (e.g., Makosz (PDK), and Leech and McCuaig (MCS), all previously with Gulf Canada Resources) and firms of consultants (as many as you might name) have developed proprietorial methodologies. Procedures vary. Workshops may be preceded by surveys, interviews or training. In conduct, some workshops are template-driven or use other methods of systematically analysing business objectives, processes, risks, controls and environment. Others are free-form, and benefit from open discussion and brain-storming techniques. Often control models such as COSO or CoCo[10] are used as a basis for comparison, evaluation and re-design. A range of technical, procedural and behavioural techniques may be employed, including risk mapping, electronic voting, group stimulation and the like. Some methods owe much to quality management techniques. Or you can do your own thing.

Results of workshops may be used to inform senior management or audit committees, to provide assurances for public reporting, to prepare local action plans for improvement, or to enable auditors and others to direct resources to problems and identified weaknesses.

More sophisticated approaches seek to explore issues other than 'pure' control, and to integrate control frameworks with other paradigms such as the Baldridge and European quality models. The advocates of workshops stress the aims and advantages of an open, group process approach, in that it helps to:

- harness group knowledge
- identify different perspectives
- stimulate ideas
- elicit information which otherwise would not have been provided
- form a consensus view on the issues raised
- create group commitment to action
- clarify operational roles and responsibilities
- promote ownership of processes, controls and change
- highlight 'soft' issues such as business ethics, informal controls, and individual, group and corporate behaviour
- build and mend relationships.

In short, workshops profit from the power of people.

Organising, running and facilitating workshops is not easy nor is it necessarily comfortable for the participants. The contributions which follow provide lessons and advice on managing and participating in workshops, especially from an audit perspective.

## 6 Sole Searching

This is the ultimate form of CSA.

> Thanks very much for helping and showing us the way. But you can leave it to us now. Call in from time to time: we would still welcome the occasional objective opinion, impartial advice and practical assistance from experts such

> as yourselves. And naturally we recognise your right and duty to provide independent assurance and validation to the board. But, rest assured, we can cope. You can rely on us from now on.

So assert those line managers who accept and feel able to discharge their control responsibilities and conduct their own control reviews: the sign of successful audit efforts.

As mentioned earlier, all auditors must plan to disengage, to ensure the correct allocation of control responsibilities and to avoid the practical consequences of over-dependence on audit and excessive participation in CSA programmes. Auditors can then simply audit CSA as an embedded part of the control framework, helping and intervening only when appropriate (do not forget, CSA may be just one part of the overall control jigsaw). Before withdrawing, auditors may have a lot of hard work to do.

## IMPLICATIONS FOR INTERNAL AUDIT

Obviously the consequences for internal audit depend on the extent of involvement and the roles and responsibilities assumed. On the positive side, CSA may take some of the pressure off internal audit as resources struggle to keep pace with demand. It may revitalise its processes and staff, demonstrate audit's usefulness at management and corporate levels, transfer control responsibilities to where they rightly belong, give a sharper focus to audit work, help audit discharge new tasks such as the provision of an annual controls assurance, and provide another string to their bow (which may bring in new business or at least preserve audit's presence). As a useful by-product, CSA may also help the co-ordination of the various audit and review functions within an organisation. It can be shown to be useful and timely for the organisation and audit's 'customers' in so far as it can be integrated with quality management and empowerment initiatives.

On the other hand, some fear that audit objectivity may be compromised and independent assurance lost. Savings in audit time through the introduction of CSA tend to prove illusory, at least in the short term. Indeed, the opposite is normally the case. CSA can be immensely time consuming, as several of our contributors attest.

Many worry that quality may suffer; that without conventional audit probing and support, significant issues will be missed. Some auditors are attracted by the thought of completing a 30-day audit in 8 hours. Others believe that depth is inevitably sacrificed, objectivity lost and professional expertise wasted, and that the productivity and information gains cannot compensate for the flaws in the process. By relying on the assessment and judgement of others, who are inevitably biased, untrained and too close to their own operations, auditors are distancing themselves even further from the direct examination of performance. Auditors are criticised for reducing the levels of their own substantive tests. How can the truth surface in a brief talk-shop? The 'cut-and-thrust' of a traditional audit is lost. Confrontation and conflict can be healthy and productive. In the words of IIA-UK (Professional Briefing Note 7), conventionally, 'the veracity of internal audit findings and the aptness of audit recommendations are tested in the crucible of an often sceptical line management. No equivalently rigorous "validity testing" may apply to control self assessment.'

Few now advocate CSA as a complete replacement for conventional audit work. Where rock-solid assurance is required, materiality and risk are high and in other circumstances, where incontestable 'hard' facts are required, professional audit expertise using standards methods and painstaking examination will be necessary.

Such doubts often linger even when CSA is introduced, causing some auditors to seek to validate workshop results or follow up with a 'proper audit'. Often one of the biggest problems believers experience in introducing CSA is convincing certain audit staff. And audit clients may prefer the 'old-style' audit approach.

Critics point to other limitations which are examined by Andy Wynne in the final chapter of this book. In reply, proponents bemoan that if CSA is not adopted, auditors and managers will continue in their same old ways, a golden opportunity will have been missed and in a changing world audit runs the risk of becoming more and more isolated from organisational requirements.

Changing attitudes is never easy and there are new skills to acquire. The advent of CSA has led to a boom in facilitation skills training. In one UK government department, internal auditors have become so proficient in the art that their services are in demand to facilitate other forms of workshop such as quality circles. Appendix 1.3 summarises the possible roles and responsibilities of internal audit regarding CSA.

## IMPLEMENTING A CSA PROGRAMME

Motives determine methods. It is one thing to tinker with new audit techniques. It is another to use CSA as a catalyst to change the culture of the organisation. CSA successes, benefits, limitations and the occasional failure are documented in the pages which follow, leaving readers to judge its worth and appropriateness for themselves.

Many of the difficulties experienced in introducing and sustaining CSA have been caused not by inherent flaws in the concept, but by failures in project management, at both levels; implementing a CSA programme, and organising specific events such as workshops. Herein lie many of the lessons to be learned in this book. Studies and experiences stress the importance of:

- making the right decision in the first place, taking account of the organisation's business culture, policies and circumstances
- proper planning based on clear objectives and meticulous preparation
- effective consultation
- careful choice of the business area in which to try out CSA
- marketing
- selecting and training the right staff, especially in facilitation skills
- realistic assessment of the time it will consume
- patience

INTRODUCING CSA

1. Decide objectives, reasons and benefits for the organisation as a whole, management at various levels, internal audit and other stakeholders.
2. Objectively assess the potential difficulties and limitations, and the appropriateness of the technique in general and for particular parts or aspects of the organisation.
3. Establish the business case, just like any other project, and in competition with other possible ideas and claims on resources.
4. Decide the best strategy, tactics and approach after identifying the options, anticipating reactions and consequences, and considering resource implications.
5. Identify responsibilities and interests. Who should 'own' CSA? What role(s) should audit play?
6. Assuming the decision is made to proceed, sell the idea, responsibilities and the preferred approach.
7. Organise the management and implementation of the project.
8. Communicate: consult, inform, explain, educate and train where necessary.
9. Implement phase one: pilot scheme in selected area (a workshop, survey, risk mapping or whatever approach selected).
10. Learn lessons: revise approach as necessary, use champions from phase one.
11. Implement subsequent phases/full operation.
12. Integrate with other projects and activities, e.g., business planning.
13. Monitor: learn lessons, correct as necessary.
14. Develop: further extension and refinement as appropriate.
15. Transfer appropriate skills and responsibilities.
16. Disengage.
17. Audit.

**Figure 1.3** CSA from an internal audit perspective.

- making allowance for the learning curve (shortened by benefiting from the experiences of others)
- efficient mechanisms to handle the large amounts of data generated
- avoiding an over-dependence on IT, which may fail and detract from the main purpose
- efficient, effective and fair reporting and use of results
- incorporating validation and quality assurance mechanisms into the CSA process
- being innovative and taking controlled risks
- visible senior and line management support
- developing ways of keeping the momentum going with minimal dependence on audit
- realising there is no single 'best way' of introducing CSA; the approach adopted must be suitable and tailored for the needs of the organisation.

Figure 1.3 summarises the essential stages of planning, implementing and withdrawing from a CSA project from an internal audit perspective.

## PRACTICAL MATTERS

A number of practicalities need to be addressed. Should all auditors be trained as facilitators, or just a group? Not all auditors make good facilitators, and audit recruitment policies may need to be revised. There may be feelings of élitism. How is consistency to be obtained? Should documentation and procedures be standardised? Should auditors be allowed to experiment?

How can the process be made more efficient and less time consuming? Using technology, handling large amounts of data, providing useful analyses and reports are issues which have caused problems for CSA users. Marketing CSA, training, preparing documentation, learning lessons and changing procedures all consume time. CSA will almost certainly not lead to a reduction in audit costs.

What should be the balance between 'normal' audit work and CSA? How quickly should coverage be extended, and on what basis? What should be the frequency and length of the workshops? Above all, how is it to be 'sold' to directors, managers and clients as a useful and cost-effective tool? For many audit functions this is the major challenge, especially if the aim is to get CSA and participative risk management into the organisation's 'bloodstream'. And once introduced, how will its success be measured? How long will it take?

The place of CSA within the organisation needs to be established. For some it is simply another audit tool. For others it is a management philosophy. It may be a passing phase, an evolution or a revolution. Many who have tried it state they have not realised its full potential. Some are now seeking to draw customers, suppliers, business partners, external auditors and other review groups into the process and to explore the application of CSA in non-discrete areas.

Both CSA and audit's attitude to it are maturing. Five years ago it was a curiosity. For many it is now a reality. Lessons are being learned from the initial attempts at its implementation. There is greater awareness and a more objective and considered view. More and more auditors now realise it is nothing new. New words and powerful selling do not necessarily bring new ideas, more appropriate practices or better results.

Major projects have been initiated in several organisations, some centrally driven such as the pilot schemes in healthcare trusts sponsored by the NHS Executive. Managers are now recognising the benefits and increasingly are taking over administration and ownership of the process. CSA is here to stay.

CSA, and the role of internal audit, needs also to be set in the broader context of the whole raft of control and corporate governance initiatives affecting, directly or indirectly, organisations. Many issues (e.g., requirements post-Hampel) remain unresolved. Will New Labour introduce legislation to govern companies' behaviour and reporting requirements? Regulators are flexing their muscles. Codes of corporate conduct and audit committees have been introduced more widely into the public sector. Information technology developments press inexorably onwards. Integrated management and control systems are now realities, not aspirations. The control bandwagon seems set to roll for ever.

The prime purpose of CSA must be as an integral part of a comprehensive control framework and a key element in a systematic assurance programme. It should reinforce a constructive relationship between auditors and their clients, and line managers and their superiors and subordinates. As an essential part of the management process, and as expectations rise and external pressures mount, it is rightly here to stay. As a part of the audit process, in most organisations it will complement other audit work, being an element of both individual assignments and the overall operations of the audit service. Management of CSA, however, should lie outside the audit function. Audit involvement should be scaled back after the initial setting-up phase.

Audit too is here to stay, where it has earned the right. The theoretical case for the retention of internal audit can always be made. How objective the arguments are, however, remains to be seen. And poor auditing, out of touch with the business, its environment and the needs of its managers, does not deserve to survive.

## NOTES

1. *Control Self Assessment and Internal Audit*, Professional Briefing Note 7, IIA UK, 1995.
2. IIA Inc – Research conducted for the IIA Ottowa chapter by Arthur Andersen, published in 1996. ('Dedicated to all those who choose to see the future as it can be, and dare to make it that way.')
3. Committee of the Sponsoring Organisations of The Treadway Commission. The 'COSO model' appears in the 1992 publication *An Integrated Control Framework.* The 'Control Criteria' recommended in the Cadbury and Rutteman reports are derived from the COSO model.
4. Report of the Committee on the Financial Aspects of Corporate Governance chaired by Sir Adrian Cadbury.
5. *Internal Control and Financial Reporting – Guidance for Directors* published by ICAE&W, December 1994.
6. Committee on Corporate Governance – The Combined Code published by Gee Publishers, June 1998.
7. Lord Nolan chaired the Committee on Standards in Public Life, set up in October 1994 as an 'ethical workshop' by John Major. It is now a standing committee chaired by Lord Neill.
8. 'COSO-Based Auditing' by Mark R. Simmon, *Internal Auditor*, December 1997.
9. See note 3.
10. The model developed by the Criteria of Control Committee of the Canadian Institute of Chartered Accountants.

## APPENDIX 1.1

# Definitions of Control Self Assessment

- 'Liberating management from audit.' Anon
- 'A work-shop based approach using facilitated group processes to examine business risks and controls and gain commitment through shared responsibility to action and improvement.' Paraphrase of IIA Research Foundation Study
- 'A process (including a trained facilitator using a structured methodology supported by computer technology) that allows groups of audit customers to more clearly identify the most important business risks, problems, control issues, solutions and opportunities within each business process or function.'
  Loach and Julien *Facilitation Techniques for Self-Assessment*
- 'The involvement of management and staff in the assessment of internal controls within their work group.' David and Fran McNamee *Facilitated Self-Assessment*
- 'A leading edge process which yields reliable, quantitative information regarding achievement of operational, financial reporting and legal compliance objectives. Teams of employees – the experts – are personally involved in facilitated workshops to determine their business unit's control strengths, weaknesses and opportunities for improvement.' Deloitte and Touche
- 'Control and Risk Self Assessment is a process that allows groups to identify and refine the business and quality objectives that they should be fulfilling, while assessing the adequacy of plans and controls that are in place to meet those objectives.' Tim Leech, MCS
- 'Control self-assessment operates on two levels as follows:
  - Team level
    Teams getting together with their manager and a specialist facilitator to analyse, within a control framework, the strengths, obstacles, and risks which impact their ability to achieve their objectives, and to decide upon appropriate action.
  - Organisational (or systematic) level
    Analysing the results from all the team CSA workshops across the organisation to define cultural strengths, weaknesses, and propensities to risk, find linkages between them, and identify root causes for the current state of control.' Paul Makosz, PDK

## APPENDIX 1.2

# Control Self Management and Assessment

Management's acceptance and discharge of their responsibilities for the whole control process, including their obligation to establish appropriate control arrangements, monitor their application, and periodically review their adequacy and effectiveness. Managers are entitled to specialist advice, professional help where necessary and independent assurance. This does not relieve them of their duties and they are obliged to demonstrate that they have established an appropriate framework and process, and are in control. K. W. Wade 1995

## ELEMENTS OF CSMA

### Overall Arrangements

- attitudes and commitment to control; control standards and priorities; the control environment
- reasons for control; range of objectives and issues; external and internal drivers and requirements; business needs, accountability and governance
- relation to business objectives, principles, tone and culture
- the overall internal control framework: integration within the organisation; co-ordination of the various control issues and elements within the framework
- responsibilities for control at all levels; respective roles of board, senior and line managers, internal audit, other specialists and advisers, external audit, audit committee, etc.
- control structures, systems and procedures.

### The Control Process

1. Determination and specification of need:
   - internal and external pressures to establish and demonstrate control
   - clarifying objectives, determining relative importance of control and main control issues
   - understanding control
   - risk assessment (related to business objectives).

2. Design of appropriate control framework:
   - acceptance of need for overall control framework
   - agreement on control criteria, standards and values
   - determination of scope of control and key control objectives
   - recognition of controllable and uncontrollable factors
   - construction of control framework and systems, using generic models where relevant
   - development of specific key controls, hard and soft
   - recognition of practicalities and residual risk
   - coping with change
   - integration with other frameworks, systems and initiatives.
3. Establishment of the control procedures:
   - testing of proposed arrangements
   - training, gaining commitment; changing attitudes
   - implementation.
4. Operation of controls:
   - day-to-day running
   - recognition, acceptance and application of control
   - embedding.
5. Maintaining control:
   - monitoring adequacy and continuing suitability
   - ensuring proper application
   - checking effectiveness
   - dealing with variances.
6. Reviewing the control system:
   - periodic appraisal (annual?): CSA
   - forming the opinion; is it still appropriate and robust given original design, day-to-day operation and change?
7. Re-designing control; revision or redesign where necessary:
8. Demonstrating control:
   - controls assurance
   - being accountable for control, control review, control effectiveness and ultimate performance

- documentation/evidence of effective control and review
- management representations, disclosures and reports
- independent reviews of control and validation of statements
- external reporting and other requirements
- external audit, validation and inspection
- reactions.

## APPENDIX 1.3

# Roles and Responsibilities of Internal Audit in CSA

Duties, activities, authorities and expectations will depend on the form of CSA adopted, the audit function's policy towards it, and any specific roles assigned to audit by the organisation. The key message should be clear by now: audit may initially drive CSA, but must not own it.

Three strands can be discerned when considering the role of and implications for internal audit:

1. options for audit involvement in CSA
2. using CSA for audit purposes
3. auditing CSA.

These are briefly explained in turn. Comment, analysis and advice will be found in the main text.

## OPTIONS FOR AUDIT INVOLVEMENT

1. Initiation and promotion: as experts in control, being aware of latest developments; (we have already observed that many still see CSA narrowly as an audit technique).
2. Project management: normally a consequence of the above.
3. Ownership: a serious risk; following from items 1 and 2. IIA-UK's uncompromising view is that: 'If it is the organisation's intention to maintain internal audit as an independent appraisal activity, then we consider it inappropriate for internal audit to be involved in the day-to-day management of the control self-assessment programme.'
4. Workshop facilitation: requiring new skills and reactions. (Note that IIA were not 'comfortable' with this either, in their view 'making internal audit a component part of the execution of CSA' and compromising audit objectivity. 'It will also be clear' the Institute states 'that it is harmful to the best interests of the business for internal audit to abandon a conventional internal audit programme of work in favour of exclusively committing to facilitating a control self assessment programme.')
5. Providing other forms of workshop support (e.g., organising the meeting(s), note-taking, providing the technology, issuing the report).

6. Giving advice and guidance to line management and staff on control and risk and control assessment techniques, and to all relevant parties on CSA itself; acting as a consultant at various stages of the implementation of CSA and the operation of CSA exercises.
7. Educating and training: as experts in control and control evaluation auditors can go further and provide useful practical coaching outside and within a CSA programme.

## USING CSA FOR AUDIT PURPOSES

The use of CSA as an audit tool was considered earlier. In summary it can be employed as follows:

1. To replace internal audit totally: in theory abolition is the long-term aim of internal audit, but the case for an independent form of assurance and source of specialist advice can always be argued.
2. To replace certain audits: where it is decided that CSA is a more efficient or effective approach.
3. To reduce audit work, if audit decides the results of a CSA exercise can be relied upon.
4. To extend audit coverage into business issues (e.g., ethical and environmental) and activities (e.g., commercial operations) which otherwise would not have been covered at all or to the desired depth, through lack of support, resources or ambition.
5. To modify (or revolutionise) the audit approach by introducing aspects of CSA into normal audit assignments, encouraging the ownership rather than the imposition of control.
6. To perform certain assignments; CSA may be felt to be of especial relevance in particular circumstances (e.g., organisational re-structuring), areas (e.g., health and safety) or operations (e.g., where considerable authority is devolved to a business unit).
7. To add to audit knowledge; a CSA workshop can inform future assignments and confirm existing opinions.
8. To point audit to areas of concern or interest; the results of CSA programmes can highlight weaknesses for subsequent audit investigation and reporting (managers and staff may not be too keen on this!).

## AUDITING CSA

1. Auditing CSA as a project; assessing the procedures and controls before, during and after implementation.
2. Auditing the CSA process; once established, assessing its adequacy, application and effectiveness as part of the organisation's control framework.
3. Auditing the results; assessing the benefits derived from the programme as a whole, verifying the results of individual CSA activities, e.g., the validity of management representations, the quality of workshops and reports and the extent to which agreed corrective actions have been successfully implemented.

# 2

# CRSA
## Current State of the Art, its Origins and Impacts

*Tim Leech and Bruce McCuaig*

## CURRENT STATE OF THE ART

Anyone contrasting today's array of leading-edge assurance services available to clients internally or externally compared to ten years ago could easily be forgiven for wondering if they were not looking at a totally different profession. We believe that the Control and Risk Self Assessment movement is the primary force having a dramatic and irreversible impact on the auditing profession.

Once a profession dominated by low value added compliance testing and reporting, auditors are now routinely using and adapting sophisticated conceptual control models to assess, design and report on the status of control and risk in their organisations. Beginning with COSO in the USA and Cadbury in the UK, these models have evolved into powerful tools to enable root cause analysis and powerful profiling of behavioural forces at work in organisations.

Training in control and risk concepts has become an important assurance strategy. Leading-edge auditing and assurance organisations now dedicate a significant portion of their resources to training other staff in control and risk concepts, usually using these same models.

Even better, the best of the models align the organisation's view of control and in many cases form a vocabulary of control and risk concepts and terms far more articulate than that of the past. Auditors no longer need to talk only about 'preventative', 'detective' or 'management' controls.

Accounting credentials are becoming far less important than in the past. Assurance services are no longer limited to evaluating financial, accounting or systems controls. Leading-edge professionals are providing assurance on a wide range of objectives such as those listed below.

## Business/Quality Objective Families

- Product Quality (PQ)
- Customer Service (CS)
- Minimising Unnecessary Costs (MUC)
- Revenue/Profit Maximisation (RPM)
- Reliable Business Information (RBI)
- Asset Safeguarding (AS)
- Safety (S)
- Regulatory Compliance (RC)
- Fraud Prevention/Detection (FPD)
- Continuity of Operations (COO)
- Unintentional Risk Exposure (URE)
- Internal Compliance (IC).

Providing assurance on these objectives is stretching many auditing organisations to adopt new skill sets and acquire new credentials.

Accounting and traditional auditing skills, while still valued, are being supplemented by other professional backgrounds and by extensive industry knowledge. For example, oil and gas clients typically have audit staff with geological, geophysical or engineering backgrounds. And these technical staff are not waiting out the balance of their career until they retire. They are highly valued by their professional peers.

Equally important are the softer skills associated with facilitating workshops, training skills and conflict resolution. Some internal audit clients now have as a goal the virtual elimination of traditional audit activity, relying instead on quality assuring information from CRSA workshops. A few even plan to go one step further and train their organisations to conduct these workshops themselves. Audit would not even be present in the workshops. While few organisations are going this far, it marks a stark contrast with traditional thinking of a few short years ago.

What tools are leading-edge organisations using? The use of a variety of anonymous voting groupware in workshops is common. Software products are now available to capture detailed control and risk status information and to build content rich control and risk universe databases containing much more and different information than anything imagined ten years ago.

Finally, most leading-edge assurance organisations are recognising risk assessment and reporting as a key part of their domain. Some have merged the audit function with the risk-management function, not just to manage insurable risk, but to understand and manage all risks associated with corporate strategy, insurable or not.

How are clients of audit and assurance organisations reacting? Our experience is that they are literally overjoyed with the changes and clamouring for more.

Audit and assurance work is becoming responsive and demand driven by knowledgeable clients – the trait of a dynamic profession. The service is focused on helping organisations reach their business objectives. Examining and reporting on the existence of, or breakdowns in, controls as a primary focus is increasingly recognised as low value.

## EARLIER STATE OF THE ART

To understand the contrast with ten years ago compare the factors shown in Table 2.1. These changes have had a significant influence on the behaviour of auditors.

## ORIGINS OF CRSA AT GULF CANADA

In 1985 Gulf Canada, located in Toronto, Canada was a mid-sized integrated oil and gas company. Publicly listed on the Toronto and American stock exchanges Gulf Canada was purchased by a Canadian investor from the real estate sector. By late 1985 Gulf had largely sold its downstream refining and marketing businesses. What was left of the company was in the process of moving its head office to Calgary, Alberta where its remaining business, finding and producing hydrocarbons, was based. Even in the years between 1980 and 1985 Gulf had experienced significant change that influenced the authors' view of control, the role of internal audit and the manner in which control was assessed and reported.

Two major events at Gulf serve to explain our growing dissatisfaction with traditional approaches to audit. It was this dissatisfaction that eventually led to the initiation of CRSA several years later.

Between 1980 and 1985 severe competition developed with respect to refining, marketing, distributing gasoline and other consumer and industrial petroleum products. High costs and low margins drove significant restructuring within the industry. Within Gulf this meant the closure or sale of refineries, consolidation of bulk terminals and closure of many service stations. Other changes included significant staff reductions, increased reliance on information technology, the development of more powerful information systems, and the decentralisation of decision making. The result was much more authority for things like product pricing delegated to front-

**Table 2.1** Traditional and leading-edge CRSA.

| Factor | Traditional | Leading-edge CRSA |
|---|---|---|
| Candour | Candour from auditees not expected or rewarded and often punished. Why would a work unit volunteer problems and control deficiencies? | Candour from work units essential and rewarded by assurance providers. Work units not willing or able to be candid about their control and risk status are high risk. |
| Work unit self analysis | Auditors play the role of primary analysts and reporters of controls. Control is seen as accounting. It is not directly linked in the minds of work units with operating the business. | Work units have accountability for control and risk. Audit plays a supporting role to guide the process, build capability and synthesise issues for reporting. Control is what it takes to mitigate risks and achieve business objectives. |
| Management/ Stakeholder confidence | Audit failures common. Leading financial institutions are devastated by misplaced confidence in traditional control thinking and approaches to auditing. | Enthusiastic work group, management, regulatory and stakeholder support emerging. |
| Reliability of results | Judgements expressed on control effectiveness based on individual auditor assessment of what they (the auditors) think is adequate. Opinions are highly variable by individual, based on flawed notions of what constitutes effective control. Control opinions are not comparable year over year or across the organisation. | Criteria of control, defined in control models, are used to assess control and risk. Effective control is defined as an acceptable level of residual risk. Work groups and management decide how much control is enough. Assurance groups report on control and risk status, not on control adequacy. |
| Receptivity to continuous improvement | Minimum control standards become ceilings. Don't do more than is mandatory. 'Catch me if you can' attitude prevails. Audit is responsible for control and following up on those not complying with recommendations. | Focus is on balancing control and risk and continuously updating control and risk status information to reflect new information and drive down the cost of control. |

line sales reps, the delegation of authority to sign binding contracts to mid-level distribution staff, and a decline in the role of formal policy and layers of supervision in the management structure. There was much more reliance on people, information and clear objectives and much less reliance on supervisory review, policy compliance and centralised decision making and approval processes.

Historically, our audit findings related to policy and procedural compliance and improper approval processes. The key indicator was stock losses, particularly stock losses at agent-operated bulk stations and service stations.

By 1985, the business was showing clear signs of turning around. In spite of the shift in the control environment all parts of the business were performing better. Stock losses dropped dramatically in spite of reduced audits. Internal Audit had cut staff and reduced audit frequency. We found on the audits we did perform, the frequency and amount of stock losses had decreased. Marketing staff and agents seemed to be accepting more accountability for control.

The second major event that shook our thinking was a major fraud in a large subsidiary. Staff did not perpetrate the fraud. It was perpetrated by the company's President, its Chairman and some of its Vice Presidents, some of whom were also on the Board. Some of the perpetrators had actually helped establish the company and all had an active role in its day-to-day management. External auditors had audited the company each year and its own internal auditors and Gulf internal auditors had also conducted regular audits. While it was never given a clean bill of health, no one imagined the fraudulent activities. Ironically, one of the last audit reports issued by the internal auditors contained the management comment: '... control systems are operating as intended by management.'

All the traditional controls were present. Approval processes were in place. Traditional segregation of duties seemed to exist. Accounting controls seemed to be in place. The Board seemed to be meeting its governance responsibilities. The company was profitable and growing.

Unfortunately, senior management had created a number of contracts between the company and other companies they owned privately and caused the company to do business for many years on terms and conditions that were clearly not at arms' length. Direct losses were calculated in the many millions. True economic losses, including opportunity costs, were several times that amount.

All the traditional formal controls which auditors viewed as fundamental were in place. But the fraud had lasted many years. While only a few employees at the top were involved, we could not believe that many more employees had not had suspicions or knowledge they were willing to live with and not disclose.

We had seen significant business success where many traditional formal controls were abandoned with positive effects and we had seen massive fraud where traditional formal controls were in place but provided false assurance.

This phenomenon (the failure of traditional control thinking) was not unique to Gulf. It has been amply demonstrated time and time again around the world. We needed to find a way to answer some basic questions: What is control? How can it be measured? How much is enough? Who should decide?

## EVOLUTION OF GENERALLY ACCEPTED CONTROL CRITERIA

The authors maintain that their primary innovation at Gulf Canada in 1985 to 1987 was not CRSA. The primary contribution was actually the development and application of control models for training, assessing, designing and reporting on internal control and risk. In short, the early recognition of the need for and development of criteria of control.

Control and risk self assessment emerged as one way to gather reliable information on the status of control and risk in an organisation. We continue to believe that the development and use of better model-based approaches to understanding and reporting on control and risk will be recognised as being at least as important as the evolution of CRSA.

## COMMAND/CONTROL MODEL

A simple but useful way to portray the implied assumptions of traditional direct report auditing is to look at what is commonly called the command/control model illustrated in Figure 2.1.

This model shaped the control systems of many large corporations and the audit programs of many internal audit departments. It has come under serious attack over the past ten years as organisations move from command and control methods to frameworks based more on empowerment, teamwork and accountability. Traditional direct report audit practices call for the auditor to assess the level of formal controls on the vertical axis by testing compliance, enforcing segregation of duties and formal approval processes, etc. We have found that, when asked, most auditors will agree that between 80% to 90% of their findings and recommendations deal with these types of controls. We call them direct controls.

In effect, by making recommendations in these areas, auditors actually try to maintain and probably increase the level of these direct controls. The model implies that the higher the level of formal or direct controls, the more effective the control environment. Our experience at Gulf did not support this model of control. We found that, by themselves, direct controls could

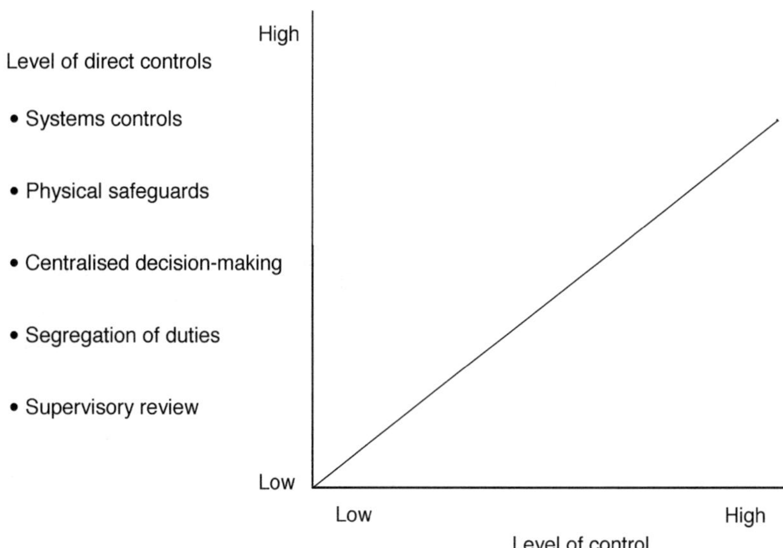


**Figure 2.1** Command/control model.

not explain or predict control failures and reliance on direct controls alone provided dangerously false assurance.

In Gulf, our restructured marketing and distribution organisation contradicted this model. Direct controls dramatically declined. Measured by business results, control had improved. In the subsidiary where the massive fraud took place, all the direct controls were there but proved totally unreliable.

## B. J. WHITE MODEL OF CONTROL EFFECTIVENESS

In 1980 the Financial Executive Research Foundation published a study of internal control in US corporations. It represented one of the first significant challenges to the command/control model.

This model (shown in Figure 2.2) was published in 1980 as part of a study done on US corporations. It was one of the first significant challenges to the core assumptions in the command and control framework. The innovation of the B. J. White Model was to recognise the existence and give equal importance to informal controls. This four-quadrant model recognised the formal direct controls of the command/control model on the vertical axis but also recognised informal controls such as competence, trust, shared values, etc., on the horizontal axis. According to this view some combination of both formal and informal controls is necessary. The proportions would vary situationally.

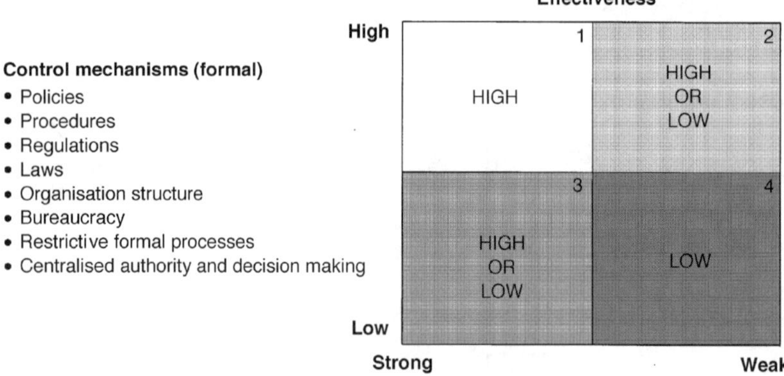


**Figure 2.2** B. J. White model of control effectiveness. (*Source*: B. J. White, *Internal Control in US Corporation Financial Executive Research Foundation*, New York, 1980.)

One can easily imagine a small software design firm with highly competent inspired staff achieving great success with little in the way of formal controls. In fact formal controls might be stifling in such an environment. It is also easy to imagine a global fast-food business with strong informal controls but equally strong formal controls governing quality and growth.

Auditors tended to spend little time examining or relying on informal controls. In fact there was a belief that because informal controls appeared intangible, they could not be observed or measured. Our view was that evidence of the existence of informal controls lay in the ability and willingness of employees to describe their control environment and in particular their control concerns, or known control risks. Our view was that disclosure of control concerns was a good proxy for the existence of informal controls. Work groups who could not or would not describe their concerns or risk issues, were in our minds, high-risk work groups. It did not matter whether the issue was the ability to disclose and report or the group's willingness. Absence of candid disclosure for any reason meant to us that the informal environment was a problem.

The marketing organisation could candidly disclose and resolve issues. In the subsidiary where the major fraud occurred there was no willingness to disclose issues. In fact issues were hidden.

## R. J. ANDERSON CONTROL MODEL

In the fall of 1986 the authors were faced with reporting to the Board Audit Committee on the state of control in the newly structured and relocated company. In the previous year the company had sold virtually all of its refining and marketing assets and relocated to Calgary with only a small fraction of its former head office staff. The company had new owners from outside the oil and gas business. In the meantime oil prices had tumbled drastically in the first quarter of the year and the government, which had previously been the buyer for all oil and gas production, had deregulated the market and opened it to competition. It was fair to say the company was reeling. How could we explain the control environment of the company in a way that reflected reality? The approach we took was to use a model-based approach. The format of reports is illustrated in Figure 2.3.

We had located in a Canadian auditing text a seven-element description of internal control. We simply converted the elements to a bar graph representation.

At this point self-assessment did not exist. We built the bars in the model based on the relative reliance we believed the organisation was placing on each

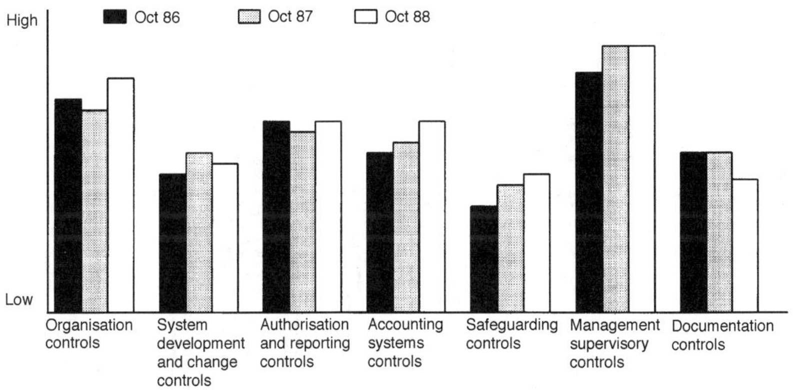


- **Organisation controls**
  - Personnel standards
  - Plan of organisation
  - Corporate culture
- **System development and change controls**
- **Authorisation and reporting controls**
  - Planning and budgeting
  - Accountability
- **Accounting systems controls**
- **Safeguarding controls**
  - Protection of assets
  - Avoidance of unintentional risk
- **Management supervisory controls**
  - Supervision
  - Management information
- **Documentation controls**
  - Formal policies, procedures
  - Systems documentation

**Figure 2.3** Internal control adequacy – changes over time at Gulf Canada Resources 1986–7.

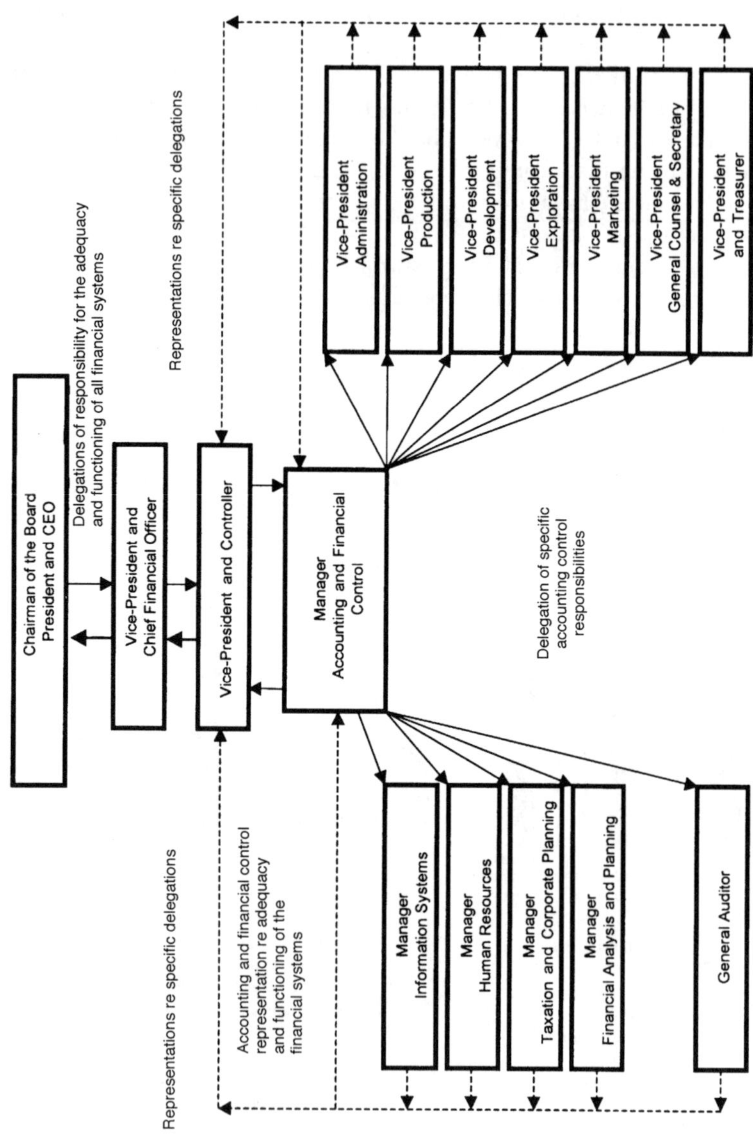


**Figure 2.4** Accounting Control Delegation and Representation Framework.

control element. We grounded our conclusions by summarising every source of control information we could find. Audit reports both internal and external, corporate policies, internal studies, news articles and task force reports were all reviewed and assessed. Most importantly, we tested our observations with both staff and senior managers before presenting and explaining it to the Chief Financial Officer and Chief Executive Officer in advance of the Audit Committee meeting. It had to be intuitively obvious as well as objectively defendable. We needed to find a way to incorporate information from all sources, not just audit reports. We also needed to ensure we gave a high weight to informal controls. The R. J. Anderson model provided both these attributes.

After our successful audit committee presentation using the seven-category model we developed and proposed the early version of CSA that later evolved into CRSA. In early 1987 we proposed the Accounting Control Delegation and Representation Framework illustrated in Figure 2.4. This framework called for cascading representations by Officers and Senior Managers on the adequacy of controls as they related to the specific areas of each executive's responsibilities. While the focus was on accounting controls it penetrated deep into the organisation. For example, in order to account for revenue and sales, the Calgary Accounting Centre relied on volumes reported by partners and field offices. The Vice President, Production was required to represent to the accuracy of the instruments and procedures used in measuring oil and gas production volumes. The Vice President, Exploration had to represent to the accuracy of information supporting expenditure accruals or drilling programmes as well as the accuracy and completeness of reserve calculations. Supplementing the Accounting Control Delegation & Representation Framework was a Control Concerns

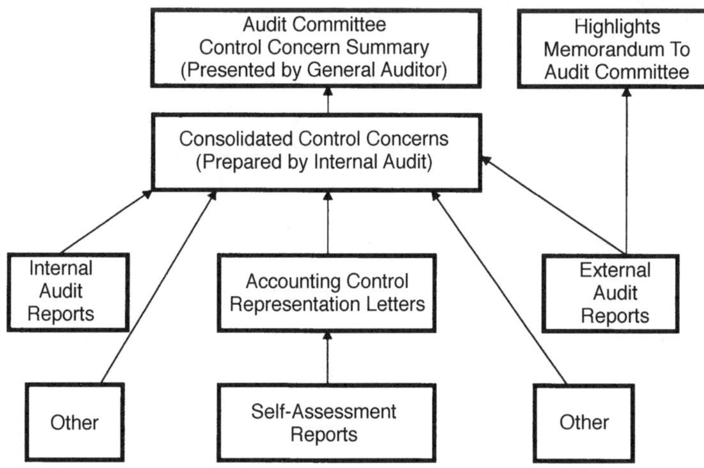


**Figure 2.5** Control Concerns Report roll-up.

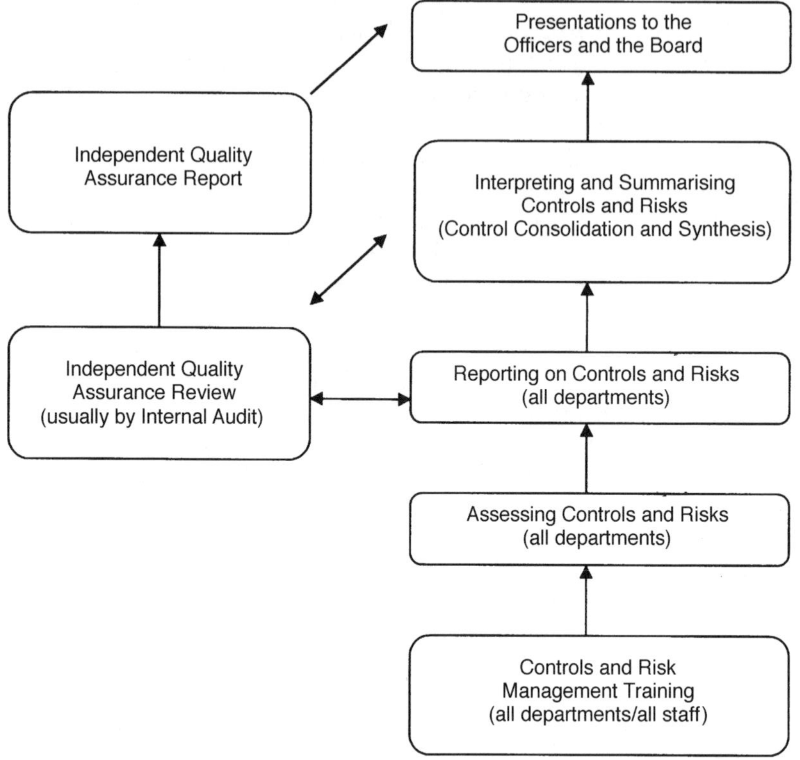


**Figure 2.6** CRSA: the fully implemented approach.

Report designed to funnel information in the representation process to the Audit Committee through the General Auditor (see Figure 2.5).

From our initial efforts to install this framework it quickly became apparent that field staff lacked any real understanding of how to assess control. Beginning in June of 1987 the Internal Audit Department began to run a series of seminars and workshops. In the balance of the year we covered the entire organisation to explain basic control and risk concepts using the R. J. Anderson control model and lead objective focused CRSA workshops. The fully implemented CRSA approach as it has evolved in our clients is shown in Figure 2.6.

Third-generation CRSA workshops follow the Card®line approach illustrated in Figure 2.7 and uses as a control model the MCS Card®model, an international model designed to incorporate the features and principles of subsequent internal models like COSO, Cadbury, and CoCo as well as most of the international quality models such as Baldridge and the EFQM framework.

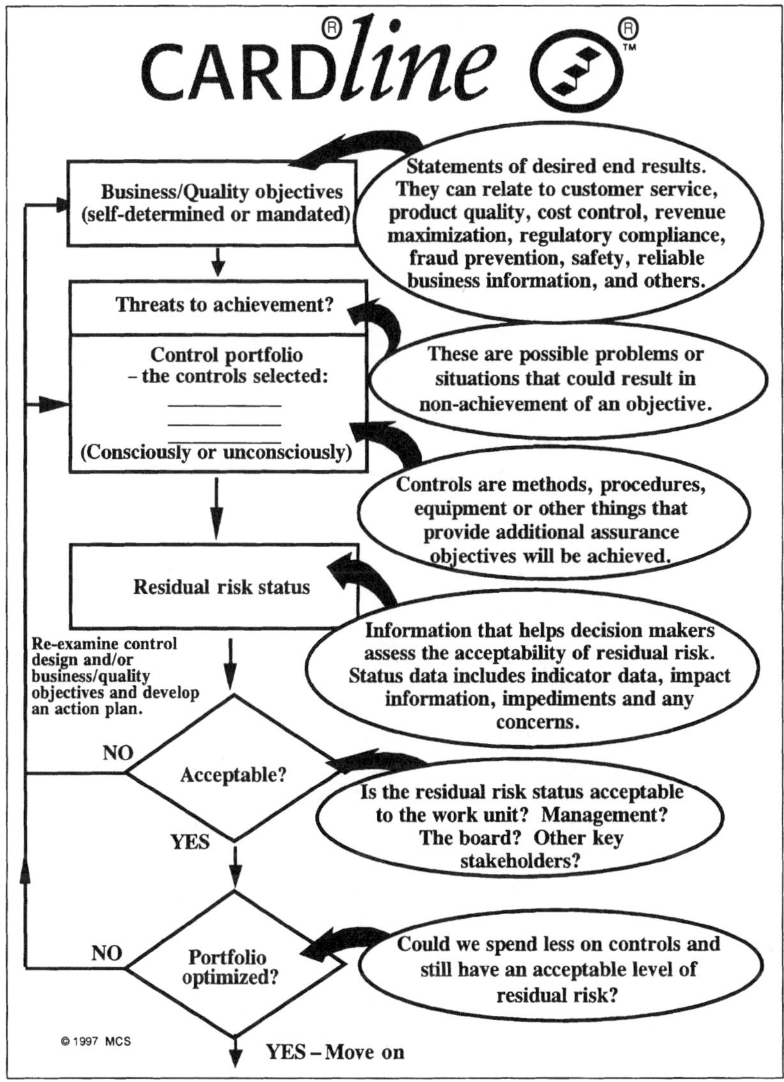


**Figure 2.7** The Cardline approach.

## KEY LESSONS FOR THE FUTURE

We have learned that while it can be very powerful, CRSA is simply a tool, and for many organisations it is not the best tool. Only about 60% of our

**Table 2.2** Organisational cultures.

| Historical/traditional | The new vision |
|---|---|
| • Assign duties/supervise staff | • Empowered/accountable employees |
| • Policy/rule driven | • Continuous improvement/learning culture |
| • Limited employee participation and training | • Extensive employee participation and training |
| • Narrow stakeholder focus | • Broad stakeholder focus |
| • Auditors and other specialists are the primary control analysts/reporters | • Staff at all levels, in all functions, are the primary control analysts/ reporters |

clients are ready to implement CRSA when we first begin working with them. Table 2.2 illustrates two extreme types of cultures. Companies who show a clear preference for the historical/traditional approach are poor candidates. CRSA seems to work in the long-term only with companies who clearly want to make a shift to move at least part way to a New Vision approach.

Even where companies are poor candidates for CRSA, traditional audit using a risk focused, control model based approach can produce many of the same results as CRSA and can be the beginning of a natural evolution to CRSA. Control models form the criteria of control on which to base an assessment of control and risk. An individual auditor can ask the same questions in a series of one-on-one interviews as a facilitator can ask during a workshop. The task may be more time consuming but most of the same issues should result.

Control models have evolved tremendously during the last decade, providing a far better fundamental understanding of control and risk and a basis to expand well beyond the traditional financial accounting control review. Control models are looking more and more like quality and safety models used by operating staff with great results for years. Suddenly auditors and operating staff have a common definition of control, essential for shifting accountability for control assessment to where it belongs. We have learned that audit's most valuable role is to move away from providing opinions on control effectiveness and to move instead to seeking consensus opinions on residual risk status disclosures. Work groups and management tend to make extremely responsible risk acceptance decisions based on complete and comprehensive residual risk status data. Our observations are that work groups may be overly cautious in their risk acceptance decisions. They do not need auditors to assess the effectiveness of their controls. They need better information to make decisions themselves. The definition of effective control is an acceptable level of risk. Work groups can and do make great risk acceptance decisions.

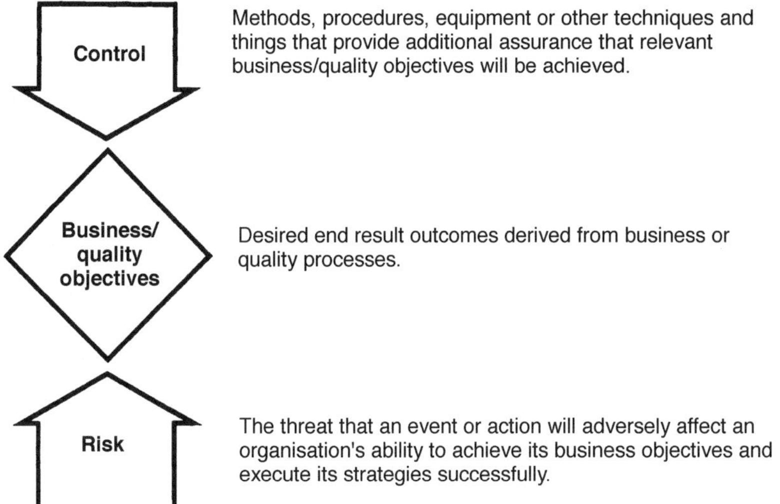


**Figure 2.8** Linking risks/objectives and control.

Risk assessment is undergoing the same fundamental rethinking as internal control experienced over the last decade. Risk is no longer necessarily linked to insurance exclusively. We are beginning to see audit and risk management functions combined and providing strategic input to their corporations. Generally accepted risk criteria are evolving in much the same way as generally accepted criteria of control.

## THE FUTURE

The link between controls, risks and business objectives is illustrated in Figure 2.8. Standards for control and risk assurance reporting are evolving quickly, particularly in the public accounting world. Assurance strategies can consist of everything from CRSA workshops to training in control and risk concepts. There is no longer a single inflexible approach to assurance services. Finally, increasing demands are being placed on Directors and Boards to provide better oversight. Providing the kind of information to respond to the questions they are now expected to ask is a far greater challenge than can be answered by traditional audit methodologies.

Much more sophisticated audit planning and reporting frameworks are necessary. Leading-edge assurance professionals will need sophisticated database technology to capture control and risk status information and link it to work groups and objectives throughout the organisation.

The next decade will show that control assurance professionals are capable of delivering far greater value than has been the case to date. The future for assurance professionals with a willingness to embrace these new ideas and tools has never been brighter. More demanding and knowledgeable customers will provide the catalyst for change.

# 3

# Control Self Assessment
## Risk Panacea or Fee Developer?

*Phil Tarling*

## INTRODUCTION

The term Control and Risk Self Assessment (CRSA) or Control Self Assessment (CSA) has gained currency in the world of internal auditing over the past five years. The basis of this chapter takes the view (based on Keith Wade's definition, see page 6) that Control Self Assessment is a structured approach to a regular fundamental review by both managers and staff of the control systems designed to assist in the achievement of objectives and the elimination of risk. I have resisted the temptation to use superlatives, such as 'innovative' or 'liberating' because I am not certain that any of them can be justified. When they are used it may say more about the organisation that is using them than about CSA itself.

When superlatives are used to describe anything it makes me suspicious and I have a deep distrust of the way such words are being used to market the introduction of CSA. Taking the hype at face value, it is as though no one had ever before thought about internal audit adding value, concentrating on management's objectives or being a positive input to an organisation. This is strange because since 1941 there has been a world-wide internal audit professional body (and since 1948 a UK version) which has been promoting the need for internal audit to concentrate upon providing a service to management. Is CSA, one should ask, only such a brilliant wheeze because organisations are willing to spend money on implementing it? Or have we seen the elements of CSA in other guises so that the approach is little more than a re-package of best practice.

Unfortunately, CSA appears to be developing in the UK as a panacea for internal control when it is clear to all but the most ardent fan that it is not and never can be. We need to explore why this is so and why internal auditors appear to have failed to convince their organisations that they are the experts in control and that the work carried out by internal audit can add value to the organisation. It is this failure that probably accounts for the fact that CSA appears innovative. But is it anything substantial or just an empty package?

## WHAT IS CSA?

To give us an idea what this is all about, perhaps we need to examine why CSA was developed. Most of the literature describes its birthplace as being with Gulf Oil of Canada and it would be fair to say that the impact that CSA has had in the last decade has been due to the work carried out at Gulf, and taken forward by their ex-employees Tim Leech and Bruce McCuaig (in one form – see Chapter 2) and Paul Makosz (in another).

Why did Gulf have a need to introduce something to replace conventional internal auditing? Tim Leech has been quoted saying that one major factor in establishing CSA was as an answer to the requirement for Gulf Corporation to enter into a US Securities Exchange Commission consent degree 'as a result of questionable business practices'.[1] The consent degree involved the production of quarterly reports from officers on internal control. In the interview with Glenda Jordan, Leech goes on to suggest he had concerns over the effectiveness of traditional internal auditing methods to help with this process. The CSA model was therefore developed as a mechanism to impart the lessons of internal control throughout the operational areas, by putting the onus on individuals to be responsible for the control of risk. However, it could be argued that internal auditing, if carried out properly on a risk basis, should detect questionable business practices which will arise through a lack of control. It is perhaps an indication of the real value of CSA that Paul Makosz has said that in '1988 I threw out all our audit practices. By 1989 we stopped doing direct report audits. In 1990 I brought traditional auditing back because workshop participants asked for it.'[2] It is interesting to note that a return to auditing was requested by the same managers and staff who were the main beneficiaries of the CSA approach.

It could be argued that one of the main approaches promulgated in the UK was developed as a response in an environment where the consequences of control failure had considerable regulatory impact involving external scrutiny of the subsequent measures established to ensure future compliance. The introduction of a new methodology within this type of environment might well be successful if it introduced staff to the concept of control which was perceived as previously invested solely in the internal audit department. The technique gives managers and staff a chance to participate; provoking an enthusiastic response.

## CSA AND INTERNAL AUDIT

Is CSA then a vehicle for internal audit or is it a fundamental part of the management tool-kit? It is not a cop out to suggest that it is both. Management should be in a position where they understand what their risks and control scenarios are; internal audit should be in a position where it understands management's objectives and is in the business of assisting their achievement. It is this latter suggestion that might cause problems for some internal audit departments, particularly those that have still to learn that audit has no objective other than to assist managers to achieve theirs. It is hard to believe that it is still possible to see audit reports outlining audit's objectives as though audit has a role that is different from that of the organisation.

Could the real force behind the introduction of CSA therefore be that in many internal audit departments the move to system-based, risk-orientated auditing of management's control objectives has yet to occur? Could systems-based auditing have been poorly understood by staff brought up on the need for extensive testing of the financial systems and with little grasp of the operational processes within the company? There is a suspicion that the introduction of CSA may be little more than an admission that internal audit has failed the organisation. CSA can also be the approach favoured where the auditors have failed to extend their sphere of influence beyond the financial arena and have neglected the need to evaluate the whole system of organisational internal control. It would be interesting for research to be undertaken to see if there is a relationship between the extent of internal audit coverage and approach and the introduction of CSA. Certainly there is some anecdotal evidence to suggest this.

In my view CSA emphasises the importance of informal controls which the proponents of CSA have argued that the traditional internal audit approach will not identify. I believe that with a more thorough internal audit approach, based upon detailed interviewing in addition to document review, these informal controls can be identified, recorded and evaluated by internal audit giving a clearer picture of the internal control framework. This, to my mind, is the essence of systems-based auditing, involving the customer in the process and producing ownership of the internal audit report. If this is done by internal audit properly, there should be no need for an extensive CSA workshop or questionnaire portfolio. The work is already undertaken by properly trained internal audit staff working with the managers and the staff involved in the process, identifying the total system for managing risk and taking control. The important aspect of this approach is consultation between the auditor and the auditee, harnessing the knowledge of the control expert with the operational expert.

Some of the enthusiasts of CSA would appear to suggest that internal audit had no grasp of the organisation's risks and objectives, did not talk to anyone when conducting the audit, made recommendations that were not discussed with and agreed by managers, and perpetuated the old-style policemen role. Whilst that may be true of some internal audit units it certainly has not been, for many a year, the profession's recommended method of practising internal audit. With the development of many very good internal audit units into risk management functions, why is it that CSA suddenly is the answer to control and risk?

So where has the thrust for CSA come from? In some areas of the public sector it has certainly been emphasised by political pressure as a result of control failures. In the NHS the thrust came in response to the damning Public Accounts Committee report into the Wessex computer affair. A solution was therefore required by politicians to satisfy Parliament. My own preference would have been for a detailed study to be undertaken asking why internal audit had not detected the various problems that were finally identified with the project in question. The outcome of such a study would have identified the problems and allowed a focused approach to improvement, setting standards for the overall improvement of NHS Internal Audit. Unfortunately this was not done and CSA has been put forward as a solution. But are we aware of what the problem was?

Where internal audit has been truly carrying out its role, across all operational systems and evaluating risk and control against managerial objectives, there is often no demand for CSA. There is therefore I believe clearly a link between the internal audit service received and the call for CSA input. No one should be surprised that the customer who has had an internal audit service bashing away at the payroll for 20 years jumps up and down for CSA which they see as having the potential to add benefit to the organisation which the tick and bash approach has failed to provide. But the vast majority of internal auditors changed their style many years ago, ridding themselves of the 'tick and bash' image and encouraging the development of participative 'whole organisation' auditing. Is that not what CSA is, but by another name?

One also has to be a little careful about the extent that CSA draws internal audit away from its mission. Much of the methodology being suggested is similar to that in use for Total Quality Management (TQM) and the Business Excellence Model (BEM) – see also Chapters 4 and 21. In these instances participants are encouraged to assess their own methods of working, coming together in workshops to exploit the inherent knowledge of the whole work-force and to establish effective, efficient working methods. Translate this into a workshop examining risk and control and you have CSA. The mechanism is a quality review of processes but often lacks the objectivity that can be brought to the process by an outsider. Internal audit can and should, but does not always, provide that objectivity; an independence from the hurly-burly of day-to-day routines.

The independence question is one that constantly raises its head, and it is clear that the reaction of some within the profession to the introduction of CSA is not helpful. Some commentators see the process as lacking the objectivity and independence which is seen to be essential to auditing. Despite this, CSA is seen as being beneficial to management practice, even though it may not be internal audit. Whilst the arguments on objectivity are difficult to refute I do not believe that internal auditors should constantly hide behind their independence, which in many cases is a thin shield anyway. No, perhaps we should be upfront and acknowledge that an assessment by both operational staff and management of risk and control could be extremely beneficial to the work of internal audit, particularly if the assessment is honest and sincere. My internal auditors are encouraged to meet with managers and staff before the system objective is written or the control objectives are discussed, and discover from them what the danger areas are. This can then focus the work of the audit so that it has valid direction and can help to improve the value-added nature of the audit outcome. It also means that in practical terms managers and staff already feel involved before the audit has really started. And as the whole purpose of the audit is to assist them, is not that what we need to achieve? Perhaps the solution is to improve the consultative nature of the internal audit approach rather than replace it altogether.

The link with TQM and the Business Excellence Model means that CSA should generally be considered to be a management practice and should not be regarded as a substitute for internal audit. This needs to be emphasised with the increasing popularity of CSA and the perception that it is an internal audit function. As a management practice it can work alongside and complement the work of internal audit; risks and controls identified during CSA workshops can be tested and validated as part of the audit process, but the same could happen with TQM or BEM workshops. One of the dangers with the introduction of CSA is that it is seen as yet another management task, which in the real world there is no time to complete. With modern organisations down-sizing and extending the span of control for middle management, control becomes more important. It is, however, likely that CSA would be one of the areas to suffer because of a lack of managerial time to make the necessary commitment.

I believe, however, that it is important that we try to avoid the route that some are suggesting, that internal audit becomes the quality assessment process for CSA, advising management on the validity of the process. The dangers of this are numerous but primarily relate to the loss of a true evaluative role and its replacement by a compliance regime. This is what internal audit has spent the last 20 years trying to get away from but now some are assisting its return. The biggest danger though is that the process of the CSA workshop, survey (or whatever) may have been in line with best practice, but who is to assess the input into the process? Did all the risks come to light? Were the individuals participating fully involved or just supporting a management line? We all know how difficult it can be to convince staff that these views mean something, that their input is needed. Can we really keep this level of enthusiasm going year in, year out particularly if staff remain the same? And if we cannot, do not we still have to carry on with internal audit, thereby incurring an additional cost?

Consider the situation that you may find your organisation in. The production team are now on their third CSA workshop. They are the same people who were on the previous two workshops. What are they likely to identify? In the majority of cases, they will identify the same things. Is this adding value? Perhaps it was the reason why Paul Makosz reintroduced direct audit reports within a year of abolishing them.

## WHAT IS THE FUTURE?

With internal audit continuing as a service to management I see CSA as an opportunity to increase managerial understanding of the value of internal control in achieving business objectives. It has the potential to provide the internal auditor with new and current information on risk and control direct from the coal face. It also ensures, if undertaken correctly, that managers and staff assume responsibility and accountability for the control environment and internal audit can work with them to ensure that the environment remains controlled. But it is important to accept that there needs to be some external influence, some evaluation from outside the normal activity, in order to make sure that the organisation gains some value from the work being done.

The Cadbury Committee report defined internal control on a restricted basis when compared to its counterparts in the US and Canada. In this country it was assumed that internal control related to the internal financial controls whilst in the others this boundary was more widespread with a dynamic approach to organisational control. The NHS in the UK has insisted on directors making assurance statements, initially on financial controls but for 1999–2000 this will be extended to all internal controls. If internal audit, as a service, reported directly to the chief executive and was responsible for a broader role in the field of risk management it is likely that CSA/Quality Self Assessment/Quality Circles will become normal input routines to the internal audit work.

I believe that internal audit has a role to play in evaluating controls over business risk which transcends the requirement for pure financial control. I am convinced that a broad-based, organisation-wide approach to internal audit provides a major input to the control needs of the directors and can contribute a great deal to the strength of the company's control framework. It is clear that a consultative approach to the planning and execution of internal audit can have much the same effect as the use of CSA workshops. The internal auditor within this context has the opportunity, at the initial stages, to identify business risk with the assistance of the operational experts. This co-operation ensures that the focus of internal audit evaluation is on the fundamental concerns of the business.

There is also the added advantage that the discussions between the auditor and operational staff, which form part of the everyday process of the audit, will act as a catalyst to retain an interest in both business risk and its control. My experience suggests that when this process is carried out correctly, it often results in unsolicited requests from managers for further assistance from the internal audit team. If the internal audit team are unable, for whatever reason, to establish this one-to-one approach then CSA may then have a role. The use of CSA as an integral part of the internal audit toolkit, either as a formalised process of workshop facilitation or through a questionnaire approach, could have a part to play in ensuring that risk and control remain in the mind set of managers, but perhaps not to the extent that the personal approach to internal audit would have done.

It is clear though that CSA is only a process that can assist internal control, not the answer to the absence of control. The danger behind the hype is that organisations will believe it is control in itself and disasters will recur. After all, would Nick Leeson, attending the Barings CSA facilitated workshop, have indicated that there was a weakness in the way that futures were being dealt with? I do not think he would have and that is a major reason why CSA remains an internal audit tool, not a replacement for internal audit.

## NOTES

1. *Control Self Assessment – Making the Choice*. Glenda Jordan, IIA Inc, page 38.
2. Ibid., page 49.

# 4

# Quality, Governance and Conduct are Important Control Drivers

*Jeff Ridley*

## CONTROL SELF ASSESSMENT IS GOOD MANAGEMENT

Understanding how organisations are controlled to achieve objectives is fundamental to good management. All regulators and organisation stakeholders require those that manage to assess risks in their environments, and to have competence to control those risks. All auditors are required by their standards of professionalism to assess control and risk during their audit work. These fundamental statements on control and risk form the base upon which the process of control and risk assessment has developed over recent years.

Control and risk assessments must be based on a good understanding of organisation objectives, threats to achievement and control activities. Collecting data for these assessments, and facilitating discussions to identify weaknesses in control, is an important role for both managers and auditors. This chapter provides a personal view of the theoretical and empirical foundations of CSA, and seeks to establish the importance of always including quality, governance and conduct objectives in every control and risk assessment. Each drives important control activities. Each can gain strength from the other. Together they can be integrated into strong control environments.

Yet, is this always so? Not all organisations demonstrate links between quality, governance and conduct in their published statements. Many still report on each separately. Few integrate the strengths from each into their statements on good management.

## QUALITY, GOVERNANCE AND CONDUCT AS OBJECTIVES

Most research and practices show that quality, governance and conduct have many shared control activities. Many of these share aims of economy, efficiency and effectiveness. Each can have a powerful influence over the others' control activities. If missions for each are integrated at strategic, tactical and operational levels, they become more powerful in control frameworks.

The Institute of Internal Auditors (IIA) Certified Internal Auditor[1] (CIA®) examination programme now includes questions concerning quality programmes and their impact on control. The following question from one of the CIA® recent examination papers demonstrates this. (The suggested answer is given at the end of this chapter.)

> Question: Auditors are operating in organisations in which management is in the process of 'reengineering' operations with strong emphasis on total quality management techniques. In their quest to gain efficiency in processing, many of the traditional control procedures are being deleted from the organisation's control structure. As part of this change, management is:
>
> (a) Placing more emphasis on monitoring control activities.
> (b) Making different assumptions about human performance and the nature of human motivation than was done under traditional control techniques.
> (c) Placing more emphasis on self-correcting control activities and process automation.
> (d) All of the above.
>
> Which is the correct answer?

In your own organisation it is worth considering:

- How does it communicate its quality, governance and conduct objectives?
- Are they integrated each with the other?
- Do quality, governance and codes of conduct assist the organisation to achieve its objectives?

## EVIDENCE OF QUALITY, GOVERNANCE AND CONDUCT OBJECTIVES IN ORGANISATIONS

Quality and governance are now well studied and researched pathways to success, even survival, in today's government and business operations. Use of quality as a control is not new. Omachonu and Ross (1994)[2] recognise control for quality is different from the use of traditional control concepts for financial statements.

> The classical control process will require significant change if TQM is to be successful. Traditionally, control systems have been directed to the end use of

> preparation of financial statements. Focus has been on the components of the profit-and-loss statement. Quality control has historically followed a three-step process consisting of (1) setting standards, (2) reporting variances and (3) correcting deviations ... In an organization that perceives control systems in this way, there is the danger that the system will become the end rather than the means. This is not to say that classical control does not have a place in quality management.

The authors explore what place classical control has in quality management activities at strategic, tactical and operational levels but not as an integrated approach. Nor is classical control defined to include the wider aspects of governance or external controls over an organisation's activities. Recent research by Bain and Band (1996)[3] into governance, demonstrates some recognition of quality and governance integration:

> We hold the view that corporate governance is very much about adding value. Companies and other enterprises with a professional and positive attitude to governance are stronger and have a greater record of achievement. In fact, some company directors, like Allan Sykes, in his article 'Proposals for Internationally Competitive Corporate Governance in Britain and America', suggest that there is an important direct relationship between a country's corporate governance system and its economic success.

Conduct is a less well researched objective in organisations. For many organisations codes of conduct are new. Yet evidence is beginning to emerge linking control activities for good conduct into quality and governance missions. Current examples of links between quality, governance and conduct are shown in Appendix 4.1. Consider the implications of each in your organisation, and compare them with statements by your own management.

## QUALITY PROGRAMMES AND CONTROL

Control is essential for all quality programmes. Consider:

- Quality management cultures focus on controlling satisfaction of customer expectations.
- ISO 9000 (1994)[4] requires clear responsibilities, controlled process and monitoring activities.
- All quality awards require controlled objectives and self assessments.

The USA Treadway Commission (1987)[5] researched '... environments in which fraudulent (financial) reporting occurs ...'. This research established a demand for control guidance in the USA, resulting in COSO (1992)[6], which developed control theory with six control elements '... control environment, objectives and risks, control activities and monitoring; all linked by accurate and timely information systems and communications'. All the quality programmes mentioned above have in common many, if not all, the integrated control elements built into the COSO model. Management, accountants and auditors now use these elements and their underlying theory to guide their risk assessments. They form the basis of control models in many sectors and countries providing internal control frameworks for many organisations with quality management cultures.

The impact of ISO 9000 on control in an organisation with systems registered to the standard, is significant. Each of its quality requirements can influence all the elements in the COSO 'Internal Control – Integrated Framework'. This framework has become a recognised reference on control across the world. Its elements span all the control requirements for any type or size of organisation. Comparison of the ISO 9000 quality requirements with the COSO control elements shows important links, each with the other, see Appendix 4.2. Referencing the quality requirements of ISO 9000 into the COSO control framework can be an excellent learning exercise for those who review control in an organisation. Quality principles of customer focus, leadership, teamwork, analysis and continuous improvement can apply to each of the COSO elements. Quality, although not specifically mentioned in COSO, is also an important requirement of the objectives in COSO's following definition of control objectives:

- effectiveness and efficiency of operations
- reliability of financial reporting
- compliance with applicable laws and regulations.

In the early 1990s, government and industry sponsored European and national annual competition programmes for quality awards and organisations in the private sector across Europe (European Foundation for Quality Management) researched and created a quality framework with eight criteria focused on achieving excellent business results – The European Quality Model. The British Quality Award (1994)[7] followed, set up with the aim of enhancing the '... performance and effectiveness of all types of organisations in the UK through the promotion of Total Quality Management'. It uses a quality award process based on the European Quality Model. In 1995 the scope of this award was extended to the public and voluntary sectors. The assessment criteria used in these awards measure commitment, culture and control, and how each impacts performance.

These criteria have also been used by the British Quality Foundation to develop their Business Excellence Model. This is linked to a self assessment tool and has been used across private and public sectors in the UK. Recently it has gained added impetus by being endorsed by the Government's Best

Value initiative (for further details see Chapter 21).

CoCo (1995)[8], provides additional guidance on designing, assessing and reporting on the control systems of organisations. It uses a control framework similar to the first four elements of COSO, also addressing control in business re-engineering processes and quality environments. It links its internal control framework to the criteria needed to win the USA Malcolm Baldrige National Quality Award (MBNQA). The MBNQA criteria framework has seven categories, none of which make any reference to ISO 9000. In Europe, Model, mentioned above, the European Quality with its criteria framework of nine similar categories references into ISO 9000 as a recognised achievement in the Processes category. Other Quality Award programmes exist world-wide and it is probable, if they do not already do so, their self-assessment and external review processes will start to recognise ISO 9000.

Ridley and Stephens (1996)[9], in their study of ISO 9000 implications for internal auditing, commented on links between quality programmes and COSO:

> There is no evidence to indicate that development of the COSO internal control model, leading to its publication in 1992, took into account any of the control developments taking place at the same time, in the quality environments in organizations. Nor, is there any evidence controls designed into quality programmes were developed taking into account the COSO study. Each of the studies of control, COSO and quality, has developed separately, but in parallel. There have been some studies of links between quality management and ISO 9000, but few published studies of links between the COSO control model and specific quality programs.

## ASSESSING LINKS BETWEEN QUALITY AND CONTROL

UK government interest in quality as a driver for change in the private sector started in the early 1980s, National Audit Office (1990)[10] – 'A recognition that success in world markets increasingly depends on quality as well as price led the Government in 1982 to publish the White Paper "Standards: Quality and International Competitiveness".' This White Paper came from research studies by The Department of Trade and Industry, which ended with promotion of quality standards as a way forward for British industry in international markets. UK government promotion of BS 5750 – the quality management system standard followed. This standard, like all standards, was researched by working groups of practitioners and academics. It was sold as a UK symbol of achievement in the design and implementation of quality systems. This same standard was adopted throughout Europe as EN 29000 and in 1987 revised by international working groups and adopted across the world by the International Standards Organization, as ISO 9000. In 1995 all three standards became the one standard BS EN ISO 9000. Another quality management standard also developed in the UK – BS 7850: Total Quality Management (1992)[11] defines TQM as:

> Total quality management assures maximum effectiveness and efficiency within an organisation by putting in place processes and systems which will ensure that every aspect of its activity is aligned to satisfy customer needs and all other objectives without waste of effort and using the full potential of every person in the organisation. This philosophy recognises that customer satisfaction, health, safety, environmental considerations and business objectives are mutually dependent. It is applicable within any organisation.

Links between quality and performance are recognised in the rationale behind SEPSU (1994)[12] which studied the practice of quality management in UK organisations covering ISO 9000, TQM and other approaches to quality achievement, SEPSU recognised the links between quality and performance in the rationale of its study as:

> . . . quality is self-evidently important in all spheres of human endeavour. In the sphere of organised work, quality is now one of the central determinants of competitive survival and thus of national prosperity. This leads to a widespread interest in the management of quality as a dimension of corporate behaviour. . . .

## ASSESSING LINKS BETWEEN GOVERNANCE AND CONTROL

Financial, social, quality and environmental aspects of governance are now international issues, across all supply chains. They embrace ethics, fairness, honesty, caring and sustaining. Cadbury (1992)[13], develops a definition of governance that embraces openness, integrity and accountability, stating that '. . . governance is the system by which companies are directed and controlled'.

Governance is based on law and regulation; direction, prevention and detection; monitoring, feedback and correction; punishment and reward. Control, as part of governance, is always seen as an essential management activity. It applies, and is applied, across all levels of an organisation and impacts performance in the achievement of all objectives.

A study by the Institute of Internal Auditors – UK (1994)[14], of world-wide internal control principles and practices, contends that:

- the primary purpose of an internal control system is to enable directors to drive their companies forward with confidence, at an appropriate speed and direction, in both good and bad times;

- the secondary, but no less important, purpose is to safeguard resources and ensure the adequacy of records and systems of accountability.

## ASSESSING LINKS BETWEEN CONDUCT AND CONTROL

Corporate concerns and public disenchantment with behaviour in some major businesses world-wide during the 1980s, led to a growing demand for improved ethical standards to be adopted publicly by many organisations. These demands have increased, moving into governments and their supporting administrations. Many organisations now publicly declare codes of ethics to their stakeholders, linking these to some, if not all, of their other objectives. The Institute of Business Ethics (1992)[15] includes the following statement in its proposed ethics code:

> We will provide products and services of good value and consistent quality, reliability and safety. . . . We will avoid practices which seek to increase sales by any means other than fair merchandising efforts based on quality, design features, productivity, price and product support. . . . We will provide a high standard of service in our efforts to maintain customer satisfaction and co-operation.

In recent years, a series of new and eventful organisation malpractices in both the private and public sectors across the world has given conduct issues a higher profile. Malpractices that have damaged stakeholders and often the public, to whom they provide their products and services. Sheridan and Kendall (1992)[16] see this scene with some unease:

> When we observe the corporate scene these days we are aware of a vague sense of unease. As business people and industrialists, as professional advisers or as senior managers, we are conscious that all is not well in the way many large concerns are run . . . how many more problems may lurk in the smaller companies.

Recently, many organisations have been influenced by external stakeholder pressures to reinforce existing conduct practices or adopt new ones. Tricker (1994)[17] sees governance and conduct, not as separate theories, but as a development of both 'stewardship theory' and 'agency theory', emphasising 'Research in this area has hardly begun. . .'. He sees both mainly based on two bodies of knowledge '. . . the legal and the operational perspectives'. Looking to the future he adds another theoretical focus 'essentially ideological and political', deriving 'insights from the worlds of political science, sociology and philosophy', leading 'to insights into the importance of values, beliefs and culture. . .'

In its study of corporate governance in the public sector, CIPFA (1995)[18] considers both Cadbury and published findings from the Committee on

Standards of Conduct in Public Life (1995)[19], then chaired by Lord Nolan. CIPFA designs a framework of principles and standards of corporate governance in the context of public services. This framework defines corporate governance as being concerned with '... structures and processes for decision-making and accountability, controls, and behaviour, at the top of organisations'. For the purposes of its governance framework, 'openness, integrity and accountability' are defined by CIPFA in terms of 'holders of public office' as shown in Appendix 4.3.

Nolan addresses aspects of corporate governance in the public sector. His first report has been followed by others and more are expected. He identifies and defines seven general principles of conduct that should underpin public life, and recommends that all public service bodies should draw up codes of conduct incorporating these principles. These principles of selflessness, integrity, objectivity, accountability, openness, honesty and leadership are shown in Appendix 4.4.

## CONCLUSIONS

Control objectives for quality, governance and conduct will continue to integrate and have an impact on all risks. Links between the control frameworks for each will be needed to reduce and avoid most risks. Those that assess risk in any organisation will need to build reviews of these links into their review process. Auditors will need to ensure that their audits cover the control objectives for quality, governance and conduct across the total supply chain, including customers and suppliers.

Ridley and Chambers (1998)[20], address quality, governance and conduct as they impact both control objectives and internal auditing. They develop *Principia* for leading-edge internal auditing, which include the following:

> The financial, social, quality and environmental aspects of control are international issues, across all supply chains.
> Control embraces all aspects of governance, including ethics, equality, honesty, caring and sustaining.

The growing interest in risk assessment across all types and sizes of organisations, led by consultants and internal auditors, is fuelled by new demands from managers and regulators for position statements on internal control. These new demands are encouraging a wider view of control, linked to all organisation objectives and associated risks. Tim Leech (see also Chapter 2) sees evidence of the integration of control and quality objectives in a growing number of companies. In 1994,[21] he reported on emerging evidence of an integration of control and quality strategies, predicting that for many organisations: '... they must integrate their control and quality management strategies if they are to be successful in the longer term and the needs of a wider range of stakeholders are to be met.'

The messages from this chapter are:

- quality, governance and conduct objectives strengthen each other and the control frameworks established for their achievement
- quality, governance and conduct should be considered during all control and risk assessments
- auditors, managers, audit committees and governing bodies should consider the importance of integrating all control frameworks in the organisations they serve.

(Suggested answer to the CIA® examination question on page 62 is (d).)

## NOTES

1 The IIA Certified Internal Auditor examinations are in four parts and set twice each year at centres across the world. Currently they are available in English, French, Hebrew and Spanish. Details can be obtained from The IIA, 249 Maitland Avenue, Altimonte Springs, Florida 32701-4201, USA.

2 Omachonu V.K. and Ross J.E. (1994) *Principles of Total Quality*. St. Lucia Press, Florida, USA.
3 Bain N. and Band D. (1996) *Winning Ways Through Corporate Governance*. Macmillan Business, London.
4 International Standards Organisation (1994) *BS EN ISO 9000 series of Quality Systems Standards, ISO, Switzerland.*
5 Treadway Commission (1987) *Report of the National Commission on Fraudulent Financial Reporting*. AICPA, New Jersey, USA.
6 Committee of Sponsoring Organizations of the Treadway Commission (1992) *Internal Control – Integrated Framework*. American Institute of Certified Public Accountants, New Jersey, USA.
7 The British Quality Foundation (1994) *The UK Quality Award*. BQF, London.
8 The Canadian Institute of Chartered Accountants (CICA) (1995) *Guidance on Criteria of Control (CoCo), Toronto, Canada.*
9 Ridley J. and Stephens K. (1996) *International Quality Standards: Implications for Internal Auditing*, The Institute of Internal Auditors Inc. Altimonte Springs, Florida, USA.
10 National Audit Office (1990) *Department of Trade and Industry: Promotion of Quality and Standards*. HMSO, London.
11 BS 7850 (1992) *Total Quality Management*. BSI, London.

12 SEPSU Policy Study No. 10 (1994) *UK Quality Management – Policy Options*, Science and Engineering Policy Studies Unit, The Royal Society and the Royal Academy of Engineering, London.
13 Cadbury (1992) *The Financial Aspects of Corporate Governance*. GEE, London.
14 The Institute of Internal Auditors – UK (1994) *Internal Control*. IIA-UK, London.
15 The Institute of Business Ethics (1992) *Business Ethics and Company Codes*. IBE, London.
16 Sheridan T. and Kendall N. (1992) *Corporate Governance – An Action Plan for Profitability and Business Success*. Financial Times/Pitman, London.
17 Tricker R.I. (1994) *International Corporate Governance*. Prentice Hall, Singapore.
18 The Chartered Institute of Public Finance and Accountability (1995) *Corporate Governance – A Framework for Public Service Bodies*. CIPFA, London.
19 Nolan (1995) *Standards in Public Life*. HMSO, London.
20 Ridley J. and Chambers A.D. (1998) *Leading Edge Internal Auditing*, ICSA Publishing Limited, London.
21 Leech T. J. (1994) paper presented at the 48th Annual Quality Congress of the American Society for Quality Control, at Las Vegas, Nevada, USA. (ASQ are in Milwaukee, Wisconsin, USA).

## APPENDIX 4.1

# Selection of Evidence that Control Environments for Quality, Governance and Conduct are Integrating

### SELF-ASSESSMENT GUIDE FOR THE EUROPEAN QUALITY AWARD – CRITERION 2: POLICY AND STRATEGY

- The organisation's mission, values, vision and strategic direction and the manner in which it achieves them.
- How the organisation's policy and strategy reflect the concept of Total Quality and how the principles of Total Quality are used in the determination, deployment, review and improvement of policy and strategy.

### ANNUAL REPORT ADVERTISEMENT IN THE *FINANCIAL TIMES* 2 FEBRUARY 1996

We are striving to make our group exemplary. Commitment to our code of business ethics defines our fundamental values. For our customer it means being attentive to their needs, guaranteeing our quality, and above all keeping our word. For our shareholders it means protecting their investment. For our staff members it means ensuring mutual respect and developing personal skills. and across the board it means transparency *Lyonnaise Des Eaux*

### 1995 ANNUAL REPORT – THE BOC GROUP

The group policy requires all business units to co-operate fully with their country's regulatory authorities, comply with all applicable laws and regulations, and prepare and follow a continuous improvement programme for its operations, customers and suppliers.

## GUIDANCE FOR DIRECTORS – GOVERNANCE PROCESSES FOR CONTROL: DECEMBER 1995

> The values of an organisation affect everything it does. They encompass ethical values, as well as matters such as creativity, innovation, quality and avoidance of bias. Values affect relationships with shareholders, customers, suppliers, employees and other stakeholders. They also affect the organization's approach to matters such as compliance with the law, financial reporting and product quality. The Canadian Institute of Chartered Accountants

## ADVERTISED MAY 1996 CONFERENCE FINAL AGENDA: PRESENTED BY THE CONFERENCE BOARD AND EUROPEAN FOUNDATION FOR QUALITY MANAGEMENT

> Quality, safety and environment – a common standard: In this session you'll hear how companies with mature quality initiatives are focusing on integration of quality, safety and environment. The voices of stakeholders are clearly identifying these three initiatives as essential to the business success of the organisation. Senior executives will share the role of these key initiatives, reflect on their experiences, and their evolving importance and impact on day-to-day operations and business performance.

## EXHIBITS FROM THE CADBURY CODE OF BEST PRACTICE (1992)

1.1 The board should ... retain full and effective control ... and monitor ...

1.6 All directors should have access to ... advice and services ... ensure that board procedures are followed and that applicable rules and regulations are complied with.

4.1 It is the board's duty to present a balanced and understandable assessment of the company's position.

4.3 The board should ensure that an objective and professional relationship is maintained with auditors.

4.5 The directors should report on the effectiveness of the company's system of internal control.

4.6 The directors should report that the business is a going concern, with supporting assumptions or qualifications as necessary.

## APPENDIX 4.2

# Comparison of ISO 9000 Quality Requirements with COSO Control Elements

ISO 9000

Management responsibility
Quality system
Contract review
Design control
Document and data control
Purchasing
Control of customer-supplied product
Product identification and traceability
Process control
Inspection and testing
Control of inspection, measuring and test equipment
Inspection of test status
Control of nonconforming product
Corrective and preventive action
Handling, storage, packaging, preservation and delivery
Control of quality records
Internal quality audits
Training
Servicing
Statistical techniques

COSO

Control environment
Risk assessment
Control activities
Monitoring
Information systems
Communication

## APPENDIX 4.3

# CIPFA Governance Definitions

## GOVERNANCE

Governance is currently defined as being the structures, systems and policies in an organisation, designed and established to direct and control all operations and relationships on a continuing basis, in an honest and caring manner, taking into account the interests of all stakeholders and compliance with all applicable laws and regulatory requirements. Governance is based on the following principles of openness, integrity and accountability:

## OPENNESS

Openness is required to ensure that stakeholders can have confidence in the decision-making processes and actions of public service bodies, in the management of their activities, and in the individuals within them. Being open through meaningful consultation with stakeholders and communication of full, accurate and clear information leads to effective and timely action and lends itself to necessary scrutiny.

## INTEGRITY

Integrity comprises both straightforward dealing and completeness. It is based upon honesty, selflessness and objectivity, and high standards of propriety and probity in the stewardship of public funds and management of a body's affairs. It is dependent on the effectiveness of the control framework and on the personal standards and professionalism of the individuals within the body. It is reflected both in the body's decision-making procedures and in the quality of its financial and performance reporting.

## ACCOUNTABILITY

Accountability is the process whereby public service bodies, and the individuals within them are responsible for their decisions and actions, including their stewardship of public funds and all aspects of performance, and submit themselves to appropriate scrutiny. It is achieved by all parties having a clear understanding of those responsibilities, and having clearly defined roles through a robust structure.

## APPENDIX 4.4

# Standards in Public Life: Nolan's Seven Principles

(Standards in Public Life, Second Report of the Committee on Standards in Public Life, Chairman Lord Nolan, May 1996, Cm 3270-1; Crown copyright reproduced with the permission of the Controller of Her Majesty's Stationary Office)

### SELFLESSNESS

Holders of public office should take decisions solely in terms of the public interest. They should not do so in order to gain financial or other material benefits for themselves, their families, or their friends.

### INTEGRITY

Holders of public office should not place themselves under any financial or other obligation to outside individuals or organisations that might influence them in the performance of their official duties.

### OBJECTIVITY

In carrying out public business, including making public appointments, awarding contracts, or recommending individuals for rewards and benefits, holders of public office should make choices on merit.

### ACCOUNTABILITY

Holders of public office are accountable for their decisions and actions to the public and must submit themselves to whatever scrutiny is appropriate to their office.

## OPENNESS

Holders of public office should be as open as possible about all the decisions and actions they take. They should give reasons for their decisions and restrict information only when the wider public interest clearly demands.

## HONESTY

Holders of public office have a duty to declare any private interests relating to their public duties and to take steps to resolve any conflicts arising in a way that protects the public interest.

## LEADERSHIP

Holders of public office should promote and support these principles by leadership and example.

# 5

# Control Self Assessment
## Its Stakeholders and Beneficiaries

*John Rowson*

## INTRODUCTION

The requirement for many public- and private-sector organisations to provide an annual statement on internal control has provided the main impetus for Control Self Assessment (CSA). However, the effort involved in a full implementation of CSA can be fully justified only if there are other benefits to the business. This chapter explores the benefits that can be obtained by various groups of people, the stakeholders. In discussing the interests of the various stakeholders, the question of ownership and process drivers is also explored.

There are quite a number of different sets of people who have both an interest and therefore a stake in the implementation of an effective programme of CSA. Whilst this chapter emphasises the benefits, there may also be disadvantages and also a number of the benefits could be achieved by alternative routes and processes.

Examples of some disadvantages are included later in this chapter, others are:

- cost
- duplication with other 'assurers' unless properly managed; such management requires adequate resources
- the discoverable nature of the documentation produced in the event of litigation.

## EXTERNAL STAKEHOLDERS

### Shareholders/Potential Shareholders/Predators

Potential benefits are:

- confidence, comfort and assurance
- increased share value/ better dividends
- investment opportunity
- more information
- increased future potential.

The intention of the Cadbury recommendations, as reflected in the statement in the annual accounts, was to provide assurance for the shareholders that an adequate system of internal control was in place during the period covered by the financial statements. This then enables the shareholders to make decisions about the security of their investment and may influence any decision on retention of their shares. Potential shareholders and predators may also gain information about the organisation and its attitude to control from the statement.

### Regulators

Potential benefits are:

- confidence in quality
- better assurance
- more focus in their overall work.

Regulators exist to ensure proper safeguards exist for the public. Evidence of proper business controls which help to ensure business objectives, that have been defined to consider regulators requirements, should enhance their reputation and enable regulators to focus attention where it is needed most. This in itself should reduce the cost of regulation.

### External Auditors

For potential benefits see page 87.

## Customers/Partnerships/Clients

Potential benefits are:

- confidence/peace of mind
- improved service
- better value for money
- better products
- dependability.

Customers such as suppliers, business alliances or retail buyers, distributors/agents/intermediaries are likely to have valid comments on their own perception of how well the business operates. This could either come from complaint/compliment analysis, questionnaires (providing there is a proper selection process), or even from a direct involvement in an assessment programme where applicable.

## Insurers

Potential benefits are:

- confidence
- fewer claims
- increased profits leading to lower premiums.

## Suppliers

Potential benefits are:

- overall improved confidence/assurance (e.g., over millennium IT problem)
- image to potential customers
- belief in confidentiality
- more (but possibly less) business
- clarity of service.

Confidence will be seen in the demand for further services resulting from business growth. Suppliers can rely on confidentiality and know what services are expected. Additionally suppliers will be able to identify with a successful organisation when seeking business from others.

### Distributors, Agents, Intermediaries, Retailers

Potential benefits are:

- overall improved confidence
- dependability
- clarity of service.

### Business Partners

Potential benefits are:

- overall improved confidence
- optimisation of partnership
- increased profits.

### The Public/Taxpayers/Society

Potential benefits are:

- additional confidence
- assurance that the business takes its responsibilities seriously
- proper use of public money.

### The Environment

Potential benefits are:

- reduced risk of catastrophe
- environmental sustainability.

Some industries are such that failures can have a significant impact on the environment (e.g., nuclear/gas/oil). Confirmed control processes are likely to reduce the chance of that ever-present risk becoming a reality.

## INTERNAL STAKEHOLDERS

### The Board – Executive Directors Prime Owner of CSA/Support

Potential benefits are:

- assurance/peace of mind/no big surprises
- meeting corporate governance requirements
- clarity of business objectives/objectives achieved
- clarification of the risks faced
- cost-effective control
- better understanding and awareness of risk and control
- buy in to better control from managers
- better working environment
- improved communication
- enhanced performance
- comfort and potential job security (although the opposite might be true)
- better investor relations
- potentially better information about risks, controls and weaknesses
- assurance that risks taken are acceptable
- improved status/salary as company progresses
- opportunity for assessing management.

The Directors have the ultimate responsibility for the systems of control within an organisation, as indicated by the internal control statement in the annual accounts. An effective control system will involve all levels of management within the organisation. The directors will be involved with high-level issues and controls and other levels of management will deal with other aspects of control.

The Directors will require assurance that there is an adequate system of control in place and that it is operating effectively. In particular, they will need this assurance before the statement in the annual accounts is signed. There are a number of ways this can be provided. Internal Audit is one and CSA is another. Control of the process is likely to be delegated, but high-level reporting will need to be in place so that the Directors can be certain that the CSA process has been carried out adequately and they have been made aware of the key issues arising.

## Audit Committees/Non-Executive Directors

Potential benefits are:

- ability to meet specific responsibilities effectively
- more information/no big surprises/better understanding of the risks run
- potentially better information about risks, controls and weaknesses
- wider coverage
- better focus/decision making.

The Audit Committee, involving non-executive directors, is used to ensuring that audit work is conducted in a satisfactory manner and that issues arising are receiving the appropriate level of attention from within the organisation. As an extension of this role they may oversee the CSA process. In performing this role they will concentrate on the Cadbury requirements rather than any wider implementation of CSA. This will involve ensuring CSA is applied consistently across all parts of the organisation. They should also make sure reporting mechanisms are adequate and that any action plans arising from the assessment are followed up and completed. It is likely that the more detailed work will be delegated to Internal Audit with a report-back mechanism.

## Senior Management — Prime Owner of CSA/Support

Potential benefits are:

- clarification of issues at their level
- work prioritisation
- improved understanding followed by more effectiveness
- clarification of responsibility for control
- recognition of known residual risk
- more frequent review possible
- status/salary improvements as company progresses.

Executive Directors and/or senior managers may be directly involved in some high-level areas of assessment but within other areas may provide only support, prioritisation and guidance.

## Finance Director/Finance Department

A traditional role of Finance in many organisations is that of the 'custodians of control'. This is because of the interface with External Audit and the fact that they prepare the accounts. Finance therefore requires assurance about the quality of the underlying records. This has resulted, in many organisations, in the Finance Department taking a leading role with CSA.

This need to be satisfied with the quality of the company's records means that Finance will be interested in that part of CSA which affects such satisfaction. However, such interest may not extend to improving the business and looking for business opportunities directly. Except in a limited number of areas, their expertise in the overall business process is relatively narrow and concentrated on financial aspects. A wider coverage of overall business issues will be achieved if people from other areas of the business are actively involved in driving CSA. This is explored on page 89 under 'Steering groups'.

## Line Management — Prime Owner of CSA

Potential benefits are:

- clarification of issues at local level
- work prioritisation
- improved understanding of risk and control and clarity of processes, followed by more effectiveness
- support for empowerment
- clarification of responsibility for control and knowledge of accountability
- better decision making
- fulfilling responsibilities
- more reliable achievement of objectives (or chance of missing objectives identified early)
- use of effective and efficient controls
- increased skills and competencies
- promotion of teamwork
- service improvements
- participation

- recognition of known risk
- more frequent review possible
- status/salary improvements as company progresses
- direction for improvement and ownership of corrective action
- empowerment to make risk decisions
- increased operational efficiency and effectiveness
- cost savings.

Line management have day-to-day responsibility for the business processes and the successful operation of these processes. The system of internal control is one of the ways that the successful operation of business processes is ensured. The nature of these controls will depend on both the operating structure of the organisation and the effectiveness of the control design. For example, the devolved responsibility involved in empowerment should change the way in which the process is controlled.

## Staff (and Systems Developers) Assistance to Prime Owner of CSA

Potential benefits are:

- a voice
- better understanding of process/risk and control
- buy in to better control
- better working environment
- improved communication
- enhanced performance
- comfort and potential job security (although the opposite might be true)
- use of effective and efficient controls
- increased skills and competencies
- promotion of teamwork
- service improvements
- pride in their organisation
- being valued
- understanding their jobs better
- status/salary improvements as company progresses

- clarity of purpose
- participation
- recognition of known risk
- enfranchisement
- knowing management are serious about control
- additional skills
- sharing of best practice
- protection from reported problems.

The staff have an interest in the success of their unit and the organisation as a whole. Performance-related pay and job descriptions may reinforce that interest. As a result it is in the interests of staff involved in a process that the controls relating to that process are well designed, effective and efficient.

The people who have a day-to-day responsibility for controlling and operating a system have the most detailed knowledge of that system and potential flaws, although they may be less aware of its context in the overall organisation. The CSA process provides a tool that enables staff to review their processes, methods of operation, standards of control and validate the control processes. Redundant controls can be eliminated and control focused on the real business risks. Other benefits which arise from an assessment are identifying areas for service improvement (perhaps for competitive edge) or business opportunities.

The maximum benefit from the process is achieved by adopting a wide interpretation of the risks evaluated so that all business objectives and issues are included. The final Hampel Report states that a wider perspective of internal control, rather than just internal financial control, is appropriate.

## Assurance Groups — Assistance to Prime Owner of CSA

Examples are External Audit, Internal Audit, compliance, quality assurance, security, special investigation units, risk managers.

Potential benefits are:

- help with primary functions
- more focused effort
- alternative list of issues/information
- better coverage of risks
- more cost-effective assurance/better use of resource

- working with better control environment
- more interesting work
- leverage for more resource
- honesty in the process by workshop attendees
- an improved understanding of the business, obtained more quickly.

A good deal has been heard about how Internal Audit are implementing control self assessment and the reduction of audit time and resources that result from this. A potential reduction in audit effort (or more likely a refocusing) might be a side benefit of an effective CSA programme but is not a reason for implementing CSA.

As the title implies, Control Self Assessment is a process which involves an assessment by people within the organisation of their own controls. Internal Audit, with their knowledge and experience, have a lot to offer in assisting the process. However, self assessment will work effectively only if it is owned and driven forward by the business areas responsible for the controls. Otherwise CSA will both be seen as, and will become, merely another audit technique. Care needs to be exercised to ensure that Internal Audit appears independent of the CSA process.

An effective CSA process produces two main benefits that can influence the effort required from Internal and External Audit:

- improved documentation of the systems, how they are controlled and where, at least some, weaknesses lie
- improved control awareness and a more effective control environment.

The overall level of risk should be reduced as a result of the improved control awareness and control techniques. Additionally, improvements in the effectiveness of the control environment will result. This will increase the assurance that can be gained by auditors about the organisation's systems and this should reduce the overall audit effort required to provide the same level of coverage. The improved documentation enables audit effort to be concentrated where it will provide most benefit. There will be less need for systems to be documented by audit and areas of high risk can be identified more readily.

As suggested above, Internal Audit should not own the process. Maintaining independence from control of the process offers other benefits:

- the process owner should define and own the corrective actions
- audit can provide advice, evaluate the effectiveness and consistency of the process without being compromised. This should provide greater comfort to other stakeholders.

### The Company Generally

Potential benefits are:

- retention of customers/loyalty
- re-sales.

Any company that can demonstrate value for money, reliability and service is likely to retain its customers. Existing customers are less likely to shop round in future if they are satisfied with the quality and service that they have received.

## WHAT NEEDS TO BE CONSIDERED?

The above suggests that it is line management and their staff who should own the process. However, are these people in a position to undertake a programme of Control Self-Assessment without help?

### Steering Groups

A steering group will provide focus and direction for a programme of CSA workshops within the organisation. Their decisions may be based on risk-management concerns fed from senior executives and possibly the Audit Committee.

#### *Membership*

The membership needs to reflect the business areas of the organisation from which process owners will be derived and drive the execution of CSA. Finance have a specific interest in a wider context and may therefore require representation. Internal Audit are likely to be required to provide assurance to the Audit Committee on the CSA process and will therefore need to be in attendance. There may be a CSA manager who will have day-to-day responsibility for the programme.

It is imperative that there should be a proper balance on the steering group if it is to be effective, process buy-in is obtained by all participants and CSA seen as supporting the business in meeting its objectives.

#### *Responsibilities*

Typically these may include:

- prioritisation of coverage at workshops

**Table 5.1** Responsibilities for CSA

| Area | Actioned by |
|---|---|
| Method of assessment – checklist or workshop? | This is pre-decided at a more senior level, but it is most unlikely that a checklist, which had not been prepared through a consulting process (e.g., a workshop), would be adequate. Hence I have shown a workshop approach below |
| Evaluate which areas first? | Directors/Audit Committee steer, perhaps basing their decisions on risk-management techniques |
| How should all areas be covered adequately? | Business universe analysis and logical sub-division |
| Getting executive support and evidence of this | Steering group. Line executive to open workshop/attend selected parts of workshops |
| Control expertise | Workshop attendance by Internal Audit |
| Facilitator | Professionally trained CSA facilitator who is impartial. Could come from another business unit |
| Detailed process expertise | Attendance by properly selected and empowered staff |
| Interlinking processes | Attendance by properly selected and empowered staff from interlinked areas |
| Assessment mechanisms and consistency across units and processes | Pre-defined by steering group and consistently applied – checked by Internal Audit |
| Standardised documentation which is re-usable during annual re-assessments | Pre-defined by steering group and consistently applied – checked by Internal Audit |
| Output timetable | Pre-defined by steering group and consistently applied – test-checked by Internal Audit |
| Getting corrective action | Line executive approval of output including action points, target dates and responsibilities |
| Key issues reporting mechanism | Pre-defined by steering group and consistently applied – checked by Internal Audit |

- assessing submissions to the Board for the annual statement
- agreeing standardised processes such as documentation layouts, timescales for workshop output, line management acceptance of workshop output and corrective activity, facilitation standards, etc.

- reviewing action plan activity against agreed targets
- setting/agreeing plans for the re-evaluation of areas for the annual statement.

## CONCLUSION

The CSA process needs to have clear ownership, clearly documented standardised outputs which are subject to quality checks and partnership involvement to identify and address issues arising. Subject to satisfactory implementation CSA should provide positive results for all the stakeholders.

It is possible that many of the benefits of CSA could be achieved by alternative means. It is essential that any possible duplication is avoided and that information from such alternative sources is fed in to the CSA process. However, it is unlikely that many of these benefits will be achieved as effectively as during an open and honest CSA workshop.

## ACKNOWLEDGEMENT

John Rowson of Guardian Financial Services would like to acknowledge the invaluable assistance provided by his colleague, Graeme Taylor, also of Guardian Financial Services.

# Part 2

## Approaches to CSA

# 6

# Workshop Techniques

*Darryl Clark*

The information included in this chapter includes research findings completed by the author in 1997,[1] supplemented by experience gained through his Chair of the UK CSA User Group. For the purposes of this chapter, CSA is defined as 'a participative approach in avoiding or suppressing risks that can threaten the achievement of stated objectives'.

Running a successful workshop can be the most exhilarating and job-satisfying experience in an auditor's career and as a *modus operandi* there is no comparison with traditional audit. However, the thought of failure can also be frightening and it is therefore crucial that workshops are prepared and structured in a way that ensures they run smoothly, and become an enjoyable experience for all concerned. This is generally regarded as 'facilitation' skills, with the auditor[2] in the role of 'facilitator'.

It needs to be recognised that innate facilitation skills will vary among individuals although anyone can be an effective facilitator provided adequate planning goes into the exercise. As a basis for comparison, a natural facilitator is capable of walking into a workshop without having previously met the attendees or possessing an understanding of the subject matter, and produce quality results with everybody walking away feeling motivated by their efforts.

For specific facilitation skills refer to Chapter 11. The purpose of this chapter is to describe tried-and-tested techniques that will help ensure workshops have a workable structure and content.

## STRUCTURAL CONSIDERATIONS

### How Many Should Attend the Workshop?

Practical considerations such as the size of the meeting room available will influence the size of a workshop. Practical considerations aside, there would seem to be no 'magic number' for the optimal number of participants,

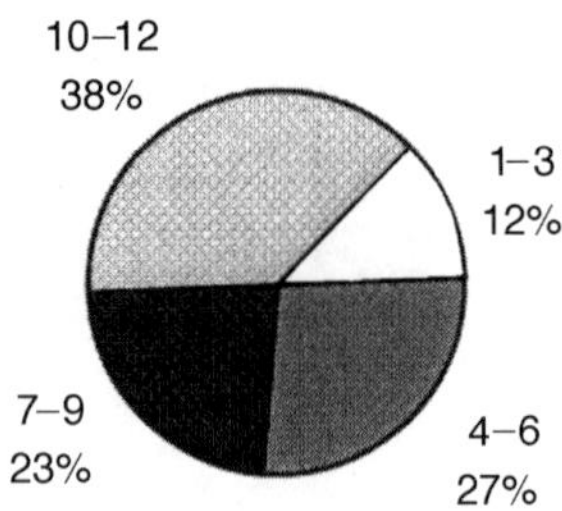


**Figure 6.1** CSA practitioner's preferred number of attendees.

although research among CSA practitioners suggests that groups of 10–12 are preferred (see Figure 6.1)

These disparate views could arise because of conflicting aims in the way a CSA programme should be implemented:

- The 'indoctrination' tendency: a desire to include as many people as possible so that the gospel of CSA permeates deep into the organisation, in an effort to make it cultural.
- The 'resistance' tendency: management wanting to restrict numbers to minimise the impact on the department's normal workloads.
- The 'expert' tendency: a desire to restrict the numbers to those who are highly knowledgeable in the process/subject under review, so as to optimise the man-time/results ratio.

The 'indoctrination' dimension might typically be observed in an organisation where internal audit is championing CSA (and with the altruistic interests of the business uppermost). The 'resistance' dimension might be seen in an organisation where CSA is not given the full unequivocal support of senior management, and the 'expert' dimension might be observed in a 'process' rather than 'functional' approach to CSA (where experts along the cross-departmental process chain are drawn together).

A conclusion that may be made is that the number decided upon will, *inter alia*, be influenced by the tendency that exerts the greatest pressure and perhaps, therefore, be influenced by who is championing and sponsoring the CSA programme. The overall CSA approach is therefore an important strategic decision, to ensure the optimum number of participants in CSA workshops given the resources available.

## How Long Should Workshops Last?

There is no hard-and-fast rule for how long a workshop should last. Their duration usually depends on either the content of the workshop and ground to be covered[3] or the practical consideration of how much time management is willing to invest in the exercise.

Again, there are disparate views among UK CSA practitioners about the optimal duration, although 3–4 hours is marginally preferred (ratified by the experience of the CSA guru, Tim Leech) (see Figure 6.2).

The 26% with a workshop duration of more than 6 hours tended to be where CSAs were completed in one sitting, and where effort was made to make the exercise 'special' for the attendees (organised logistically like external training). United Friendly and BT, for example, adopt this approach (see Chapter 13).

Whilst practitioners will have their own ideas about the duration best suited to their organisations, good facilitation skills will detect when it is time to close the workshop. It would be a mistake to prolong a workshop simply because there is the time allotted. Doing so would result in the workshop becoming 'your', not 'their', workshop. Ownership is an essential ingredient of any successful CSA programme and facilitators must guard against hijacking the exercise for their own purposes. However, this viewpoint presupposes that CSA is being introduced because of a desire by the *business* to have a participative approach to risk management. If, on the other hand, CSA is being used as a means by which *internal audit* unilaterally wishes to change its audit approach, the need to treat 'ownership' so sensitively may not be as great. It is therefore important for those wishing to implement CSA to understand and agree their motives beforehand.

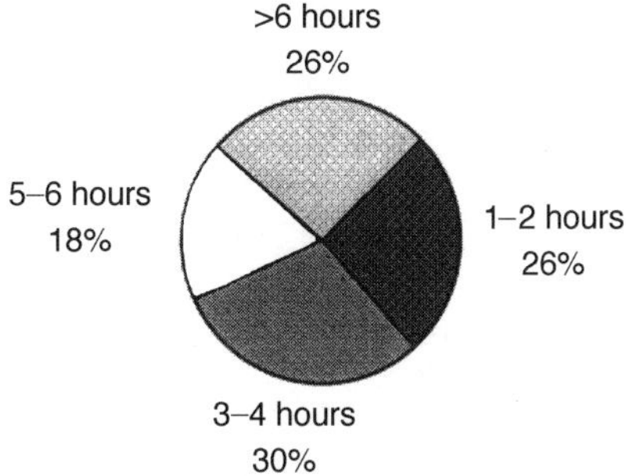


**Figure 6.2** CSA practitioner's preferred workshop duration.

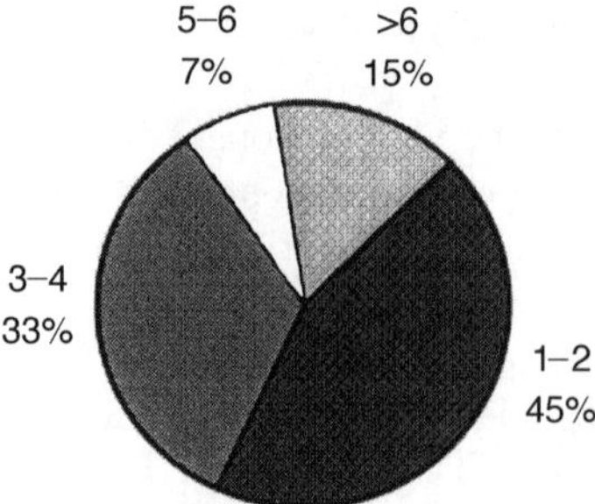


**Figure 6.3** Preferred number of workshops.

## How Many Workshops Should be Run?

Obviously, the more workshops that are conducted the greater the volume of output, since the level of analysis can increase. However, the more workshops conducted the more it is likely that participants will absent themselves (or simply not participate effectively when they are present). Similarly, there is a Pareto effect in that the more significant findings are likely to be identified sooner rather than later and an experienced auditor (and facilitator) will sense when the salient risk and control issues have surfaced (see Figure 6.3).

Auditors should also give consideration to the subject matter or group they are dealing with. Whilst one group could be satisfied with one or two workshops, other groups may require more. It is therefore useful to work with an average number of workshops for annual planning purposes, and accommodate the needs of each group individually. It could certainly be dangerous to fix the number of workshops with every group without regard to their individual requirements and complexity. Doing so would do more to satisfy expediency of the CSA programme, than proper business interests. Participants will instinctively feel when they have not been given long enough, which in the worst case could result in them feeling that no-one is really interested in hearing what they have to say. However, resources are never infinite and after a few pilots each organisation should be able to tailor their individual preferences.

## Who Should Attend Workshops?

This is perhaps the most complex structural consideration, and draws on a number of issues covered earlier. There are broadly four questions that need to be considered.

### 1. *What skills need to be present?*

Anyone implementing a CSA programme is likely to have just two primary ambitions, (a) to bring about a cultural change in the way their organisation manages risk and (b) to demonstrate impressive results from the exercise. Ambition (a) stems from an innate belief in the process, whereas ambition (b) is to provide evidence that one's belief in (a) was justified! No doubt there will be other objectives, but these are likely to be included in one or other of the above two ambitions.

This question is therefore highly relevant because in some ways (a) conflicts with (b). Inviting whole departments would certainly further (a), however, certain essential skills and views may be drowned by the sheer volume of views that will percolate from the group, jeopardising ambition (b). Similarly, restricting the workshop to a small handful of recognised 'experts' will help fulfil (b), but the cultural gospel of (a) will be preached to only an elite congregation. For publicity purposes, (b) is probably more important in the short term.[4] Nevertheless, one needs to be careful with the selection of 'experts'. (There is the classic story of an American dog-food company that spent a fortune on marketing a new product, which failed miserably, only for the office cleaner to point out that dogs didn't like it.) One of CSA's greatest strengths is that anyone from any level is capable of making a full and valuable contribution – provided they are given the opportunity to be heard. Consequently, it needs to be recognised that excluding anyone (which is inevitable to some extent on practical grounds alone) will have an indeterminable impact.

The decision on whom to invite (from a skill-base perspective) will, therefore, in part depend on which influence (ambition (a) or (b)) predominates.

### 2. *What are the pros and cons of inviting management?*

The advantages of having management in attendance are that it:

- demonstrates explicit endorsement of the CSA process
- provides a reasonably 'safe' environment for staff to air their views and concerns to their manager (albeit directed at the facilitator)
- provides a multi-level staff/manager communication opportunity that might otherwise not have occurred
- provides management with the opportunity to demonstrate they are genuinely willing and able to empower their staff.

Out of 49 CSA practitioners surveyed, none operated workshops without the presence of management. (The one caveat here is that it is not known whether management insisted on attending, or that practitioners would have preferred their absence.)

Some disadvantages of having management in attendance are that:

- they may not like what they hear and may defensively attempt to discredit the process
- staff might be reluctant to view their opinions for fear of ridicule or fear of loss of credibility with their manager
- political considerations may prevent real issues from surfacing
- staff may fear that any 'recommendation' may be perceived as criticism of the effectiveness of their manager, and behave reticently
- a sensitive issue could surface which, if not handled properly by the facilitator, could quite seriously damage staff/manager relations.

Although no specific research has been done on this subject, I would suspect that there is a correlation between management's propensity to attend, with the autocratic/democratic culture of the organisation. I would suggest that the more autocratic an organisational culture, the more likely the manager/decision-maker is to attend (and vice versa). Interestingly, I would further argue that from an auditor's perspective, the more autocratic the organisation the more the auditor should aim to exclude management!

The decision on whether to include management may in part, therefore, depend on the management culture. Of course, even within autocratic organisations 'democratic' managers will exist, and this will need to be taken into account.

### *3. What level of management support will carry conviction with the attendees?*

Certain groups sometimes need assurance that what they are involved with is fully supported 'from the top'. This 'from the top' endorsement is by no means essential (CSAs run for the exclusive benefit of the internal audit department have been highly successful), but any form of management endorsement will always be helpful in underpinning the programme's credibility. A small group of junior staff can be highly motivated by being involved in something that a senior manager is enthusiastically encouraging them to contribute towards. This can be achieved through a number of mediums, but quite often is achieved by a manager addressing the group and introducing CSA and the aims of the workshop. If this approach is to be adopted, the issue is then to decide which manager will provide the 'punch' required (departmental manager, regional director, CEO, etc.).

### *4. How many attendees will it take to convince management that their views have to be taken seriously?*

During the period when approval for a CSA programme is being sought,[5] it can be useful to obtain feedback on how many staff senior management feel the need to attend a workshop. Once this estimate is mentioned, the following question can then be asked: 'If we ensure that many attend, would you have comfort in the veracity of the results produced from the workshops?' To an extent this becomes a rhetorical question; what is actually being said is 'If we have that many attending, you will have to take their views seriously'. Consequently, the decision on who should attend a workshop, might in part depend on how many senior management prefer should attend (so that they have personal confidence in the results produced). This is clearly a political consideration.

### Recommended Structure

As a *de facto* standard the most popular structure is two workshops of 3–4 hour duration involving 10–12 participants. It also seems to be obligatory to include management in the workshops. However, since a 'quick win' can be highly beneficial in getting the programme off to a hot start, it may be advisable to begin with a small group of 'experts' to CSA, a particularly discrete topic.

## WORKSHOP CONTENT

### Breaking Down Jargon

In order successfully to engage a workshop into the cut-and-thrust of control design and risk evaluation, it is clearly imperative that the participants understand both the context and content of 'internal controls'.

It is easy for auditors to forget that what is to them second nature may be quite unintelligible to others. Do not underestimate your own knowledge. It will be necessary to define, describe and give examples of 'objectives', 'risks' and 'controls'. As auditors, we could construct some pretty fancy definitions of these, but the language we would use is likely to be convoluted. For example, a classic definition of 'control' is

> the employment of all the means devised in an enterprise to promote, direct, restrain, govern and check upon its various activities for the purpose of seeing that enterprise objectives are met. These means of control include, but are not limited to, form of organisation, policies, systems, procedures, instructions,

standards, committees, charts of account, forecasts, budgets, schedules, reports, records, checklists, methods, devices, and internal audit.[6]

Workshops, on the other hand, require something far more digestible. For example:

Objectives = The reasons behind what we do (for example, 'to provide a high-quality customer service').

Risks = The things that can, and sometimes do, go wrong and which therefore jeopardise our objective (for example, not knowing the product well enough to answer a customer's query).

Controls = The things we must do, and have in place, to stop risks from happening, or minimise the damage they cause (for example, product training).

The above explanations will be much better received than the 'official' definition mentioned earlier (there are no points to be won by being clever). Note the deliberate mention of a 'soft' control (product training). This will help attendees appreciate controls beyond the 'hard' platform of checking, authorisation, etc.

The sections that follow conform with the 'de-jargonise' principle. However, caution must be exercised; whilst one group will appreciate a 'Noddy meets CSA' approach, others might view it as patronising. Consideration might therefore need to be given to the audience being facilitated, with perhaps more than one set of CSA introductions.

## Describing Controls

Depending on the depth of preparatory work decided upon, it may also be useful to provide a more detailed explanation of the three key variables (objectives, controls, risks) described above. Internal auditors, for example, might typically describe the nature of controls as:

- detective
- preventative or
- directive.

If this detail is considered appropriate/helpful, an example will help describe their distinction. Use of analogies can be an effective tool in this respect (see Table 6.1).

Whilst exhaustive lists of different control types are widely available and often distributed to attendees, my experience is that they have limited practical value during the workshops themselves. This is not to say that the

**Table 6.1** Detective, preventative and directive controls.

| | For a car! | Business equivalent |
|---|---|---|
| Detective control | the dashboard (things that provide diagnosis as it happens, but, unfortunately, often after it has happened). | An exception report (i.e., it detects that a 'risk' – something wrong – might or has happened). |
| Preventative control | the steering wheel, mirrors and lights (things and actions that keep the car on the road, and avoid accidents). | A computer data validation, for example, input of an incorrect post-code prevents the user from continuing (i.e., it prevents a 'risk' – something wrong – happening). |
| Directive control | the owner's handbook and highway code (maintenance-type issues and other 'rules', for example 'check tyre pressure monthly' and 'drive with two hands on the steering wheel'). | A procedure, policy or other similar instruction (if properly written and understood) ensures that 'Risks' – something wrong – are being managed. |

lists are flawed, but because there is usually so much going on that participants become saturated with new concepts and information. Although these control lists/menus can be useful as *aides mémoire*, complete dependence can make the process too mechanical and may stifle free expression and provocative thinking. However, other practitioners find them indispensable so, as is usually the case with CSA, it comes down to what works best for you.

## Describing Risks

Before we can begin a discussion on risks there is one crucial point in all workshops that must be emphasised, which is that all risks need to be identified. The reason for this is manifest – an abundance of sophisticated controls would be useless against risks that were not contemplated. For this reason it is far more important to allocate limited workshop time to identifying risks, than it would be to spend that time elaborating on the controls already in place and the design of additional controls. This is because if workshop time is fully consumed the group can always, at a later date, complete the controls against risks that were not discussed. Better a half-finished series of workshops than to leave the group prey to unattended risks.

In describing risks, one should differentiate between types of risk and the concept of residual risk. To help participants, types of risks are sometimes presented, of which the following might be typical:

- financial risk (loss of income, unnecessary expenditure, wasted or under-performing capital)
- legal and regulatory risk (statutory, contractual, industrial or civil exposure)
- process risk (duplication, procrastination, over-supervision, elongation and IT deprivation)
- product risk (not fit for purpose, incorrect pricing)
- market risk (change in consumer tastes, lifestyles and industrial structure, innovation)
- governmental risk (changes in economic and fiscal policy, political bias or instability)
- technological risk (changes in, or entirely new, technologies)
- competitive risk (threat from competitors, substitutes, suppliers, new entrants).

Clearly, this inventory of risks could be added to or built upon, but in all likelihood would be irrelevant to a typical workshop. I first built this list for a CSA of corporate strategy, but having tried it on a 'normal' workshop, and failed, it was assigned to the scrap heap. Even if I were able to complete a perfect inventory of risks on an obscure business process, I should resist the temptation to do so. This is because it is not my understanding of the process that is important, but that of the workshop; it is the participants who add value to the exercise, without which the exercise becomes a pure surrogate for traditional audit. The more one tries to set frameworks and boundaries, the more one imposes one's own view and will, and ironically, the more one begins to restrict those who are being consulted.

'Residual' risk is a classic example of CSA jargon. It is, as the term suggests, those risks that prevail despite the existing controls being in place. Once additional controls have been agreed to neutralise these residual risks, what remains, if anything, is 'acceptable risk'. Personally, I have never experienced problems with this item of jargon; indeed, it can possibly be beneficial to have some jargon that the workshop can take away with it as a means of making them party to a new ideology.

## The Conceptual Model

To help ensure the programme passes the test of time, one should aim to implant a 'picture' in the mind of the workshop participants. This is so that the exercise is seen as something superior to 'yet another process'. One very common approach is to draw an iterative model by way of a flowchart (see Figure 6.4).

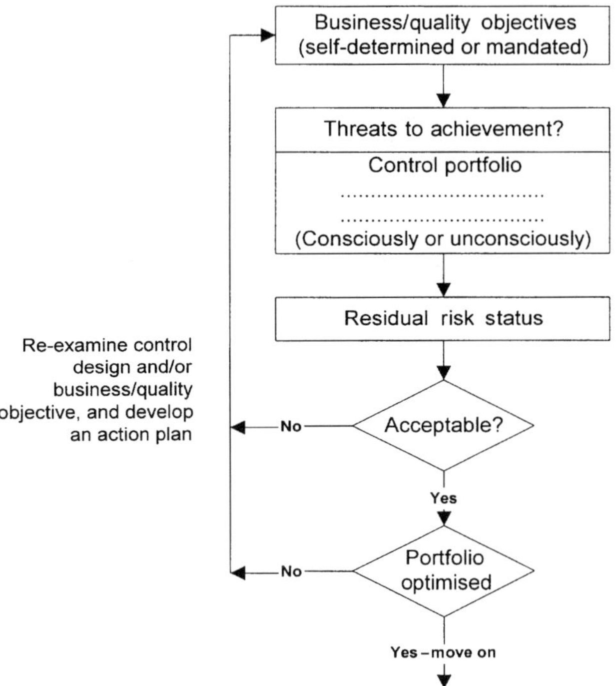


**Figure 6.4** Iterative model of risk management process (Copyright © 1995–8 MCS. Reprinted with permission from MSC Control Design and Training Inc.)

However, this model better describes the CSA process, rather than being a conceptual representation. Organisational effort is about accomplishing objectives, sometimes frustrated and impeded by risks, but managed through control. I have developed a model (Figure 6.5) to describe this conceptual representation; its purpose is to emphasise that objectives, risks and controls are three parts of the same whole.

The triangle attempts to demonstrate the separate pressures exerted by the three forces and their mutual dependencies. When in equilibrium, one could imagine these three forces as sides on a triangle filled with air such that the pressure from inside the triangle equals the pressure outside. In this steady state the triangle holds its shape and accomplishment is inevitable (assuming the objective is not deprived of resources). As soon as the mistaken assumption is made that any one of the forces is any more or less important than any other, disequilibrium results, the triangle loses its shape and accomplishment of the objective(s) is placed in peril.

In reality of course, the three forces act simultaneously against one another in constant struggle. But if the pressure can be held in balance by identifying and evaluating all the risks attached to the objective, and then

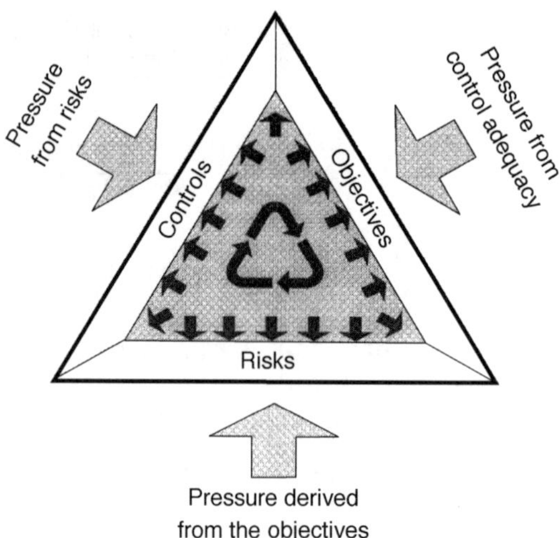


**Figure 6.5** The Folgate Insurance Accomplishment Control Model (ACM).

controlling those risks, accomplishment is achieved. So-called 'business risk' emanates from a *conscious* decision not fully to suppress or eliminate risk through the medium of control. Poor management could be said to derive from *unconscious* business risk. Additionally, if the pressure from outside the triangle is in equilibrium with that inside, it can sustain an infinite amount of pressure. In business terms, this means that there is theoretically no limit to the ambition of a particular objective, provided pressure equilibrium is successfully managed.

In practice, and whatever the description applied to it, pressure equilibrium is not a natural phenomenon but requires explicit intervention to maintain the status quo. This might also be described as a thermostatic or cybernetic control system. In whatever way the facilitator chooses to describe this phenomenon (there are less technical ways of describing the ACM), this understanding is necessary to appreciate CSA's *raison d'être*. In so doing, the workshop has a solid point of reference from which to navigate its efforts.

## PULLING IT ALL TOGETHER

There are as many different approaches to carrying out workshops as there are practitioners using the technique. However, in most cases the approach is broadly similar. I use a hierarchical style and structure, which tends to require four to five three-hour workshops. The following approach can therefore be tailored to meet your own needs. Taken chronologically, the steps are:

1. CSA introduction
   - benchmarking exercise ('where are we now?')
   - describing objectives (using obscure examples such as the objectives of a car, a garden, a zoo)
   - describing risks (with obscure examples such as speeding in a built-up area)
   - describing controls (i.e., solutions to the obscure examples above).
2. Agree the objectives of the department/process/function under review (with sub-objectives if necessary).
3. Agree the major risks associated with each objective.[7]
4. Agree other risks associated with the major risk.
5. List the controls currently in place, and list the residual risks (if any).
6. Decide upon additional control requirements.
7. Agree that the controls listed are appropriate/commensurate with the risk, and assign these to an 'action item' list.
8. Agree that the CSA is completed.
9. Agree accountability for each 'action item'.
10. Agree timing for completion of 'action items'.
11. Write and issue report.

This approach is represented pictorially in Appendix 6.1.

## Tools of the Trade

### *Databases and computers*

Practitioners have attempted to automate or provide additional structure to workshops (and their output) by employing database techniques using PCs. Such systems are used either as direct input during the workshops themselves, or used to store and sort the results subsequently. In the latter case, these systems are typically maintained by internal audit, and I know of only one example where business managers have attempted to build database solutions. The anecdotal evidence is that computers and databases provide little added value, given the development and maintenance effort involved. Those who have gone down this road have often either:

- discovered it to be a cul-de-sac
- failed to find a practical solution or

- ended up over-proceduralising the whole CSA process.

Indeed, some practitioners have reported drowning in all the paperwork produced from CSA.

My preference is to keep the whole exercise as simple as possible (although I can sympathise with the seductive temptation to try and find a PC solution). I have found there really is no substitute for a flip-chart, coloured marker pens and sticky tape. Apart from the simplicity of this approach, it is a medium that easily engages the group. For workshops that are going well, it is even quite easy to pass over the facilitator's role to one of the participants.

Automation, on the other hand, tends to rank process above people, when CSA is quite definitely a 'people thing'. However, if you are tempted to go the computer route, it might be valuable first to search out someone who has already attempted, or is using, this approach. This will at least help reduce the development effort.

### *Computer voting technology*

More of these systems are now coming onto the market. Whilst my 'keep it simple' approach means that I do not use this technology, I have seen it work and I have met many practitioners who report how effective and useful it is. An observation seems to be that a balance is required between using the technology to obviate protracted discussion, against it becoming a 'trigger-happy' session such that CSA becomes a mere push-button exercise.

For the above reasons, voting technology has the advantage of protecting democracy within the group, which could be a distinctly effective strategy in an autocratic culture. On the other hand, overdependence could remove discussion, along with the nuggets of gold that often emanate from it.

### *Benchmarking*

If it is considered important to monitor the progress of the CSA programme over the long term, it is clearly necessary to evaluate where the organisation is currently. There are a number of tools used to do this and I developed the approach provided in Appendix 6.2 ('Risk management maturity ladder'). As part of the introduction to the workshop, the five statements can be answered by each participant in a matter of moments. The data can then be monitored over time to determine whether perceptions (if not actions) have changed. Benchmarking can also be useful for giving impetus to the initiative, which can wane over time.

## CONCLUSIONS AND RECOMMENDATIONS

De-jargonise all of your audit understanding to help carry your audience with you. Describe objectives, risks and controls separately but emphasise their mutual dependencies. If an objective changes, different risks will emerge requiring new controls; if new risks manifest themselves the feasibility of the objective needs to be re-visited; if controls are circumvented or weakened, risks will operate unmolested thereby placing the objective in direct jeopardy.

Decide in advance the level of 'education' required, but be sure not to patronise the group. In terms of delivery keep things as simple as possible, at least at the outset. There is no evidence I am aware of that high-tech programmes are any more effective than shoestring operations.

Use what tools you feel are appropriate, but do not over do it. There will be a surprising amount the workshop will be getting to grips with, without cluttering the exercise with lots of tools simply because individually they look or sound useful. Consider computer voting technology but be sure you understand in advance why it is that this tool will be beneficial to your particular approach or organisation.

## NOTES

1 Clark, D. J., 'Control Self-Assessment – an explorative analysis and comparative study to traditional audit', Kingston University, post-graduate research, 1997, Surrey, England.
2 Or other individual or manager running the CSA programme.
3 Some practitioners provide very little background or introduction to the CSA methodology, whereas others might dedicate a whole workshop to this subject.
4 This approach is generally part of what is termed a 'quick wins' tactic.
5 Approval from the Board, or similar, is not a prerequisite: an internal audit function could adopt CSA simply because it feels it is a more effective *modus operandi*.
6 Sawyer, L. B., 'The Anatomy of Control', *The Internal Auditor*, Spring 1964, pp. 15–16.
7 These are often termed 'inherent risks'.

## APPENDIX 6.1

# Hierarchical Approach to CSA Workshops

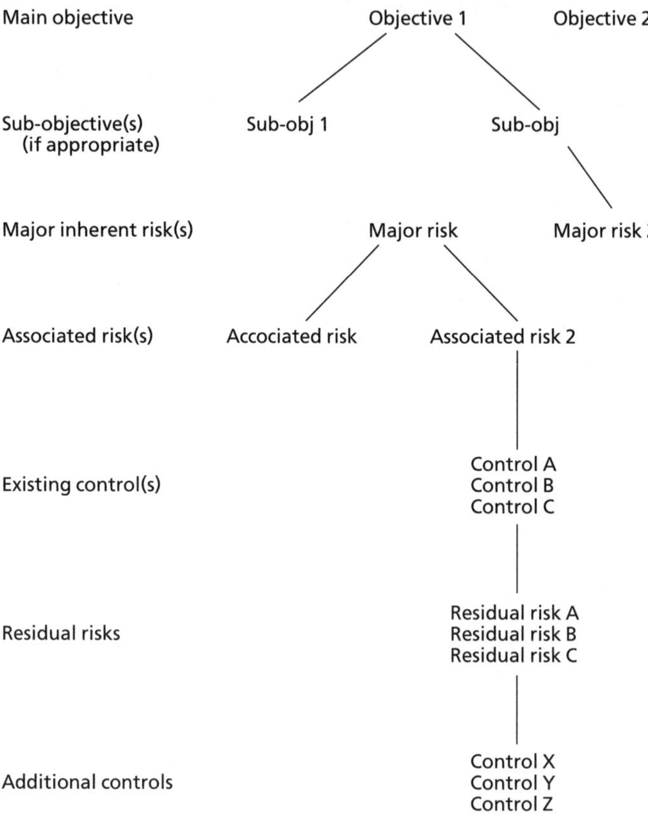

## APPENDIX 6.2

# Risk Management Maturity Ladder

### *Which of the following statements best describes the status of risk management in your organisation?*

Note that for practical use, the statements should be jumbled and use only the quoted statements (removing the 'Status', 'Maxim' and description headings. The maturity ladder can be used at an organisational, functional or process level and will need amending accordingly. It may also be useful to monitor changes over time.

Status 1: Insecurity
'We do not know (or properly understand) the risks we face as an organisation.'
Maxim: fortune favours the bold.

Status 2: Awaking
'We are currently discussing the potential benefits of implementing some form of structured risk management process, or programme.'
Maxim: forewarned is forearmed.

Status 3: Enlightenment
'We have started to consciously and systematically identify and evaluate our risks, and as a result have suppressed or eliminated some of them.'
Maxim: look before you leap.

Status 4: Wisdom
'With strong management support, we systematically evaluate our risks, and their suppression or elimination is a routine part of what we do.'
Maxim: prevention is better than cure.

Status 5: Security
'Through systematic evaluation and strong management support, we know the risks we face, and have appropriately protected and/or prepared ourselves should any of them occur.'
Maxim: better safe than sorry.

# 7

# Using Control Self Assessment to Evaluate the Effectiveness of an Organisation's Control Environment

*Martin Reinecke*

## INTRODUCTION

The impact of an ineffective control environment could be far reaching, possibly resulting in financial losses, a tarnished corporate image or even failure of the entire business. Consider, for example, the following hypothetical case of an airline generally considered to have an effective internal control system.

> The airline has well-defined information systems and control activities, comprehensive policy manuals prescribing control functions, and extensive reconciliation and supervisory duties. Its internal audit function performs frequent risk-based financial audits. The control environment, however, is significantly flawed. Senior management is extremely cost conscious and places middle management under tremendous pressure to save costs by setting unrealistic cost-cutting targets and objectives. The maintenance manager decides to save costs by lengthening the routine replacement cycle of certain high-value parts, even though this practice constitutes unethical behaviour in putting the lives of thousands of passengers at risk. His subordinates are aware of this but fearful of retaliation, they are not willing to report it to his superiors. After an aircraft crash, the investigation reveals the cause as being inadequate maintenance. Should this information become public knowledge, it is certain that the airline will be criticised, lose many passengers and may even have to close down.

If the board, audit committee, top management and internal and external audit in the above example did not take the condition of the control environment into account, all of them may have concluded that the airline had a sound system of internal control. All of them may have concurred with a statement in the annual report that 'nothing has come to their attention to indicate a significant breakdown in internal control'. Should they then not be held accountable to stakeholders for ignoring one of the fundamental and pervasive elements of internal control?

This chapter describes the workshop-based control self assessment (CSA) process that is used by Deloitte & Touche's Corporate Governance Services Division in South Africa to evaluate the effectiveness of an organisation's control environment.

## DEFINING CONTROL ENVIRONMENT

The COSO Report (*Internal Control – Integrated Framework*) defines the control environment as follows:

> The control environment sets the tone of an organization, influencing the control consciousness of its people. It is the foundation for all other components of internal control, providing discipline and structure. Control environment factors include the integrity, ethical values and competence of the entity's people; management's philosophy and operating style; the way management assigns authority and responsibility, and organizes and develops its people; and the attention and direction provided by the board of directors.

The individual elements of the control environment are not be dealt with further in this chapter, but readers may gain an appreciation of their flavour from Appendix 7.3.

## WHY USE CSA TO EVALUATE THE CONTROL ENVIRONMENT?

The answer to this question is relatively simple: people. The control environment is about the behaviour of an organisation. CSA is a process that focuses on an organisation's people and their knowledge and understanding of the conditions within that organisation. Hence our motto for CSA: 'The power of people'.

## OVERVIEW OF THE PROCESS

The process we use consists of the following five phases:

- gaining commitment
- process design

- conducting fieldwork
- reporting
- action plans and follow-up.

This chapter focuses primarily on the process design and conducting fieldwork phases as the other three are dealt with extensively elsewhere in CSA literature. However, some thoughts on these three phases have been included for completeness.

## SKILLS AND TOOLS REQUIRED FOR THE ASSESSMENT

Before we examine the process, it is important to consider the skills and tools that are required to perform this assessment. Many current and prospective CSA practitioners seem to hold the view that the tools, based around technology, are more important than the skills involved in performing CSA. This is not true; many CSA workshops and projects fail, for example, as a result of a lack in facilitation skills.

A skilled facilitator must recognise and understand individual and group behaviour in order to intervene when the process requires intervention. The golden rule is therefore for facilitators to focus on the process and not get involved in the content. For example, one of the worst mistakes a facilitator can make is to get involved in a debate or argue with participants when their views are not the same as that of the facilitator.

Although some people have natural facilitation skills that they can develop and improve over time, I would recommend that all CSA practitioners should participate in some form of formal facilitation training. Partnering with a team of clinical psychologists, Deloitte & Touche in South Africa has established a development programme for CSA facilitators, which is consistently rated by clients as the most valuable section of the CSA implementation programme.

We usually have two facilitators participating in CSA workshops. The role of the first facilitator is to ensure the process is effective. Hence this person will focus exclusively on the group and their actions and will not take formal notes. This person will ask questions, listen and intervene where necessary.

The role of the second facilitator is more challenging. This person will capture the information discussed by the group as well as acting as a 'lifeline' for the first facilitator, i.e., 'rescue' the first facilitator if (s)he is pulled into the content of the discussion.

As far as tools are concerned, we recommend that the group discussion is captured electronically and displayed for all participants to see and discuss.

Typically, a notebook computer and a data projector are used for this purpose. However, flipcharts and/or an overhead projector could also be used effectively. The advantage of electronic capturing is that the time spent on producing the report is dramatically reduced. A simple template for capturing discussion is included in Appendix 7.1.

If possible, anonymous voting technology should be utilised to obtain participants' ratings (more about this later). However, if the budget does not allow for electronic voting technology, paper-based questionnaires, such as the ones used in surveys, are just as effective, but take longer to process.

Finally, the rooms in which the workshops are held should have enough space for the facilitators to move around and allow all participants equal access to visual aids. We have found that a room that is set up in a U-shape or horseshoe works best.

## GAINING COMMITMENT

This phase extends far beyond merely obtaining approval to go ahead with the assessment. The project team needs to ensure that senior management has a clear understanding of the nature and extent of the evaluation process. CSA workshops create huge expectations amongst managers and employees that something will subsequently be done to address their concerns, i.e., senior management will take action.

Failing this, managers and employees may lose faith in CSA and be unwilling to participate in future projects. However, history has proved that where appropriate steps are taken, there is a significant improvement in attitudes, motivation and commitment within the organisation. We consider that it is therefore important to start by making a formal presentation to senior management to explain:

- the importance of assessing the control environment; for example, it should be quite easy to customise the above airline scenario to suit the organisation concerned
- why CSA is an appropriate evaluation tool
- the importance of having senior management's commitment
- how the assessment will be performed; it is always a good idea to perform a live demonstration.

It almost goes without saying that the CSA team should carefully listen to senior management's concerns and ensure that all these are adequately dealt with before starting the project.

## PROCESS DESIGN

In brief, our workshops typically run as follows: participants are requested to indicate through voting (or a survey questionnaire), the extent to which they agree or disagree that a series of statements are applicable to their work group, division or organisation. The three to four statements with the lowest scores are then discussed individually to determine the obstacles that prevent that statement from being accepted and, more importantly, the impact on internal control. It is therefore of utmost importance to ensure that the statements address the right issues, both in breadth and in depth. Examples of statements are given in Appendices 7.2 and 7.3. The focus of the process is usually based on one of two models, either:

- a high-level assessment of the control culture of the organisation, i.e., the existence of effective management processes for control as described in the 'Guidance on Control' (CoCo) framework issued by the Canadian Institute of Chartered Accountants or
- an assessment of the elements of the control environment as described in the COSO evaluation tools.

At a glance the two focus areas appear to overlap extensively. This is true to a degree. The main difference between the two is that the CoCo-based assessment is broad in scope as it includes areas such as establishing performance objectives and monitoring. The COSO-based approach focus is narrower but delves deeper into control environment elements. It is therefore necessary to have a basic understanding of the two control models and how they differ from each other when deciding which one of the two is to be used. The reason we differentiate between the two assessments is to meet the individual needs of the clients where the assessments are performed. The key is to discuss both options with senior management and to agree on a format that may include elements of both or even additional elements if requested by senior management.

Appendix 7.2 reflects a hybrid approach. It contains statements derived from the CoCo framework but regrouped into the COSO components (the generic CoCo categories are Purpose, Commitment, Capability and Monitoring and Learning).

Appendix 7.3 contains statements that were derived from the COSO evaluation tools, analysing the control environment into its component parts. The example statements are not cast in stone. They should be tailored to meet individual circumstances such as the level of education, experience and understanding of the people that participate in the workshops. The key objective is that workshop participants are able to relate each statement to their own situation at work.

The following scale is used to rate the extent that participants agree that each statement applies to their workteam/organisation:

1. I strongly disagree that this statement is true for my workteam/organisation.
2. I disagree that this statement is true for my workteam/organisation.
3. I somewhat disagree that this statement is true for my workteam/organisation.
4. I am not sure if this statement is true for my workteam/organisation.
5. I somewhat agree that this statement is true for my workteam/organisation.
6. I agree that this statement is true for my workteam/organisation.
7. I strongly agree that this statement is true for my workteam/organisation.

The average ratings are then categorised into three areas; acceptable, cautionary or dangerous. We usually use the following cut-off points: from 4.5 to 7 is 'acceptable' because participants are, overall, in agreement that the statement applies to their workteam/organisation. Between 3.5 and 4.5 is '*cautionary*' because participants are, overall, not in agreement that the statement applies to their workteam/organisation. From 1 to 3.5 is 'dangerous' because participants are, overall, in agreement that the statement does not apply to their workteam/organisation. In this case the workshop participants should be able to provide good explanations why these statements are not applicable. It is essential that only statements relevant to the organisation are assessed in the workshops. An example of the graph from a CSA workshop is included in Appendix 7.4. The recommended cut-off points are also not fixed and should be agreed with senior management prior to the workshops. We also find it useful to hold an initial workshop with senior managers to obtain their feedback and input on the process design in order to make any required changes before the process is rolled out to the rest of the organisation.

## CONDUCTING FIELDWORK

Fieldwork consists mainly of running the CSA workshops. However, it is recommended that CSA practitioners gain a good understanding of the business processes and issues faced by managers and employees on a daily basis prior to conducting workshops. This knowledge will allow them to be more effective facilitators by being able to demonstrate to workshop participants how the issues discussed could affect them. Ultimately, a sound knowledge of the business will enhance the participants' trust in the facilitators and the CSA process. The typical assessment for a small enterprise or a division of a large organisation therefore consists of a minimum of four workshops; one with senior management, one with middle management and two with other employees.

Senior management (and sometimes middle management) should also be consulted when selecting the participants. This is done to identify 'undesirable' participants such as people who are known for 'loose talk in the passage', i.e., those who would easily share confidential and/or sensitive information with anyone that may care to listen. Such people have a detrimental effect on CSA workshops as the other participants will not trust them to adhere to the ground rule of confidentiality and therefore the other participants may not share all their thoughts. It is also not wise to have people that directly report to one another in the same workshop as this may stifle participation. Subordinates may fear subsequent retribution if they raise sensitive issues.

Our workshops begin with the facilitators explaining the workshop process and establishing ground rules. Typically they are as follows:

- Be open and honest – tell it like it is!
- Focus on the issue, not the person.
- Do not speak about an individual (i.e., disclose the name) who is not in the room.
- The outcome of the ratings and the content of the discussion are not to be repeated outside the workshop.
- Participants may disclose the process to their colleagues.
- Everyone in the workshop will be treated equally and will receive equal opportunity to contribute.
- Comments should be clear, concise and specific and should not repeat what has already been said.

Participants are usually given an opportunity to add their own rules in addition to the above.

The next step is to obtain the ratings on the list of statements. The summarised ratings are categorised and displayed in a graphical format (see Appendix 7.4) for all participants to reflect on. The three or four statements with the lowest scores (typically 'danger' areas) are then selected for individual discussion. In cases where there are a large number of low scores, the facilitators should help the group to decide on the areas for discussion.

Each of the three or four statements is discussed individually. The facilitator will start the discussion by asking an open-ended question such as 'what is preventing the workteam/organisation from implementing this statement?'. This question should also be followed up by a series of 'why?' questions to ensure that the root cause or obstacle is clearly identified and captured in the worksheet (see Appendix 7.1).

The facilitator then asks a question such as 'how does this prevent you from doing your job?' for each obstacle to determine its impact on control. The impact is also best illustrated by actual examples that should also be captured on the worksheet. This information is of utmost importance. In some of the earlier projects, only obstacles were identified and it was found to be very difficult to explain the impact of these 'soft issues' to senior management.

The typical response from senior management was that a weakness such as a breakdown in communication does not have an impact on financial results and therefore it should be dealt with by the human resources function. However, if we can demonstrate that specific decisions that were based on inaccurate information and subsequently resulted in financial losses were caused by the breakdown in communication, senior managers usually start listening and become committed to taking action.

In addition, the worksheet in Appendix 7.1 caters for capturing recommendations. This can be somewhat of a thorny issue as feeble recommendations or ones that have failed in the past will cause senior managers to lose trust in both the CSA process and the team. Hence the appropriateness and feasibility of recommendations should be tested with the group before they are noted on the worksheets.

Once discussions have been concluded, the facilitators should thank the participants for their contributions, and explain the next steps in the process (usually all participants will receive copies of their worksheets and/or the full report as agreed with senior management). Participants should also be reminded of the ground rules that would apply after the workshop, i.e., confidentiality.

## REPORTING

The first step in the reporting phase is to circulate the workshop worksheets to each participant. They will usually receive only the worksheets of the workshop that they attended, and distribution will be limited to those attending. However, there have been cases where the senior management team wanted the formal report to be distributed to all employees, and for information to be circulated covering other workshops.

The formal reporting phase consists of two steps; developing a written report and presenting the findings in a debrief workshop. The format and content of the written report may vary according to the needs of the senior management team for which the project was conducted. Typically our reports will consist of the following:

- a summarised report which includes:
  - summarised assessment graph
  - major obstacles identified in all the workshops, i.e., common themes
  - the impact of these obstacles on current control activities, including examples
  - recommendations to address the obstacles
- an appendix for each workshop containing
  - assessment graphs (see Appendix 7.4)
  - workshop worksheets (see Appendix 7.1)
- an appendix containing a list of all recommendations that were identified in the workshops.

The senior management team should be encouraged to respond to each recommendation in writing, referring to an action plan or explaining why the recommendation cannot be implemented. This step is necessary to manage the expectations of the participants that raised the recommendations. Hence the earlier warning to ensure that all recommendations are appropriate and feasible.

The above report is usually rather lengthy and therefore we usually present it to the senior management team by way of a debriefing workshop. The purpose of this workshop is to discuss and clarify the main obstacles that are causing breakdowns in the control environment. The senior management team usually asks many detailed questions during this workshop and therefore the CSA team needs to be well prepared.

The CSA team should also aim to establish the formalised action-planning process. They should not drive this process because the ownership for ensuring that the control environment is effective always remains with senior management. However, the CSA team should participate in this process by fulfilling a monitoring role. It is usually a good idea to agree on a date for an action-planning workshop that may be facilitated by the CSA team if they are comfortable with their skills to do so, i.e., whether or not they have sufficient facilitation skills to perform the task.

## ACTION PLANS AND FOLLOW-UP

The steps in this phase will be determined by the outcome of what was agreed in the debrief workshop. We usually undertake a follow-up assessment to measure the success or impact of the action steps that are to be implemented. The timing of the follow-up is very important. On the one hand it should not be scheduled too soon because action steps may not have been fully implemented or the effect may not yet be visible. On the other hand it should not be left too late because this may place the implementation of the action plan too low on senior management's priority list. Our experience indicates that six months after the original assessment is usually optional.

## CONCLUSION

CSA is indeed a powerful assessment tool as it has the ability quickly and effectively to identify root causes of control problems in any organisation. The process described in this chapter represents only one example of how CSA can serve as a catalyst for changing corporate cultures.

## APPENDIX 7.1

# Example Worksheet

| Discussion Area 1: Example Comments | |
|---|---|
| Obstacles | Impact on control |
| Many controls have been formulated but not implemented properly, for example, budgets that are not monitored. | People 'test' the system resulting in large budget variances and financial losses. |
| There is a lack of understanding of certain control mechanisms such as month-end reports and budget variances. | Controls are disregarded or not used effectively, for example, continuous production defects resulting from a poor-quality raw material component. |
| Nothing is done about non-compliance with controls as a result of a lack of discipline. | Control breakdowns such as documents being signed for approval of payment without proper review. |
| Errors are not tolerated and people are punished without being given the opportunity to learn from mistakes. | People are not willing to take on additional responsibilities (they only do the minimum) or display any initiative as a result of a fear of retaliation. |
| Policies and procedures are revised without being communicated properly. | People apply policies and procedures selectively and inconsistently. In addition, it could result in questionable actions. |
| Information is not shared and properly co-ordinated as a result of departments functioning in isolation. | Information will be deliberately withheld or delayed to make certain departments appear to be under-achievers. |

Recommendations

Clarify authority and responsibility levels.
Implement a formal performance management system.
Establish formal communication processes to deal with changes in policies and procedures

## APPENDIX 7.2

# Control Culture Statements Derived from CoCo

## Control Environment

Shared ethical values are practised throughout the organisation.
Our people are treated with integrity and respect.
Our authority and responsibilities are clearly set out.
We trust each other and communicate openly.
We have sufficient knowledge, skills and tools to do our jobs.

## Risk Assessment

We understand what the business aims to achieve.
We know what can go wrong in the business.
We have measurable performance targets.
We adapt quickly to changes in the business environment.

## Control Activities

Our policies help us to achieve our objectives.
We understand what is expected of us as individuals.
Decisions are made by the right people.
Decisions are made timeously.
Decisions and actions are properly co-ordinated.
There are sufficient controls in the business.

## Information and Communication

The way we communicate helps us to achieve our objectives.
We have sufficient information to do our jobs properly.
We have plans in place to help us achieve our objectives.
Our information needs are continuously assessed to take into account changes in the business.

## Monitoring

We monitor our performance against our performance targets.
We question why we have to do things in specific ways.
We make sure that required changes are implemented.
We report regularly to ensure that we achieve our business objectives.

APPENDIX 7.3

# Control Environment Statements Derived from COSO Evaluation Tools

## Integrity and Ethical Values

We are familiar with the expected standards of ethical and moral behaviour.
Our top management sets an appropriate example of expected ethical and moral behaviour.
We treat customers, suppliers, employees and other business associates with honesty and fairness.
We take appropriate action when we become aware of unacceptable behaviour.
We do not override policies and procedures without documenting and explaining it.
When our compensation is based on meeting performance targets, the performance targets are realistic.

## Commitment to Competence

We know what is required from us in the workplace.
The knowledge and skills required to perform our jobs is known and assessed frequently.
We have sufficient knowledge, skills and tools to do our jobs adequately.

## Management's Philosophy and Operating Style

We know what can go wrong in the business.
We retain our good people.
Our accounting function is a vehicle for exercising control over business activities.
Our assets, including intellectual assets, are protected from unauthorised access or use.
We meet with our managers on a regular basis to report on our activities.
We give our managers the facts, even if it is not what they want to hear.

## Organisational Structure

The organisational structure ensures that the right people get the right information on time.
The organisational structure changes if there are significant changes in our business.
We have sufficient time to carry out our responsibilities.

## Assignment of Authority and Responsibility

Our authority and responsibilities are clearly set out.
We are familiar with the controls that we are responsible for.
We have enough people to achieve our mission.
Where appropriate, we do not need to obtain our superiors' permission to perform certain tasks.

## Human Resource Policies and Practices

We have appropriate policies and procedures for hiring, training, promoting and compensating our people.
Integrity and ethical values form part of our performance measures.
We know what we need to do and how we need to behave to obtain promotions and salary increases.

## APPENDIX 7.4

# Example CSA Workshop Graphs

Figure A7.1 shows the ratings for each of the Control Environment Statements (detailed in Appendix 7.3) averaged across the four workshops. The ratings indicate the extent that the workshop participants agreed with each statment – 1.0 indicating strong disagreement and 7.0 indicating strong agreement that the statement is true for the participant's workteam or organisation (see also page 118). The four workshops were one with senior management, one with middle management and two with employees.

Figure A7.2 shows the extent to which the workshops for each group of staff is in alignment. Differences and similarities in the ratings from each workshop could form the basis for further discussion.

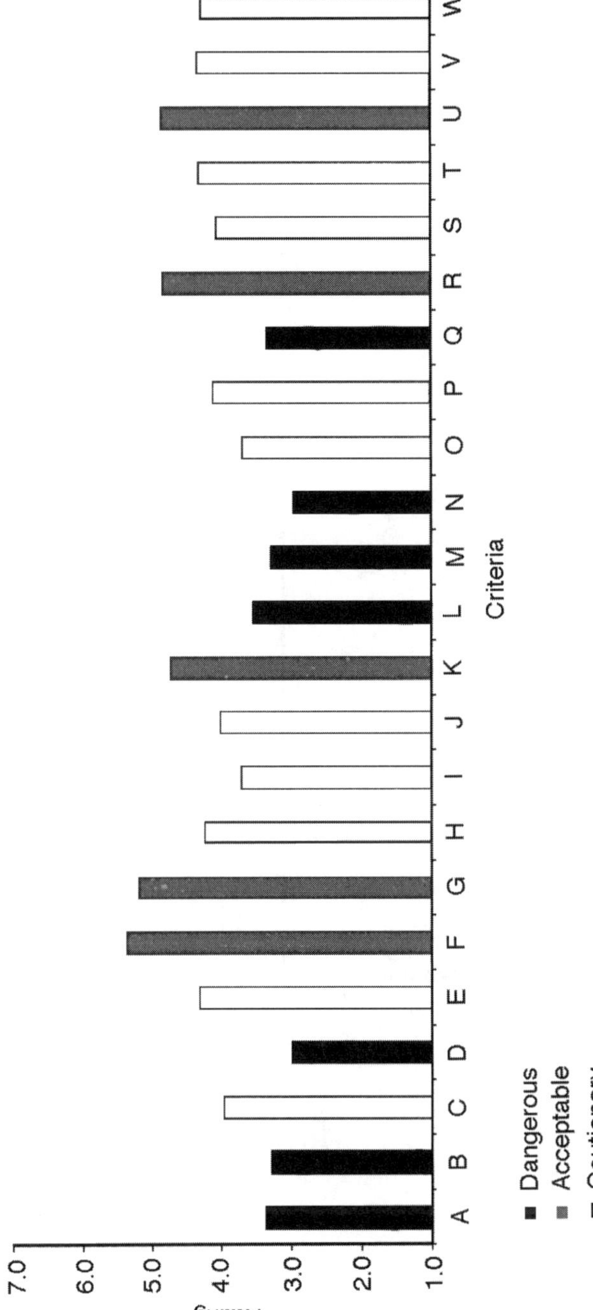


**Figure A7.1** Average ratings for the four workshops.

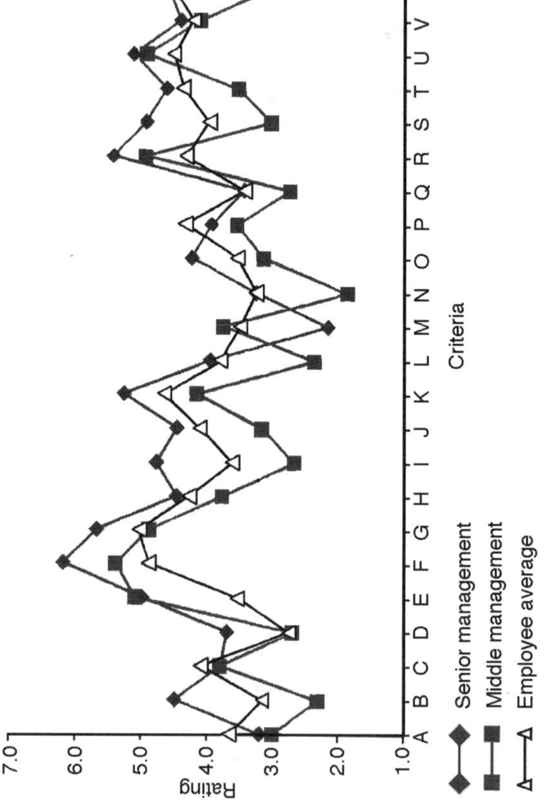


**Figure A7.2** Aignment

# 8

# The Use of CSA Workshops as Part of an Integrated Risk-Management Strategy

*Dave Gammon*

## INTRODUCTION

Many organisations have experienced some degree of success in implementing control self assessment (CSA) strategies but few can lay claim to embedding successfully the culture and supporting management organisation and procedures that will ensure ongoing identification and management of the organisation's major business risks.

The key driver behind the development of most CSA strategies in the UK has undoubtedly been the Cadbury Committee's control reporting requirements. The interpretation of these requirements has led to the development of a myriad of CSA techniques which have been used to gather information about the effectiveness of organisations' internal control systems. The information-gathering techniques and scope of coverage afforded by the CSA strategies vary so much from organisation to organisation that few common principles can be established.

One common theme apparent in most organisations' approaches to CSA is the use of risks as the basis for control identification and assessment. Whether using workshops or questionnaires, the grouping of control system elements against business risks helps management understand the need for certain control components as well as providing a method by which a control system can be conveniently classified. Some organisations have expanded their CSA programmes to address wider issues than those required to meet Cadbury reporting requirements and a few have seen the potential for aligning their CSA programme to a wider integrated risk-management process.

Implementation of a CSA programme within the organisation presents an excellent opportunity to integrate and co-ordinate the organisation risk-management efforts and provide clear competitive advantage through improved understanding and management of risk. The tools developed for CSA programmes, particularly the use of workshop and structured interview techniques readily lend themselves to a comprehensive risk-management programme.

## INTEGRATED RISK MANAGEMENT

The term integrated risk management has been used to describe an organisation-wide, common approach to the identification, assessment and management of business risk. It encompasses the development of a risk-management strategy and policy at board level which provides the mandate and basis for a cohesive and consistent approach to the management of organisational risk. It requires comprehensive assessment of risk through establishing a risk-focused organisational culture and the establishment of appropriate risk-reporting structures (see Figure 8.1).

CSA programmes are undoubtedly improving the level of information that organisations have about the status of internal control. How successful such programmes have been in raising awareness, and improving the quality, of risk management across the whole organisation is more questionable. Experience indicates that while management show initial enthusiasm for CSA the process does not embed itself within the organisation and ultimately the assessments become an 'administrative chore' or disappear altogether. The programmes fail because:

- They are not addressing the business risk-management issues that are foremost in the minds of management. Many CRSA programmes still have a largely financial control focus resulting from the key driver

**Figure 8.1** The integrated approach to managing risk.

behind such programmes being the requirements for corporate governance reporting. Other programmes focus on the negative 'what can go wrong' interpretation of risk, ignoring the risks inherent in business strategies that will directly impact organisational performance.

- They are driven by internal audit functions as opposed to management. The programme is perceived to be something that management have to do as opposed to something that will deliver value to them.
- The programmes are not driven and actively sponsored by the board. Few CSA programmes start with a board-level assessment of the strategic risks that could impact the ability of the organisation to deliver its strategy.
- They do not align with organisations' existing planning and control processes. Most CSA programmes are carried out as stand-alone programmes with their own reporting structure. This leads to them being considered as an 'initiative' rather than an element of normal organisational operations.
- Insufficient investment of energy and support required to embed risk management and make it an organisational competency; CSA programmes are providing a snapshot of the status of risk in an organisation. Effective risk management results from ensuring that people understand risk and their responsibilities in relation to managing it, combined with effective reporting procedures that ensure risk levels are continually monitored. Achieving this in many organisations requires an extensive change of management programme and cannot be achieved overnight.
- The programmes fail to account for the activities and *modus operandi* of other review bodies and risk-managing functions within the organisation. Many CSA programmes are failing to link themselves with the activities of other risk-management functions. Indeed there are many examples of internal audit led CSA programmes that fail to link back to internal audit's own work programmes!

An examination of the arrangements for assessment and management of risk in many organisations will reveal inconsistencies in personal attitudes towards risk and unco-ordinated arrangements. Organisations are beginning to examine their current arrangements and moving towards an integrated and organisational-wide view of business risk.

Many of the tools and techniques used in CSA programmes can be of potential value in a wider and more holistic risk-management strategy. The use of workshop-style approaches to CSA has provided a mechanism for prompt identification and assessment of business risks. Such approaches to risk assessment bring additional benefits to organisations by:

- raising the level of organisational awareness of risk issues and critical control components
- promoting cross-functional and hierarchical discussion of business risks thereby improving organisational communication and understanding of risk levels
- enabling assessment and improvement of 'soft' control mechanisms such as communication, training, accountability and motivation mechanisms
- providing opportunities for the transfer of risk assessment skills to organisational management and personnel.

Successful risk-assessment workshops do not just happen. They are carefully designed and planned to allow the maximum opportunity for success and minimise the risk of failure. If the potential benefits of running a workshop are to be realised there are four areas which must be effectively addressed.

## Planning

The time required to prepare properly for a risk management workshop should not be underestimated. The planning phase can be divided into two distinct elements:

- Technical research to understand the specific issues likely to be discussed during the workshop; such research includes developing the workshop objectives and scope as well as research into the organisation, its markets, products, value chain, competitors, major change programmes and the key issues it faces.
- Process preparation involves designing the workshop process and addressing the administrative arrangements for running the event. Key elements of process preparation include planning the agenda, dry running the workshop, contingency planning and workshop materials preparation. In designing a workshop agenda attempts should be made to match existing methods of operation used by the department. I conducted a workshop with a management team who were in the middle of preparing their business units strategic plan. The team were using a force field analysis planning style which incorporated an analysis of risk. Our workshop structure was moulded to fit within this process. The management team thereby benefited from facilitation of their strategic planning sessions and avoided duplication of effort.

## Quality Facilitation

Ensuring the workshop achieves its objectives and includes everyone's perspective of the organisation's risk portfolio requires skilled and disciplined facilitation. The facilitator has to manage the discussions, timescales and the group dynamics to maximise the value obtained from the workshop.

The importance of good facilitation training and the benefits of practice in a 'safe' environment before performing a risk management workshop cannot be overstated. Facilitators involved in delivering risk assessments should have excellent communication skills, a thorough understanding of risk and control principles and a genuine enthusiasm for, and commitment to, delivering quality workshop results.

## Content Challenge

The role of 'challenger' in a workshop is to provide a level of quality assurance over the content of discussions in the workshop, ensuring that:

- all significant risks are considered by the group
- discussions of control elements and residual risk levels are robust and comprehensive.

The role of challenger can be performed by the facilitator but is generally more effective when performed by a second party. It is particularly useful to have a specialist in the subject being assessed who can bring an independent perspective or best practice to the issues being discussed.

## Effective Participants

For a workshop to produce a balanced and accurate assessment it is important that representation is obtained from all areas of the organisation, in the correct proportion. Careful consideration should be given to the development of the participants' list ensuring all functions, hierarchical levels and specialists necessary to attain a comprehensive and accurate assessment are represented. By way of example, a workshop held to review new product development should include representation from sales, marketing, production, quality assurance, research and development and finance. If any of these areas were not represented it may raise a question mark around the balance and accuracy of the assessment. It may also result in a lack of buy-in to the actions proposed from those functions that were not represented.

The selected participants should be fully briefed in advance about the workshop process and the area they are assessing. This should considerably reduce the amount of time spent answering process questions during the workshop. It also allows participants to consider some of the issues in advance of the workshop. Experience shows that a pre-workshop meeting is a more preferable method of delivering these briefings than the use of documentation packs. It enables participants to meet each other and ensures they are briefed. Sending briefing packs on the other hand does not provide assurance that they will be read!

## STAGES OF A RISK MANAGEMENT WORKSHOP

Whilst the format of workshop programmes must be designed with the organisations normal operating standards and preferences in mind, there are a number of common modules within such programmes for which guidance can be provided. Current practice frequently favours splitting the workshops over two sessions, one covering the identification and profiling of risks and the second session dealing with controls and residual risk levels. A further emerging practice is to conduct risk identification and profiling as a separate exercise, using the workshop to validate the risks identified and their relative priority.

The risk management workshop can be broken down into three key modules:

- risk identification and profiling
- control and residual risk assessment
- action planning.

### Risk Identification/Profiling

When prompted to identify key business risks, without guidance, most people have an almost natural inclination to identify issues that they know are currently problems in their work environment. Whilst this approach may yield some insights into current business issues it is not an effective basis for compiling a comprehensive risk profile as it is:

- subject to individual interpretation and bias in selecting what are significant issues
- likely to omit serious risks which have not yet caused direct operational problems for the organisation.

For these reasons it is important that guidance is provided to help participants understand the meaning of risks, in the context of the workshop. This guidance can consist of the following:

- A definition of risk – to help participants understand the type of issues they should be considering. Definitions of risk frequently point to the relationship between risk and the organisation's objectives. This approach allows people to frame their thoughts around a point of reference with which they should, hopefully, be very familiar.
- A risk framework – this is used to provide headings under which specific risks can be considered and grouped. Whilst general guidance frameworks are commonly available they should always be tailored to the specific organisation and its activities or they will lack relevance, and ultimately credibility, with management. An example we developed with a public sector body contained the three broad categories in Table 8.1.
- 'Cause' and 'effect' definitions – used to ensure that risks identified are properly defined and lend themselves fully to the assessment process. A common problem when asking participants to brainstorm risks is that the effects of risk, as opposed to their causes are identified.

Having identified risks it is useful to consider and record the impacts they could have on the organisation. This provides a means of helping participants clarify the nature and importance of the risk to the organisation. This information also assists the ranking of risks against each other, a vital step in the creation of the risk profile.

In order to focus the workshop on the issues of most importance to the organisation it is necessary to attempt to put the identified risks into some logical priority. This generally involves using scales against which each risk can be measured and compared. Scales in common use for this purpose are:

- significance – the potential impact, financial or otherwise, that the risk would have on the organisation
- likelihood – the probability that the risk would occur in the organisation

**Table 8.1** Risk framework for public sector body.

| External | Internal | Output |
|---|---|---|
| Economic | Staffing and management | Policy and Regulation |
| Political | Information and communication | Advice and information |
| Legal | Systems and physical assets | Financial assistance |
| | Financial information | |

- management – the extent to which the organisation has the ability to influence the impact or likelihood of the risk occurring.

Using a combination of these or similar scales, identified risks can be profiled. This profile will enable participants to understand the importance of the risks identified in relation to each other and to plan the issues upon which management time should be focused. Graphical images such as bar charts or risk matrices are commonly used to display and facilitate discussion of the risk profile (see Figure 8.2). The risk matrix enables the group to visualise the risk profile and the importance of individual issues in relation to others. It is a powerful tool enabling the group quickly to focus on the biggest risks. From the risk matrix in Figure 8.2 it can clearly be seen that the critical risks are G, B and C.

Various methods can be adopted for profiling risks from sophisticated voting technology to simple paper-based scoring. Whatever mechanism is used it is important to understand the extent of disagreement amongst participants when calculating the average. Disagreements when scoring risks can often reveal misunderstanding amongst participants about the nature of the risk or organisational communication issues. These may warrant further discussion before finalising the risk profile and using it to carry certain risks forward into more detailed discussion.

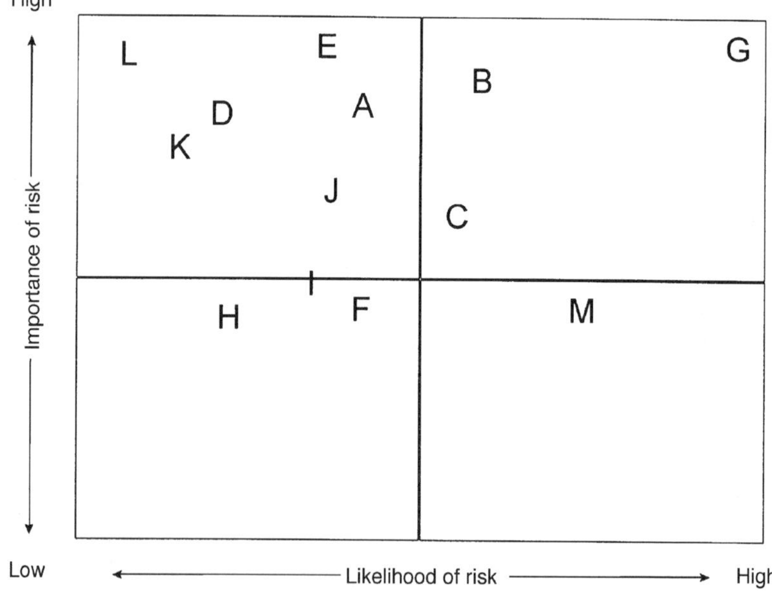


**Figure 8.2** Risk matrix.

## Control and Residual Risk Assessment

The identification and profiling stage establishes a picture of the key risks faced by the organisation, disregarding the management processes and controls currently in force to manage them. The risk profile enables the participants to identify and select the risks that the workshop should discuss in detail. This discussion should establish:

- the control mechanisms in place to manage the risk and the extent to which they consistently operate
- the level of risk that still exists in spite of the control mechanisms in effect (residual risk)
- the extent to which the current balance between residual risk and control is acceptable to the organisation.

These discussions are conducted on a risk-by-risk basis, although it may be possible to aggregate some risks together where commonality exists.

It is useful for participants to be provided with guidance on the identification of control mechanisms, preferably in advance of the workshop. This guidance should define controls and provide a framework of areas for consideration with appropriate examples. Existing control frameworks such as the COSO (see Appendix A) and CoCo (see Appendices B and C) models can be useful in providing a structure and reference point for participants to consider control within.

The facilitator and challenger, as part of their preparation, should consider and schedule the risks and control mechanisms that are likely to exist. This information can be used during the workshop as a prompt for discussions and quality control of the issues identified. As well as identifying the control mechanisms in place the facilitation team should prompt discussion of the extent to which those mechanisms identified operate and are effective.

Having established and recorded the control mechanisms employed to manage risks the facilitation team should encourage a discussion amongst participants of the problems that still, or potentially could, exist in relation to the risk in spite of the control mechanisms. This discussion provides an indication of the nature and level of residual risk and assists participants in forming an opinion about its acceptability. Issues to be considered as part of this discussion may include:

- the extent and materiality of problems experienced in relation to the risk, e.g., known losses and historical performance
- time, money and other resource constraints that may prevent effective management of risks

- levels of uncertainty and change in the organisation's operating environment that impact its ability to manage its risks
- the level of information available with which to measure residual risk levels.

The combination of information about current control mechanisms and residual risk levels should put participants in a position to assess the commercial acceptability of the current situation. A summary of this assessment can be captured using a simple acceptability scale:

*LOW* Acceptable level of risk – no action currently needed.

*MEDIUM* Some reduction in risk level required – monitor position and plan action.

*HIGH* Unacceptable risk level – action required.

This enables identification of risks that require management action to reduce residual risk back to a commercially acceptable level.

## Action Planning

Where unacceptable levels of residual risk have been identified the workshop should focus on improvement planning. It is unlikely that the workshop will result in the development of detailed improvement strategies because of time constraints, lack of information or the absence of management levels sufficient to authorise significant change.

Efforts should be focused on identifying the steps that are required to develop an appropriate solution. It is common for improvement plans developed in workshops to consist of further research, development of cost models or establishment of teams to tackle risk levels as opposed to defining detailed management action.

It is important to ensure that improvement plans are time framed and that responsibility for their completion is identified. A single point of responsibility for the output of the workshop and subsequent co-ordination of actions should be established before the workshop takes place. This sponsor should be of sufficient seniority to ensure full consideration of the workshop outputs and approval for the action plans. The facilitation team should invest sufficient time in both advance and post workshop briefing of the sponsor. The improvement planning session of the workshop should also be used to agree the actions to be taken on residual risks identified but not discussed in detail during the session.

Following the workshop a report should be issued summarising the risks identified, the resulting profile, residual risk levels and improvement plans.

This information should also be absorbed into the risk management reporting structure to enable ongoing measurement and monitoring. An example output report is shown in Figure 8.3.

**Business risk**

Inaccurate and untimely sales forecasts.

Significance 4.7 Likelihood 4.9 Manageability 4.2

Impacts.
Stock unavailable to meet customer demand.
Excessive stock levels and associated stockholding costs.
Excessive product wastage.

**Controls identified**

- Monthly forecasts are prepared by marketing and are updated quarterly.
- Supply/demand meetings are held bi-annually with production and finance personnel.
- Informal production planning/marketing discussions are held as required (reactive not proactive).
- Forecasting accuracy is computed monthly by production personnel.

**Residual risks**

- Demand is particularly volatile for these product lines as consumer preference is influenced by many changing factors.
- Procedures for updating forecasts are poor and not formalised.
- The sales department is not involved in supply/demand meetings.
- Information from supply/demand meetings is not always communicated to marketing managers, who are responsible for completing the forecasts.
- Sales forecasts are not synchronised with financial forecasts.
- Accurate forecasting is not a priority for marketing as it is not included in their key performance measures.
- Marketing is not formally responsible for forecasting.
- Forecasts are produced solely by marketing rather than by a cross functional team.
- Poor communication across functions is leading to missed sales opportunities.
- Forecasts are not updated frequently enough.

**Residual risk status:** HIGH (unacceptable risk level – action required)

**Action plans**

- Establish a consistent and defined monthly process for forecasting by region (PD 06/94).
- Establish accountability for, and a higher priority of, forecasting within the sales and marketing functions (DT 05/94).
- Determine a single point of responsibility for forecasting accuracy (PD Immediate).
- Set up a cross-functional team including sales, marketing and finance to conduct reviews of monthly forecasts (PD 05/94).
- Include forecasting accuracy as a key performance measurement (DT Immediate).
- Review status of risk: 10/94 – cross-functional team.

**Figure 8.3** CSA workshop report.

## CONCLUSION

Many organisations have successfully implemented CSA programmes in response to internal control reporting requirements. In implementing these programmes there has been considerable focus on developing tools and techniques to deliver risk and control assessments. In many cases these CSA programmes have overlooked the wider picture of how an organisation manages its risk base. The result is an unco-ordinated approach to managing risks and inconsistent attitudes towards risk acceptance and mitigation.

One valuable technique to emerge from the development of CSA programmes has been the use of workshop-style meetings to identify and assess risk. Such an approach is consistent with the empowerment and involvement ethics adopted by many organisations. Such techniques enable cross-functional discussion and understanding of organisational risk levels as well as the development of risk awareness in individuals.

For most organisations there is a need to examine what their fundamental strategic risks are and to use this knowledge as the basis from which to build an effective risk management strategy. A programme of workshops in isolation of a wider risk-management strategy will not be effective in delivering competitive advantage and building a risk-competent organisation.

# 9

# A Questionnaire-based Approach
## Key Internal Controls and Systems

*Gus Cottell*

'Nothing endures but change' *Heracleitus* (540–480 BC)

## BACKGROUND

Prior to joining the research councils my internal audit experience had been in local government. The local authority that I worked for had a strong financial approach to internal audit. Audits were allocated according to cost centres and throughout a three-year cycle all of the cost centres of the authority were covered. The move to the research councils was a bit of a culture shock. The audit plan was called the Audit Needs Assessment (ANA) and the focus was not financial but on systems. The systems that existed within each research council were identified and then scheduled to be reviewed over a three-year period. In a lot of the audits it was not even necessary to comment on the financial aspects of the system.

This move from concentrating purely on the finances of a system provided a lot more scope to develop and try new techniques. In addition, the sheer size of the research councils and the comparatively small amount of internal audit resource meant that some other avenue had to be explored to optimise the time available. It did not take long to alight on the idea of control self assessment (CSA) as a tool to achieve this.

## THE RESEARCH COUNCILS

The research councils are non-departmental public bodies (NDPBs), or as they are more commonly known – 'Quangos'. There are seven research councils and they are responsible for the channelling of Government money to scientific research projects. The seven research councils, together with their annual budgets, are shown in Table 9.1.

**Table 9.1** Annual budgets for the seven research councils.

| | £m. |
|---|---|
| 1. Biotechnology and Biological Sciences Research Council (BBSRC) | 183.3 |
| 2. Council for the Central Laboratories Research Council (CCLRC) | 1.45* |
| 3. Economic and Social Research Council (ESRC) | 64.9 |
| 4. Engineering and Physical Sciences Research Council (EPSRC) | 386.4 |
| 5. Medical Research Council (MRC) | 289.1 |
| 6. Natural Environment Research Council (NERC) | 165.1 |
| 7. Particle Physics and Astronomy Research Council (PPARC) | 200.7 |

* Receives funding from the other research councils who use their facilities.

The head office of each research council is based in Swindon with the exception of MRC which is based in London and CCLRC which is based outside Oxford. Some of the research councils have institutes and sites all over the country. These can range in size from a few people to several hundred people. There are also sites abroad ranging from such diverse locations as the Antarctic and Hawaii.

## THE RESEARCH COUNCILS' INTERNAL AUDIT SECTION (RCIAS)

RCIAS has an overall complement of 14 staff, comprising ten in-house staff and under a partnering arrangement with an accountancy firm, an additional resource equivalent to four staff. This arrangement came about as a result of market testing of the internal audit unit. The accountancy firm are involved in the management and direction of the unit in addition to supplying an audit resource, particularly in specialist areas where a full-time auditor cannot be justified as part of the in-house team.

RCIAS is run by the Head of Internal Audit, a deputy and a service delivery manager from the accountancy firm. Below the Deputy Head of Internal Audit is a flat structure of Senior Auditors. RCIAS is governed by an Internal Audit Supervisory Board (IASB), comprising seven finance directors of each research council. It meets twice a year and provides strategic direction for the unit. RCIAS also reports to each research council's audit committee. Each audit committee meets up to three times a year.

## CSA IN THE RESEARCH COUNCILS

The concept of CSA was first introduced to one of the research councils, BBSRC, in 1993 by Anthony Jacobus, then Head of Internal Audit. Anthony's history was of being educated and working in America and then in the City. The concept was not introduced to the research councils as CSA, but as KICS – Key Internal Control and Systems. 'The role of KICS audits is to provide a method by which the adequacy of internal control is measured by the management of the organisation itself in conjunction with RCIAS.'

KICS was initially developed at BBSRC because of the need to provide an annual level of assurance across some twenty sites. Tailored audit (KICS) programmes were developed in collaboration with line managers which are designed to aid the evaluation of the key components that must be present to sustain an adequate level of internal control at any location.

The KICS process rests on thorough consultation with auditees so that it is not seen as something imposed by the auditors. Its purpose was seen as not only to provide guidance on internal control but also to promote greater involvement of management in its ownership of the operation. This was seen as key to sound management and good corporate governance. The KICS audit concepts are based on a risk analysis which

- provides a rational basis for prioritising controls around what really matters to the organisation
- is essential to ensuring that controls are cost effective and that being in control is a real source of strategic advantage
- avoids control evaluation becoming entangled in a morass of detailed control procedures.

Drafting and discussing the tailored KICS audit documentation within BBSRC and its affiliated institutes, including involvement of management at various levels, lasted about six months. It was initiated by a KICS template prepared by internal audit which altered at every meeting. It grew and shrank as the views of management changed from wanting to cover everything to recognising the need to focus on *key* controls and systems. Ultimately the documentation covered the following systems:

- organisation and planning
- research
- finance
- human resources
- computer installations and systems.

The final KICS document looked like an Internal Control Questionnaire (ICQ). It was different in many respects though. The ICQ is generally focused in one particular area (e.g., creditors) and has standard controls listed that would be expected to be seen in the system. These controls stem from audit authoritative knowledge. The KICS document on the other hand is a negotiated document with management that has been through an iterative process. It provides coverage over the whole organisation and is tailored to the organisation's specific requirements.

## DOCUMENTATION AND PLANNING

An example of the KICS document is provided in Appendix 9.1 used at BBSRC institutes. The KICS document used at BBSRC Central Office in Swindon has a comparable structure but also covers a number of corporate governance issues.

Some 70 days of senior internal auditor time is usually budgeted for KICS audits across BBSRC and its affiliated institutes and locations out of a total of 350 audit days for BBSRC. All 21 locations across BBSRC are to be covered over a three-year cycle with the main eight institute sites covered every two years (four each year). The subsequent visits are to follow up on what has been previously agreed to ensure that the appropriate controls have been put in place. As with any other organisation today, BBSRC is operating in a dynamic environment, even the public sector feels the winds of change. Therefore the subsequent visits can look at what has changed at the institute and address their new control issues.

It should always be remembered that the KICS document was an agreed document designed to be tailored to a specific organisation. As such it is pointless to use the same document year in year out. It has to be updated to reflect the changes that have occurred in the organisational environment. This means going back to management and asking if the areas covered are still appropriate. In RCIAS we review the documents every three years.

## PRACTICAL APPLICATION IN THE FIELD

Carrying out the audit is quite simple once the CSA document has been developed providing, of course, that all the preliminaries have been attended too. Contact is usually made with the Institute Secretary to arrange a week when the auditor can visit. For an institute audit the form we would use would be the one in Appendix 9.1.

We would expect the Institute Secretary to select a week when most of the people we would need to see during the audit would be on site. In reality this is probably not possible in which case we would have to make arrangements with their deputies. The people we would need to see relating to each KICS document are shown in Table 9.2.

The best way to start the audit is to meet the Institute Secretary on the Monday morning. As this is the first time on site there is a need for formal

**Table 9.2** Staff to see to complete each KICS document.

| | |
|---|---|
| Section 1, Organisation and Planning | Institute Secretary |
| Section 2, Research | Institute Director |
| Section 3, Finance | Finance Officer |
| | Institute Engineer |
| | Payroll Manager |
| | Stores Manager |
| Section 4, Human Resources | Personnel Officer |
| | Payroll Manager |
| | Health and Safety Officer |
| Section 5, Computer Installation | Institute Computer Manager |

introductions. It is from this initial meeting that the auditor will be given the timetable and a background of the peculiarities of the institute and/or the people to be encountered during the week. It is crucial that this meeting goes well as an initial report will be submitted to the Institute Secretary at the end of the week. At the initial meeting a closure meeting will also be arranged for the Institute Secretary to advise of the findings and proposed recommendations.

The Organisation and Planning section of the KICS form provides an overview of the institute. This interview may last an hour or so at which the auditor may be provided with, or directed to, committee meeting minutes, charters, etc. The information picked up here prepares the auditor to speak authoritatively with other staff of the institute.

Next on the list should be a visit to the Finance Officer. The Finance section of the KICS form is quite broad in scope. The interview with the Finance Officer will be quite lengthy (two hours plus) and there will be a need to return to discuss issues that require explaining. In addition, not all the work can be completed in discussion with the Finance Officer. The auditor will be directed to speak to his staff for more of the detailed information in particular areas.

The Research section of the KICS form requires an interview with the Institute Director. The responses to the questions here are usually quite different from the responses gained from other members of staff encountered during the audit. Often the Director will be taking a different view from the administrative and support staff. He will be a world-leading scientist with broader concerns. This may require a mind shift for the auditor when considering the responses received and their interpretation.

Dealing with the section concerning Human Resources is usually straightforward, but requires a good understanding of personnel and payroll systems. Usually the control issues encountered in this area are typical of all organisations. The Personnel Officer will talk about how people are recruited at the institute and how leavers are dealt with. They will explain the systems in place that can be traced through to the payroll systems. The Payroll Manager will explain the notifications they receive when someone starts and leaves and about payroll processes.

The Computing section of the KICS form does presuppose that the auditor has some basic computer audit skills. Without them they are unlikely to make much impact in the area. An outline knowledge of the computer set up and the systems used is necessary. Fortunately, all institutes follow broadly similar structures although with devolved management of institutes there is currently a desire for each institute to exercise some autonomy.

When carrying out the audit the responses are typed directly onto the KICS form (any finding or recommendations are appended to this document). This has the benefit of alerting the auditor to any tests that need carrying out. When completing the form the auditor should always ask himself 'if management take me to task on this point will I have the evidence to back up what I have said?'.

The preparation of working papers is an important issue during the audit. As a lot of ground is covered during a KICS audit the auditor has to grasp quickly the systems that are being explained to them. Again it is essential that the auditor has had experience of all these systems before. It saves time and enables the auditor to home in on the real control issues.

At the end of the week the Institute Secretary should be presented with a draft of the completed KICS form and any recommendations made. In RCIAS we operate a 'no surprises' policy. We do not leave the site without having discussed the audit with institute management. The formal report is issued within twenty days of completion of the fieldwork after approval from internal audit management.

The closure meeting should be a two-way process. It is not inconceivable that an auditor may have made a mistake. It is at this stage that the Institute Secretary can point this out to the auditor and save a lot of embarrassment later.

## PITFALLS TO AVOID

KICS is not a universal panacea. It would be wrong to give the impression that the KICS approach could replace other forms of auditing. This is definitely not the case. In some respects KICS can be regarded as a somewhat superficial approach. It provides coverage, but it is covering the whole of the organisation. It is a high-level review giving a broad internal audit assurance.

KICS is best utilised alongside other forms of auditing. It must be seen as another technique at the auditor's disposal to achieve the objectives of the internal audit service. The traditional systems-based approach to auditing is at the other end of the spectrum from KICS. It is a contrast because it is very focused at what it looks at but it is also able to provide considerable depth.

KICS complements the systems-based approach giving broad annual assurance supplemented from assurance gained from systems audits as part of the longer-term plan. The results of either audit approach should feed into the other thereby providing an efficient process. The approaches should not be used in isolation, but should be used in a structured way so that they support each other.

A KICS audit cannot be carried out by junior or inexperienced staff. The KICS document, in order to keep it a manageable piece of work, asks some pretty general questions. The more senior and experienced auditor will be able to work with the auditee and explore the issues raised by a question with them, rather than just ask it and receive a yes or no answer.

The auditor will be dealing with senior management and, in the research councils, some of the most eminent scientists in the world. The task of operating at this sort of level does require some tact. The Heads of Internal Audit sending staff out on such audits must ask themselves 'how will this auditor be perceived and what will the effect be on the image of internal audit'.

## QUESTIONS TO ASK ON THE INTRODUCTION OF KICS

The main question to ask is 'will the KICS approach be suitable for us?'. CSA is only one way of carrying out audit reviews; there are many others (e.g., financial, systems-based). The factors to consider are:

- the organisational environment
- what method of delivery of CSA is to be used.

The organisational environment is crucial in deciding whether to adopt KICS or not. For example, in an industry that processes a high level of financial transactions like a bank there will naturally be a requirement to do a lot of substantive testing. In such an environment there may be less requirement to take the high-level KICS approach when assurance is required at the lower level. On this basis the organisation will want to spend more money on auditors for this function to be able to get the level of assurance that they need.

On the other hand, an organisation such as a Civil Service department will be interested in other less tangible and rather more general aspects (e.g., ensuring that parliamentary questions are addressed effectively). Where this is the case they may well be looking for an increased level of this broader assurance supplemented with a smaller amount of compliance and substantive testing in specific areas.

If the decision is 'yes, we will go ahead with CSA', the decision has to be made about how internal audit is going to deliver the approach. Broadly these divide into two approaches:

- questionnaire, interviews etc.
- using a workshop approach.

Using a questionnaire-based approach enables coverage of a wide range of topics and it is the responsibility of the auditor to arrange to see the individuals they need to see. The workshop approach requires the setting aside of a period for all managers to be in the same place at the same time. Although important issues may be tackled there may be some restrictions on the number of issues that can be dealt with though crucial high-level issues may be addressed.

## INTRODUCING KICS

The introduction of KICS requires 'buy in' at various levels. Firstly, it requires buy in from management who overview the running of the internal audit service, usually the Audit Committee and/or the Finance Director. CSA requires the abandonment of more traditional approaches.

Audit Committees and/or Finance Directors have to be made aware of the consequences of their decisions. They are sacrificing some in-depth audit assurance for less depth but broader coverage audit assurance. Naturally, they want to know how the KICS approach is to be applied and what the end product will be like. To this end some examples and plans of what is intended to be carried out should be presented. This may include:

- identifying the organisations or parts of the organisation to be audited
- an example of the KICS document
- time schedules and costs, what audits are proposed to be sacrificed for KICS audits
- what is the deliverable; how the report is going to look and be issued.

Once the strategic decision has been made that a KICS approach is going to happen, internal audit has to win over the hearts and minds of the auditees they are going to be working with. 'Champions' were identified within the institute who were to be links. More often than not this was the Institute Secretary, the administrative expert who liaises with the scientists on a day-to-day basis and is able to bridge the communication gap that auditors could not as 'outsiders'. Having explained the concept to them and won them over, KICS would then be raised as an agenda item for the senior management meeting of the institute. This requires a presentation by the Head of Internal Audit.

What about the auditors, the people who have to do the work? Their buy-in is crucial as they are the KICS sales staff. As mentioned above, the requirement is that auditors applying the KICS approach have to be experienced and tactful. They also have to be able to have the foresight to recognise that this is a technique that is here to stay and be alert to making recommendations to update the KICS questionnaire.

The next stage is developing the template, the initial discussion document. This has to be done by someone who has been with the organisation for some time and has real knowledge of the systems. The reason for this is that the 'first-cut' KICS document is a demonstration of internal audit's knowledge of their business. If the template document is poor then a lot of credibility will be lost at the outset. This ground may be difficult to regain and may threaten the success or introduction of KICS.

The iterative process should take place with senior management. When preparing the BBSRC Institute KICS document the senior management selected were two Institute Secretaries. At the outset we had in mind that the site visit to the institute would take a week. Consequently the final outcome concerning the KICS document is that it had to be manageable and able to be completed within that timescale by the auditor. There is a balance that has to be struck. The KICS document has to be of sufficient size for it to provide coverage, yet it should not be so large that the auditor does not have sufficient time to explore the questions with the auditee.

When the KICS document has been agreed it then has to be put to the Finance Director or Audit Committee (depending on what has been agreed at the outset). Once approval has been granted the KICS document is suitable for use in the field. The first audit using the KICS document should be carefully planned. It is probably best to start with an 'audit-friendly' site. The auditor carrying out the audit should be familiar with the site and management. The purpose of this is to minimise risk and increase the chances of a successful audit.

When the auditor returns from the field they should be 'de-briefed'. It is important to find out how the audit went, if anything went wrong and if improvement of the delivery of the audit work can be improved the next time a KICS audit is carried out. It may also be worth while, at the end of the reporting process, to send a customer satisfaction survey out.

## SUCCESS

The application of the KICS approach in BBSRC has been a complete success. This has been proved by the desire of management to have a Central

Office KICS questionnaire designed for them and by the demand of other research councils to want the same type of audit.

In spreading the KICS approach to other research councils we employed the communicative skills of Keith Wade from Consultancy and Audit Training Services. Each year RCIAS has an 'awayday'. This is a period when we go off site for a couple of days. We take stock of what has happened over the past year and decide the future direction of our internal audit service.

On occasions we invite a research council's Finance Director along as well. It is a useful time to meet informally for both parties and build good working relationships. Keith Wade was instrumental in explaining the future role of CSA and the importance it has as a technique for the internal auditor to use on occasions. Through his work Keith sold the idea to the Finance Directors.

## SUMMARY

Although the following looks like a long 'to do' list in implementing the KICS approach, as always it is really just a matter of common sense and professionalism. The various steps may not be the most appropriate for your organisation though, and like the KICS document, may have to be tailored to your specific circumstances.

- Get approval for the approach from the Finance Director and/or the Audit Committee.
- Present the proposal to the senior management of the business unit that you will be auditing and get their approval.
- Get the buy-in from senior auditors in the internal audit service.
- Develop a template KICS questionnaire.
- Enter into an iterative process with senior management of the business unit.
- Finalise the KICS questionnaire.
- Carry out the first KICS audit.
- Analyse the approach and the results with the auditor.
- Get feedback from the auditee.
- Improve delivery of the next KICS audit.

A questionnaire-based approach such as KICS is bound to be a success. It provides members of management with the opportunity to discuss their job in a structured way and most people enjoy talking about their work. In doing so they identify the risks they have in their systems and can devise controls to redress those risks with the auditor – true teamwork!

# APPENDIX 9.1

# KICS Document for BBSRC Institutes

| Control objective | Yes/ No | Comments/cross-reference to any attachments |
|---|---|---|

## 1. ORGANISATION AND PLANNING

### Overall organisation

1.1 Is the overall management and departmental structure, including the duties, lines of responsibility and accountability defined in:

1.1.1 Organisation charts?
1.1.2 Written job descriptions?

### Organisation of operating departments

1.2 Are the duties, lines of responsibility and accountability of staff adequately defined in:

1.2.1 Organisation charts?
1.2.2 Written job descriptions?

1.3 In respect of all staff:

1.3.1 Has a 'Delegation of Authority' been prepared showing control responsibilities and cash limits?
1.3.2 Are there clear instructions relating to the delegation of duties when staff are absent?

### Business planning

1.4 With regard to the planning process:

1.4.1 Are the links between Council science priorities and policies, and detailed institute plans adequately documented and dealt with?
1.4.2 Are assessments made about categories of work (e.g., basic research/contract research/wealth creation/support services/etc.)?

1.4.3 Are plans and budgets projected forward beyond the current year for at least two more years?
1.4.4 Are 'SWOT' (Strengths – Weaknesses – Opportunities – Threats) or other analytical approaches to strategic planning utilised or valid?

1.5 Are planning, budgeting and the management accounts linked to form an interactive whole and are they exposed to independent review (e.g. Institute Governing Body)?

Completed/updated by:

HEAD OF RESEARCH:
AUDITOR:
DATE:

## 2. RESEARCH

2.1 When planning research activities, are the following taken into consideration and, if so, how:

2.1.1 Scientific relevance?
2.1.2 Council policies?
2.1.3 Costs and facilities?
2.1.4 Capabilities to manage research?
2.1.5 Flexibility and responsiveness?

Are any other criteria utilised and, if so, how?

2.2 Are there adequate systems in place for decision-making purposes with regard to resource allocation between basic, strategic and applied research?

2.3 Research work also needs to be considered in terms of its potential for direct and more immediate results and market applicability. Are there systems in place to make appropriate decisions about:

2.3.1 The current or future utility of contract work?
2.3.2 Commercial and other potentially wealth-creating opportunities?
2.3.3 How potential Intellectual Property Rights (IPR) are dealt with (see also Fixed Assets, Section 3.20-22)?

2.4 Is there a system for regular internal review of research projects in progress or planned, covering Science Budget funded projects, MAFF commissioned work plus other contracts?

2.5 With regard to the Peer Review procedures (both science and support systems):

2.5.1 Note date(s) of latest review
2.5.2 In respect of findings and proposals for any resulting action, have these been dealt with?
2.5.3 Are there matters outstanding or carried forward from the Peer Review(s)? (note/obtain brief details)

2.6 OASIS forms the basis for significant assessment of scientific research output. Are there satisfactory controls over

2.6.1 Completeness, accuracy and timeliness of input information
2.6.2 Other factors relevant to its effectiveness in information and assessment terms for decision-making purposes?

Completed/updated by:

HEAD OF RESEARCH:
AUDITOR:
DATE:

## 3. FINANCE

### Accounting manuals

3.1 Are there to hand the Government and Council:

3.1.1 Manuals of procedures and policies?

3.1.2 List of account codes?

3.1.3 Local budget instructions and 'desk' procedures, and have these been approved by a senior official (who?), regularly reviewed (latest date?); and made available to relevant personnel?

3.1.4 Accounting and other calendars showing due dates (plus recording actual performance) for reports, key reconciliations and other important checks/reviews?

**Monthly reports and accounts**

3.2 Are these produced promptly after the end of the relevant accounting period? To whom are they distributed? (e.g., to the Director, Secretary and others plus to budget holders).

3.3 Are meaningful written explanations, for example, explaining the reasons underlying significant changes from budget and/or previous periods, routinely prepared?

3.4 Is a record maintained (e.g., board/committee minutes) of:

3.4.1 Any actions required
3.4.2 Those actually taken

following the review of the accounts?

**Preparation of operating budgets**

3.5 Does a senior official have overall responsibility for the direction and preparation of operating budgets? (State his/her position.)

3.6 If the budgets are revised during the year, do the procedures in 3.3 above also apply to the revisions? (State how often the revisions are made and whether the actual results are compared with the original budgets and/or the revised budgets.)

3.7 Are the budgets covered by a written statement of assumptions made?

3.8 Are reasonable steps taken to formulate the assumptions which are most critical to the reliability of the budgets/establish the areas most sensitive to change? (E.g., by comparing the budgeted and actual results for the past two years.)

**Income and expenditure**

3.9 Are income budgets:

3.9.1 Analysed in an appropriate manner? (State how they are analysed e.g., by type of research or section head.)
3.9.2 Approved by the relevant department heads or similar persons? (State their positions.)

3.10 Are expenditure budgets:

3.10.1 Determined with sufficient accuracy, e.g., by reference to actual forecast costs? (State how they are prepared.)
3.10.2 Analysed in a manner appropriate to the operations? (State how they are analysed.)
3.10.3 Approved by the relevant department heads or similar persons? (State their positions.)

**Overheads**

3.11 Are overhead budgets:

3.11.1 Determined with sufficient accuracy, e.g., by reference to actual forecast costs? (State how they are prepared.)
3.11.2 Analysed in a manner appropriate to the business? (State how they are analysed.)

3.12 Are actual overheads:

3.12.1 Analysed between appropriate expenditure classifications? (e.g., administration, marketing, accommodation and support services.)
3.12.2 Allocated between departments or other cost centres?
3.12.3 Measured by suitable methods?

**Other items**

3.13 Where applicable, do the budgets deal adequately with the following (specify how):

3.13.1 Significant amounts of 'other' income and expenditure?
3.13.2 Provisions for debtors and other assets plus contingencies?
3.13.3 Procedures for dealing with and approving

non-routine contracts, grants and other such items where both income and liabilities (e.g., for performance) may be involved?

3.14 With respect to the monthly reports and accounts:

3.14.1 Do they include a comparison of actual and budgeted cash flow?
3.14.2 Are nominal ledger accounts (also PGO/Bank accounts and debtors/creditors) reconciled with narrative explanations for any differences?
3.14.3 Are they routinely scrutinised and suspense items/accounts agreed by an independent senior officer?

**Receipts cycle**

3.15 Can any:

3.15.1 Goods leave the premises without being recorded?
3.15.2 Monies be received and not recorded or banked?
3.15.3 Work be done/sales made for a bad credit risk?
3.15.4 Sales be invoiced but not recorded?
3.15.5 Overdue accounts escape follow-up?

**Payments cycle**

3.16 Could:

3.16.1 Unauthorised payments be made? (E.g., how are accountable documents controlled.)
3.16.2 Liabilities be incurred for goods or services not authorised/received?
3.16.3 Liabilities be incurred but not recorded?
3.16.4 Charges be allocated to the wrong accounts?
3.16.5 Goods be returned to suppliers without this having been recorded?

**Inventories, stores and cash**

3.17 Are stock and cash takes undertaken? (Note: frequency, organisation, nature and locations.)

3.18 Can persons with custodial functions undertake recording and accounting functions? (including not only physical goods and consumables but also cash and accountable documents, such as POs and cheques).

3.19 Are inventories, stores and cash on hand excessive when compared with rates of consumption?

**Fixed assets, including intangibles (e.g., IPR)**

3.20 With regard to fixed assets including intangibles:

3.20.1 Can they be acquired or disposed of without proper authority?
3.20.2 Is adequate distinction made between additions/disposals and repairs and maintenance/ non-capital items?

3.21 Is there a systematic approach to maintenance of:

3.21.1 The built estate?
3.21.2 Other fixed assets?

3.22 With regard to capital and other projects, including IPR, are there systems in place for the proper recording and control of

3.22.1 Actual and anticipated costs to be incurred to completion, plus in-house costs?
3.22.2 Comparisons with budgets, contractors' estimates and the like?
3.22.3 Other matters covered in 'Capital Works Procedures' circulated by Estates Branch of BBSRC?
3.22.4 Legal matters and costs related thereto?

**Purchasing**

3.23 Are standard purchasing routines established and rigidly adhered to?

3.24 Are all purchase commitments, including contracts approved at an appropriate level *before* liability is created? (See also 1.3.1 Organisation and planning, above.)

3.25 Are there procedures in force to ensure optimum purchasing in terms of lowest cost, consistent with quality and service requirements, taking into consideration economic lot sizes, delivery locations, storage, payment terms, quantity and other discounts, etc.?

**Financial audits**

3.26 In respect of management letters resulting from the most recent financial audits by the NAO and/or external auditors

3.26.1 Has a response been made to all matters raised?
3.26.2 Have actions resulting therefrom been implemented?
3.26.3 Are there any matters still outstanding?

Completed/updated by:

FINANCE OFFICER:
AUDITOR:
DATE:

## 4. HUMAN RESOURCES

4.1 Are there to hand:

4.1.1 Manuals of personnel procedures and policies?
4.1.2 Health and safety rules and regulations?
4.1.3 Laboratory procedures relating to safety and the conduct of experiments?

4.2 Are the policies and regulations per 4.1 above adequately communicated to all personnel and reflected in location/operation procedures?

4.3 Are there regular inspections and how are the recommendations resulting therefrom dealt with? (Note latest and obtain details of findings/actions taken.)

4.4 Is there a system in force for reporting and evaluating accidents? (See also 4.1.2 and 4.1.3 above.)

**Personnel and payroll**

4.5 Examine the system and controls for new posts, regradings, changes in rates of pay, leavers and new recruits and, in regard to staff information generally:

4.5.1 Is PERFAST in use? (If not, how are staff records maintained.)
4.5.2 Are there controls to ensure the completeness and accuracy of staff details?
4.5.3 Does the system used for pension entitlement information deal with all the necessary requirements? (E.g., unpaid or special leave, overtime and/or allowances.)

4.6 In regard to payroll information:

4.6.1 Are there satisfactory links between staff information and payroll?
4.6.2 Are payrolls run on PAYSOLVE or independently processed? (E.g., by Chessington, or other bureau.)
4.6.3 Are the controls to ensure completeness, accuracy and authorisation procedures, satisfactory?
4.6.4 Is summary information for decision making purposes, forecasting and the like, readily available and adequate?

4.7 Consider the following in connection with personnel records and the payroll cycle:

4.7.1 Could unauthorised employees get paid?
4.7.2 Can employees receive unauthorised payments?
4.7.3 Can deductions from gross pay be improperly made or misappropriated?

Completed/updated by:

PERSONNEL/PAYROLL OFFICER:
AUDITOR:
DATE:

## 5. COMPUTER INSTALLATIONS AND SYSTEMS

5.1 Are details of the major computerised systems at the location (particularly those related to the various activities and cycles covered by KICS herein) readily available? (E.g., outline system descriptions.)

5.2 With regard to systems which cover accounting, research, personnel and other key records, are these records **adequately** safeguarded/ backed-up against loss or destruction?

5.3 Is the 'Security Tool Kit' software being used by management for control purposes, including the exception reporting facility? (Note how and where used.)

5.4 Is there a local computer department and if so are:

5.4.1 Administrative procedures documented, understood and followed by the staff of the department?
5.4.2 Are controls established and operating over the development and maintenance of systems and programmes?
5.4.3 Are processing controls documented and understood by operators?

5.5 Where local processing is involved are there controls over:

5.5.1 Data input?
5.5.2 Standing data?
5.5.3 Transaction data?
5.5.4 Data output?
5.5.6 Exception reporting?

5.6 With regard to on-line systems:

5.6.1 Are terminals used for input of transaction(s); enquiries only; or both? (Obtain details of who can do which and to what systems.)
5.6.2 Is access to terminals restricted? (Specify controls.)
5.6.3 Are all transactions logged by the computer and does the log record from which terminal data was received?
5.6.4 Are there adequate stand-by facilities in the event of line failure?
5.6.5 If VDUs are in use, is the display of certain confidential data capable of being suppressed?

5.6.6 Can printed hard copies be obtained from output displayed on the VDUs?
5.6.7 Can programmes be created or amended via a terminal?
5.6.8 Are all creations and amendments logged by the computer?

Completed/updated by:

COMPUTING MANAGER:
AUDITOR:
DATE:

# 10

# Effective Risk Management in a Complex Environment using Electronic meetings

*Glyn Rodgers*

## INTRODUCTION

This chapter describes how CSA has been developed at The United Leeds Teaching Hospitals NHS Trust using the techniques of electronic meetings. At such events participants each have a laptop computer and are able to enter their thoughts and ideas directly via their computer. This well established meeting technique has significant advantages of speed, accuracy and completeness. The fact that input can be anonymous has particular benefits in CSA in ensuring that risks are not glossed over.

## UNITED LEEDS TEACHING HOSPITALS NHS TRUST (ULTH)

ULTH is Britain's largest NHS trust, employing 13,000 staff over eight different sites. It has recently opened a new £90 million wing which during its construction was the largest building project in the NHS and provides some of the best facilities available in the world.

ULTH is dedicated to providing a wide range of first-class hospital services to the people of Leeds and beyond. It is governed by a Board of Directors, composed of executive and non-executive directors in roughly equal proportions. In common with many NHS Trusts, ULTH faces severe financial challenges which the Board is vigorously tackling in a number of ways, including moving decision making closer to the patient by a major restructuring into 11 subsidiaries. The subsidiaries are changing the nature of ULTH, meeting the need to increase efficiency, reduce costs and modernise services so that the standards of care for the patients can be maintained and improved. Each subsidiary is responsible for its own income and expenditure – and risk management.

Risk management has been specifically identified as an important activity nationally by the NHS Executive. The Executive describes risk management as 'an essential part of line management which enables line managers to manage their services more effectively and to a higher standard'. The consequences of failing to be proactive toward risk management include losing quality and reputation for patient care, and 'paying out for claims, fines, staff costs and patient costs'.

The ULTH Trust has taken a leading part in an NHS pilot Controls Assurance project to develop and implement risk-management techniques. During this project the Trust has used the computerised technique of electronic meetings in order to help staff identify and discuss risks and the actions needed to manage them. The ULTH project focuses on empowering departments to review their own risk environment and providing a framework whereby a devolved team can take appropriate actions to manage risk more effectively.

A Risk Management Group under Len Wright, the Director of Finance and Performance, has been set up to lead the pilot project, formed of key representatives from the areas where risk management work was being undertaken. This helps ensure that the risk management programme is integrated into the major restructuring activities that are taking place across the Trust.

As an introduction to risk management a professional 20-minute video was made, demonstrating the business risks of doctors with falsified qualifications, hackers accessing a hospital's computer system and the consequences of mixing patients notes. Medical staff are very familiar with risk assessment and management in the context of day-to-day individual patient relationships, but there are new types of risk that now need to be evaluated as a business responsibility of the Trust and its subsidiaries.

## RISK MANAGEMENT FRAMEWORK

A simple model, the generic risk cycle, has been used as a framework. This model has four phases:

1. risk identification
2. risk analysis
3. risk management
4. risk audit.

These four phases are outlined in Figure 10.1. The model allows for 'bottom up' risk identification at the departmental level and a top-down review of risks from the Board's perspective.

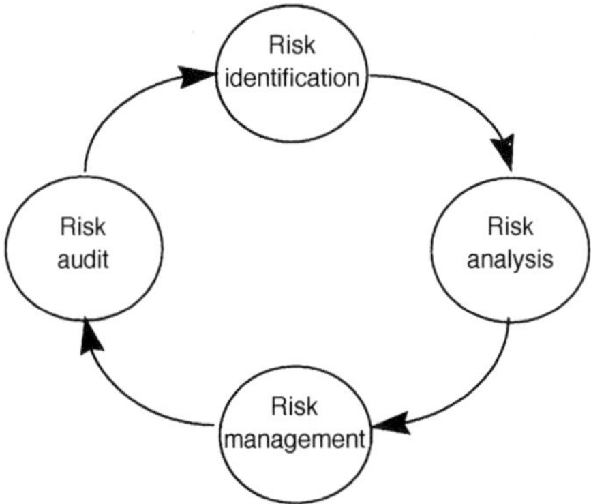


**Figure 10.1** Generic risk cycle.

For the first phase, each department, directorate or service delivery organisation identifies its own risks at a meeting of key people. The risks identified may be confirmed by further one-to-one interviews. Staff in certain areas may require expert assistance to identify effectively all the risks. The output of this phase includes an outline 'risk library'. The process is shown in Figure 10.2.

The second phase is risk analysis, as illustrated in Figure 10.3. In addition to direct costs such as repair and replacement, intangible losses are considered such as loss of customer goodwill, reduced supplier confidence or employee dissatisfaction. Two dimensions of risk are evaluated: *probability* and *consequence*. Using these characteristics, each risk can be evaluated in a two by two matrix. There are a number of techniques to assess probability, including historical data and subjective assessment.

**Figure 10.2** Risk identification.

**Figure 10.3** Risk analysis.

At a Board level, the following risk areas are addressed:

- property risks (buildings and equipment)
- security risks (physical, personnel and information)
- occupational health and safety and environmental risks
- business interruption.

The third phase, risk management, establishes whether the controls in place are appropriate and whether responsibility for a control is generally accepted. This is shown in Figure 10.4. The current monitoring arrangements are assessed to ascertain whether they provide the Board with the assurance it requires. This involves

- an evaluation of existing control measures
- the identification of areas of concern with these measures and an assessment of the potential for improvement
- providing recommendations on areas for improvement, including priorities for action
- drawing up an action plan to address the issues raised.

Action plans to reduce risks would be noted in the business plan of the department.

The fourth phase is risk audit, to ensure that the framework of policies and standards within the organisation is being adhered to. This process rests with line management, directors and the Board of each subsidiary. This stage is outside the scope of the current project.

In conjunction with Price Waterhouse, ULTH decided to take a new approach and to use electronic meetings for some of the meetings to identify and analyse risks. These meetings have very specific advantages in this area in encouraging open discussion and reducing the length of meetings. It is clear that candour in risk analysis is essential; everyone who has a possible contribution must be able to do so in a stress-free environment. Also the cost and time involvement of busy specialists must be kept to a minimum. The software and methodology developed by GroupSystems was selected as being well established, especially in the US, where tens of thousands of meetings have been run.

**Figure 10.4** Risk management.

## OVERVIEW OF THE PROCESS

In an electronic meeting the participants use a personal computer (PC), usually a laptop, to enter facts, opinions, suggestions and votes. The PCs are linked together in a network and all the input is collected on one of the PCs. A facilitator is often present to help run the meeting. He or she has responsibility for the organisation of the meeting, not for the output.

An agenda for an electronic meeting includes a number of sessions that are started and stopped by the facilitator from one of the PCs on the network. To start a session the facilitator sends questions, statements or subject headings to the PCs, asking for answers or comments or votes from each participant. The participants type their input into the PC, check it and then send it across the network using the mouse or a function key. At this point the input can be available for all participants to see, usually anonymously so no one knows who made a particular comment. The input can be shown on each participant's PC and also on a large screen such as one would find in any conference room.

Typing skills are not important. In fact the slow typist, by keeping input short in order to reduce the typing required, can communicate as effectively as an expert typist who enters long sentences. Length of input does not equate to quality or ease of understanding! At the end of the meeting, all the information gathered during the meeting is available. Reports can be printed out and transferred to e-mail or diskette for distribution to all interested parties. Most electronic meetings conclude with an anonymous participant survey to ensure that participants have said all they want to say and are committed to the output of the meeting.

## ADVANTAGES

Electronic meetings have considerable advantages over conventional meetings, as can be seen from a number of specific features.

*Shared input*
Suggestions, facts or opinions entered by participants are shown on all the PCs and can be projected onto a large screen. This avoids duplication of input and saves time.

*Parallel input*
Participants type in their contributions at the same time, rather than talking one after the other. This saves time.

*Keyboard input*
Making one's contribution to a meeting, via the keyboard gives participants time to consider their input and to be sure that they are typing what they really mean.

*Anonymous input*
As distinct from a conventional meeting, all the input can be anonymous. This is particularly valuable in the process of risk assessment since it means that all possible risks can be freely identified.

*Electronic voting*
Electronic voting allows risks to be quickly and easily prioritised. One technique of electronic voting is called matrix voting, whereby participants can vote using multiple criteria. In the field of risk assessment two criteria frequently used are 'how likely is it to happen?' and 'how great are the consequences if it does happen?'.

*Action planning and commitment*
Participants can enter proposed actions for all to see, which ensures that actions are clearly understood and that commitments are shared. This building of consensus in the meeting enhances teamwork.

*Large meetings*
Large electronic meetings are very effective, which means that everyone involved can get together at the same time.

*Participants feedback*
This is designed to ask questions such as:

- did you feel able to contribute to the meeting?
- how confident are you that we have identified all the risks?
- do you think the actions that we have planned are adequate?

The answers to these questions are shared instantly with the participants before the meeting closes. These questions ensure that participants are satisfied that all the risks have been found and that appropriate actions have been set in place.

*Electronic record*
At the end of an electronic meeting, all the risks, comments, votes and actions are recorded on the computer. This record of the meeting is immediately available for participants to take away with them.

*Distributed meetings*

The Internet and related networking technologies make it possible to run electronic meetings with participants distributed around the country, or indeed the world. This means that external experts on specific subjects can make their contribution to risk management meetings without needing to travel to the meeting. This facility has not yet been used at ULTH.

## RISK WORKSHOPS RUN AS ELECTRONIC MEETINGS

The first stage in setting up a risk workshop is for the leader of the workshop to discuss and agree the benefits with the Department Head. The scope of the workshop can then be agreed, and participants identified with a suitable span of skills and knowledge. The workshop leader can be an experienced external consultant or someone from the organisation with appropriate position and training (see the section 'Practical information' near the end of this chapter for more discussion on the position of workshop leader).

A summarised agenda of a risk workshop when run as an electronic meeting is shown in Figure 10.5. This agenda shows a timescale of half a day, though these workshops have been run in two hours when participants are particularly busy. The first activity in the meeting is to watch the risk management video and introduce participants to the electronic meetings technology, which usually consists of a short ice-breaker session lasting 5–10 minutes. The next activity is for participants to review the objectives of the department and ensure that there is agreement on them. Participants are then invited to input risks by adding to a set of risks already entered into the computer. The risks already in the computer have been collected from some or all of the participants before the meeting. The objectives of this preparation are to encourage the participants to think about risk issues before the meeting and also to keep the meeting as short as possible by avoiding duplicate entry of the obvious risks during the meeting.

Agenda – typical departmental risk assessment workshop

| | |
|---|---|
| 9:00 | Introduction, including video and icebreaker. |
| 9:20 | Review and agree department objectives (discussion and vote). |
| 9:40 | Brainstorm the risks (participants add risks to those already entered). |
| 10:15 | Electronic discussion of the risks. |
| 10:45 | Electronically assess risks by likelihood and impact. |
| 11:00 | Discussion – identify risks which are already controlled. |
| 11:30 | Enter actions to manage the high-priority remaining risks. |
| 12:00 | Feedback survey on effectiveness of meeting. |
| 12:15 | Adjourn meeting. |

**Figure 10.5** Agenda – risk assessment workshop.

Participants type a description of a risk in approximately a dozen words, with unlimited space to add a further description if required. Once a participant has entered a risk it can be seen by all the others who know immediately that they do not need to re-enter the same risk. All participants can make comments on any of the risks, for example to develop a description in more detail or to ask a question. The risks are then categorised in order to help analyse them. Typical categories for a clinical department could be:

- equipment
- procedures
- inpatient issues
- outpatient issues
- training
- patient information.

Participants are then asked to vote on the seriousness of the risks, indicating both the likelihood of the risk occurring and the impact if the risk occurs. The votes are on a scale of one to ten. The facilitator gives guidance to the participants on how to express likelihood and impact on a 1–10 scale. Alternatively, scales of 'very likely', 'likely', 'possible', 'unlikely' can be used for likelihood and 'high', 'medium', 'low' and 'negligible' for impact. An example of the result of a vote for eight risks is shown in Table 10.1.

The risks can be displayed in a two-by-two matrix showing high and low risk, and high and low impact. The results of this vote make it very easy to identify the risks that are both high likelihood and high impact, i.e., those that need to be tackled first. An example of this type of matrix is shown in Figure 10.6.

The spread of the votes for each risk can be analysed to identify where there is significant disagreement about likelihood or impact. If some participants think a risk will have high impact and others think it will have

**Table 10.1** Votes on the likelihood and impact of risks.

| Risk | | Likelihood | Impact |
|---|---|---|---|
| 1 | Lack of flexibility to reward staff appropriately | 7.33 | 6.67 |
| 2 | fraud in complex technical area | 4.15 | 7.11 |
| 3 | Poor training for middle management | 2.44 | 7.05 |
| 4 | Time wasted in badly organised meetings | 8.10 | 8.82 |
| 5 | Lack of funds for projects to improve quality | 6.27 | 4.46 |
| 6 | Internal transport problems | 3.77 | 3.61 |
| 7 | Failure to communicate new procedures | 3.87 | 7.23 |
| 8 | Trainee staff not adequately supervised | 7.45 | 5.26 |

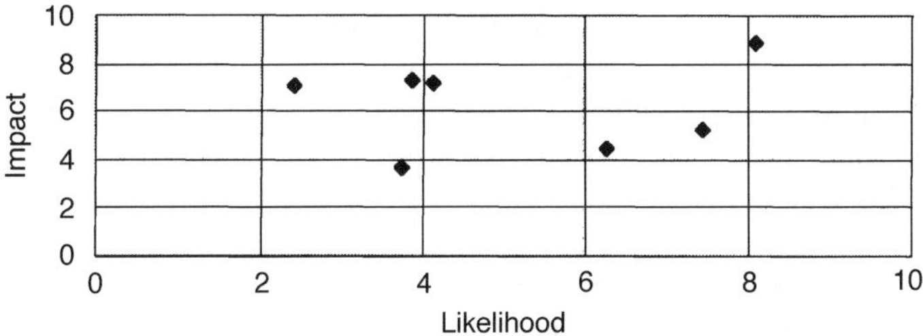


**Figure 10.6** Scatter diagram of likelihood and impact of risks.

low impact, then more analysis is needed so that everyone has the same perception before actions are proposed. In this way the electronic meeting technology helps the meeting participants focus discussion on the important issues.

The anonymity across different disciplines within a speciality ensures that all opinions are considered on their merits. Hence when actions are agreed, there is real consensus among the meeting participants. Participants do not vote on risks where they have no opinion or knowledge.

The next stage is to identify the controls which are already in place for the most significant risks. Again all participants are free to enter their knowledge and opinions. Actions are then listed to manage the important risks. These actions are then assigned to people or departments and everybody involved makes a visible and public commitment.

## ELECTRONIC MEETING RISK WORKSHOPS AT ULTH

At ULTH, electronic meeting risk workshops were run for the Board, the Institute of Pathology and the Departments of Obstetrics and Gynaecology. For the Board, 58 risks were listed and then categorised under four objectives:

- Advance the Trust's leading role as a centre of innovation and excellence in service provision, teaching and research.
- Secure the Trust's future in a changing external environment by transforming the Trust.
- Ensure financial viability.
- Develop as a good employer.

Not surprisingly, the most urgent risks for the Board came from the financial and cost pressures on the Trust. With appropriate preparation a Board can in a three-hour session get a good overview of its risk position and be sure it is in control.

The electronic meeting workshop for the Institute of Pathology was led by the Senior Chief Bio-Medical Scientist, and facilitated by a consultant from Price Waterhouse. Pathology is a diverse and complex area, with a wide range of staff groups, making it difficult to get a common view of risks for the whole department. Hence this group was very suitable for an electronic meeting.

At the end of the day, over 250 risks had been identified and discussed so that there was common understanding and prioritised by impact and likelihood. The risks were sorted into the following categories:

- political
- commercial
- construction
- operational
- financial
- health and safety
- corporate issues.

Prioritising the risks in these categories avoids the impracticality of comparing completely different risks, e.g., political risks with Health and Safety risks.

A specific outcome of this workshop was the realisation that although *accidents* were carefully recorded, there was insufficient monitoring of *incidents*, such as a theft, loss of a specimen or an error made with a specimen. Consequently a form for incident reporting was developed with an appropriate Standard Operating Procedure.

The largest risk category in the Institute of Pathology was 'operational'. One particular benefit of the process was that it enabled a comparison to be made across the Institute of how comparable risks were handled in different departments. An edited set of risks in the 'operational' category is shown in Figure 10.7.

A similar approach was used for the Obstetrics Risk Management Workshop. This workshop was led by the then Assistant Director of Business Planning at ULTH. Facilitation support was again provided by an external consultant from Price Waterhouse. Before the workshop, the leader circulated all participants by letter and interviewed a number of them to collect their view of the department's risks and these risks had been entered into the computer before the workshop began. Hence the participants had only to enter additional risks and to comment on those already entered. This preparation allowed the workshop in two hours to discuss 46 risks and classify them into 'equipment & procedures', 'communications' and 'training & staffing'. The participants then voted to identify the top ten

Operational risks

1. Workload does not allow adequate time for personnel or service development.
2. Key members of staff do not have IT facilities.
3. Communication matters need addressing.
4. Separate sites impact on efficiency – transport, lack of contact, IT, teamwork.
5. Failure of information cascade of standard Trust procedures.
6. Adequate supervision of trainee staff.
7. Cost of updating equipment/purchasing new equipment.
8. New policies – time required to formulate.
9. Lack of information limits monitoring of SLAs.
10. Quality of backup from other departments e.g., personnel, finance, supplies.
11. Breakdown of major items of equipment.
12. Time wasted travelling between sites for meetings.
13. IT must be improved and integrated.
    - Mismatch of IT in institute and trust.
    - Response time has to be improved to ensure quality of service – IT?
    - Poor information technology leading to poor report time.
14. Ensuring continued staff training.
15. Transport systems for remote laboratory.
16. Computer crash.
17. Staff transport difficulties.
18. Transport problems – both manual and automated (transport delays affecting result time).
19. Difficulty in obtaining required grades of staff (difficulty in staff recruitment).
20. Need in some areas to multi-skill/rotate – resourcing problem.
21. Changes in treatment regimes requiring different tests/emphasis in reporting.
22. Wrong skill mix.
23. Motivation of staff due to low morale.
24. Keeping pace with technology – changing so fast, needs finances to keep up to date.
25. Physical layout – impacts on efficiency.

**Figure 10.7** **Edited operational risks from Institute of Pathology workshop.**

risks. These were brought before the Obstetrics Audit Group to establish an action programme. As a result, a particular piece of equipment was audited, emergency drills were arranged, more consultant-led labour ward sessions were held, 'near-miss' review sessions were rescheduled and some additional training sessions were organised.

The doctors and nurses involved in the Obstetrics electronic meeting found it such a useful exchange that they persuaded their colleagues in Gynaecology to hold a similar meeting.

## PRACTICAL INFORMATION

The facilitator of the meeting needs to understand the business implications of risk analysis and have reasonable knowledge of the subject under discussion. The facilitator must have sufficient personal status and experience to brief the head of the department concerned and to help manage the meeting. The role of the facilitator may not be straightforward if uncomfortable areas of risk are brought out or there is disagreement among participants.

When introducing this technique it is important to brief participants in advance of meetings and it is helpful to ask them to prepare risk definitions which can be entered into the computer beforehand. The scope of risks to be covered needs to be carefully defined. The participants should be from related business areas, it is not usually productive for the meeting to discuss dissimilar risks, e.g., technical and financial risks, in the same meeting.

It is important to set the tone of the meeting so that all risks can be discussed. The anonymity of electronic meetings is, of course, very helpful in this regard but the point is still worth emphasising. To ensure the successful introduction of this technique it is important as in any project to prepare and to train people effectively. To achieve optimum efficiency, advice should be obtained from people with experience in the field. Managers in the organisation need to be prepared to face up to risks that are identified and to develop appropriate action plans.

## CONCLUSIONS

Providing computers to help run meetings clearly involves higher expenditure than is incurred for flipcharts and pens in a conventional meeting. It is therefore important to establish the benefits of using electronic meeting technology. One benefit is speed, since with appropriate preparation it is possible in a two-hour electronic meeting to list, discuss and prioritise the risks in a complex medical department. Another benefit is that the discussion is recorded in complete detail and available for further review after the meeting if required.

The anonymity of input has a significant value in showing that management is not attempting to brush anything under the table or allow any 'conspiracies of silence' to develop. Follow-up meetings to define and audit actions do not necessarily have to be run with electronic meeting technology because the risks are now defined and on the table. The follow-up activities are essential to ensure that all the information collected in the electronic meeting is properly acted upon.

The response of the participants to the new technology, although not recorded formally, was generally very positive. Hence we can conclude that the use of computer technology in the process of risk management at ULTH has been a success. As with most computer applications costs will fall with the passage of time and the outcome will improve as users develop more confidence with the process. We can expect therefore to see electronic meetings playing an increasing role in risk management.

# 11

# Facilitation Skills

*Arnie Skelton*

## WHAT IS FACILITATION?

> Facilitation means drawing out the ideas, experience and beliefs of a group so that they arrive at conclusions and decisions that are really theirs and that they are willing and able to take responsibility for' *Warren Redman*.

Quite simply, facilitation is helping and assisting others to reach their own conclusions and decisions. A facilitator would be a key player in any Control Self Assessment process. Facilitators help the group or meeting work through an agenda of relevant control and/or assessments, and reach suitable conclusions.

When asked to consider the implications of workshop-based approaches to CSA, most auditors tend to place the need for appropriate facilitation skills and training in such techniques at the top of the list. If auditors have been used to the more traditional styles of auditing or are personally lacking in confidence in their ability to encourage others to debate issues and work together in making assessments and decisions, there may be some reluctance to participate in facilitated workshops, use this technique in CSA programmes, or even consider the adoption of CSA at all. Understanding of the various roles of the facilitator and others involved in the process will help. This chapter seeks to provide this and to give practical tips on conducting facilitated meetings. It concentrates on those meetings where technology is not used to any great extent, although the principles and practice still apply. Other considerations apply where technology is used, these are covered in Chapter 10.

## ROLES AND RESPONSIBILITIES OF THOSE INVOLVED

### CSA Group Members

The group members are the main contributors in the meeting; they should:

- describe key elements of the process
- offer ideas and solutions
- listen to others
- debate, analyse and discuss
- make and agree decisions
- agree on an action plan
- take responsibility for implementing any agreements within the action plan.

## CSA Facilitator

The facilitator's role is to help group members achieve the above, without becoming a participant in the meeting.

## Referee or Captain?

The main role of a facilitator is to chair the meeting in a non-directive, neutral way in order to:

- maintain the flow of 'the game'
- ensure agreed values, rules and procedures are adhered to
- ensure fair play (e.g., everyone has the opportunity to contribute)
- maintain discipline / order, and manage conflict positively
- help the group manage and allocate their time
- record decisions, actions and outcomes.

Overall, the facilitator acts as referee, rather than captain. It is *not* the role of the facilitator to:

- make decisions
- lead the group
- argue the case
- persuade the others to their own point of view.

However, the following may be added to the facilitator's role, with the express agreement and approval of the group:

- contributing ideas/suggestions

- acting as devil's advocate, i.e., challenging their assumptions / thinking
- acting as observer of the group's dynamics, and offering feedback as appropriate.

### The Auditor as Facilitator

In CSA projects, the facilitator might often be from the audit team, possibly chosen as someone who has the relevant CSA expertise and inter-personal skills and who can offer appropriate advice. In such cases, the facilitaor will have to tread a fine line between offering their audit, control and assessment expertise, and leading/dominating the group. For most CSA meetings, the auditor as facilitator has two key roles:

1. To offer their professional expertise as control and risk assessment specialists (consultative role).
2. To manage the group in a facilitative (referee-style) manner, to ensure the group achieve its stated objectives (facilitative role).

It is reasonable – possibly essential – that the audit specialist offers the group the benefit of their expertise; but it is eventually the group's responsibility to decide what to do with this advice. The auditor as facilitator must take care to ensure the CSA group (the client) accepts and retains ownership of the decisions taken, and of their implementation. It is a good idea to have an initial meeting of the CSA group to clarify and agree key roles and responsibilities.

## BENEFITS OF FACILITATION

Effective facilitation of a group can lead to the following benefits:

- greater involvement by and in the group
- more opportunities for more people to be involved
- encourages people to speak up
- more ideas / suggestions / comments likely to be made
- more chance of everyone having their say
- improved teamwork
- more group discipline
- better group management
- greater empowerment within the group
- greater ownership by the group.

## ORGANISING A CSA MEETING

It may be your role, as facilitator, to arrange the relevant meetings. The following is offered as a set of steps to take.

### *Initial discussion with key participants*

This is to establish the membership of the group; this could be done face to face or over the telephone.

### *Initial pre-meeting*

This is a very important meeting, since it will establish the templates for all future meetings. It should have all members present. The purpose of this meeting is to:

- discuss and clarify roles and responsibilities of the group and the facilitator
- establish common values and ground rules for the group
- define the purpose, scope, objectives and timeframe for the CSA project
- set an agenda for the next meeting
- agree documentation to be collected and distributed, and by whom
- agree any other action
- agree venue and time.

This is a full agenda, and you can allow a half-day for such a meeting. Time spent well in this meeting will pay huge dividends later.

### *Substantive meetings*

These are at the heart of the CSA process (any detailed CSA is likely to require more than one such meeting). It is up to the group to decide how it wishes to work through its business though it should begin with a reconfirmation made at pre-meeting (ideally have these agreements to hand, typed and copied for each member, and/or put up on the wall).

Thereafter, one useful approach might be 'OPRA'. For each system or procedure under investigation

O: confirm the key Objectives of the system

P: identify / describe the Process stages

RA: carry out a Risk Assessment of each stage (or simply identify the top half-dozen risks within each system).

Within the risk assessment, follow the 'WAGER' approach:

W: **W**hat is the element under discussion?

A: **A**ssess the element in terms of control/risk

G: are there **G**aps – i.e. risks which need to be covered?

E: should some of the controls be **E**nhanced?

R: should some of the controls be **R**emoved or **R**educed?

## SPECIALIST FACILITATOR SKILLS

### *Skill area 1: maintaining the flow*

#### *Control against repetition or waffling*

'Does anyone else want to come in here?'
'So, (Alan) – can I just summarise the point you're making here?'
'Can I just check that everyone is clear about the point Alan is making'

#### *Keep the group focused and on track*

'I think we are moving off the point here ...'
'I'm not sure how this is contributing to the issue in hand ...'
'Is this what we want to be discussing right now ...?'

#### *Sort issues*

Ensure the issues are clear in everyone's mind; be prepared to break down a complex issue and a vague issue into several smaller but discrete issues. Involve the group in this process and record the issues on the board then ask the group to arrange and prioritise them.

#### *Summarise and recap*

'Can I just summarise what's been said so far'
'So, just to recap what's been said ...'

Recapping and summarising are also effective ways of regaining control if the group discussion is getting out of hand.

### *Skill area 2: ensuring values and rules are maintained*

- Agree common group values, e.g., openness, being solution centred (see list at Appendix 11.3)
- Agree common 'best practice' principles or rules, e.g., no interrupting.
- Produce lists or flipchart, and pin them up somewhere in the room where everyone can see them.

### *Skill area 3: ensuring fairness/equality of opportunity*

Seek to involve people whose body language suggests they may want to say something, but who perhaps lack confidence to speak up.

> 'Martin, is there anything you want to say on this issue?'
> 'Jenny, you look as though you might want to say something here'

Consider 'going round the group', which means that everyone will have their turn (but be sensitive to the order in which you go round the room). Alternatively, ask everyone to write down their views and submit them to you.

### *Skill area 4: maintaining order/managing conflict*

Remember that the group have agreed to your role, which includes intervening in certain situations (i.e., they are on your side if you intervene). Describe what's happening, before suggesting an appropriate action:

> 'I think the meeing's getting a little heated; can I suggest we take a short break ...'
> 'I think there are two meetings going on at once here; can I suggest we all focus on the topic we are meant to be discussing, and only have one person speaking at a time ...'

Always seek the group's approval for any action:

> 'It seems that we can't reach consensus on this issue: (to group) do you agree?'
> ' I feel some people are unhappy to continue with this discussion: (to group) do you agree?'

### *Skill area 5: helping the group manage time*

Announce at some point how long they have left on a particular item and if they are likely to over-run, give them a choice:

> 'You've only got five minutes left; do you want to come to a decision now, or carry on and take the time off a later item?'

Never stop the discussion (that would be taking over). Instead, point out the consequences of the choice they are making:

> 'Can I remind the group that you said you were going to stop, but you are in fact carrying on. Is that what you want to do?'

### *Skill area 6: recording decisions*

Do not get sucked into the argument: stay detached enough to keep an ear out for key decisions; listen effectively. Put the key issues (that need a decision) on the board – it acts as a reminder to you and the group what has to be discussed / decided. Make sure you are recording the group's decisions: do not be swayed by a strong but single voice or a vocal minority:

'Does everyone agree with that view?'
'Does anyone want to offer an alternative, or opposite view?'

If there is no obvious concensus, ask for a vote.

## Optional Roles

### *Skill area 7: offering ideas/suggestions*

Ask permission first:

'Can I offer a suggestion here?'
'I have an idea that might help, if you'd like to hear it.'

Be careful not to appear too passive and see if you can build on others' suggestions:

'To develop Dave's point, maybe you could...'
'I'd like to take Janet's idea one stage further...'

Once you have made your suggestion and explained it, let it go. It is not your role to be an advocate of the idea.

### *Skill area 8: acting as devil's advocate*

First ensure you have permission for this role, then get them to act as devil's advocate if you can – i.e. encourage them to take a balanced view of their own ideas:

'What would anyone who is unsympathetic to this idea say?'
'Can you think of any reasons why anyone would not support this idea?'

If offering criticisms of your own, be constructive, rather than destructive:

'If someone thought (name the criticism), what would you say?'
'How would you react to the criticism that . . .?'

### *Skill area 9: observing group dynamics*

Most people find it difficult to watch and take part at the same time; your main role is to facilitate, so focus on that. If you feel it would be counterproductive to intervene at the time, make a specific note of the key incident/behaviour, and report back at the end of the day/session. It is vital you know what is causing the problem – don't just report that 'the meeting got sticky on that issue' – they will accept that, but will want to know from you *why* it got sticky

### *Skill area 10: giving feedback on group dynamics*

Follow the principles of giving constructive feedback given in Appendix 11.5. Ensure that you leave sufficient time (agenda space) for feedback, if that is what the group want. People need time to absorb and reflect on feedback – especially if it is at all critical; do not expect immediate improvements.

## GENERAL 'FOUNDATION' SKILLS

In addition to the specialist skills identified above, there are a set of generic skills which all good facilitators will have, simply to ensure they work well and effectively with others in the group. A number of these skills are given below.

*Active listening*
Showing another person that you are paying attention will encourage the other person to continue talking. You can actively demonstrate that you are listening by:

- warm eye contact (not glaring or staring)
- nodding
- open body posture – arms and legs uncrossed
- focused body posture – body turned towards the person who is talking
- recapping and summarising.

*Clarifying/checking understanding*
This is an excellent way of showing you are listening, and also maintaining the control and pace of the discussion. It is also important to check with the group that they all (or most) agree to anything written down which has the status of a 'decision'. Distinguish between 'collecting ideas on the flipchart' and 'confirming decisions on the flipchart'. It may be helpful to say which of these two processes you are engaged in ('I'm just collecting your ideas...' 'I'd like to confirm these decisions with you...').

*Asking questions*
Ask a suitable mixture of open, closed and probing questions; open questions to get others talking, closed questions to focus and check detail, and probing questions to delve more deeply.

*Sorting issues*
This is an effective management skill. Often the discussion (particularly in its early stages) will bring up a range of issues in a random way; it is a facilitator's job to sort these issues into some order, and then (perhaps) ask the group to prioritise the issues for further discussion.

*Maintaining control*
You must maintain control of the group discussion and behaviour, and of yourself. It is easy for a facilitator to get sucked into the discussion by either participating or simply following the debate thereby losing sight of the main purpose of a facilitator. Good facilitators will also need to remain calm in difficult situations.

*Problem solving*
The group may get stuck; your role is to offer ways forward to help the group 'problem solve'. There are a whole host of such techniques, well represented in the literature. Examples include:

- brainstorming (quick-fire generation of ideas from the group)
- reversals (take any relationship within, or description of, the process, and reverse it to see if it offers fresh insights)
- analogy ('in what way is the process like...?')
- imaginative comparisons (compare the process to...)
- imaging (draw the process).

*Recording accurately*
Ensure, as owner of the pen, that you accurately record what is being said. This means using the group's words on the board. If you feel you can phrase things better or, more succinctly seek their permission/approval. Do not subconsciously edit; record all the ideas, not just the ones you support or understand.

## TYPICAL PROBLEMS AND POSSIBLE SOLUTIONS

*Setting, sorting and sticking to an agenda*

- get (contributions for) the agenda beforehand
- confirm/prioritise the agenda at the outset
- make sure everyone understands the agenda
- confirm preferred/desired outcomes with the group

- allocate time to agenda items
- review progress against the agenda regularly
- do not allow drift – manage it through the group.

*Hierarchy/authority getting in the way (direct/indirect)*

- old cultures die hard – expect this
- possibly tackle through use of values, e.g.,
  - everyone has equal voice
  - every contribution is valued
  - no deference to hierarchy or expertise (Appendix 11.3)
- express your concerns, if you see this problem occurring
- ensure all get their say
- point out your concerns, but leave them with ownership – no-one is forced to contribute
- acknowledge their right to stay quiet, but point out the consequences of this.

*Deference to expertise*

- same as above
- expain that all ideas are valued, whether from an expert or not
- role model by contributing ideas yourself (but beware of leading the group).

*Passive participants*

- expect a slow start
- use brainstorming technique to get participation
- have icebreaker, for example, ask each group member for their hopes and fears for this group session
- be firm and asssertive on put-downs or negative responses
- bring people in, but in a non-confrontational way (e.g. by going around the table)
- divide into smaller groups, possibly putting quieter members together; quiet people tend to say more in smaller groups (but remember the need to keep the whole group working together).

*Dominant individuals*

- acknowledge their contribution, then link to someone else
- be firm/calm (your role you should have the support of the group)
- go around the group, ensuring the dominant person goes last
- have a word with the person in the break, or beforehand.

*Lack of belief that anything will happen*

- clarify the purpose and responsibility of the group (i.e. to come up with ideas and suggestions)
- ask the group if they wish you to carry this message to senior management
- refocus the group on what they are there for, and that they should fulfil their role as professionally and positively as possible
- don't get sidetracked into this ... some negative group members might be happy to discuss this rather than the main agenda items.

*Lack of (any) practical suggestions*

- brainstorm
- offer clues or suggestions
- ask them to describe how it currently is, then take each item in turn
- ask how it could be better or different
- use some problem-solving techniques.

## CONCLUSION

Facilitation comes naturally to some, and auditors who are used to a participative style of auditing – encouraging others to make a contribution, and remaining silent where necessary – may be perfectly comfortable with the process, although all sessions need careful planning and controlling.

Other auditors may not take to this style of auditing. Some still may not be suitable for the task, others may even disagree with the approach. Therefore, care needs to be taken in the selection of auditors for workshop facilitation (and in the appointment of audit staff in the first instance if facilitation is to figure largely in the audit process). Appropriate guidance and training are essential, and our own experience has shown that even those who initially think they will be comfortable in the role often underestimate the requirements of the task.

Once reluctance and any other early problems are overcome, and following training, simulated workshops and practice, many come to regard facilitation group sessions as stimulating, rewarding and useful and conclude that, after all, audit can be fun!

APPENDIX 11.1

# Preparing for a Workshop: Checklist

- Group identity known?
- Group membership known (numbers)?
- Have I provided facilitation for this group before?
- If 'no', do they know what a facilitator does?
- Venue?
- Seating arrangements?
- Refreshments?
- Time: from to
- Equipment: flipchart, paper, pens
- Other?
- Agenda?
- Desired outcomes?
- Any known difficulties, e.g., group dynamics?
- Contentious issues?
- Own personal needs: reading paperwork?
- Talking to those involved?
- Thinking, e.g., handling difficulties

*Notes/comments*

## APPENDIX 11.2

# Running a Workshop: Checklist

- Check seating is as preferred
- Check equipment
- Clarify your role and expectations with the group
- Agree values, rules and good practice
- Identify, sort and agree agenda, and rough time allocations
- Keep an eye on:
  - time
  - non-participants
  - poor behaviour
- Before intervening, think:
  - what am I going to say?
  - why?
  - how am I going to say it?
- Be constantly prepared to:
  - record
  - clarify
  - summarise
- At the end, recap decisions and agree an action plan / next steps
- Clarify who owns the flipchart notes

*Notes/comments*

## APPENDIX 11.3

# Common values

Possible common values include

- openness
- honesty
- being solution centred
- being positive
- support of and for each other
- action, rather than sentiment
- accepting personal responsibility (rather than blaming others).

## APPENDIX 11.4

# Good Practice (Rules and Procedures)

Examples of good practice might include

- no interruptions
- silence is affirmative
- decisions by consensus, then voting if no clear consensus
- keep to allocated time
- no waffling
- no put downs (e.g., sarcasm, patronising, belittling).

**APPENDIX 11.5**

# Principles of Constructive Feedback

Remember that the purpose of all feedback is to give the other person or group the opportunity to learn about themselves. It is their responsiblilty to decide what they do with the feedback.

- Choose a time that's suitable to the individual / group, but give your feedback sooner rather than later.
- Choose a private venue.
- Be specific: avoid generalisations, vagueness or exaggerations.
- Focus on behaviour, not personality or attitude.
- Be open and honest.
- Be direct; don't beat around the bush.
- Give feedback only on issues or behaviours that the person or group can change.
- If invited, offer suggestions about how the other person could improve or be different.

If you find giving feedback embarrassing, consider the following:

- How would you like to receive feedback? Use that as your model.
- It may be impossible to avoid embarrassment for both parties but …
- … short-term pain, long-term gain (or short-term gain, long-term pain!).

# Part 3

## The Private-Sector Experience

# 12

# Internal Audit's Role in Developing CSA

## The Securicor Story

*David Nowell-Withers* (an interview, March 1998)

### WHAT IS THE RELEVANT BACKGROUND OF SECURICOR AND YOURSELF?

The origins of Securicor date back to a private security company formed in London in 1935. Securicor plc is now a company with an annual turnover of £1.2 billion and over 56,000 employees worldwide. Its activities are in three divisions – security, distribution and communications – with overseas operations in 35 countries.

The internal audit function is based in Sutton, Surrey, with a staff of 15.

### WHAT PROMPTED SECURICOR TO LOOK AT CSA?

There were a variety of issues stemming from the Cadbury report and the expectations placed by management on Internal Audit to help meet the reporting requirements that the Stock Exchange required. We had to find a better way of using Internal Audit in the evaluation of controls, in order to give to the Board the assurances required to enable them to make their statements in the Annual Report and Accounts.

We also wanted to introduce an additional demonstration of the value that Internal Audit can bring to the management process. Essentially, we wanted to look at the prospect of business benefit from a better run organisation based on the balance of risk and control. That is not an easy message to sell, but certainly it was an important one to put across. So there were both external and internal drivers which prompted us to look at this route.

## WHAT IS YOUR DEFINITION OF CSA?

Based on the IIA definition, it has been roughly interpreted as a process by which line managers and staff identify and evaluate risks and review existing controls that address them, leading to a written report with prioritised points for action.

### How Did You Get Started With CSA?

Internal Audit had introduced CSA via the questionnaire route some years previously. A standard format was introduced for subsidiaries to indicate on a quarterly basis the status of specific financial controls such as dates when bank reconciliations were last prepared, physical stock checked and bad debt provisions reviewed. These were signed off by both the Finance Director and General Manager of each operating unit in the UK and overseas. The individual unit's reports were reviewed at divisional level and any serious anomalies reported through to the Audit Committee. The same approach is being taken with IT operational controls with exception reports to the Audit Committee.

A further development was the introduction of a format for reporting each half year the self assessment of internal financial controls (see Appendix 12.1). This analysis covers eight financial cycles and nine elements of control that relate to each financial cycle. Again, there is a sign-off by both Finance Director and General Manager of each company and critical review at divisional level. To establish a consistency, definitions of the cycles, controls and the basis of assessment were necessary and reference was also made to guidelines to good management practice in these areas that had been developed previously. The completed forms are compiled and analysed by Internal Audit into reports that highlight exceptions and trend changes, which are reported to divisional management and, by exception, to the Audit Committee.

## WHAT ABOUT THE WORKSHOP APPROACH TO CSA?

Internal Audit became aware of this through attending seminars, reading articles, and discussions with peers. We saw that potentially benefits could be achieved from adopting this approach. But *how* to do it was the question. It was recognised that, in Securicor, we were not going to have an overall top-down approach which made it mandatory to adopt this process; this is not the sort of culture that prevails. So we had to introduce the concept and see how it would work out in a diversified business environment.

To start us off, the Internal Audit Department had external training from Keith Wade of CATS International, on what CSA was. Conceptually, it was easy to grasp, but it was not until we did a practical workshop on our own department's activities that staff members realised the complexity of the process and the skills involved.

We went away from that workshop with the message that we needed some further assistance if Internal Audit were to offer this as a service to management. In order to take this further, we took advice from external consultants, specifically Coopers & Lybrand, who advised us on a structured format for CSA workshop procedures and provided us with an experienced facilitator for the initial exercise.

## HOW DID YOU INTRODUCE CSA WORKSHOPS?

We decided to take a pilot exercise approach by running a CSA workshop on three levels. The first one was on a company basis, aligned to the achievement of their overall objectives as stated in their three-year business plan. The second was in relation to a specific business objective of a company which related to the merger of a recently acquired business with that company. The third one was in preparation for an internal audit review of the basic financial controls of a company that had not been visited before. Each of the three workshops was in a different Securicor division.

## WHAT WAS THE PLANNING AND FORMAT FOR THESE WORKSHOPS?

With the first two workshops, we aimed to involve management from the start. This included agreement on its purpose and focus as well as the date, timing and participants. Essentially, we wanted management to feel they owned the process and its outcome.

Timing was for a one-day workshop and preparatory interviews with not more than twelve participants that included an internal auditor for input on control matters. There were one or two facilitators and a recorder using laptop IT to capture information, sort and project on screen or printout. It was agreed that the workshop report would be to the General Manager who participated in the workshop, for his use and distribution. In all cases, workshops were run away from the normal place of business.

## HOW DID THESE WORK OUT?

We learned from the first workshop that it would be far too ambitious to consider all the business objectives of an operating subsidiary in a day. We had to consolidate objectives under general headings and then go through the process of identifying risks, prioritising them under these headings and identifying mitigating controls. This one-day workshop exhausted all parties involved and we covered only three of the four prescribed areas (market position, cost, efficiency, quality of service). We were satisfied that the process worked and produced satisfactory results in the areas covered.

The second workshop was more focused on a specific business objective (the merger of two companies). It was rewarding and we felt that the company had been provided with an operating template with which it could work out a programme which balanced the risks and controls that had been identified. In practice, the merger of these two activities was regarded as highly successful and we like to think that the CSA workshop played a part in this.

The third one, in relation to preparation for an audit, was a mixed success. Internal Audit benefited from it because, as a result, we were well prepared to focus on important issues when we went on site to carry out the audit. It enabled the auditors to do more in-depth review of identified areas of weakness. Whether management perceived this as a benefit for themselves would be for discussion.

## WITH THESE EXPERIENCES, WHERE DID YOU GO FROM THERE?

It was apparent that the effort involved by both Internal Audit and management was considerable. Each workshop took at least two staff/weeks of auditor time and probably two days for each participant. To roll the process out throughout the group would not be readily accepted by busy management and Internal Audit were not staffed to concentrate on this approach. We did not feel that the case for proposing that this be done throughout the group had been substantiated.

## WAS THAT THE END?

No, it wasn't, in the sense that really we evolved from that to the wider consideration of risk management.

## HOW DID YOU BECOME AWARE OF THAT?

Again, it was by a variety of influences, namely attendances at seminars, networking in general and overall being aware of the climate of change that was taking place in the auditing profession.

## WHAT WAS YOUR APPROACH TO RISK MANAGEMENT?

We decided that, logically, in structuring an approach to reviewing risk management, the evaluation of risk is the precursor of assessing controls and we named this exercise RACE – Risk And Control Evaluation. To start the RACE project a proposal was presented to the Group Board for a risk-mapping exercise to take place at Board level as an introduction to the methodology and thought processes involved, which could then be rolled out throughout the group. This was accepted, and in 1997 it was carried out by external consultants, namely Coopers & Lybrand, and presented to the Group Board with various observations on how improvements could be made. These matters have been actively addressed by a Group Risk Management Steering Committee. We are now at the stage where risk management is being rolled out to the individual divisions and, more specifically, to the business units within the divisions and this is where Internal Audit come in again.

## WHAT IS INTERNAL AUDIT'S ROLE?

It is to put on their risk-management consultancy hats and establish risk maps with the mitigating controls that are prepared in a structured manner and can be consolidated and presented in a uniform format. This has been accepted at Group Board level and is what is currently taking place.

We have the high-level risk matrix that resulted from the review at group level, which categorises risks from the highest groupings of Strategic, Operating, Financial and Information down through sub-categories to specific business risks. Internal Audit have formed a central database of this and are involved in reviewing its application and relationship within each division.

## DO YOU PROPOSE TO USE CSA WORKSHOPS IN THIS PROCESS?

Initially, no. This is based on the fact that we found them difficult and time consuming, but they cannot be ruled out in the future once all parties involved are more comfortable with the processes involved. For the moment, individual members of Internal Audit, a maximum team of four people, will be involved in interviewing and laying out in common format the risks/controls involved in carrying out our various businesses. This is to be co-ordinated into the common database and analysed and used by management at all levels. Whether this work is best carried out in a series of self-assessment workshops at business unit level has yet to be decided. We can, however, foresee that this will probably be the case with larger units.

## HOW IS THIS GOING TO AFFECT INTERNAL AUDIT?

Specifically, we shall be heavily involved in a consultancy role, probably for about 12 months until this methodology is integrated into management processes and they take ownership of it. Once this has been achieved, and it will not be something that will happen immediately, then Internal Audit will be addressing the risk-management processes adopted by management rather than emphasising the review of controls.

## HOW WOULD ADOPTING CSA AFFECT THE BUSINESS?

The ultimate accolade for CSA would be its acceptance as a normal part of management's processes and activities, by which interested parties can focus on the strengths of controls in relation to an agreed acceptance of risk, be this at Group Board, divisional or individual company levels. Internal Audit would assist management by reviewing their risk-management activities which form a natural part of management's various processes for the running of businesses. That is the position we want to get to within two years.

## WHAT ARE THE LESSONS LEARNED FROM CSA TO DATE?

In short, they are:

1. Do not underestimate the selling of the process that has to take place – it is not a natural thought process for management to isolate and analyse the various elements of risk and controls in this manner. What's more, they may not see the need to do this anyway.
2. Do not underestimate the time involved in preparing for and carrying out workshops, or indeed, just the analysis of questionnaires being used in self assessment.

3. Do not assume that there are inherent skills within Internal Audit to carry out the facilitating role involved. Have specific training in this area and note those who are comfortable doing this for applied use.
4. Get early results to demonstrate what the end product is and can be. By doing this you will get further support from management to pursue the exercise.
5. Change the approach when Internal Audit act as consultants, so that they become more assertive in driving to obtain the information necessary and the opinions required within tight timeframes. This really applies both to workshops and interviews with senior management. It is also important to get the results of these processes back to management as quickly as possible. This is a consultant's approach, rather than an internal auditor's approach and the difference needs to be recognised.
6. Attempt to differentiate the presence of Internal Audit as a consultant or a facilitator from that of being a member of Internal Audit. This is difficult to do and has to be positively stated and worked out in order to achieve the differentiation. It should not be ignored, otherwise the acceptance and motivation of participants may become confused.

In general, the adoption of risk and control self assessment practices must be regarded as a journey which evolves, to a destination that changes. As long it as delivers value to the business *en route*, it will succeed.

## APPENDIX 12.1

# Assessment of Internal Financial Controls

Please rate the controls operated in the following areas on a scale of 1 to 4 as follows:

1 = Very confident (no reservations)
2 = Overaall confidence (minor reservations)
3 = Limited confidence (some significant reservations)
4 = Not confident (Several significant reservations)

| | Financial cycles | | | | | | | |
|---|---|---|---|---|---|---|---|---|
| Elements of control | Credit control and debtors | Contracts adminstration and invoicing | Purchases/ expenses and creditors | Payroll | Cash and bank | Fixed assets | Stock | Deferred expenditure/ accrued income |
| Organisation | | | | | | | | |
| Segregation of duties | | | | | | | | |
| Physical | | N/A | N/A | | | | | N/A |
| Authorisation and approval | | | | | | | | |
| Arithmetical and accounting | | | | | | | | |
| Personnel | | | | | | | | |
| Supervision | | | | | | | | |
| Management | | | | | | | | |
| Information and communication | | | | | | | | |

| Assessment of overall control in relation to exposure | | | | | | | | |
|---|---|---|---|---|---|---|---|---|

Prepared by: Reviewed by: Company:

Financial Director: Managing Director:

Date: Date:

# 13

# CSA and the Audit of Formal Controls

*Jane Shipway*

At the end of March 1997 BT employed around 127,000 people in over 40 countries, and with a turnover of £14,935 million. The size of the internal audit department, at just 100 strong, seems small by comparison.

## BACKGROUND TO CSA AT BT

At BT, CSA is

> An innovative approach to Internal Auditing which enlists the support of all people in the business both to review existing controls for effectiveness and in implementing improvements.

This may not be your definition, or one that you are comfortable with, indeed many people have many differing views about what CSA is; there is no correct answer.

In the Autumn of 1993 our Chief Internal Auditor, Graham Sheppard, saw Paul Makosz giving a presentation on CSA. At that time Paul still worked for Gulf Canada Resources in Calgary. Paul's enthusiasm for CSA and his natural charisma sold the concept to Graham. Here was a technique that promised to help us at a time when, because of organisational changes including much joint venture work and the increasing pressure to do more with the same number of people, we needed to review our ways of working. The final selling point for Graham was the fact that to use CSA effectively we needed to combine traditional auditing skills with facilitation skills, and we were fortunate to have that skill set; we just needed to know more about CSA. That led to my visit to Calgary to work with Paul and his CSA team for eight weeks in late 1994.

I returned from Calgary with many ideas about how to run CSA workshops. However, BT was not Gulf Canada Resources and the CSA process as I saw it in Gulf, although very good, I knew would not fit well in BT. At that time Gulf was a 650-man outfit, all based in one building and all experiencing a CSA workshop every year. An almost impossible task for us in BT. Together with the Senior Audit Managers I decided on a methodology which would best suit our company and clients. I was not entirely happy with the initial approach which concentrated on formal, process-based controls and avoided the equally important informal controls but it was right for the BT culture and right for a process owned by internal audit, and it was a beginning.

After several months of trying to find a suitable client and process to pilot CSA (there was some reluctance, mainly from our internal auditors who viewed CSA rather cautiously), Graham made a suggestion and a client was chosen. We had a good relationship with the chosen client who had been very supportive of audit in the past and was open to new ideas on the way to improve auditing techniques. We held several pre-workshop meetings where the agenda and proposed controls were thrashed out and in October 1995, almost two years from when Graham had seen Paul's presentation, we ran three pilot workshops. The workshops were extremely hard work but very successful and we could not have achieved such levels without the use of a computerised anonymous voting system and the consultants who worked with us to operate the technology.

Following the pilots we carried out an evaluation. Feedback was sought from the delegates who had attended the events, the client management who were on the receiving end of the audit findings and from the auditors who had participated in the events. All feedback was very positive and on this basis we decided to buy the software and draw up plans for a further 12-month trial where we could expose CSA to a wide number of clients, covering a diverse number of processes and give exposure to as many auditors as possible.

All the pilot workshops and the workshops held in the 12-month trial were facilitated by myself, mainly because one of the fear elements of CSA stemmed from the fact that many audit people did not want to become CSA presenters and facilitators. Following the trial our approach was to seek volunteers from the audit department for a small team of 'CSA experts' who would build and run CSA events for the whole audit division. We now have a team of four. This approach works well and has gone a long way to alleviating the fears of the more traditional auditors.

## BT APPROACH TO CSA

Our current approach to CSA is very much process driven. We run workshops on a particular process, system or part of the process/system. For example, if we are carrying out an audit of our accounts payable system we would bring together a number of people who work on the system e.g., AP clerks, and use CSA with them to evaluate the controls over the AP process and to make recommendations for improvement. We are concentrating on formal controls, e.g., all invoices are date stamped on receipt; all invoices are processed promptly, etc. We do not cover informal controls such as leadership, teamwork, training, etc. That having been said one thing I have pushed for is the inclusion of an ethics session on the workshop. This session is optional and this will be covered later. We use the computerised anonymous voting technology, as seen in Canada, which helps us quickly to evaluate the controls and also adds an element of enjoyment to the day, something which has been sadly lacking from audits in the past! Our CSA approach has four distinct phases; planning, the workshop, testing and reporting.

## Planning

Planning, as with any style of auditing, is key to the process. The first stage of planning for a CSA job is to meet with the client management, usually 2–3 levels above the workshop delegates, and sell the CSA process to them. This is usually done some 6–8 weeks before the audit is due to start. The meeting is usually attended by the Lead Auditor for the job and a member of the CSA team. If the selling is successful, and we have not yet had any failures, we would also discuss the logistics of the event, e.g., location, attendees, agenda, etc.

The second stage of planning for CSA involves both the Lead Auditor and the same client agreeing a set of control questions to be used at the workshop. Normally we supply a list to the client and they update as necessary. I think it is worth mentioning at this stage that most of the system/processes we have audited using CSA have been well documented and audited before, making this stage of our process relatively easy. Having said that, we have used CSA on a system not audited before, and on that occasion we drew up list of anticipated controls from the process procedures. Once the control questions have been agreed with the client, the workshop software can be built around OptionFinder®, anonymous voting technology, and agendas and CSA brochures go out to each of the delegates. Whilst the foregoing is taking place traditional audit planning is also carried out.

## The Workshop

A typical workshop runs between 10a.m. and 3p.m., is supported by one of the four trained CSA teams and an auditor with knowledge of the process/system being examined. We try to encourage 12–16 delegates to attend but leave selection of delegates to the client. The delegates may include people from a number of locations, e.g., if we are covering a national process we may hold a workshop in one central location and invite delegates from around the country. If possible we try to get a senior manager from the client unit to open the event, this shows commitment to the process. Introductions are informal and following an introduction to CSA we use an 'icebreaker' to get the day off to a good start.

Since we are asking the delegates to evaluate the controls operating over their process/system, we feel it is important to educate them on what we mean by Internal Control. We therefore run a short session on Internal Control, highlighting the different elements and giving particular emphasis to responsibility for control. We also give examples of controls that should be operating in their own process.

The evaluation of a control session is where the computerised anonymous voting technology comes into use again. The controls are shown to the delegates one at a time, explanations given if needed, and then the two criteria questions are asked: How well is the control currently working? How important is the control? People can abstain if they do not know the answers to the questions. We are not looking for people to guess about the controls, we want facts only. When all the controls have been evaluated we usually break for lunch.

After lunch we begin with the short session on ethics. This starts with a brief presentation given by one of the auditors on the importance of high ethical standards. A case-study scenario is then given to the delegates and they are posed several ethical dilemmas related to their own work area which they anonymously vote on. The session is light-hearted but the message is clear.

The next session is the key session of the day, areas for improvement. In this we discuss the controls evaluated earlier in order of priority, e.g., we start with controls that the delegates have indicated are high in importance but low in deployment. We do not use the computerised anonymous voting technology but by this stage we have created an environment in which all the delegates feel comfortable and the discussions are always open and honest. Recommendations are discussed and agreed by the very people who will have to make changes at the workplace, making implementation much easier. The workshop ends with an evaluation session where eight key questions are asked using the voting technology. The results are used exclusively by the CSA team continually to improve the workshops.

Although I have given the outline of a typical workshop, no two events are the same. The main message is that the facilitator must be flexible and manage the day to ensure that the key sessions are completed.

## Testing

Testing is carried out by the audit team usually on the days immediately following the workshop. Where delegates have told us that a control is not working we would not normally test to confirm that this was the case unless we wanted to quantify the effect of non-operation. Where delegates have said that a control is working, we carry out testing depending on circumstances, e.g., importance of control, risk to business, gut feel, etc.

## Reporting

Traditional reporting methods are used making reference to the CSA workshop and graphs produced by the technology are included if appropriate. Our reporting targets are to issue the draft report within ten working days of site work completion and final reports within ten working days of receipt of client responses. Reports are issued to senior clients but may be copied to all interested parties if requested.

## BENEFITS

For Audit the main benefit has been the man-day savings which have been as high as 75% against a traditional-style audit. In addition, the approach is more client-centred particularly for people on the shop floor who feel more involved in the whole audit process. A spin-off benefit for audit is that the new technique is an exciting development opportunity for audit people. I believe CSA will never replace traditional auditing techniques but will increasingly become a preferred methodology to support that traditional role.

The main advantages for our clients are reduced audit time on site, increased awareness of internal control and controls over their own jobs and, most importantly, recommendations are formulated by the people who will have to implement them thus easing implementation.

## PITFALLS

On the whole, so far, our CSA journey has been relatively trouble free. That said, the biggest obstacle we have had to overcome, and in some respects are still battling with, is the reluctance of some of our own audit people fully to support the CSA process.

Change is not easy for anyone, and for auditors changes to techniques and approaches which they feel threaten their very being are particularly difficult to come to terms with. Here was an innovative approach to auditing that required presentation and facilitation experience. The safe haven of one to one interviews and quiet testing was being threatened. Another, quite valid, view was that our customers were, in the main, very happy with the existing approach, so why 'upset the apple cart'.

CSA awareness sessions were given to groups of auditors prior to implementation, but only if they requested it. I am aware of pockets of auditors who have never had CSA awareness training, do not want it, and still do not know what the concept is all about. Needless to say, they are not using CSA as fully as they might be. We are addressing this in 1998/99 by running training CSA workshops for all our audit staff.

My advice to anyone considering using CSA in their department would be to ensure that everyone has a full understanding of the concepts of CSA. I do not mean that everyone is trained to run CSA events, since I firmly believe that good facilitators are born not made, but that everyone is given a good enough understanding of CSA to allow them to consider using the technique every time they undertake an audit.

## Questions to Ask before Introducing CSA in Your Own Organisation

I believe there are two key questions to ask before you embark on the road to CSA.

### *Do we have the right skills?*

From my experience it is unlikely that the skills of the existing audit team will be adequate in the areas of facilitation and presentation. Presentation skills may not be such a big issue but good facilitators are hard to find and difficult to cultivate.

### *What approach is best?*

There are many, varied approaches to CSA. My advice would be to research as many different approaches as time allows and select the approach (or even design your own) which best suits your own environment and company culture. Do not try to force another company's approach on your own organisation, inevitably it will not work!

## THE WAY FORWARD IN BT

CSA continues to develop within BT and as I write we are exploring the concepts of stand-alone CSA workshops with no testing, risk-based CSA workshops which concentrate on identification of risks by the clients and CSA for follow-up audits. I am sure that as time goes by CSA in BT will continue to evolve even further.

## SUMMARY

I have tried, in this Chapter, to give you an understanding of the background and approach to CSA in BT. I have also tried to give you a few pointers on pitfalls and key questions to ask before implementing a CSA approach. Hopefully, you will gain from my experiences in what I can only say have been a very exciting few years.

# 14

# Developing Effective Controls with CSA

*Raj K. Pradhan*

## INTRODUCTION

Risk assessment was first introduced as a planning tool for audit in 1989 and has since evolved into a risk management approach to audit. This process comprises the identification of risk and the assessment of these risks and the related internal controls jointly with management (a form of CRSA). This approach to audit has been in place at BOC for some five years and is continually improving and evolving with the ever-changing needs of the business and its environment.

The BOC Group is one of only a handful of British companies that are truly 'global' in terms of their markets, management, technology and production. The Group comprises a portfolio of four businesses – Industrial & Special Gases, Health Care, Vacuum Technology and Distribution Services. BOC has operations in some 70 countries, employs over 40,000 people around the world, has a turnover of approximately £4,000 million and generates an operating profit of some £540 million.

Within BOC, Control Self Assessment (CSA) is defined as a methodology for identifying critical areas of risk for the business and the related controls and assessing their appropriateness and effectiveness in meeting the Group's broad objectives. It is very much a top-down process requiring the application of good business and common sense and like all tools it is only as effective as its user. Within BOC this process has many facets and has been made easier by the culture of the company where internal controls are very much the responsibility of management.

Risk identification and assessment of the related controls are the result of teamwork. They require the involvement of all functions and activities ranging from finance, marketing and engineering to audit and insurance. Risk covers every aspect of the business from health and safety and the environment to human resources and finance. It is not confined to financial risk. There is therefore no simple prescription for establishing effective controls as the needs of each organisation will be different.

In BOC all businesses have their own specific system of internal controls some of which are predicated from the group centre, others which are determined by the business concerned and are specific to that business and others which are established at the unit level and are both generic and/or specific to that unit. CSA, whether part of the risk management approach to audit or part of another process (e.g., identification and evaluation of property or catastrophe risks for insurance purposes) only helps to ascertain whether controls are in place and whether they are appropriate and effective. It is only in certain situations (new businesses, acquisitions and major computer systems changes) that the use of CSA will result in the fundamental re-engineering of the processes concerned and the related control systems.

In BOC the emphasis is on getting the basics right and then continually evolving and improving the process to manage proactively the challenges and risks of a constantly changing and competitive global environment. The basic principles set out below are therefore applied to all internal control systems. These are in addition to the principle that all controls should be appropriate to the business concerned, easy to implement and administer and be measurable in terms of their effectiveness. This is a very important aspect of the BOC approach and is a fundamental requirement if the process is to be owned by the business jointly with others, such as internal audit, in the organisation. If the process is perceived to be one that is initiated and imposed by the finance community it will fail, as it will not have the buy-in (ownership) of the business as a whole.

## DEFINITION OF CONTROLS

The concept of control as applied in BOC is based on the generally accepted definition of internal controls in both the USA and the UK as well as in other countries around the world and may be summarised as an integrated framework of processes established by management which will result in the achievement of business objectives in relation to:

- the effectiveness and efficiency of operations where the focus is on continual improvement
- the reliability and integrity of information, i.e., all data whether financial or otherwise whether originating internally or externally and whether for use internally or by third parties

- compliance with applicable laws and regulations in all the countries in which BOC operates.

Whilst this appears to be 'motherhood' stuff it is very important to keep these objectives in sight when establishing effective controls. Everyone concerned must be familiar with these objectives. There are six basic components of an effective system of internal controls that may be summarised from COSO.

### 1. *Competent personnel*

Competent people are an essential element of any successful and well-managed enterprise. It would be impossible to achieve good internal controls as defined above without competent, well-trained motivated personnel. This element is not included in the COSO definition but is, I believe, assumed to be integral to it.

Within BOC this has led to the establishment of an award-winning Financial Management Training Programme for graduates of all disciplines, succession planning, personal development plans and the identification of developmental jobs etc. The Group continues to focus on this area as one of the key components of a successful business.

### 2. *The control environment*

This is the tone set within the organisation and begins with the Board of Directors. Integrity, ethical values, compliance with laws and regulations, quality, etc., are all essential components of a good control environment. A booklet documenting the vision objectives and values of the BOC Group has been published and distributed to all personnel throughout the organisation world-wide so that all are aware of the Group's vision, objectives and values and can focus their efforts accordingly.

### 3. *Risk management*

This is an essential ingredient of a good control system. It is the process of identifying the critical activities of the business (all the activities that must work faultlessly) and managing them to ensure success in meeting the business's objectives. Within BOC risk has been defined and its component parts identified, e.g., catastrophic, strategic risk, etc., as a means of focusing on the critical areas of the business (see page 220). This classification has been discussed and agreed by the Executive Management Board and the Senior Business Executives as the basis for identifying and tracking the management of these risks.

### 4. *Control activities*

These comprise the policies, processes and procedures established by management and executed by all concerned to ensure that the risks identified are addressed and managed successfully. Within BOC the prime responsibility for this rests with management. However, as part of the risk management approach to audit, Internal Audit work closely with management to assess their appropriateness and effectiveness.

### 5. *Information and communications*

The essential components of any system of internal controls. This is a process by which management set out their expectations to their employees and receive relevant, reliable and timely information. This enables them to ensure that the key risks are being addressed, to communicate their decisions and to ensure that they are implemented. This takes several forms and ranges from monthly operational reports and staff briefings, tracking and reporting of key projects to the identification of key management measures such as 'critical success factors' and 'key performance indicators' for both strategic and annual plan purposes.

### 6. *Monitoring*

A key aspect of the process enabling management continually to review their decisions and actions, assess the appropriateness and effectiveness of internal controls and adapt them to changing circumstances. This is done through normal management channels of reports etc. and through internal audit work.

The above elements of good internal control are an inherent part of business processes and reflect good management practices as illustrated by the Management Process Model in Figure 14.1. This figure was developed by internal audit and is used to demonstrate that the management process comprises all the elements of internal control. Good business management will therefore result in good internal controls and vice versa as well as meeting the requirements of good corporate governance. Demonstrating this has been an important element of the process in establishing effective controls as management have accepted that controls are an integral part of management and taken ownership of them.

## MANAGEMENT RESPONSIBILITY

As stated in the definition above, internal controls comprise an integrated framework of processes and procedures that must be established by

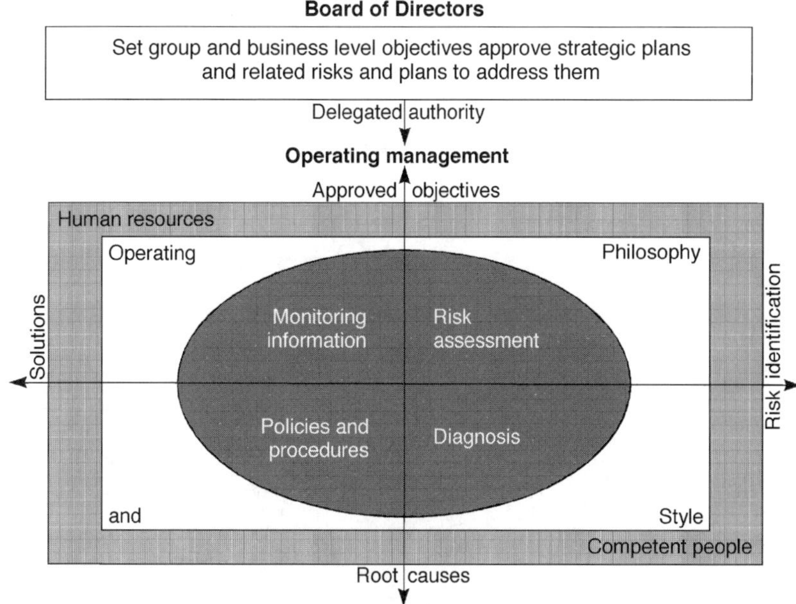


**Figure 14.1** Management process model.

management. Whilst everyone in the organisation has some responsibility for controls it remains primarily the responsibility of management. Management have to own and be responsible and accountable for internal controls on an ongoing basis if they are to be appropriate and effective.

## MANAGEMENT PROCESS

One of the basic elements of good management is the recruitment and retention of competent personnel (including managers). Without capable people the business will be unable to manage its affairs effectively nor will it achieve its objectives. Figure 14.1 shows this as a very specific element of management whereas this is not included as a specific element of internal control, being, I think, inherent in the model. The process used by internal auditors in reviewing a business has this element as a specific aspect of their work and their discussions with management.

In establishing appropriate and effective controls, management must of necessity set out a framework /environment for the business to operate in. Such an environment will form the foundation of the business culture and the platform for communicating common standards, values and objectives. In terms of the management process illustrated in Figure 14.1, the

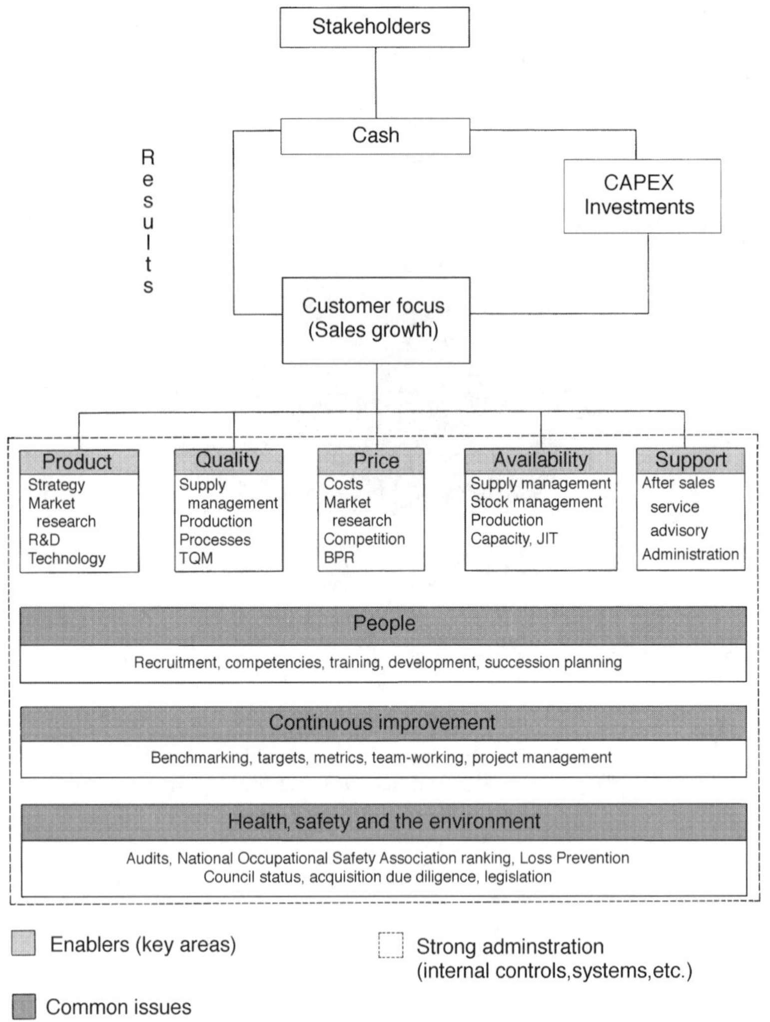


**Figure 14.2** Objectives, risks and controls.

establishment of such an environment is described as 'Operating philosophy and style' and equates to the 'control environment' element of internal controls.

Once the above two elements have been achieved, management need to identify all the key aspects of the business which must be executed well in order to achieve the approved objectives. This will also include the assessment of associated risks in order to develop a prioritised action plan to address these. For example, if the objective is to focus on customers and generate cash for investment and the stakeholders the risks/results of not achieving this objective are inability to pay employees, suppliers, bankers etc., and inability to make new investments (see Figure 14.2). Risk identification/assessment is just the result of identifying key objectives and looking at their consequences. This process equates exactly to the 'risk assessment' element of good internal controls.

The next step is to diagnose the root causes of the risks and their various elements and associated risks and to prioritise them and to seek solutions for them. As illustrated in the model, these can be broadly categorised as product, quality, price, availability and support. Each of these broad categories has different, and some common, elements to be considered. For example, under the category of product one needs to consider customer needs, competition, research and development, technology, product strategy, materials, etc. Once these elements have been identified and prioritised, management can then develop a strategy and put into place relevant policies, processes and procedures to manage them.

Action plans to control and manage the risks identified will of necessity consider the three key elements which are inherent in and/or affect all aspects of the business. In BOC these are people; continuous improvement; and health, safety and the environment. Finally management will need to put into place a process of measuring and monitoring to ensure that the actions taken and the control processes established and implemented are having the desired effect and that they are achieving their objectives.

## RISK ASSESSMENT

As indicated by both Figure 14.1 and the elements of control, risk assessment is a key aspect of developing key controls. In order to assess risk we must first understand what we mean by risk. Risk is generally considered to have a negative connotation. For the purposes of developing effective controls we must consider not only the possible negative effects of risk but also the benefits that can be derived by taking and managing risk. For this purpose risk is defined as follows:

> An event, a contingent event, process or set of circumstances which may give rise, either directly or indirectly, to a loss of wealth or opportunity and /or some other negative impact arising therefrom.

Risk may be categorised in many ways. However, for the purposes of developing effective controls I have found the following elements/categories to be useful in determining and assessing risk.

*Catastrophic*

These are risks that are out of your control and cannot be managed, e.g., acts of God, floods, earthquakes, etc. Catastrophes are generally insured against but may also need contingency plans, etc., for damage-limitation purposes.

*Strategic*

These are risks that are also out of your control but they can be managed, e.g., economic conditions, customer expectations, etc. These are difficult to control as they can be dynamic, may necessitate change and management actions may need to be reactive. They need constant attention as the repercussions from not managing these risks may well be significant.

*Business generic*

These are day-to-day operational risks which are generic to all businesses, e.g., bad debts, quality issues, supplier issues, etc. These need to be segregated into two specific types of risks; (a) housekeeping, e.g., late invoicing, whilst not desirable, will not have a significant effect on the business and (b) critical, e.g., installing faulty equipment in a customer's plant resulting in the stoppage of production. This latter type of risk must be strictly controlled preferably on a zero-tolerance basis.

*Business specific*

These risks are specific to a particular business, e.g., legislation and health-care regulations (e.g., Food and Drug Administration or Department of Health, in a health-care operation; hazardous chemicals regulations in a chemical business, etc). Generally speaking these are reasonably controlled and do not represent a high risk but can give rise to complacency.

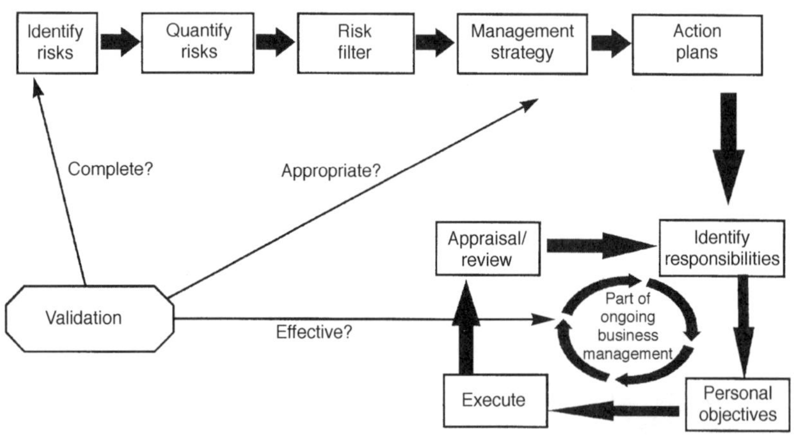


**Figure 14.3** The risk-management process.

All the above risks need to be managed to the level appropriate in a particular business. The risk management process, as illustrated in Figure 14.3 has the same elements as the management model in that it requires that risks be identified and assessed, prioritised, actioned and monitored.

## RISK-MANAGEMENT APPROACH TO AUDIT

The risk-management approach to audit incorporates all the elements of Figures 14.1–3. It works with operational and executive managers to identify the operations which require audit attention using a generic risk model (see Figure 14.4). Each business and/or geographical region of BOC has an audit manager responsible for it. This structure parallels the management structure of BOC and allows the audit manager to develop good relations with the management team of the business concerned based on mutual trust and respect and on his sound understanding of that business. The audit manager has continual dialogue with the business he is responsible and accountable for and meets them at least once each quarter. The purpose of the meetings is to review and agree the risk profile of the business, follow up prior action plans, discuss and review business developments, e.g., new projects, significant future plans, etc. This allows the business and audit to work closely together to identify all significant risks and issue reviewed action plans and to plan and focus audit effort to address them as part of a joint effort.

The audit process developed in BOC includes a 'health check' of all significant processes and functions of the operation being audited (see Figure 14.5). The results of this health check are then used in discussions with management to confirm areas of risk already identified by the audit management process and to identify other risks (generally external, e.g., competition) that may have been overlooked or not previously identified as such. These areas of risk and the related controls are then audited and recommendations for improvement are then agreed and implemented by management. These actions are monitored continually by internal audit through the audit-management process.

## COST VERSUS BENEFIT

In developing any system of internal control one must be aware of the cost / benefit of the control and the level of risk one is prepared to accept in order to manage the process. For example, ensuring all cheque payments are supported by original invoices and require two signatories minimises the possibility of improper payments but does not mitigate the possibility of the

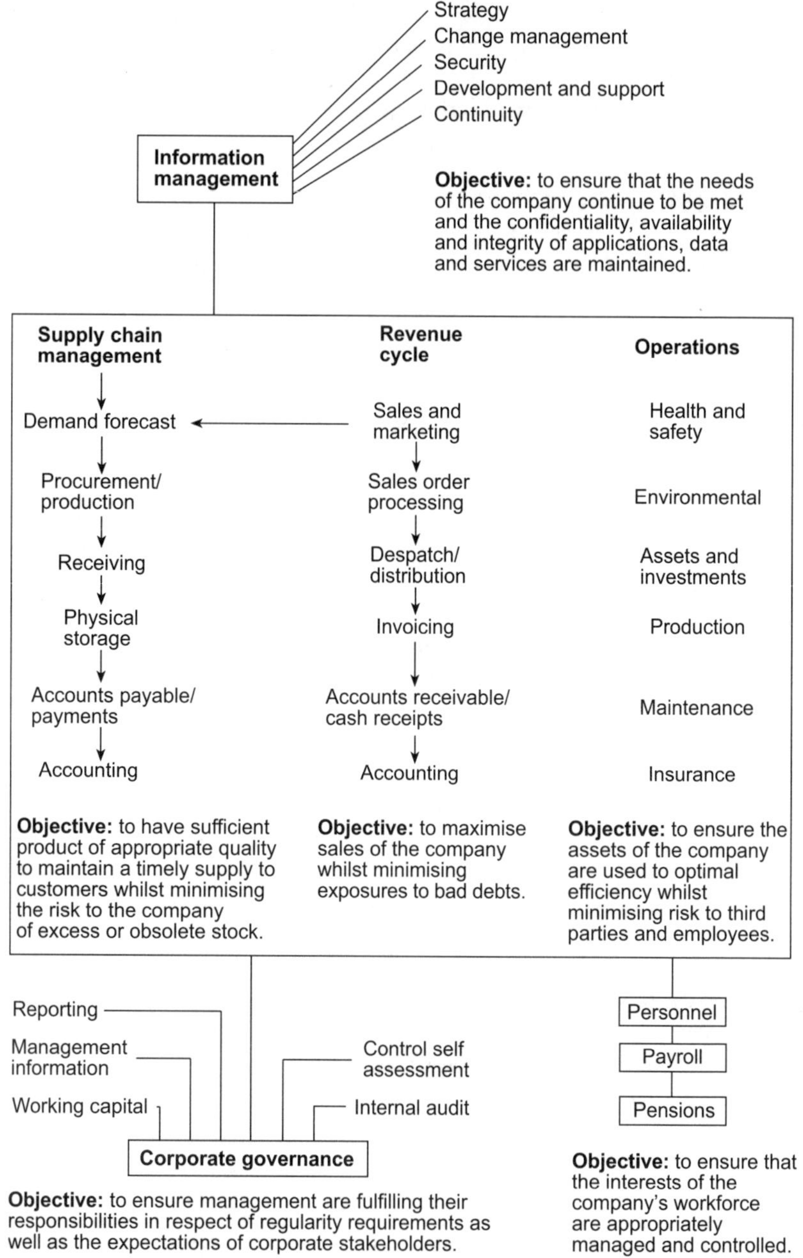


**Figure 14.4** Generic risk model.

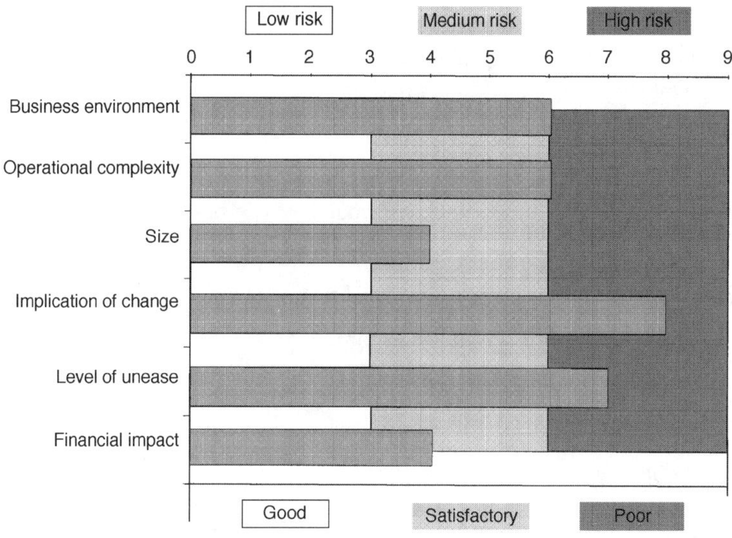


**Figure 14.5** Health check of processes and functions.

cheque being intercepted and cashed by someone other than the intended recipient. This latter risk is taken either knowingly or unknowingly by the business.

Ascertaining the cost-benefit of a system of internal controls is not easy. Unless one takes a 'helicopter view' of the process and its objectives it is difficult to ascertain whether or not the control is achieving the desired effect. For example, the objective of a good supply management process is to ensure that the required goods or services are received on a timely basis, are of the required quality and price and do not require a heavy investment in stock. Various controls will be required over this process, e.g., ensuring accurate demand forecasting, qualifying suppliers, etc. However, ensuring accurate demand forecasting may not achieve the objective of supplying your customer on a timely basis with the right quality goods at the right time and at the right price if the purchasing of the forecasted demand is not well controlled. Cost versus benefit and the related risks must therefore be looked at for the process as a whole.

Whilst individual controls will be required to manage specific aspects of a process, the combination of these controls and their effectiveness in meeting the principal business objectives is what needs to be measured and monitored. The true benefit of the process generally lies at the end of the process, i.e., when the product is delivered to a customer and he is satisfied to the degree that he returns to your business and not the competition to fulfil his needs.

In reviewing cost versus benefit it is essential therefore to take a top-down perspective of the process in question and the related controls. The following questions will help you determine whether or not the relevant controls are effective and cost effective:

- Does the system of controls achieve the business objective?
- What effect does it have on other aspects of the business?
- Is it dependent on other aspects of the business?
- What benefits does it bring – does it add value to the process as a whole?
- Is it simple to administer and maintain?
- Is it mandatory, i.e., required by law?

## CONCLUSION

Controls Self Assessment (CSA) is a very useful tool in helping management ascertain and assess the risks to the business and the effectiveness of related controls. Like any tool it has to be used judiciously and with the application of good common and business sense. It also needs to be adapted to the circumstances of a particular business and its control environment, geography and culture. Remember the tool is only as good as its user.

There is no simple prescriptive method for developing effective controls as the needs of each particular business and the risks facing it are different. In the BOC culture, management are responsible and accountable for internal controls. The approach taken to CSA has been to capitalise on this and the matrix organisation structure. Consequently, management and functional areas such internal audit, insurance, health & safety, environment, etc., are continually in contact to ensure that all significant risks are identified, and actions are taken to manage these risks, to monitor their progress and where necessary to establish and implement new policies and procedures. Experience has taught us that the following statements are a true reflection of reality:

- The management process, the risk-management process and the elements of internal controls are synonymous. Together, they are the foundation of a well-managed organisation whose management meet all the requirements of good corporate governance. They are not separate processes but an integral part of the whole process of management. The best and most effective controls are those which form an integral part of the management process and are therefore owned by management.
- Good controls also have to be cost effective as well as addressing the needs of the business. The cost/benefit of controls is not easy to

determine. It is necessary to take a top-down approach to ensure that the business processes concerned and the related controls meet the objectives of the business effectively. Controls must be commensurate with the risks involved and the benefits to the business.

- The development of effective controls does not require 'rocket science'. Application of basic principles, good old common sense and a good understanding of the business can achieve all that is desired. The application of the KISS (keep it simple) principle works wonders.

# 15

# Embedding Control Self Assessment in the Organisation

## 'SAS' – The ASDA Experience

*Duncan Stephenson*

This chapter relates the experience of implementing a control self assessment system at ASDA, the UK's third largest supermarket chain (£7bn turnover). This is our own story which will, we hope, prove helpful to the reader in reviewing their own experience, or in girding themselves for the coming challenge of implementing CSA in their own organisation.

### WHERE HAVE WE GOT TO?

ASDA has a chain of over 200 superstores which are serviced by a distribution network comprising 12 warehouses or distribution centres. Internal audit's self assessment system ('SAS') is in operation throughout the chain of superstores. The system currently covers stock and cash and a pilot is now running on self assessment for the new ASDA quality programme called 'ASDA Best Way', or ABW for short. Self assessment by stores of their controls over stock (termed retail accountability in ASDA) has now been in place for 14 months. Cash SAS came in 9 months ago. SAS modules for product ordering (an operation very susceptible to dysfunction as a result of poor operating standards) and front-end (check-outs and customer service desk) are ready to go. Self assessment for distribution centre best practice is in development. The trend is toward expansion.

### WHAT IS SAS?

In the language of control self assessment, SAS is an on-screen, survey-based system for self assessment. The system currently runs on the Unix box in stores and is a hybrid of Lotus 1-2-3 with hypertext help facility. It was written over a long period of time, in the background, in the spare time of the stores audit manager with some spare-time, unofficial help from IT. All the same, it not only works, but works well.

We have now re-written it in Microsoft Access so we can produce run-time versions that can be 'plopped' into any pc or onto almost any network without Access having to be there. This can be done at speed; the time requirement comes from mapping the processes, identifying the key controls, writing the questions, writing the background reference material, etc. With a lot of this now under our belt, we can do this pretty efficiently too. So, the benefit I am drawing out here is that once you have done it, you can replicate the process again and again without all the pain of the first time; what American management gurus love to refer to as 'leverage'.

## SAS *IN UTERO*

If we had told the Board, or the Audit Committee, or the Operations Director what we were planning to do, we would have got nowhere. Talking merely conceptually would have been the kiss of death to the project. It had to be done by stealth. We had to have the product, the system, something to show, something to touch before we could start talking about it or, more importantly, before we would be listened to. The system is very visual and very colourful, almost everyone who looks at it makes some admiring comment, it sells itself when you see it.

There were various crucial points. The Audit Committee had asked the head of internal audit how he could confirm the state of controls in the chain. That was the starting point for the long, careful process of research and development. A year and a half later, rather a long, elephantine gestation period, we had something to show, or to show off.

The first, rather vague statement of organisational need or frustration was that mentioned above: how do we know what the state of controls is across the chain, and how do we know if it is improving? The second statement of need was a realisation that the control fabric was breaking down and that something was needed to strengthen it. The Operations Director wanted more auditors in the field, others were more sceptical of the benefits of such a move. The issue of a weak control fabric appeared to explain wildly varying stock results across the chain. The concern was what to do about it.

At this point we pulled the covers off SAS and showed anyone who cared to see, what the audit team could deliver and what we thought that would do for the business. Once you know what the state of controls actually is, right across the chain, at any time, and from one moment in time to another, then you have the basis for improvement. What gets measured, gets improved.

Those concerned all bought the concept because they could see, hear and touch it, and therefore understand and appreciate it.

## QUESTIONNARE VERSUS WORKSHOP

Workshops tend to be top-down views, although they do not have to be. At ASDA we do them for business risk reviews with board members, or at the start of major audits. Questionnaires tend to be bottom-up views, although they do not have to be.

To get the detail from over 200 stores on a regular basis, it had to be the survey, or questionnaire approach. Workshops take too much time to get the coverage. Whilst the group workshop dynamic can produce creative results, you do not usually get the view, both aggregate and individual, that you need to weave some strength into your control framework. At least not in a multi-site situation.

The experience of questionnaire surveys is chequered, at least that is what our research seemed to indicate. At another major retailer, control books (a series of checklists) were introduced to stores. It seemed to work well for about six months and then died a death. In general terms, there seems to be little longevity in the checklist approach.

It is not just CSA questionnaires. Much the same can be said for any questionnaires that head offices put out to their branches, that organisations put out to their employees, that businesses put out to their customers. The first problem is actually getting a response; 30–50% appears to be an average rate of response after a couple of reminders. That is not good enough for CSA. Then, if you do get a response, how truthful is it? How valid is it? It is easy to fill something in without too much thought, in automaton fashion, and send it back. It is sometimes tempting to lie, to exaggerate, or to make joke replies. It was said that in the 1992 general election, people did not care to admit that they were going to vote Conservative and therefore opinion polls were inaccurate as forecasts of the actual result.

After some thought, we figured that the problem with questionnaires is that you are asking someone for something but you were giving them nothing. A fundamental flaw that goes against human nature. Successful market research agencies give their respondents something, if only a token. We had to give something upfront, to be able to ask for something back in the form of self assessment scores. What we gave them is detailed in the overview below.

## SAS OVERVIEW

The component parts of the Self Assessment System are shown in Figure

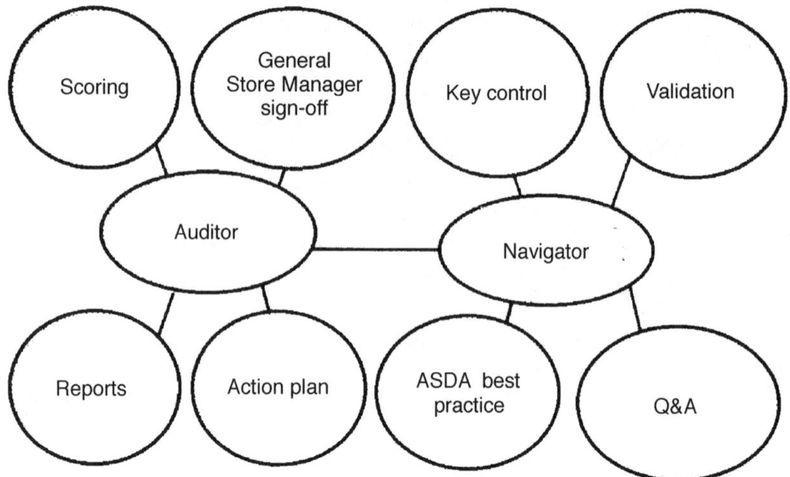


**Figure 15.1** Components of the self assessment system (GSM = general store manager; ABP = audit best practice).

15.1. The sputnik-type shape shows two major components and four parts to each major component.

## AUDITOR

The auditor is the action-oriented bit. It comprises the actual questionnaire where users score themselves, the sign-off box for the branch manager, an automatic action plan for resolving weaknesses, and a summary report of users' scores.

*Scoring*: users enter the scoring section or questionnaire and respond to a series of questions (see Figure 15.2); the response can be '1' – control is in place and working, '2' – control working partially or some of the time, '3' – control not in place, or 'N' – not applicable to this store (e.g., question relates to lottery terminals or petrol-filling station or customer café that this store does not have).

GSM *sign-off*: the GSM (General Store Manager) has to sign off the self assessment as valid and complete; comments can also be put in the box provided. When self assessments are signed off in this way, the system is closed down for the quarter (scoring and reporting is performed quarterly) and the results pulled back to the centre for analysis and reporting by internal audit.

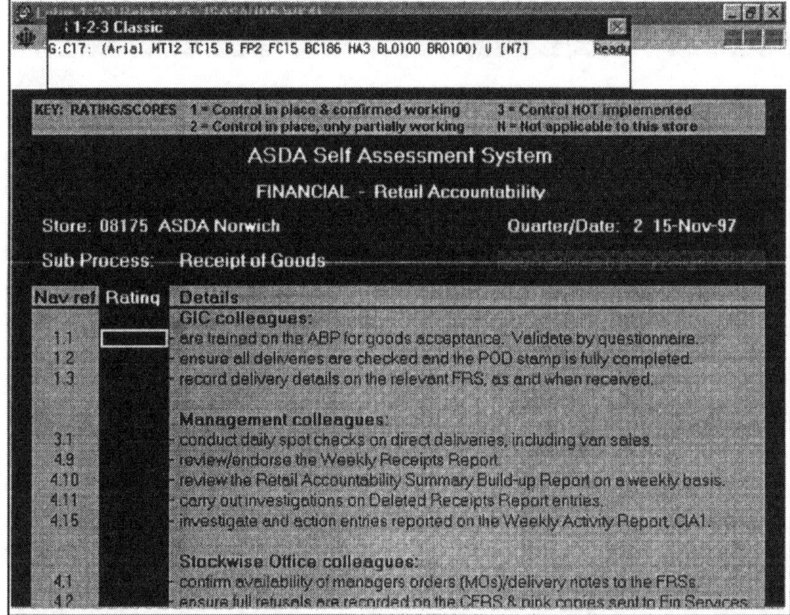


**Figure 15.2** SAS – financial – retail accountability.

*Action plans*: if the users have scored a '2' (control only working partially) or a '3' (control not in place or not working), then an automatic action plan is produced which tells them what to do to resolve those control weaknesses. This is the first element of giving them something that they can use, something that is valuable to them.

*Reporting*: as soon as users come out of the scoring part of the system, they can go into the reporting and see what their overall score is for each area (e.g., goods in, price changes, returns, etc.). The reporting tells them what they scored in that section in the last two quarters and also what proportion of the questions they have answered. If they come out of the scoring after answering half the questions, it will show their aggregate score and indicate the scoring as 50% complete (see Figure 15.3). We believe that most questionnaire approaches do not let users see how they scored nor how it relates to how they previously scored. Comparison of how they did versus other stores comes later, when all the results have been polled and analysed.

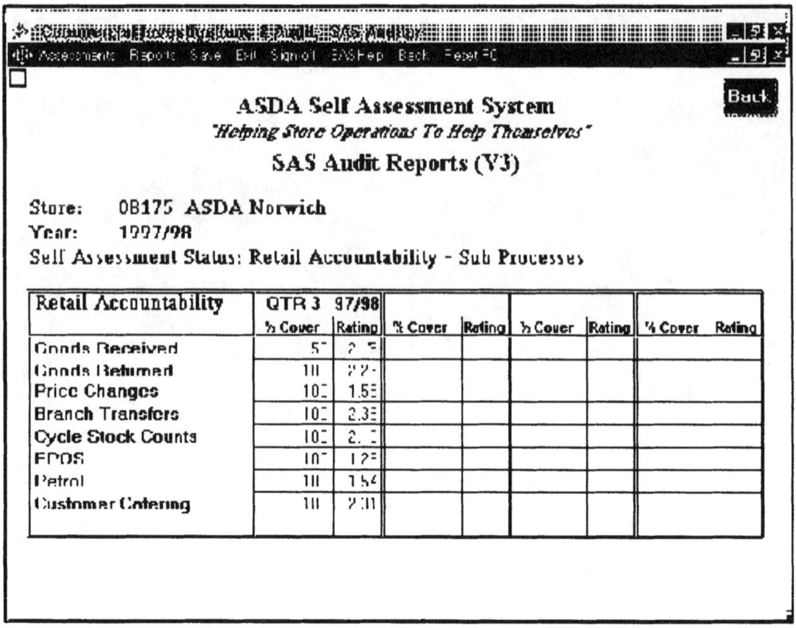

Assessments Reports Save Exit Signoff SAS Help Back Reset PC

Back

**ASDA Self Assessment System**

*"Helping Store Operations To Help Themselves"*

**SAS Audit Reports (V3)**

Store: 0B175 ASDA Norwich
Year: 1997/98
Self Assessment Status: Retail Accountability - Sub Processes

| Retail Accountability | QTR 3 97/98 | | | | | | | |
|---|---|---|---|---|---|---|---|---|
| | % Cover | Rating | % Cover | Rating | % Cover | Rating | % Cover | Rating |
| Goods Received | 5[illegible] | [illegible] | | | | | | |
| Goods Returned | [illegible] | [illegible] | | | | | | |
| Price Changes | 10[illegible] | 1.5[illegible] | | | | | | |
| Branch Transfers | 10[illegible] | 2.3[illegible] | | | | | | |
| Cycle Stock Counts | 10[illegible] | 2.[illegible] | | | | | | |
| EPOS | 10[illegible] | 1.2[illegible] | | | | | | |
| Petrol | [illegible] | 1.54 | | | | | | |
| Customer Catering | [illegible] | [illegible] | | | | | | |

**Figure 15.3** SAS – audit reports.

## NAVIGATOR

The navigator is the back-up, the reference section. In terms of the auditor–user interface, this is mainly giving something to the users that will help them complete the questionnaire, that will help them do their job, explain their job, train for their job.

*Key controls*: this backs up the question in the questionnaire. The scoring section references to this part of the navigator. Here users find the key control, that is being surveyed, explained. The risk that is being addressed is also defined. The new version links questions that are scored as '2' and '3' to these risks to produce a report of the residual risks to which the operation is exposed.

*Validation*: the scoring section asks users to check or to assess a control. The validation section of the navigator tells them precisely what they need to do to validate it, how many items they should check, how often, etc. See Figure 15.4.

*Q&A*: questions in the scoring section occasionally ask users to confirm if the person or persons performing a function know what they are doing and

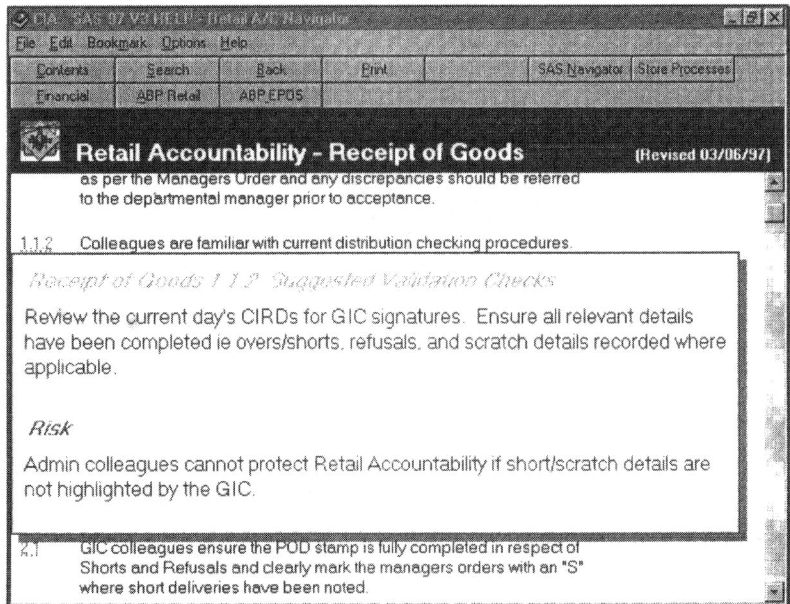


**Figure 15.4** Navigator – retail accountability – receipt of goods.

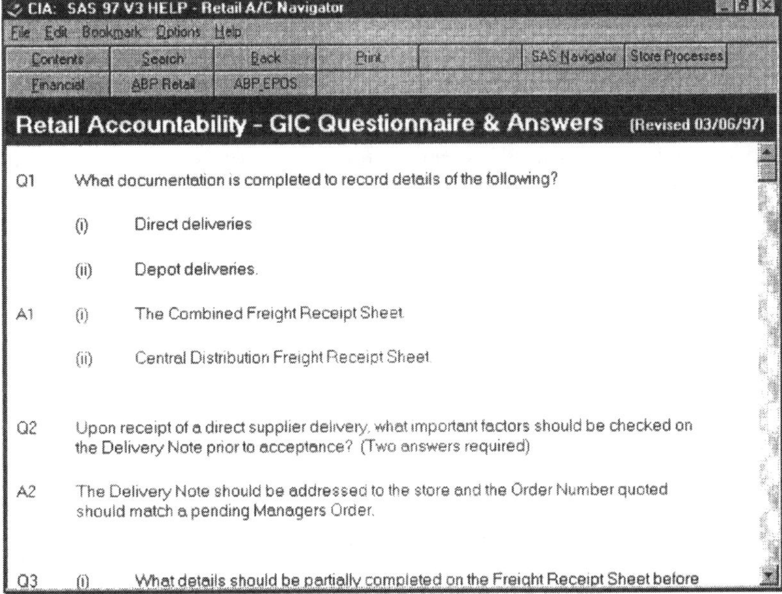


**Figure 15.5** Navigator – retail accountability – questionnaire and answers.

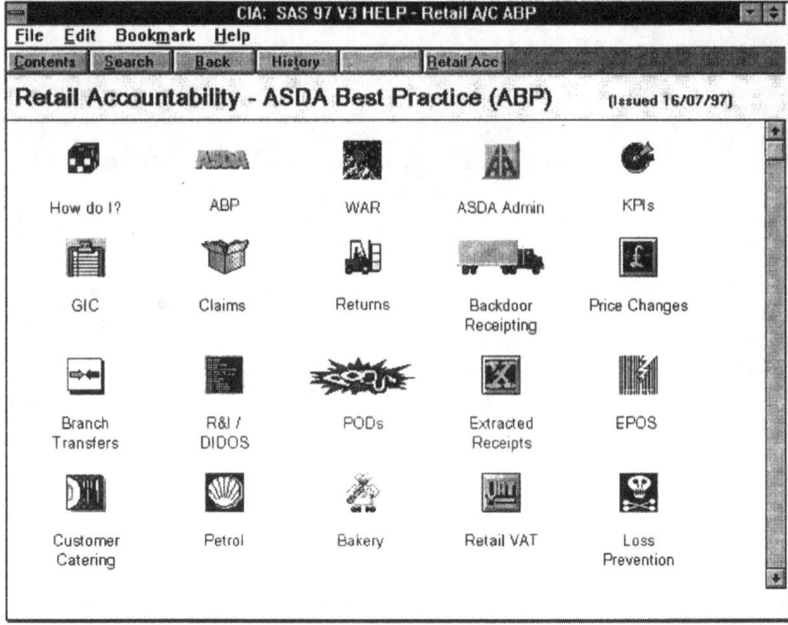


**Figure 15.6** Retail accountability – ASDA best practice.

why. Users need to test that they have been trained and that they understand. The Q&A section provides the questionnaires to confirm that understanding. See Figure 15.5.

*ABP*: this is the big win for the stores – ABP stands for ASDA Best Practice and essentially represents on-screen manuals and latest briefing documents kept up to date and accessible for the areas covered by self assessment. The gateway screen to the best-practice module is shown in Figure 15.6. The manuals still exist but they know they can go to SAS and get the latest document and the latest version of the best practice. This represents value you can touch to store personnel as it enables them to go straight to the reference that they need. It is this part of SAS which has enabled SAS to become a very valuable training tool.

## GETTING GOING

We had built the system and had been given the green light to proceed with a pilot which we carried out in ASDA's Scottish stores. We held workshops and tried to sell the concept. We introduced the questionnaire in paper format to get it going and to test it; and it got going, and we learned the arts that were required. In hindsight the more flexible system we are now building will allow us to prototype rather than work from paper questionnaires. It also gives the pilot crew a better idea of the hands-on feel and also what they are going to get. The workshops were hit and miss, and the buy-in was partial. The learning was number one: forget paper, (ASDA prides itself on its quest for the paperless operation) and number two, prepare the audit team for the workshop approach and for selling the product to a possibly sceptical audience. After all, this was foreign territory for our team in terms of approach. The auditors have to be trained to do it; they have to be prepared for a period of implementation, of training, of problem resolution, of self assessment validation which they may not relish.

Well, we did it and have come through. The result is that we can do it standing on our heads now, and swiftly too. We can take new colleagues and show them how to do it. But it was painful and if a colleague did not like it, you could bet the stores would not buy it either. That left us with remedial work we had not anticipated.

## WHAT IS A KEY CONTROL?

The first version we tested in Scotland had lots of controls to score yourself against, consequently it took too long. The other problem that reared its head was weighting; did a score of three on one control count the same as a score of three on another control? Arguments followed. The simple solution was to reduce the number of controls to those that really were the key controls. What was the set of controls which you could happily apply an even weighting to? The new system has got a weighting option which we may or may not need. Companies which find themselves stifled by suffocating control procedures may find that the mapping process that precedes SAS and the implementation of a SAS system in fact releases them from the dead hand of over-control. A benefit here may be found in the end result – suddenly you find you have a more streamlined control framework.

## FILLING IN THE BLANKS

Not until we went through process mapping in the areas covered by SAS did we find that there were some surprising omissions. What do you do with this? How do you know you are OK on this? Is this good or bad? On these occasions we came back and tried to find the answers. It sounds a bit sneaky but if we did not find answers, we just wrote the best practice ourselves. By the very inclusion of this new 'best practice' on SAS, it became the standard.

This surprised us but in retrospect it is a big benefit. The feedback loop on SAS and the continuing evolution of it, mean that we will know if this was the right policy or not.

## ROLL OUT: THE AUDITOR AS IMPLEMENTER

Some auditors hate SAS, no two ways about it. They will do it, but they do not like it. So choose your implementation team, train them in what they need to know and motivate them. A poor implementation will give you problems. An auditor may end up doing the assessments for a unit and creating a dependency. This is not self assessment. This is where the implementation manager must be really close to what is going on at the crucial stage.

## THE OUTPUTS

At the end of every quarter, the results are polled. The scores are pulled back to the centre and analysed. Here is the third graph of results we ever produced, we call it the WOW! graph (see Figure 15.7).

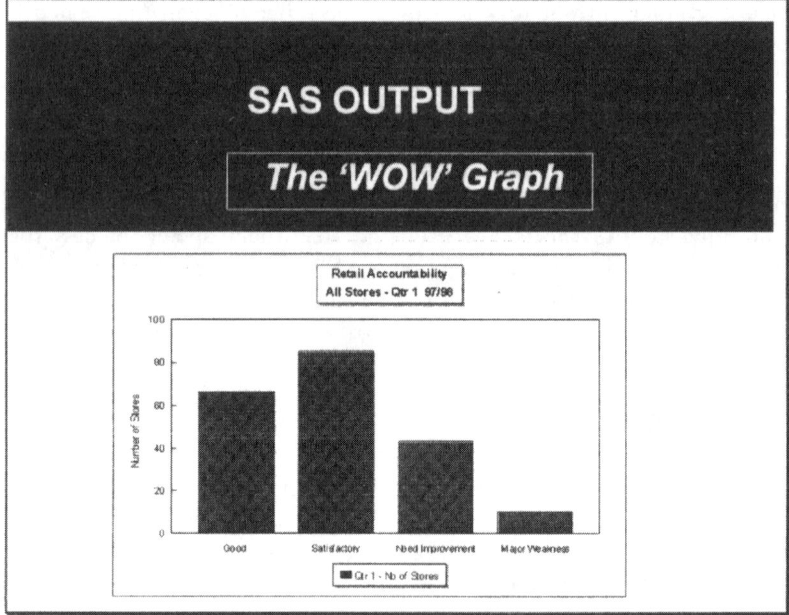


**Figure 15.7** SAS – output – the 'WOW' graph.

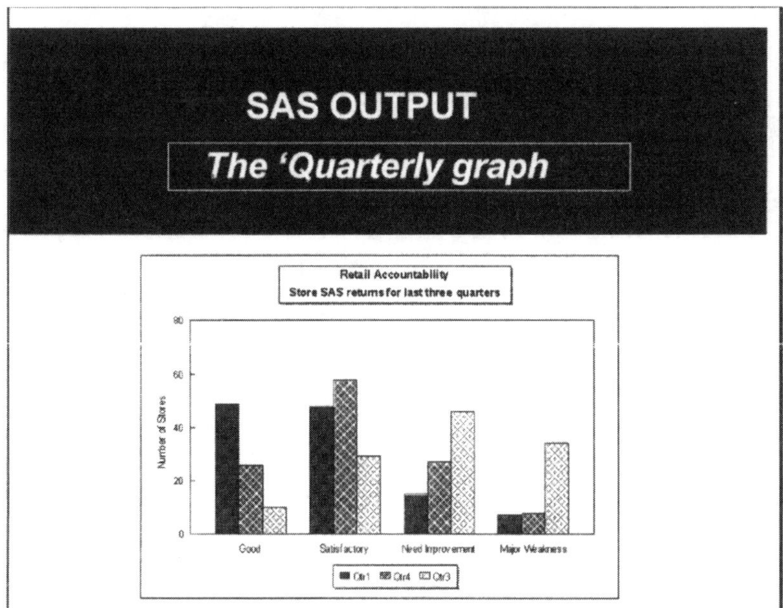


**Figure 15.8** SAS – output – the quarterly graph.

The graph shows the third-time picture of the profile of controls over stock (retail accountability in ASDA terminology) across the whole chain at any one point in time and the starting point for everything else that follows.

The WOW! graph shows one result. The next one shows how the position changes over three quarters. A gradual shift in scores to the left, an improvement in scores and an improvement in controls. Underlying these graphs is a programme of validation of the scores that stores have submitted. If we think it is too good, we go in and validate. If it is wrong, we change it. Aside from this we try to validate 5% each quarter. The stock or retail accountability graph for the first three quarters' assessments is shown in Figure 15.8.

We then split down by regional manager, comparing the aggregate for one region with the other regions, and how these change over time. The initials along the x axis of the graph relate to ASDA's regions (see Figure 15.9).

And then we drill down once again. In Figure 15.10 we see the scores for a region split by store and also by sub-process. The regional manager can see if there is a problem with a store or with a sub-process.

We are often asked where does bottom-up meet top-down. What the above outputs show is how the bottom-up builds to an aggregate company-

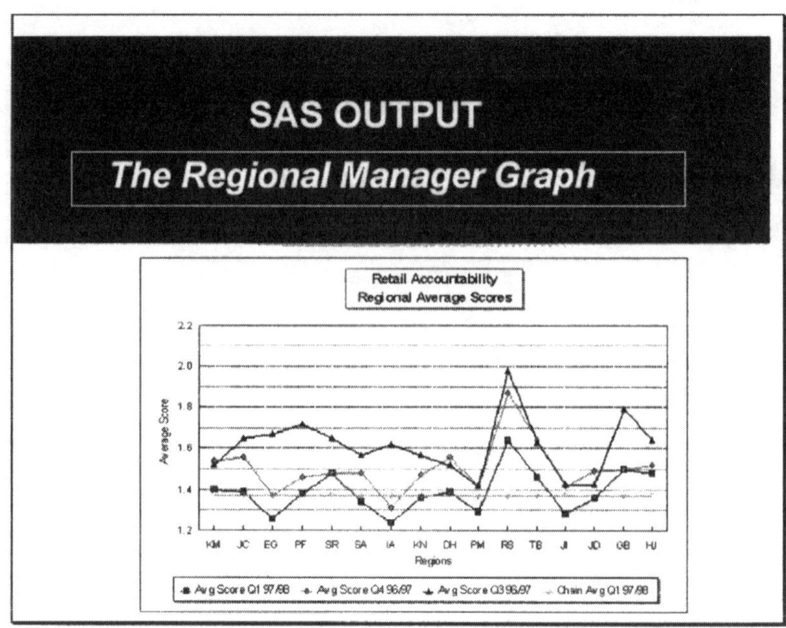


**Figure 15.9** SAS – output – the regional manager graph.

SAS OUTPUT

*The Regional Manager Matrix*

| Store Name | Total Score -Retail | Goods Received | Goods Returned | Price Changes | Branch Transfers | Cycle Stock Counts | EPoS | Petrol | Customer Catering |
|---|---|---|---|---|---|---|---|---|---|
| Corby | 1.48 | 1.44 | 1.15 | 1.16 | 1.63 | 1.45 | 1.68 | 1.77 | 1.80 |
| Coventry | 1.74 | 1.56 | 1.54 | 1.52 | 1.38 | 1.55 | 2.32 | 2.08 | 2.10 |
| Gt Yarmouth | 1.44 | 1.37 | 1.23 | 1.37 | 1.63 | 1.09 | 1.53 | 1.62 | 1.90 |
| Hinckley | 1.32 | 1.33 | 1.31 | 1.26 | 1.50 | 1.45 | 1.32 | n/a | 1.10 |
| Ipswich | 1.36 | 1.41 | 1.00 | 1.00 | 1.00 | 1.45 | 1.56 | 1.77 | 1.70 |
| Leamington Spa | 1.27 | 1.70 | 1.15 | 1.42 | 1.38 | 1.00 | 1.32 | 1.69 | 1.20 |
| Leicester | 1.39 | 1.81 | 1.62 | 1.05 | 1.63 | 1.45 | 1.58 | 2.15 | 1.80 |
| **Norwich** | **1.46** | **1.70** | **1.69** | **1.32** | **1.63** | **1.45** | **1.42** | **n/a** | **1.00** |
| Nuneaton | 1.19 | 1.22 | 1.00 | 1.16 | 1.25 | 1.18 | 1.21 | n/a | 1.30 |
| Oadby | 1.32 | 1.56 | 1.00 | 1.42 | 1.13 | 1.27 | 1.21 | n/a | 1.30 |
| Peterborough | 1.27 | 1.56 | 1.08 | 1.00 | 1.13 | 1.45 | 1.05 | n/a | 1.54 |
| Stowmarket | 1.74 | 1.85 | 2.08 | 1.16 | 1.38 | 1.45 | 2.26 | n/a | n/a |
| **Sub-total: Average** | **1.42** | **1.54** | **1.32** | **1.24** | **1.39** | **1.35** | **1.54** | **1.85** | **1.52** |

**Figure 15.10** SAS – output – the regional manager matrix.

wide picture from which you then drill down as the figures guide you. The chain-view graphs feed into the top-down risk review. The top-down review stays at a pretty high level. The bottom-up review comes up to meet it. This is the practical conclusion of the ASDA experience.

The concern is that bottom-up requires focus and follow-up, which require ongoing effort to achieve them. Our belief is that at that point many companies have pronounced the whole concept a failure. They have gone for a big-bang implementation and they have gone down in a blaze of glory. In fact it was a poor approach and a lack of consistency and constancy that brought them down.

## SATORI IN ASDA

'Satori' is the Japanese word for a sudden realisation, or a kick in the head. The satori we experienced was that SAS had gone out there and to a certain extent, taken on a life of its own.

- Stores were using it as a training tool, output from SAS was being plastered on walls to communicate issues.
- Inter-store comparisons were leading to a certain level of competitiveness in best practice. As long as we could prove that the better scores were valid, then this was no bad thing.
- SAS as a crutch. Things are going wrong, where do I start? Start with SAS to make sure everything on there is working OK, then move on and look elsewhere.
- SAS as a language of control. It is hard to encourage people to talk about controls or their control environment, it sounds pretty dull. We found, nevertheless, that people were talking about SAS and their SAS scores quite freely.

## SPONSORING AUTHORS' NETWORK

To keep the ASDA best practice piece up to date, we need a network of sponsoring authors. You therefore need to be proactive in getting hold of everything that is going on and making sure that all the latest briefings and procedures come to audit for inclusion into ABP. It can be hard work but it ensures the integrity of your product and keeps you at the heart of things. We have had stuff out there in SAS before it has appeared in any other format.

## ASSESSORS' NETWORK

The store assesses itself. We find that it is usually the administration manager who does it. This is now growing in scope as more modules are built. More managers in the stores environment are getting involved in doing assessments, particularly via the quality programme. New versions of the system have a bulletin board to tell people what is new or what they should look out for. The process of receiving feedback is also continually being worked on. At the moment it is verbal, or via update meetings. The GSM's sign-off comments are also retrieved and reviewed.

## CULTURE

There is much talk of the culture requirements of CSA. The reaction of the down-to-earth Operations Director of ASDA is that 'Culture is something that grows on top of a yoghurt'. What ASDA does have is a required way of working that is reinforced constantly with slogans and briefings. That way of working is intended to reinforce personal responsibility for doing the job. Clearly any company can create its own priorities or take responsibility by using SAS. The key in CSA is that a bad score is an opportunity to improve rather than a sacking offence. What is expected is that some effort will be made to improve as a result of a bad SAS score. That is all that is required 'culturally'.

## EXTENDING THE REMIT OF INTERNAL AUDIT

Implementing SAS in the areas of stock and cash was working on the auditors' home turf. The quality programme, front-end, and ordering are all taking them into areas which they have previously only touched. The result is that internal audit is getting involved more in other areas of the organisation.

## FLEXIBILITY AND LONGEVITY

In the world of CSA, there have been lots of quitters over the past ten years. Nevertheless, the trend is still toward expansion, as evidenced by the ever-increasing audience at the American IIA's annual CSA conference (700 delegates in 1997). The quitters, amongst whom are numerous pharmaceutical companies, banks, insurers, and oil companies, seem to have lost heart in the struggle to keep it fresh, to keep innovating. The death knell for a workshop is when they say 'but we did this last year'. Things may have changed but you have to change also.

Whilst feeling relieved to have gone past the first anniversary of SAS with the programme intact and expanding, we have to remain flexible. We have introduced assessment holidays where you get a quarter off from assessing the questions you got a 1 on last time. That way you concentrate for a quarter on your 2s and 3s. Some people like to have the discipline of a diary of when to perform which checks. If that is what they need, then we provide it. The validation programme has to continue to maintain credibility in the system also. It is not an easy ride, but if the result is that more requests come and thus you manage to cover another area of your organisation's operation, then it is worth it.

## THE BENEFITS

Who is going to sign up to this? Where are the benefits? Does it mean I can employ fewer auditors? The most successful scenario for the implementation of CSA is when there is a need or frustration within the organisation that you can latch on to. The need may be a desire to get a grip on controls in a certain area, the need to make a change programme stick and make sure everyone is doing it, or simply reassurance for the CEO or the Audit Committee chairman that things are OK.

CSA was born from the frustration of trying to keep a handle on things in a fast-changing environment. The process is highly appropriate as a monitor in the environment of change, as long as the custodians of the system keep up with it and continue to sell it.

Since SAS has been implemented in the area of stocks at store, the level of stock loss has been decreasing. The correlation is not proven but it does have something to do with it. SAS highlights training needs very quickly and although it is hard to put a figure on it, it is a benefit. And then, how do you quantify the satisfaction the Audit Committee chairman might feel when he sees the WOW! graph?

Wherever an operation is highly sensitive to operator compliance to procedures, then CSA should prove its worth. We hope to prove this in the near future in a monetary way with one of the next modules of SAS.

# 16

# CSA in a Financial Services Organisation

*Vicky Kubitscheck*

## INTRODUCTION

This chapter aims to provide an outline to my approach to CSA and, in particular, the considerations and developmental processes that are necessary for determining the right approach for an organisation.

Other chapters in this book provide many ideas on the details and contents of a CSA programme, however, to be successful, the CSA programme must recognise the 'soft issues' of the organisation such as its nature and culture, i.e., it must be specific to the organisation and its people. The influence of these issues, including organisational culture, is real; this was apparent when developing an approach for my last organisation, AXA Equity & Law and comparing best practices between the various companies within the AXA Group across Europe and America. Also, by taking into account existing management processes and tools already in place, CSA could be more readily integrated into the organisation. It must finally be stressed that CSA underlines sound management practice and that in an organisation that is already practising good governance, CSA should merely be formalising management's approach.

In this chapter, I provide the background and driving forces that have influenced my present organisation, AEGON UK (holding company of Scottish Equitable group of companies) and others in the same industry in the implementation of CSA. I concentrate on the evaluation process that I have used which may assist you in your own consideration and design of a suitable approach for your organisation.

## THE BACKGROUND

### Waking the Sleeping Giant

Logic would dictate that organisations in the financial services industry are well run with almost an instinctive sense of propriety, after all, they are handling and being entrusted with someone else's assets and possibly nest egg investment for the future. For nearly 200 years, insurance and banking organisations have operated relatively unchanged, dictating their services to consumers. Proud of their tradition, almost to a point of arrogance, the financial services industry will initially need more than mere recommended practice contained in the Cadbury report, new Combined Code or COSO report to help shake it off its podium.

Early statistics have shown that financial services organisations have, by and large, been playing the catch-up game in the corporate governance arena, with some minor exceptions in those involved with the banking industry. The many international high-profile cases of poor corporate governance, e.g., Nomura's copper trade losses, Morgan Grenfell Asset Management's difficulties, Baring's breakdown of controls and supervision, and the Orange County 'financial earthquake', may have highlighted the risks in deficient systems of control. Yet many boards in the financial services are in danger of maintaining the 'it wouldn't happen to us' syndrome.

### Financial Services – a Whole New Ball Game

Fortunately, strong undercurrents of change have been tugging at the feet of the financial services industry in the 1980s and 1990s, which even the most entrenched in cultural demeanour cannot fail to ignore. To do so would result in the ultimate penalty of being extinguished. One could identify four main driving forces of change over the last two decades:

1. **New consumer behaviour**
   Consumers are more knowledgeable for various reasons, e.g., improved standards of education and awareness of the economy, better communication through the media and technology and more active consumer rights organisations. Old reliable consumer behaviour such as loyalty and predictability will give way to choices of economy and convenience. Expanding markets and price-conscious consumers will and have driven the financial services industry to review their approach to satisfying the demands of the new breed of consumers.
2. **Technology**
   The technological revolution has affected not only the way customers

are serviced but also the way products are distributed. The advent of modern telecommunications via automatic telephone sales systems and the Internet will continue to impact on the traditional methods of management controls.

3. **Competition and globalisation**
   From the number of mergers and takeovers occurring in the financial services industry over the last ten years, companies not wanting to lose out are under pressure to lower distribution costs and increase productivity. Being more cost efficient and customer focused has been a preoccupation in a number of organisations in the drive to attain financial strength and to gain organic growth. The new breed of managers who are 'empowered', who are more aware of corporate objectives and whose accountabilities are more transparent, is growing.

4. **Regulatory and statutory requirements**
   An overwhelming influence on CSA in the insurance industry has been the introduction and extension of regulatory requirements. Regulation relating to investment advice was introduced in the late 1980s, one of its contributing factors being consumers' outcry for more accountability by product providers and financial advisors. The need to comply with the Financial Services Act 1986 prompted the growth of a new business function with specialist Compliance Officers and Compliance Auditors being trained with the aim of 'protecting the investor'.

   The transformation of statutory regulation in the financial services industry has remained under scrutiny as a continuing sign of the complexities involved in controlling the whole gambit of financial services and satisfying the consumer. Pensions mis-selling is one such example of complexity which arose, some may say, through a combination of political and economic issues. Changes in the various statutory regulations relating to the banking industry, building societies, insurance companies and investment management companies appear to contain elements of the new corporate governance culture. For example, the European Commission's Third Life and Non-life Insurance Directive requires companies to be managed 'in accordance with the principles of sound and prudent management'. The Department of Trade and Industry reinforced these principles by specifying requirements for directors to make certain disclosures in their annual returns and by issuing a series of Prudential Guidance, e.g., Note 1994/6, on controls over investments and derivatives. This regulatory function has now been taken over by HM Treasury. The Financial Services Authority (FSA) has recently been created as a 'super-regulator' of most forms of financial service, and the Labour Government has announced its intention to 'clean up the City'.

## DESIGN APPROACH

During my research and development of a CSA methodology, I found that organisations approach CSA in very different ways, though the principles and objectives remain similar. It is therefore not surprising to see a convergence in the detailed practices, with differences remaining in the way CSA is introduced and implemented in an organisation. I summarise below those factors that have influenced my approach to implementing CSA.

### Approach Checklist

#### *Executive sponsorship*

- Is CSA being sponsored at the top?
  Experience from many organisations indicates that without support from the top, implementing CSA would be almost impossible or limited in application. The need for genuine approval and sponsorship from the top is almost a prerequisite for introducing a full CSA programme in an organisation.
- Will support from the top be visible?
  Senior management and the executives not only need to sponsor the programme but also must be seen to support the effort to ensure that appropriate resources and priorities are committed. Wherever possible, senior management should front the key stages of implementation to demonstrate ownership and buy-in of the initiative. This visibility is vital to ensure that CSA is owned by management, by the business and not the facilitators, especially if the facilitators are Internal Audit. Involving management at all levels is also necessary to reinforce the educational aspect of CSA, i.e., sound management practice.
- Is there a business driver for CSA?
  Implementing CSA for a specific business objective that has been identified by senior management is a powerful lever in designing approach. The business drivers that motivated the boards in the respective organisations in which I have implemented CSA included the need to meet HM Treasury regulatory requirements, the recognition for sound systems of controls to minimise errors and loss, and as part of a continual improvement programme.

#### *Control culture or continuum*

- Is awareness of controls high, acceptable, low or indifferent?

The level of awareness of controls or the understanding of the concept of controls determines the level of initial educational content of the CSA implementation process. It is likely that some business areas are more aware than others, while some are more ready to accept controls than others. Consequently, one needs to be flexible in addressing these differences between different parts of the organisation. Nevertheless, it is prudent to introduce CSA to all parts of the business by explaining the 'concept of control', 'business risks' and 'business objectives'.

In my approach, I have sold the 'concept of control' as 'best management practice' while stressing that controls are not obstacles but ways in which we manage 'business risks' to ensure the achievement of 'business objectives'. This approach recognised the control continuum in my organisation at the time, which was going through several changes, e.g., business process re-engineering and consolidation of practices throughout the group on an international basis.

### *Cost and affordibility*

- Is the budget large, small or undefined?
  A limited budget will impact on the implementation process, e.g., use of consultants, training of facilitators and the solution, e.g., software for maintaining CSA. In my last organisation, CSA was treated on a par with other projects, requiring cost and benefit analyses for funds to support the project. It is my opinion that CSA can be successfully implemented with a limited budget but not with limited commitment from the organisation.

### *Size and complexity of the organisation*

- Is CSA to be implemented throughout the organisation?
- Are there great variations in business disciplines within the group, e.g., general insurance, life insurance, investment management, off-shore business, estate agencies, banking?
- Are they located across the country and internationally?
  These factors will influence the level of resources required as well as the approach where a consideration of local control environment should be taken into account. Also, if the control continuum and work culture is different in each entity, the way CSA will be implemented in each entity may need to be adapted, e.g., more clarification or recognition of local practices.

### *Availability of resources*

- Are there sufficient resources to facilitate the process?
- Has management committed sufficient resources to the process?
- Has management committed resources for the on-going maintenance of CSA?
  There is no doubt that implementing CSA is a time-consuming and, initially, a resource-intensive process. Momentum can be lost if resources are not properly prioritised and are pulled away from the process. The process of implementing CSA must be managed like a project, with clear objectives, timescales, deadlines and resources.

### *Supporting systems*

- Will CSA be maintained manually or assisted by software?
  The CSA process generates a tremendous amount of data and information. Manual processing of the information may limit the approach for reporting purposes, e.g., critical analyses of exposure to risks and progress achieved. Efficient capture of such data and ease of maintenance will affect the on-going success and effectiveness of CSA.

## IMPLEMENTING CSA

Of the considerations outlined above, I feel that priority should be given to addressing issues relating to ownership, commitment from the business, and resources.

### CSA Co-ordinators – a Key Feature

The key feature of the CSA programmes I have implemented, and generally continue to advocate, lies in the appointment of divisional or business risk co-ordinators. They play a key role in rolling out the programme in their respective areas and obtaining real management buy-in and ownership. By acting as focal points, they help provide a more efficient channel of communication and co-ordination with individual managers. Their appointment by top management should be visible. Ideally, these individuals know and are known within that business entity, and have the 'right attitude' towards 'doing things right first time'.

Buy-in from these coordinators from the outset is vital. This can be achieved by Internal Audit, as facilitators, providing initial training or introductory

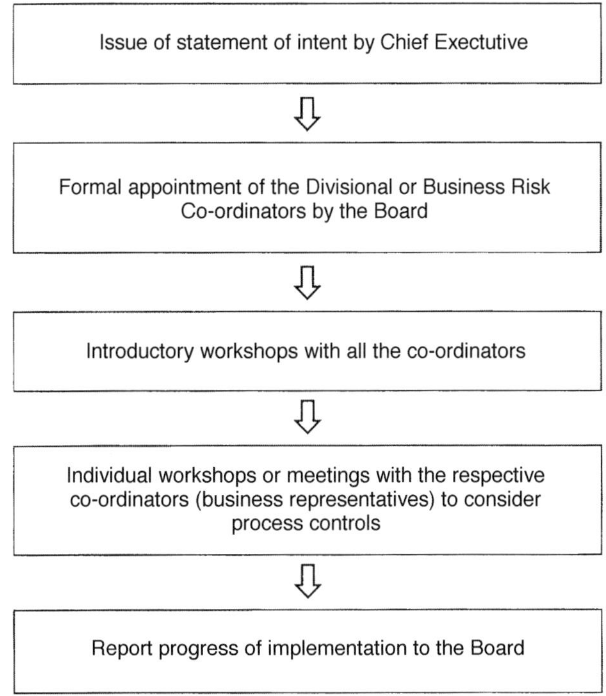


**Figure 16.1** Key stages for starting the CSA programme.

sessions at the formal appointment of the co-ordinators. A close working relationship between Internal Audit and the co-ordinators is necessary to help ensure the smooth and sustained operation of the programme.

During the initial implementation stages of the CSA programme, the co-ordinators are expected to spend a fair proportion, at least 20%–30%, of their time on the programme. It is expected that this proportion will decrease to no more than 10% as managers embed the programme in their 'tool box'. In this respect, it is important to consider the tools that managers are already using when designing one's approach to CSA to ensure that it can be integrated with existing management techniques. The key stages for starting the programme are illustrated in Figure 16.1.

## Operating Principles and Design Features

The operating principles and key design features of my CSA programme, which takes into account an assessment of the business environment and constraints as outlined above, are contained in Table 16.1.

**Table 16.1** Operating principles and key design features of a CSA programme.

| Principles | Design features of the programme |
|---|---|
| Ownership must lie with management | ■ A 'statement of intent' or mission statement is issued by the Chief Executive.<br>■ Divisional co-ordinators representing each area of the business are appointed by the respective Director. Co-ordinators are part of the management team, whose seniority is necessary to indicate the Board's commitment as well as to co-ordinate the development of the programme within their areas.<br>■ The data and information is maintained by the business area, with assistance from Internal Audit, as facilitators.<br>■ The annual reports or 'self assessments' should be issued to the Chief Executive. |
| Objectives and deadlines must be clearly stated | ■ Objectives and deadlines of the programme as they are rolled out are documented and issued to the co-ordinators.<br>■ Presentations are provided to the co-ordinators at the outset to reinforce the message.<br>■ Regular contact with the co-ordinators is maintained to ensure deadlines are met. |
| Guidance for adopting and maintaining the programme must be clear | ■ A 'Manager's Guide' is written by Internal Audit and issued to each co-ordinator. The details of the guide and underlying working principles are reinforced in the presentations or at workshops.<br>■ The guide covers all aspects of the programme from the expectations of the Board, to assessment of risks, definition of controls, control design, reporting formats and on-going maintenance of the documentation. |
| The programme must be simple to understand, implement and maintain | ■ The concept is introduced as simply as possible, using best management practice as the key approach. The fundamental questions we ask include 'What are my key responsibilities?' 'What are my objectives?', 'What risks am I facing in my area?', 'What procedures have I implemented to mitigate these risks?' and 'How am I ensuring that I am carrying out my responsibilities satisfactorily?'.<br>■ Simple proformas are used. |
| The programme must be an integral part of management practice | ■ Local practices are identified and, wherever possible, the process is integrated with local management practice, e.g., reference to existing procedure manuals, quality control checks, and discussion of controls to be included as a regular item at management team meetings.<br>■ Existing communication channels, e.g., network system or LANs, are used to maintain the documentation and facilitate monitoring of progress by the managers as well as Internal Audit. |

| | |
|---|---|
| On-going support and advice must be available | ■ Internal Audit, as facilitators, maintain regular contact with the co-ordinators, on a formal and informal basis. This ensures that progress is sustained and reporting deadlines are achieved.<br>■ Support from Internal Audit must be constant, consistent and available according to the individual needs of the co-ordinators.<br>■ Board's expectation and call for annual reports from each business area helps to reinforce the continual implementation of CRSA. |

## The Programme

The CSA programme I advocate is similar in principle with most models in the market. The difference, is in the 'delivery', i.e., via the co-ordinators in the business areas.

The programme consists of six key steps, as illustrated in Figure 16.2. Internal Audit, as facilitators, assist the Risk Co-ordinators in the review of

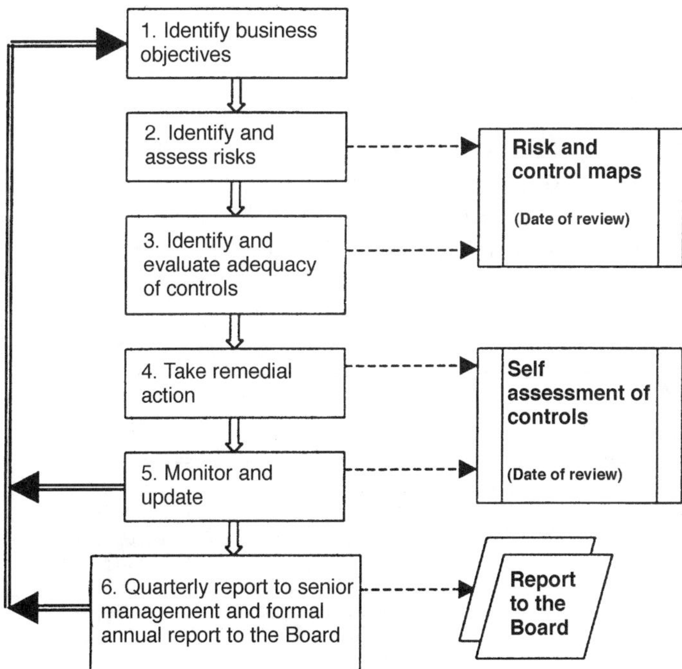


**Figure 16.2** Key Stages for the CSA programme.

each step and in producing or updating of the various 'Risk & Control Maps' and 'Self Assessments'. The auditor will readily note that these documents form a useful source of information and starting 'benchmarks' for the conduct of internal audits in the respective business areas.

## CONCLUSION: MAINTAINING THE MOMENTUM

### During Implementation

Maintaining the momentum for implementing CSA is a familiar challenge to Internal Auditors acting as facilitators. There is no easy solution. The principles outlined above, in particular, top management commitment together with strong monitoring and feedback, are most important. Building strong allies in the co-ordinators is extremely useful although without commitment from the top, conflicting priorities will soon arise. The bottom line is that Internal Audit, as facilitators, must drive the programme and demonstrate enthusiasm unfailingly, i.e., via strong marketing, negotiation and PR initiatives. Yesterday's internal auditor would not have anticipated the need for skills such as those required in today's business environment.

### On-going Maintenance

It is the role of the co-ordinators to review and update the 'Risk & Control Maps' on an on-going basis. The need for formal reporting to senior management and the Board help ensure that the process is carried out, hence the need for the commitment and support from the top at outset.

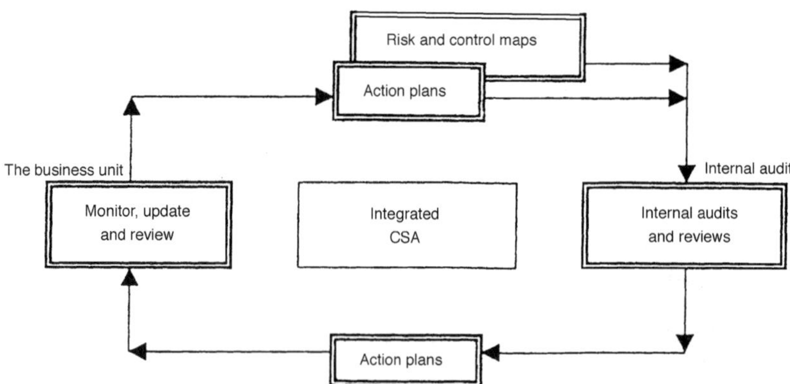


**Figure 16.3** The integrated CSA programme.

The continual input and monitoring from Internal Audit will reinforce the principles of the CSA programme. Internal Audit can actively monitor and integrate CSA in their own process by feeding back findings arising from audits to the respective co-ordinators for input into the Risk & Control Maps. Through this process, CSA in the organisation will be truly 'holistic' and integrated into the business environment. (See Figure 16.3).

## APPENDIX 16.1

# Specimen proformas

## Risk and Control Mapping

The mapping of risks and controls is conducted either by the co-ordinators with the respective managers or at workshops with all relevant parties.

**Risk & Control Maps**

**Business area:** ______________________________

**Key activity or process:** ______________________________

| Key risks | Likelihood (1-5) | Impact (1-5) | Manager responsible | Process controls:- Manual | Automated | Required action (where controls are considered weak) |
|---|---|---|---|---|---|---|
| | | | | | | |
| | | | | | | |
| | | | | | | |
| | | | | | | |
| | | | | | | |
| | | | | | | |
| | | | | | | |
| | | | | | | |
| | | | | | | |
| | | | | | | |

## Self Assessment and Monitoring

Each co-ordinator organises checks of key controls within the respective processes. Some co-ordinators in larger parts of the organisation, e.g., Customer Service, Sales, may assign help from local supervisors to perform these checks.

**Self assessment of controls**

**Business area:** ____________________

**Key activity or process:** ____________________

**Review period:** ____________________

| **Key controls** *(refer to RM as appropriate)* | **Assessment or checks conducted** *(brief description)* | **Results** ✓ Satisfactory ✗ Unsatisfactory | **Action required** | **Completion sign-off by Manager** |
|---|---|---|---|---|
| | | | | |
| | | | | |
| | | | | |
| | | | | |
| | | | | |
| | | | | |
| | | | | |
| | | | | |
| | | | | |
| | | | | |

## Reporting to the Board

On-going progress reports within each business level or entity are encouraged to be produced using existing reporting formats and frequency, e.g., existing monthly or quarterly management meetings. The report format that co-ordinators sought guidance for related to higher level reporting at Board level.

In addition, Internal Audit would express an independent opinion about the satisfactory operation of those controls either through the conduct of normal audits in those areas or specific independent verification. This statement is provided to the Chief Executive Officer.

The following are two proformas for reporting at Board level.

**Report of internal controls to the Director (at least annually)**

**To: (Name of Director)**

**From: (Name of Divisional Manager)** **Date:**

The following are the results of our annual/quarterly assessment and checks of our key systems of controls:

A: (Name of key activity)

The self review checks conducted in the period indicate that the key objectives and risks *(previously agreed/advised)* are being managed properly with the exception of ................................ etc.

As a result, the residual or unmanaged risks or exposure potentially include ......................................... etc.

Remedial action is being instigated/planned ...................................................... etc.

B: (Name of key activity)

etc.

C: (Name of key activity)

etc.

**Report of internal controls to the Chief Executive (annually)**

**To: The Chief Executive**

**From: Director of ____________________** **Date:**

**Copy to: The Chief Internal Auditor**

We have conducted our assessment of systems of controls for the year ending ____________________.

- **to provide an overall statement of the operation of key controls**
- **to state significant areas of breakdown of controls**
- **to state any significant risks that are not being managed adequately and obstacles to management of those risks**
- **to specify planned or outstanding remedial action required.**

## APPENDIX 16.2

# Specific Reference

### Insurance Companies Act

The Insurance Companies Act 1982, Schedule 2 paragraph 6(1)(b) define the criteria for 'sound and prudent management' as

6(1) The insurance company shall not be regarded as conducting business in a sound and prudent manner unless it maintains –
(a) adequate accounting and other records of its business, and
(b) adequate systems of control of its business and records

6(2) Accounting and other records and systems of control shall not be regarded as adequate unless they are such as –
(a) to enable the business of the company to be prudently managed, and
(b) to enable the company to comply with obligations imposed on it under this Act and, in the case of a UK company, enactments in the EEA States that apply to its insurance business.

Furthermore, under paragraph 6(A) of the Insurance Companies (Accounts & Statements) Regulations 1983, as amended, directors are required to certify any published guidance 'with which the systems of control established by the company comply or in accordance with which the (annual return to the HMT (was DTI) ) has been prepared'. This requirement came into effect from 1 January 1995, with the HMT (was DTI) issuing a series of Prudential Guidance Notes covering matters relating to systems of control and preparation of returns.

# Part 4

## The Public-Sector Experience

# 17

# Business Self Assessment in the Department of the Environment, Transport and the Regions (DETR)

*Mike Haselip*

## INTRODUCTION

This chapter will describe the experience of the former Department of the Environment in introducing Business Self Assessment (BSA) which, in essence, is no different from other forms of control self assessment. The terminology Business Self Assessment represents the fact that risk control is a part of business management and not an end in itself.

Successful implementation came about on the back of wider management and cultural changes which had the backing of top management. It required a change in philosophy by the auditors and was helped by the addition of a professional trainer to the audit team. The key to success was the involvement of all staff in the workshop process and their acceptance of ownership of risk management.

## BACKGROUND

The DETR internal audit service is provided by Internal Audit Services (IAS), an in-house team which, perforce, has long been in the vanguard of change. This is largely due to pressures common across all sectors of business. Primary drivers are the Government's policies for encouraging delegated management and inducing efficiencies through, for example, market testing.

Internal Audit Services is comprised of the former Internal Audit units of the Departments of Environment (DOE) and Transport (DOT) and consists of 42 staff operating out of offices in London and Hastings. In addition to providing an audit service to DETR it acts as internal auditor for other bodies, namely, the Planning Inspectorate Agency, Drivers Standards Agency, Vehicle Certification Agency, Marine Safety Agency, Office of the Rail Regulator, Historic Royal Palaces Agency, London Railway Passenger Committee and the Irish, Northern and Trinity House Lighthouse Authorities. It also provides advice and guidance to Chief Executives and internal auditors in some forty DETR Agencies and Non-Departmental Public Bodies (NDPBs).

The introduction of Business Self Assessment (BSA) represented a convergence of the Department's (DETR) wider management philosophy with the continually evolving internal audit service. The experience described below is that of the ex-DOE Management Audit Services Unit (MAS) which now forms part of Internal Audit Services. The Department of Transport Internal Audit Unit had separately developed 'control self-assessment' which was a questionnaire and interview-based approach to identifying control over a handful of basic financial systems; it did not involve workshop discussions with natural work teams and is not described further in this chapter. (As an exposition of this type of approach, see Chapter 9.)

An early mechanism for change was the integration of internal audit with the Department's job evaluation experts (staff inspectors) to form a team tasked with both audit and advisory work. This was not simple brigading but a genuine integration so that today most auditors are required to be proficient organisational analysts and job evaluators. Thus Internal Audit Services was able to broaden the range of its advice beyond systems development to embrace organisational matters. The main rationale for this policy was twofold:

- Job evaluation is an essential audit tool for assessing managers' control over pay.
- By having the ability to switch staff between (reactive) advisory work and (proactive) audit work, optimum use was made of scarce skills.

This change led to greater clarity in the way Internal Audit Services categorised its work and customers. It now has three types of client:

1. Accounting Officers (Chief Executives), on whose behalf they draw up and carry out a programme of core assurance audits.
2. Senior and central line managers who can request an audit of an area within their sphere of interest (secondary assurance audits).
3. Advisory work on request by managers throughout the Department.

The core assurance audit programme is divided into four:

1. Lateral audits where Internal Audit Services assess common functions or performance against strategic objectives, e.g., relating to departmental

training or efficiency management. The aim of such audits is to provide a high-level assessment of control across the organisation.

2. Business systems audits where it looks at a particular aspect of the Department's work. For example, an audit of a specific grant regime related, say, to housing policy, is a business systems audit whereas an audit of grant giving in general would fall under the category of lateral audit. However the trend is towards objective-based audits where Internal Audit Services examines all systems that contribute to a specific strategic objective; to that extent they are becoming more lateral in character.
3. Resource management audits where Internal Audit Services examines the way line managers control their administration budgets. It is in this type of audit that the job evaluation skills are put to best use. The purpose of these audits is primarily to help managers identify problem areas and adopt good practice.
4. Compliance audits of particularly vulnerable areas.

In developing its service Internal Audit Services has long attempted to encourage staff at all levels to participate in the audit process. This was as much a defensive move as an act of enlightenment. Along with most auditors, Internal Audit Services was subject to occasional criticism that it did not understand the business or focus on relevant issues. Auditors did not necessarily disagree with this criticism. Indeed, it was frustrating that those who understood systems best (those who designed or operated them) started to think about risk management only when the auditors came along. Even then the dialogue was mainly with managers whose attention was primarily on getting the things they wanted done without worrying too much about the relevance of tasks to objectives or the efficiency of them.

The traditional approach to auditing meant that line management had no stake in the ownership of the process and most staff were disenfranchised by it. This did not sit well with delegated management and became even more acute when the DOE Departmental Fundamental Review recommended further de-layering and empowerment. Moreover, it was not unknown for managers to employ consultants without asking their staff whether or not they had a problem and, if so, if it could be solved internally. In short, there was a lack of internal communication.

Another Internal Audit Services concern was that the practice of systems auditing was becoming increasingly mechanistic and was bumping up against other analytical tools such as process re-engineering. The basic concept of deducing the health of internal control by reference to the design and operation of systems was proving too dominant and ignored the fact that people are the most important element of control; they – not systems – are the vital factor in making things happen (or not). Auditors have generally long accepted that people can compensate for poor systems design or, conversely, make a good system fail. In short, their actions collectively determine corporate success. This was more noticeable for Internal Audit Services auditors by virtue of their deeper concern for work processes and job design brought about by their involvement in organisational and job analysis. As things stood they were becoming increasingly aware that adherence to systems auditing was divorcing them from real-world risks. But, in common with other auditors, Internal Audit Services was able to address this only as part of a general shift in management philosophy, notably policies designed to reduce hierarchical working and improve communications.

Therefore, development of the audit service coincided with wider changes in the Department. This provided an opportunity to promote audit as the means for achieving the organisation's strategic management objectives. Internal Audit Services had known about the experiments with control and risk self assessment in Gulf Canada for some years and it seemed an appropriate time to adopt it when the Department issued revised delegations to line managers which included specific responsibilities for risk management.

## PILOTING BSA

In December 1994 the DOE Audit Committee agreed to a pilot programme of BSA. It was decided at the outset that Control Self Assessment (CSA) was a non-starter because in the minds of many managers 'control' was a negative concept. Indeed, one aim of BSA was to convince them that control was a positive aid in the achievement of objectives. In any event 'business' self assessment better described what Internal Audit Services was hoping to achieve. The emphasis was to be on work processes to enable natural teams (including managers) to analyse what they do and why, as a precursor to identifying the inherent risks. Business Self Assessment was to be as much about process re-engineering (and efficiency) as the establishment of controls.

It was important that the BSA programme was not seen as a new initiative, adding further burdens on managers already caught up in change management. This was avoided by simply converting a part of the 1995/96 audit programme to Business Self Assessments. Managers were given the choice of joining in the BSA experiment or facing a traditional audit. All opted for BSA! Another important ingredient was the choice of areas. IAS unit deliberately targeted progressive managers responsible between them for disparate businesses ranging from central services to policy advice. Internal

Audit's primary concern was to test the concept in differing environments to ascertain whether or not it could be used across the Department's federal organisation.

The pilot programme gave ownership of the BSA process to the line and was an immediate success. People liked the feeling that their views were being sought and could air them in an informal atmosphere with their colleagues. Managers were often surprised by the depth and originality of suggestions from staff.

Internal Audit Services chose the low-tech approach advocated by Tim Leech. This involved using flipcharts, newsprint, etc., to record the outcome of the brainstorming sessions and subsequent risk prioritisation rather than investing in IT to ensure anonymous voting. As a result IAS was able to start up almost immediately with no extra costs attached. A professional trainer was recruited to help provide those facilitation skills which might not have come naturally to auditors although, in practice, IAS was fortunate to have staff who had the right blend of qualities to make the pilot a success.

From the point of view of credibility it was essential that line staff were not presented with an audit view of control but were allowed to arrive at their own judgements on what was a material risk and how it should be addressed. The workshops were led by Internal Audit facilitators whose task was to provide advice to the workshop team, prompt thoughts and ultimately validate the process. This last point was linked to the fact that BSA was still a part of the audit programme even though ownership of the results rested with line managers. The facilitator had to certify that the team had covered the main points and that its conclusions did not leave the organisation exposed to significant risk.

## THE BSA PROCESS EXPLAINED

There emerged a problem with terminology. Business Self Assessment came to be regarded as a particular process which was defined by its outputs; in this case an action plan which, *inter alia*, listed the organisation's objectives, key risks and agreed action for control (or an acceptance of certain risks). If, as was subsequently the case, facilitated workshops were used for different purposes the temptation was to give them different names (e.g., facilitated discussions). In practice, the core ingredient in all cases is group analysis of work processes and, to that extent, they are all 'business self assessment'. The process broadly consists of planning, workshop and report back. The following paragraphs describe them in more depth where the purpose of the exercise is to help a team develop its risk-management strategy.

## Planning

From the outset it was clear that the key to success would be thorough planning. The starting point was to identify natural teams and understand their common purpose and key objectives. This required the facilitators spending time in talking to individual team members before the workshop. This helped build up a picture of where the team stood in relation to corporate objectives and highlight potential questions. It also enabled the facilitators to learn which issues were of most interest to team members.

Before going live with the pilot, Internal Audit Services experimented with BSA on itself. The exercise enabled the facilitators to explore the process for potential pitfalls and good practice. The result was that IAS was able to have a clearer idea of what would work while benefiting from the BSA outputs.

## The Workshop

IAS soon found that the optimum number of staff in a workshop was about ten. This was manageable in taking the process forward while ensuring that all individuals had a chance to participate. Originally Internal Audit adopted a one-day workshop but it soon became clear that this was too much for all concerned; it moved to two one-half-day meetings which was found to be more conducive to incisive participation. It also meant that the process could be divided into two natural parts.

In the first session the focus was on identifying business processes, discussing the control environment and identifying risks. The heart of the session was a brainstorming of risks which were written down by the facilitators. Participants were then invited to vote for those risks they considered the most important. Here Internal Audit adopted a low-tech version of Pareto voting. Participants were provided with a number (equivalent to 20% of the number of recorded risks) of coloured sticky paper discs. The group was then invited to place the disks on those risks they considered the most important. Each participant was allowed to put only one of their discs on any one risk. Thus a prioritised group consensus of their business risks emerged.

The record of risks and voting results were then quickly written up by the facilitator and circulated to participants. This then provided the starting point for the second session which focused on how best to address the key risks. Options for this ranged from introducing new controls to living with a particular risk.

## Summary Report and Feedback

Following the second workshop the facilitators drew up a report within twenty-four hours containing graphs, discussion of the issues raised and an action plan. This document showed the team's conclusions about the scope for making procedural efficiencies and the need for new or strengthened controls. The report was then agreed by the team and their manager (if he or she did not participate in the workshop). The facilitator advised the manager of any major risks or controls which, in their view, still required attention. But they made it clear at all stages that the process and its outputs were owned by the team and Internal Audit Services's role was simply to advise, guide and act as a catalyst for discussion.

## Reporting to Management

Given that the pilot Business Self Assessment was part of the audit process it was agreed that the facilitators should certify that the team had been thorough in its discussions and that the resultant action plan (as amended following comments at the report-back stage) was sufficient to address key risks. A summary of the report with the facilitator's certificate was sent to senior line managers and Finance Divisions and reported to the Audit Committee. The Committee's main concerns were with matters relating to regularity and propriety; efficiency matters were dealt with as part of the corporate planning process.

## SUBSEQUENT DEVELOPMENT

Such was the success of BSA that the Management Board commissioned a programme of facilitated discussions to help implement some of the recommendations of the Departmental Review. These facilitated discussions differed from the pilot BSA programme in that there was greater emphasis on efficiency matters and the facilitators did not certify the outcome nor report it to Finance or the Audit Committee.

Now that self assessment is in the Department's bloodstream, Internal Audit Services is using it as part of the main audit programme. Increasingly, the scoping study that precedes most audits is being replaced by a facilitated workshop to help staff brainstorm for key risks and controls. This enables IAS to restrict subsequent audit work to those areas where validation is important for providing an independent assurance on control.

Perhaps more important, the workshops enable auditors to form a view on the local control environment. This is defined by a number of factors, e.g., ethical standards, clarity of responsibility, etc., and fed into Internal Audit Services's on-going assessment of relative risk across the Department in which the control environment is a key factor. This, in turn, helps inform the Head of Internal Audit"s annual opinion on the effectiveness of internal control which underpins the Accounting Officer's 'Cadbury' statement in the annual accounts.

## LESSONS LEARNED

### Conduct of BSA

The key is to ensure that the auditors who carry out facilitation work are prepared to trust staff to make judgements about risk and control. They must also learn to talk in simple everyday language that all can understand; audit jargon has to be dispensed with. Even words such as 'risk' and 'control' have to be defined and used with care.

In order to get full value from the process it is essential for the facilitators to get a feel for the control environment, either through discussion of ethical issues or observation. It is important for them to cover corporate issues as well as local ones. The point here is that the auditors can then play back to the Management Board the extent to which its strategic management policies – designed to support a delegated management regime – are working in practice.

### Characteristics of Successful Teams

In order for the workshop to achieve its aims it is important that between them, members of the team have the skills and knowledge required to undertake the work in question. It would be pointless to talk about risk if the only member of staff who knows about a key process is not present. And each member should have a clear understanding of their role which is essential for identifying efficiency savings by eliminating duplication or unnecessary tasks.

Communication during the workshops must be relevant, direct and frank. The facilitator's role is crucial in ensuring this comes about and that discussion is not unduly dominated by over-articulate individuals or managers. Conversely, diffident members of the team need to be encouraged to speak out. Here, the services of a trained facilitator could be invaluable in maximising individual participation. Well-directed discussion can lead to a growing interest in upgrading performance.

## Value of BSA in Improving Internal Control

Business Self Assessment is a natural part of delegated management. It helps place responsibility for control where it properly belongs. It also enhances communication at all levels and contributes to the development of empowered teams. By drawing staff into the process of risk analysis it provides balance and perspective in the context of local business objectives thereby overcoming the artificiality of centre-led risk assessment. By definition, this will lead to consideration of matters such as quality and environmental impact which are not readily considered by those auditors who tend still to see risk largely in financial terms. Another important advantage is that the workshops throw up reliable diagnostics on elements such as teamwork, leadership, objective setting, performance appraisal, process analysis, skills appraisal, etc. It also assists in developing team building by addressing inherent conflicts within the team and streamlining procedures.

From the auditors' point of view BSA enables them to get a much clearer and informed idea of internal control and the environment in which it exists. They are seen as helping to develop management processes rather than as a backward-looking checker. The auditors are able to focus on the key issues and read across the whole organisation to identify instances where two or more teams are wrestling with the same problems in isolation.

There is nothing new or original in what has been achieved in DETR. It is simply that BSA came at the point when there was a convergence in (a) the stage of Internal Audit Services's service development, (b) the demands of corporate governance brought about by the work of the Cadbury and Nolan Committees and (c) changes to the Department's corporate management strategy. Therefore timing was important but the overriding conclusion is that Business Self Assessment – and similar techniques – will succeed only if the organisation is culturally ready to use it as part of corporate management strategy.

## Key Success Factors

- Business Self Assessment should be seen as part of the corporate management strategy.
- Top managers must be receptive to cultural change.
- It is essential to involve all staff in natural teams not just managers.
- Keep the process and language simple.
- Ensure that you have the right blend of experience, skills and knowledge to undertake the task.

- Trust the team to make its own judgements.
- Do not view control as an end in itself or think that only auditors understand it.
- Above all remember the origin of the word 'audit' and LISTEN!

# 18

# CSA in Local Government

## A Study in Change

*Neil Cowan*

## RISK MANAGEMENT IN LOCAL GOVERNMENT

The concept of total risk management is relatively new to local government. History shows an *ad hoc* approach with some major or obvious risks being addressed, as, for example, in planning to cope with particular emergencies, whilst purchase of insurance has typically taken care of all other anticipated risks.

Risk management is, of course, much more than finding insurance cover for all possible risks. Even if this was good management practice, today's insurance market and the cost of premiums mitigate against such a simplistic policy. Risk management, therefore, should seek to identify and evaluate all risks faced by an authority and thereafter work to control and minimise these risks. This process will help to reduce losses – financial, physical and humanitarian – whilst improving service standards.

Managing risk means identifying all risks which may adversely affect an authority in attempting to achieve its objectives. This management activity attempts to balance the probability of a particular risk arising against the action that may be taken to either combat the risk or accept it as being of little threat. Insurance will be part of the solution, but not the whole answer.

The skills of the risk manager must also move; from an understanding of the insurance market to identifying trends in performance, undertaking benchmarking, pointing out training needs, getting the best out of loss adjustors, forecasting probabilities, initiating schemes of risk identification, undertaking insurance negotiations, maintaining a self-insurance fund and using IT to keep large volumes of data with easy access.

The history of departmentalism in local government recognises the functions of the engineer, the architect, the teacher and others, as specialists but does little to assist the corporate approach to problems that affect every operation of the authority but can least well be addressed by departmental managers. Specialist managers tend to be task-orientated and have neither the information nor the will to see beyond their remit. Thus, even if risks are recognised and action taken in the particular specialism, no cognisance will be taken of the possible impact on the rest of the organisation. Perhaps even worse, no advantage will be taken of collective knowledge and experience, or economies of scale, where these are relevant.

Risk management seeks to identify and evaluate all risks faced by an authority and take action to minimise their possible impact on an authority's operations. Risk self assessment aims to provide information on risks by utilising a bottom-up approach which will identify risks at the places and by the people where they will be faced. In other words, the intention of self assessment is to put the onus for identifying risks where it belongs; with those who see risks arising, or are exposed to them, on a day-to-day basis.

## CONTROL SELF ASSESSMENT (CSA) IN PRACTICE

The impetus for CSA in Fife Regional Council came initially from work generated by the Council's risk management group. The risk management group was set up as an initiative which would redirect the Council's historic reliance on insurance as the only mechanism for handling all statutory and other possible liabilities. Identifying and evaluating risks, i.e., managing them, had not hitherto been part of the management culture. However, factors such as the demise of the Municipal Mutual Insurance Company – with the consequent difficulty in obtaining cover at reasonable cost – and the need to set up a self-insurance fund to cater for such major risks as fire, began to concentrate minds.

Unlike the private sector, where CSA has been, in the main, a response to a board of directors' need for better control asssurance – usually so that the board can comment on internal control in its annual statement – in local government, any improvement in control *per se* has come about as a by-product of a different approach to risk management. This is certainly what happened at Fife Regional Council.

The risk management group consisted of Directorate-level representatives, with the chair being Assistant Director of Finance, (Operational Review). Departments represented included the major operating departments (and, as a consequence, the higher-spending departments), together with others with an obvious interest; transport, for example, where an upward trend in vehicle accidents was causing concern from the points of view of human suffering as well as cost.

In line with contemporary thinking, the group first agreed on its mission and its main objectives. The mission was easily formulated and, in essence, was to identify and evaluate all risks faced by the Council and take action to minimise their possible impact on Council operations. In summary, the objectives were to:

- control and reduce risk of losses
- reduce expenditure on losses
- maintain service standards
- improve employee morale.

The task of the risk management group was to seek new methods and devise new procedures for identifying all the many risks which could adversely affect the authority in attempting to meet its objectives. In tandem with this main task, the group had to review methods for internal charging (allocation) of insurance premiums and the resourcing and use of the in-house (self insurance) pool or fund.

## DEVELOPING THE RISK SELF ASSESSMENT MODEL

The risk management group was the vehicle which allowed a risk self assessment model to be developed in the authority as a means of identifying risks in all operations which had hitherto been ignored by the centre (or unknown to it) or covered by blanket – and expensive – insurance. This move sat well with the Council's developing approach to decentralisation and local empowerment and, for that reason, was seen to be politically acceptable. Departments were willing to at least pay lip service to the theory in the knowledge that the politicians would be amenable to an initiative which seemed to fit with their own emerging philosophy.

Before the establishment of the risk management group, assessment of risk – to the extent that it was undertaken – was a function of the Finance Department and its Insurance Section. Input from operating departments was minimal other than to bemoan their lack of control over allocated insurance charges; departments played little part in identifying risks or actively preventing mishaps. Thus, the intention to develop a whole new approach to managing risk, which actively involved departmental personnel at all levels, presented problems initially with management culture and approach.

The Head of the Operational Review Division (the Council's internal audit, performance review and internal consultancy division), as the chair of the risk management group, was the obvious candidate to develop and drive risk self assessment. At this stage, the tasks were twofold: (a) to research and bring forward a methodology that would work in the particular circumstances of the Council and (b) to lobby the Chief

Executive and heads of department in order to have the concept agreed in principle.

The methodology leaned heavily on published work and, in the main, already tried and tested. The foundation stone, therefore, was the concept of putting the onus for identifying risks where it belongs; with those who see risks arising, or are exposed to them, on a day-to-day basis. The intention was to devolve risk assessment to departments, divisions, sections, units and individuals with, ultimately, the information gained from these assessments being collated, evaluated and acted upon centrally.

The process required workgroups to be identified which would be relatively small and at a level both to be familiar with their immediate working environment and understand the risks faced on an everyday basis. The groups could have been, for example, a small primary school, a highways repair team, a home for the elderly or a section of a central support department.

Each group would have to establish what its work objectives were since risks would be directly related to the achievement (or non-achievement) of these objectives. The methodology accepted that the way to do this as a start was to establish the objectives of the workgroup in relation to, firstly, the council's strategic objectives and secondly, the strategy and plans of the department and/or division/section.

It was accepted that the process would make use of a particularly scarce resource, time. Personnel at all levels would have to take time out from their normal routines in order to take part in self assessment. The selling points, however, were that there would be overall benefit to the Council by undertaking the process and that, since all employees would be giving input to the undertaking, it would be seen as participative, good for employee relations and part of the move towards devolving power – a new ethos for the Council. It was accepted also that probably the largest slice of time and effort would come in setting up the self assessment process – designing systems, training and then facilitating the groups themselves in undertaking the process.

## THE SELF ASSESSMENT PROCESS

The authority's information systems were sophisticated, well developed and considered to be at the leading edge of technology. Despite this, it was decided that information gathering would be by means of paper records, at least for the pilot study. The main reason for this decision was the wide diversity of council front-line employees. Whilst many were computer literate and used keyboards in their day-to-day work, many others were not trained or ready in this way to meet the challenge of, for example, computerised hand-held voting systems.

The process began by recognising that there are two levels of risk; the macro level, i.e., corporate and departmental risks and the micro level, i.e., unit or workgroup risks. Within these two levels objectives have to be known and interrelated. Thus, working from the bottom up, each group needs to know corporate and departmental objectives. The group must then state, discuss and refine its own objectives and relate these to the macro objectives. Knowing its objectives, the group then has to consider all the risks that can be identified which may prevent the group achieving its objectives. The risks and their consequences, having been categorised as acceptable or unacceptable, require then to be prioritised.

The basic form for recording information required simply the writing down of the objectives which each work group had refined from discussions of its *raison d'être*, associated risks to attainment of the objective, the consequences of the risk, a priority and an existing or suggested control.

The Operational Review Division was to undertake training of line managers and supervisors, emphasising not just the mechanics of the process but the background to its implementation and the expected beneficial outcome. The Operational Review Division was also to undertake the role of facilitators when the process got under way at workgroup level and subsequently, to collate the data centrally on a database using existing software.

It was accepted that there would always be some residual risks and that some, because of the particular circumstances of local government, might be relatively significant. These could come about through lack of funding, environmental factors, inadequately trained staff and the motivation and morale of key employees.

It was decided that CSA should first be run as a pilot scheme in two small central departments and one major department. Clearly, however, the whole self assessment initiative depended upon heads of department enthusiastically embracing the concept and its consequences.

## IMPLEMENTING CSA

The Chief Executive could see the benefits of an holistic approach to risk management and was easily convinced of the role that CSA could play in a more unified approach to corporate management and control. The Council's approach to management depended upon a more democratic approach, however, and most decisions of a strategic management nature had to be put to and agreed by the heads of departments meeting as the Management Team. Thus, the Chief Executive agreed to 'sponsor' a paper on CSA drawn up by the Head of the Operational Review Division for presentation to the Management Team. In the meantime, the pilot sudy went ahead.

The two central departments chosen to take part in the pilot were small with only a few employees. Workgroups of six to eight staff were easily identified and training delivered quickly and with good understanding on the part of the staff being trained. This was, in all probability, because the staff concerned were trained administrators, understood technology and were close to the authority's corporate core. Having been trained, each group undertook the CSA process and returned completed forms for entry into the database.

The largest department chosen – incidentally, the authority's biggest-spending department – did not fare so well. Despite a Directorate member of that department being on the risk management group and having participated in the strategy and decision making which led to the setting up of the pilot scheme, the Head of the Department expressed strong reservations both on the utility of the CSA approach and on the large resource (as he saw it) that would be required to put the scheme into operation. The scheme was vetoed by that head of department until such time as the CSA process as a whole was agreed by the Management Team and implemented by the entire Council.

When the paper on CSA was put to the Management Team by the Chief Executive, no opportunity was given for the only real 'expert' in the process (the Head of the Operational Review Division) to give a presentation, answer questions, allay fears or amplify the bare bones of the paper. Thus, rather than seeing the medium- and longer-term benefits of CSA, both in terms of improved control and risk reduction, it appeared that the heads of departments concentrated on the dis-benefit of the time input needed to make the scheme a success. The enthusiasm of the Chief Executive on this occasion was unequal to the staid traditionalism of the rest of the management team.

The CSA initiative foundered and was wrecked at this point. Ironically, a proposal by the Council's main insurer to undertake reviews of insurable risks in the properties of the same largest-spending department which had turned down the CSA pilot, was approved. Presumably, this was because there was no up-front cost or resource input required from that department and, therefore, no obvious dis-benefit. The lack of consideration of other risks, the lack of independence of the insurer's own staff and the probable increase in short-term cost through an insurance only solution, seemed not to count.

## FUTURE OF CSA IN LOCAL GOVERNMENT

The imperative of better internal control as part of an effective corporate governance strategy in the private sector seems not yet to have been grasped by local government. Whilst many private-sector corporate governance initiatives and requirements do not apply directly to local government, nonetheless the principles of, for example, the Cadbury Code of Best Practice or the Combined Code, can be adopted with good effect. CSA may have first come to prominence in the private sector because of a board of directors' need to be more certain of its ability to report on the effectiveness of internal control; now, however, it can be seen *inter alia* as a contributor to efficiency as well as to the effectiveness of control. In this role, i.e., as an efficient process in the review of control, CSA has the potential to be embraced by all organisations, whatever the sector of the economy.

CSA can work in local government, although it should not be seen as the panacea for all ills. It has a part to play in the overall review of internal control and the limited experience of the process – as shown by this chapter – indicates that the pure mechanics are not a problem. There is potential for both improving control and reducing cost, after the initial resource implications have been taken care of, provided that the facilitators of the process gain converts at every level in the organisation. Efforts to achieve cost reduction ought to be a driving force in local government and that is without even considering the less obvious benefits of improved employee motivation and morale which are available from a well-engineered scheme.

Clearly, developing a workable scheme is not a problem for local government. What may be a problem, however, for many authorities will be gaining high-level commitment. If internal control, risk management and insurance are seen by authorities to be only within the purview of the Treasurer, then obtaining that commitment may be an even greater problem.

Managers of all disciplines and at all levels, particularly at the highest level, need to be persuaded that managing risks and being responsible for control is an essential part of their function. A move away from departmentalism to a more generalist approach to managing operations will change the face of local government in the future and make it more amenable to innovative ideas such as CSA. Local authority associations, as well as councils themselves, have a role to play in this process in developing best practice in all functions and specialities. CSA is just such a best practice; it needs to be appraised and adopted by the professional and political associations and offered as one of the means by which authorities can be managed more effectively.

## CONCLUSION

Local government is a unique area of the economy but has much in common with other sectors and, in terms of principles of management, probably varies little from any other type of organisation. There is, however, still much of tradition evident in the way that local government functions and this tends to militate against change and innovation. Long audit plan life-cycles are as prevalent in local government as elsewhere. This is one of the reasons why CSA has been seen by managements as a means for focusing on risk and devising the associated controls in such a way as to avoid overreliance on a none-too-frequent internal (or external) audit review.

CSA requires commitment from senior and middle managers but it is at much lower levels that time and, therefore, money has to be put into the process. Success depends upon being able to convince those at workgroup level that it is worth their while investing time and effort into what may be seen as yet another management initiative. And, of course, if there is no real top-level commitment, that will soon become evident to those further down the chain.

Organisations which already have a culture of devolved management and empowerment may fare better in introducing CSA than others. A well-motivated workforce used to good two-way communicaations and operating in a framework of leading-edge management practice is more likely to embrace the concept of CSA and see the benefits. The more traditional structures and practitioners are more likely to balk at the extent of change before seeing the long-term benefits that CSA can engender.

Without commitment and enthusiastic implementation, CSA will fail. Value for money is a compelling argument, however, and it is likely that, if existing resources can be used to provide better internal control assurance via CSA, then it will be a brave manager who will ignore its possibilities.

# 19

# Control Self Assessment – The UK Experience in Local Government
## Doing it the Ashford Way

*David King*

## BACKGROUND

### Changing Environment

Ashford Borough Council has, like many local authorities, been undergoing continuous transformation. A different political complexion, development of a corporate strategy, restructuring, coupled with the pursuit of improved quality, customer focus and governance have all influenced the direction, pace and shape of Ashford's business base.

### Impact on Risks and Control

As Ashford has reviewed and changed its policies and procedures against this constantly moving environment, so strategies, structures and systems have become more complex and onerous. Managers have had to cope with technological and commercial developments whilst seeking greater financial autonomy, flexibility and freedom to make informed operational judgements.

The financial and operational risks associated with service delivery have taken on new dimensions. Fresh unattended risks have been created while some existing risks have taken on greater importance, yet the adequacy of the control mechanisms and frameworks in place and management's speed of response to identify, minimise and safeguard against these risks has sometimes been challenged. In some instances, managers have tended to off-load and subordinate their responsibilities, looking towards the internal auditors to provide essential control features and act as surrogate managers.

## Internal Audit's Limitations

Before the introduction of CSA, Ashford's internal audit service, with a staffing complement of four auditors, had been run essentially on traditional lines geared towards satisfying its chief finance officer's statutory responsibility for sound financial administration. Whilst seen as relatively successful in that respect by excelling in the policing and investigation of irregularities; maintenance of standards and provision of sound advice, there was an increasing perception that the internal audit's coverage of other areas was often superficial, narrow in its scope and predictable in its approach.

There was also a perception that the internal audit service was flirting with the real risks that influence and threaten the Council's business base. Despite the development of a risk matrix and regular maintenance of audit plans, risks were often evaluated on gut feeling with important non-financial areas, where arguably the more significant risks are located, often shied away from. As a consequence, the internal audit service was in danger of missing the big issues, failing to make a proper contribution to the Council's business development and provide adequate assurances about the Council's overall governance.

## Realisation of Need for a New Approach

There was one further realisation. Unless the resources of the internal audit service were increased to match the expanding frequency, complexity and speed of change taking place in the Council, the auditors were going to become increasingly reliant on management and staff generally to maintain the essential controls that the auditors wished to see in existence.

Given such increasing reliance, how would the internal auditors know that the managers and staff charged with operating and maintaining those important controls were committed and able to do so? What did the internal auditors really know about these people? How dedicated and good were they? How sound were their communication links and the information they used? What did they really care about financial and operational matters? What were their skills and values and what quality standards did they perform to? It was clear that unless the internal auditors understood these issues, i.e., the control environment in which the managers and staff operated, then the internal auditors could not have any confidence that recommended controls would be implemented and maintained robustly and reliably.

It was evident that a new and vibrant technique was needed which brought together managerial and auditing skills and experiences to ensure that the Council's control environment was assessed properly and its business and quality objectives, associated risks and essential controls, were reviewed in such a fashion that managers and internal auditors were able to provide proper assurances to senior management and stakeholders generally. At the same time the technique needed to be able to satisfy the chief finance officer's statutory responsibility and meet the external auditor's quest for governance and managed audit status.

On the face of it, control self assessment (CSA) provided the internal auditors with a mechanism for giving those assurances and as a consequence it became one of the driving forces for the further research which ensued.

## RESEARCH

### Basis of Research

Research in the summer of 1996 endeavoured to establish the extent to which CSA could improve the management of local authority business objectives, risk and controls and therefore contribute significantly to local authority governance. The main research, based on a questionnaire followed by structured interviews with identified users, aimed to establish the extent and manner by which CSA was being developed in local government and the level of success enjoyed.

### Scope of Main Research

The questionnaire was aimed at eighty local authorities in England representing an untapped source of information. Forty-eight responded to the questionnaire, namely: 38 District Councils; 2 County Councils; 2 London Boroughs; 2 Metropolitan Borough Councils; 4 Unitary Authorities.

### Principal Outcomes of the Main Research

Eight of the local authorities (and they were all District Councils) were using some form of CSA. A further sixteen were planning pilot schemes. Structured interviews with senior auditors from the eight District Councils revealed a diverse approach to the subject. Reasons for adopting CSA ranged from District Audit pressure, the pursuit of management theory, internal audit's desire to use modern techniques, senior management's appetite for change and even simple curiosity. The technique was owned and driven by managers, by internal auditors, and in some instances by both. Financial and non-financial areas were being examined.

The self assessment methods adopted by the users differed, with some of the local authorities using formal workshops, others just relying on questionnaires but only one using both techniques (and then only infrequently). None of the users was operating secret voting arrangements to promote frank and uninhibited disclosure of unattended risks and poor controls and none had adopted arrangements to assess their organisation's control environment.

The interviews also identified some weaknesses in the way CSA was being managed. There was little regard for the cost of implementation. There was an absence of structured approach to the management of change issues arising from using CSA and little attention paid to proper training requirements for facilitators and participants. Only two of the eight users had seen fit to seek their external auditor's view on the use and acceptance of CSA. There was also insufficient attention to outputs and inadequate use of review mechanisms for testing CSA's effectiveness.

The results indicated a rather haphazard and superficial approach which was not particularly flattering to the internal audit profession in local government. Not surprisingly, the results from using CSA ranged from no improvement to moderate achievement in improving control. Only one of the eight users claimed considerable success.

On a high note, the users were unanimous in regarding CSA as a technique which complemented the traditional internal audit approach. All eight users of CSA were, at the time of the survey, committed to its development and were generally optimistic about the technique's long-term future and its eventual contribution towards local authority governance.

The research painted a picture of uncertainty. The reasons are clear. Not everyone is sufficiently conversant with the principles of CSA or convinced that existing traditional audit methods are deficient or that CSA fits within the local government culture. There is still doubt about who should own and drive the technique and whether it is an instrument for examining financial issues only or a means of addressing a wider base. There is little guidance available on how best to prepare for introducing CSA or how it is actually done. Although there is much talk about workshops there is little practical advice on how to run one and despite there being constant reference to questionnaires for assessing the control environment there is little opportunity of acquiring a suitable copy.

Finally, despite all the hype, there is little tangible evidence within local government circles to demonstrate that CSA actually works, consequently there is little enthusiasm for making the effort to get started.

## PRACTICAL ISSUES OF RUNNING CSA

### CSA – the Ashford Way

It is against the backdrop of research and uncertainty that several CSA pilot schemes have been run at Ashford Borough Council to test the principles and mechanics of the technique. The main issues arising from the pilot schemes are now presented in four parts:

- A working definition of CSA based on the way it is being developed at Ashford.
- A valuable insight into the early decisions that need to be made and issues to be considered before embarking on the introduction of CSA.
- The practical issues of actually running pilot schemes and the pitfalls and barriers that need to be overcome if CSA is to be implemented successfully.
- The real benefits of CSA – a working example.

These matters are now examined in depth and solutions offered.

### Working Definition of CSA

- Control self assessment is a practical process involving workgroups with auditors providing a facilitating role. It is not a one-to-one arrangement neither is it simply a process of sending out questionnaires for managers to complete with auditors responding to the adverse replies. Essentially, it requires people to talk to each other openly about their successes, their problems and their aspirations.
- It involves an early assessment of the control environment.
- It requires the identification and critical analysis of current business objectives, risks and controls, followed by a redefinition of the principal objectives, key risks and essential controls that will demand and justify future management and audit attention.
- It requires agreement by managers and auditors on suitable action to fulfil the principal objectives and introduce essential controls and arrangements within a reasonable and appropriate timeframe.
- It recognises that any residual unimportant risks and controls will not receive the same (or perhaps any) level of management and audit recognition in future.

## Early Decisions and Issues before Embarking on CSA

### *Why should auditors get involved?*

Irrespective of what the purists may say about CSA being a management tool, the reality is that it is unlikely to get off the ground and be sustained unless internal audit is there to organise the process, facilitate in the workshops, provide essential momentum and give support in a comprehensive and robust fashion.

There are also significant benefits to the internal auditor being involved in the process and receiving essential information about the reliability (or otherwise) of the control environment, about significant changes that have developed or are about to transpire and the changing complexion of key risks and controls. For these reasons it would seem eminently sensible for the development of and participation in CSA to be a joint effort between managers and auditors in which the identification of problems and the search for solutions are shared.

### *Why focus on the early assessment of the control environment?*

Early assessment of the control environment is essential if auditors are to understand the things that influence and colour the manner in which managers and staff function and affect the quality of the processes, controls and services emanating from their efforts.

### *What does assessment of the control environment involve?*

It is essential that those participating in the workshops are encouraged to record and give freely their views about the environment in which they work without fear of recrimination. Emphasis should be on establishing and assessing the participants'

- level of understanding of core values, work objectives and associated risks
- degree of confidence in leadership and management
- ethical standards
- level of job satisfaction
- attitudes towards their remuneration and other rewards
- views on management's recognition and encouragement of good work and ideas
- commitment to high quality and continuous improvement
- views on trust and security

- levels of skill and delegation
- sufficiency of funds, other resources, the right tools, equipment and training
- views on staffing structures
- opinions on access to information, their confidence levels in the accuracy of the information they produce and receive and the adequacy of the arrangements for securing and recovering such information
- assessment of the adequacy of their planning processes in respect of future work and use of resources
- ability to satisfy their work objectives
- views on the effectiveness of team work
- opinions on their performance measurement arrangements and the value of the work they do
- feelings towards the quality of management
- opinions on the adequacy of the arrangements to test customer and user needs and views
- ability to make changes based on their learning process
- understanding of, compliance with and confidence in the control mechanisms relating to both financial and operational activities.

Essentially, these issues have been developed at Ashford based on the four control components – Purpose, Commitment, Capability and Learning – which form the CoCo framework from The Criteria of Control Committee of the Canadian Institute of Chartered Accountants, *Guidance on Criteria Control*, August 1994.

## *How will views on the control environment be extracted?*

A comprehensive questionnaire addressing the above issues with provision for secret voting will provide participants with the means of expressing their views in confidence and enable the facilitator to consolidate the views and assess the associated strengths and weaknesses.

Constructing such a questionnaire is not easy. Questions may be clear and appropriate to senior management but ambiguous and irrelevant to junior staff leading to distortion of results and interpretation. At Ashford, the control questionnaire, which contains sixty-eight questions, has had to be reviewed and changed after each CSA pilot scheme to fine tune the content but it is unlikely that it will ever be perfected and there is no guarantee that someone in a future workshop will not point out a flaw or ambiguity or simply insist that a question is not relevant to them. Appendix 19.1 provides examples of the questions posed in the Ashford questionnaire.

Whilst the desire to use a soundly constructed questionnaire is understandable, it is equally important to appreciate that not too much emphasis should be placed on the semantics of the questionnaire and the deep meaning of the statistical analysis flowing from it. The exercise should be aimed at identifying the key but simple messages, i.e., the important strengths and weaknesses about the control environment. Experience has shown that these are often highlighted very clearly without too much of a scientific approach. There is a tendency for participants to race through the questionnaire and to discuss it amongst themselves. It is important to stress that they should take their time and that individual views are being sought at this stage of the CSA process.

Questionnaires should be completed by means of secret voting but the difficulty is deciding what form this should take. Rapid-response technology with electronic keypads for participants to punch their answers with anonymity is available but at a price to which most internal audit budgets, or perhaps even corporate budgets, might not extend.

At Ashford, secret voting is based on technology at the other end of the scale – sticky blue dots available from the local stationers which participants place against the appropriate answers on the questionnaire sheets. The blue dots are cheap, never fail to introduce a degree of lightheartedness into the proceedings (which helps relax the participants) and the method works but the downside is that the results cannot be seen immediately and need to be analysed in between the workshops.

## *What level should CSA focus on?*

Immediate use of CSA at strategic level is an appealing option. It is likely to attract much attention from senior management and Council members. If used successfully, it will be seen to be addressing the bigger picture and adding value to the authority's key business activities. Success at this level will almost guarantee future usage and development of the technique and boost the internal audit profile.

However, CSA needs to be handled carefully and the technique mastered. Inability to use CSA properly and effectively, particularly at strategic level where failure would be very public, is likely to result in loss of confidence and early termination of the technique.

CSA has a steep learning curve and logic suggests that initial trials should be pitched at smaller, more modest activities, and on friendly ground, where the gaze of senior management and Council members may not be so catastrophic in the event of default.

### *Should CSA be aimed at corporate issues or is it safer to begin with functional areas?*

Corporate application of CSA has the same attraction as using the technique at strategic level but it will almost certainly require a multi-disciplined approach to the composition of the workshop participants. This will present further challenges to auditors in their facilitating roles, not just in terms of arranging the workshops but ensuring that the workshop participants remain focused on the subject matter and progress is not compromised by departmentalism.

Applying CSA initially to smaller self-contained functional areas may not provide the same rich rewards as examining corporate issues but it is probably safer to do so until the art of running workshops is learned.

### *Should CSA be limited to traditional financial risk areas or focus on wider operational issues as well?*

Organisational business is not just about money. It is about such wider issues as strategies, people, machines, methods, research and development, information flows, improvement of standards and quality, knowing how the job gets done and the risks and problems that these issues generate. Auditors must stop thinking in purely financial terms and 'get stuck into' these wider issues if they are to understand and therefore make a valid contribution to their local authority's overall business development and governance. Therefore application of CSA in its widest sense is recommended.

### *Should CSA address such matters as quality improvement, cultural and human resource issues?*

These are matters fundamental to the successful application of CSA. The technique is all about looking at the bigger picture and any use of it which excludes these important areas will inevitably be deficient in its conclusions and contribution towards business development and control. The message is that there are no half measures with CSA and there are no limitations to its use.

### *Who needs to be consulted before CSA gets off the ground?*

Internal auditors need to think very carefully about this aspect. It is not just about consulting; it is about marketing and auditors are perhaps not very good at this. Auditors will need to get their act together and be well rehearsed if CSA is going to be promoted successfully. Selection of a champion to promote CSA, manage the change processes, overcome any resistance, and undertake the essential backstage work required to gain support for the technique and sell its potential will be critical.

Chief finance officers of local authorities, with Section 151 responsibilities, will need to be convinced that CSA fits with those obligations. Chief Executives and elected Council members should be interested in the strategic and corporate benefit of CSA to the organisation so early discussions with them is recommended. Liaison with the Head of Human Resources is critical before the control environment, with its cultural and human resource connotations, is examined and the trades unions will need to be convinced that the motives behind CSA are legitimate if resistance to it is to be avoided.

Resistance is also likely to come from some internal audit staff who may view breaking away from traditional audit coverage as sacrilege. Accordingly, it is important that internal audit staff are kept informed of the reasons for developing CSA and convinced of the benefits if they are to support the process and be asked to act as facilitators. CSA represents a radical breakaway from traditional audit thinking so external audit will need to be consulted to ensure that CSA is acknowledged as a credible part of the managed audit concept and able to contribute to improving overall governance.

The chief officer of the department in which CSA is to be piloted will need to be convinced about the paybacks if valuable staff time is to be dedicated to attendance at workshops. 'What is in it for me?' is likely to be a prominent question put to any auditor promoting CSA. Accordingly, internal audit will need to be sure what those paybacks are. They must be attractive and meaningful but not over-sold. It is also a good marketing ploy to encourage the chief officer to select the subject to be examined rather than for the auditor to be seen to be dictating the choice.

### *How will CSA be accommodated within the audit plan?*

Accommodating CSA presents a problem. Internal audit services with fixed resources or limited budgets are unlikely to be able to employ additional audit resources. Engaging consultants is doubtful for the same reasons and some consultants have yet to experience or master the technique. Most strategic audit plans are already spread thinly, some over four, five or six years, so stretching strategic plans even further to accommodate CSA will be undesirable.

Fitting CSA into existing strategic plans will mean that something will have to go. On the face of it this appears to be unacceptable but there are internal audit services which continue to cling on to non-audit duties or regularly revisit favourite audit haunts (such as officers' travel claims, inventories, petty cash and similar easy pickings) instead of stepping back and questioning the value of these audits and the need for them at all. Heads of internal audit must be prepared to look objectively at these and other 'small beer' activities and question seriously whether CSA might be a better and more rewarding proposition.

Control self assessment will never be a complete substitute for traditional audit coverage and the proportion of time that CSA takes up within audit plans will be very much for each head of internal audit to determine having regard for local circumstance. Whatever the outcome, the chief finance officer and external auditor will need to be satisfied with any revised arrangements for accommodating CSA.

At Ashford, audit resources used in implementing CSA have been equivalent to around 10% of the annual audit plan. However, as a consequence of the Council's recent restructuring arrangements, internal audit is to become part of the corporate planning and review function. Accordingly, it is likely that CSA will feature more prominently at the corporate and strategic level and therefore consume a greater part of the audit plan in future.

### *With whom will the facilitator liaise to organise the workshops?*

The workshops are not just going to happen of their own accord. They need to be planned and co-ordinated. Suitable dates for participants to attend all the workshops will need to be agreed and adequate accommodation arranged. It is important that workshop dates do not clash with main holidays and high peaks in departmental work and personal commitments. Continuity of attendance at workshops is important.

Experience has shown that appointing a liaison officer (ordinarily the service manager responsible for the subject matter to be examined) with whom the facilitator may discuss workshop preparation details and matters arising as the workshops progress is vital if the CSA process is to be managed well.

### *Who is going to attend the workshops?*

The case for the auditor acting as facilitator has already been put. What remains is to decide who else should attend. Unequivocally, the workshop should reflect the whole spectrum of officers involved in the subject matter under examination, from senior management to the clerical officers including any operatives involved.

Attendance by senior management is essential in order that they are in tune with the manner in which the workshops have developed, the problems and issues raised and the proposed solutions. The downside is that other staff may feel inhibited by their presence but that is something which the facilitator must address and hopefully overcome. Attendance by other staff is fundamental to the CSA process because it is those on the 'shop floor' responsible for the day-to-day tasks who often hold the key to identifying the real weaknesses and risks of their work and the likely business solutions. CSA should be a learning process for all who attend.

## *How many should attend a workshop?*

The Ashford experience has shown that as few as five can provide an effective forum provided all those in attendance feel sufficiently comfortable in contributing actively to the proceedings.

## *How many workshops will the CSA process need?*

This is difficult to say. The minimum experienced at Ashford to complete the CSA process has been two (involving seven participants) and the maximum has been seven workshops (involving five participants). There are several important factors that will influence the number of workshops required.

- The more complex and wide-ranging subjects under examination are likely to demand a greater number of workshops to ensure that coverage has been sound. Experience has shown that the more contained and focused subjects are likely to require fewer workshops.
- The extent to which participants are prepared to engage in free and frank discussion. Some workshop participants will never speak during the workshops whilst others will endeavour to dominate or use the occasion to raise obscure issues.
- The ability of the facilitator to keep the workshops 'on track'.
- The length of each workshop. Whole-day workshops tend to sap participants' attention spans and can be very demanding and tiring for the facilitator. Half-day sessions (lasting, say, for three hours each) can be more successful but lead to an increased number of workshops and a longer period between the start and finish of the CSA process.

## *Who needs training?*

The managers and staff participating in the workshops will require an appreciation of the principles and aims of CSA, although this may be provided briefly at the commencement of the first workshop. The main training must be aimed at those auditors who are to act as facilitators in the workshops. However, not all auditors will be capable of performing well in this unique capacity. It requires confidence and special skills to run and keep a workshop on track, develop a 'no blame' environment in which the participants feel able to speak freely and generate and maintain a steady flow of debate. CSA also demands an understanding of the technical issues and key points, ability to provide commentary and advice on proposed controls whilst maintaining essential notes of the proceedings.

The CSA workshops are 'no hiding' places. The facilitator's performance will be under scrutiny and if he or she is unable to control the proceedings and demonstrate empathy towards operational problems the workshop process will fail. Any attempt by the facilitator to 'come on strong' regarding financial (in particular, fraudulent) matters will be an instant turnoff for the participants who need to be convinced that the auditor is there to take a wide interest in their business activities and not use the occasion to 'beat the audit drum'.

Facilitators therefore need tenacity and an awareness of and sensitivity towards business issues. An understanding of the history of CSA, its principles and aims will be fundamental in preparing auditors for CSA pilot schemes. A sound appreciation of the concept of risk, the construction of the questionnaire used for assessing the control environment and ways of interpreting the results will be critical.

Every opportunity to rehearse and develop a workshop facilitating role should be taken but whilst planning and practising CSA are important, no amount of preparation will guarantee success. The workshops will stutter at times and probably take much longer to complete than anticipated.

### *Who should see the results of the CSA process?*

It is important that the results should not be restricted to senior management, e.g., the chief financial officer and the chief officer responsible for the subject matter under examination. The results have come from the contributions of the workshop participants so it is important that they see the produce of their efforts, after all it is they who will be responsible for implementing and maintaining the agreed action plan. Developing ownership of the results and remedies is fundamental to a successful CSA outcome. The external auditor will clearly need access to the results and it is likely that Council members may wish to see them too.

### *What reporting style should be used and who should produce it?*

It is probably best that the auditor drafts the CSA report as part of the facilitation. At Ashford, drafts of the report are produced after each workshop, distributed to the workshop participants and used as minutes (amended where necessary and then agreed) at the start of the next workshop. This develops the participants' feeling of ownership, enables participants to understand how the CSA process is unfolding and ensures that there are no surprises at the end of the process.

However, it is important that the report is not presented as a traditional audit report; to do so is likely to tarnish the whole process and lessen the feeling of ownership. The report must be seen as neutral, consequently a joint report is recommended, signed accordingly by both the service manager responsible for the activity under examination and the auditor acting as facilitator. Moving away from the traditionally structured audit report also affords the opportunity for introducing some flair and innovation into the style of the report to make it more attractive and agreeable.

Producing a joint report, however, can have its complications. Auditors tend to guard their independence vigorously and are not particularly renowned for their readiness to compromise, whereas CSA generally, and the signing of a joint report specifically, requires auditors to make some adjustment in their thinking.

It is fundamental for auditors to appreciate that in acting as facilitators they are part of the CSA process and linked unequivocally with the ensuing results. They cannot disband it or walk away simply because they are not comfortable with the outcome. Signing a joint report may require the auditor to put their name to issues with which they might previously have disagreed or would have preferred to be distanced from. The message to the audit fraternity is clear – do not enter the CSA kitchen unless you are prepared to take the heat!

### *Should assurance statements be used?*

The use of assurance statements to support the CSA process is favoured at Ashford. It is important that the responsible service manager should be required to state occasionally that they have implemented the agreed controls and arrangements, have maintained their effectiveness and are satisfied with the level of control in operation. Appendix 19.2 provides suggested wording for an assurance statement.

### *How often should assurance statements be produced and to whom?*

The production of assurance statements can be built into staff performance appraisal arrangements as a means of regulating the assurance procedure. At Ashford, performance appraisals are undertaken each six months and this is considered to be an ideal frequency and opportunity for chief officers to receive assurance statements and discuss any difficulties associated with them.

As CSA exercises will almost certainly address financial issues to a varying degree it seems logical that assurance statements should also be sent to the chief finance officer as part of the control process although this may only need to happen at the end of each financial year. Internal auditors (and external auditors) may wish to see the assurance statements or at least pursue instances where an assurance statement has not been produced or has been qualified. Copies of assurance statements might be made available to the Chief Executive and Council members, particularly if the CSA exercises have been focused on strategic and corporate issues.

### *Is there a need to review the CSA outcomes?*

Internal auditors are very apt at recommending review arrangements but perhaps less keen to review the effectiveness of their own work. CSA most certainly requires a review mechanism to test the soundness of the technique. Several issues must be addressed. Who is going to carry out the review, how frequent will the review be, how will the review will be carried out, what benchmarks will be used to judge the effectiveness and who will see the results of the review process? These are issues for each local authority to determine.

## Practical Issues of Actually Doing CSA

### *What is a typical order of events for a CSA exercise?*

The following list reflects the events, spread over a number of workshops, that have been (or will in future be) adopted at Ashford.

- Introduce CSA, including a brief description of its origin and history.
- Identify and discuss the typical business objectives of an organisation.
- Discuss the main elements of risk.
- Complete the control questionnaire.
- Analyse the completed control questionnaires.
- Discuss the results of the control questionnaires; identify the strengths that need to be sustained and any deficiencies that require attention.
- Identify the current business objectives of the activity under examination.
- Break the business objectives down into sub-objectives.
- Apply a SWOT analysis to each sub-objective.
- Filter the results to identify the key issues.
- Agree the residual issues.

- Redefine and agree the principal objectives, the key risks associated with the objectives and the essential controls to guard against or minimise the risks.
- Identify any shortcomings in the essential controls.
- Agree the action plan to address the shortcomings.
- Agree the action plan for developing business opportunities, for implementing any quality improvements identified during workshop discussions and for overcoming any deficiencies in the control environment.
- Agree a timetable for the action plans and assign officer responsibility for each tasks.
- Agree the wording of the assurance statement.
- Agree the final report.

Some of these events are now examined in greater depth.

### *Identifying and discussing typical business objectives of an organisation*

Experience at Ashford has shown that not all workshop participants understand the expression 'business objectives' within the context of local government. It has therefore proved useful to request participants to first identify what they believe to be typical business objectives of private-sector organisations, e.g., profit, growth, product development, customer focus and environmental compliance. Organisations such as Mothercare, Virgin, Oxfam and the water companies have been used to generate discussion.

### *Discussing the main elements of risk*

It is becoming apparent at Ashford, as CSA is developed, that it is wrong to assume participants always have a clear understanding of what is meant by risk and what types of risk they should be considering. Accordingly, future CSA pilot schemes will contain a brief session in the early stages of the first workshop, addressing the main ingredients of risk.

- A simple definition of risk, e.g., a problem or hazard caused by something not happening (that should) or something happening (that should not).
- Five strategic risks, i.e., those brought about by political and legal influence (e.g., legislation); market influences (e.g., competition);

stakeholders (e.g., customer demands); technological changes (e.g., computer software) and environmental pressures.

- Operational risks, e.g., pollution, fraud and corruption, poor quality and service delivery interruptions and delays.

### *Identifying current business objectives of the activity under examination*

Experience has shown that workshop participants are inclined to be conservative in the number of objectives they identify for their business although even with small numbers some objectives can overlap and may have to be grouped.

At Ashford, the principal objectives have tended to fall into the following categories: sound financial administration; business development; communications; staffing (and other resource issues); stakeholder interests; compliance with legislation and council policy; quality improvement. Best value must surely be added to these as a key business objective in any future CSA exercise.

### *Breaking business objectives down into sub-objectives*

Current business objectives may be broken down into sub-objectives, for instance, a typical main objective of business development might have sub-objectives of innovation, research, service development, partnership development, funding and other resources, planning and training. Again, some grouping is recommended to avoid duplication.

Clearly, the more sub-objectives the longer the CSA process will take. Accordingly, it is recommended that a limit of five sub-objectives for each principal objective be set, unless there are good grounds for extending this rule.

### *Applying a SWOT analysis to each sub-objective*

Once the sub-objectives have been identified and grouped, it has proved very useful, albeit somewhat time consuming, in encouraging workshop participants to carry out a SWOT analysis of each sub-objective. This approach has the immediate benefit that from the strengths and opportunities often spring the things that need to be sustained, exploited and taken forward to develop the business activity whilst from the weaknesses and threats normally flow the business risks that need to be addressed and controlled.

## *Filtering results to identify key issues*

Even with a limitation imposed on the number of sub-objectives, the task for the facilitator of managing a large number of SWOTs can be formidable. A recent CSA exercise at Ashford involving the Marketing, Media and Tourism Service in the Chief Executive's department produced five key objectives and 26 sub-objectives, with the workshop participants acknowledging 73 weaknesses and 40 risks whilst generating 59 opportunities relating to their business, a total of 172 issues to address.

Clearly, having a large number of issues (such as 172) to sort out is likely to be unmanageable so there is a need to filter the issues to identify the key weaknesses, risks and opportunities. The filter used at Ashford is a simple one. Participants are asked to put the issues they have identified into three categories:

1. Those they cannot do anything about (because they fall outside of their control).
2. Those which they do not wish to do anything about (because the weaknesses are not material, the risks are minimal or the rewards from developing the opportunities would be outweighed by the effort).
3. Those which are fundamental, within their control and must therefore be addressed.

Numerous risks (and threats) will be identified from the SWOT analysis of each sub-objective. The challenge for the facilitator is in encouraging the workshop participants to prioritise these risks so that the material risks can be highlighted and the others discarded. Users of CSA may therefore wish to supplement the filtering mechanism described above by taking a closer and realistic look at each risk and asking, 'What are the chances of it happening and if it did, would it result in significant loss or damage?' In other words, 'Would it really matter in the overall scheme of things?' If the risk is theoretical or would amount to small and limited loss or damage then the question must be begged, 'Would using valuable resources to guard or minimise the risk add value to the business?' If the answer is 'No' then the chances are the risks may be discarded.

## *Agreeing residual issues*

Agreeing the residual weaknesses, risks and opportunities that both managers and auditors do not consider fundamental to the governance of the business and to the organisation as a whole, and therefore do not wish to do anything about, tends to be a difficult process. The concept of materiality does not come easy, particularly to some auditors, and the thought that they should be party to agreeing that some weaknesses and risks do not justify attention may be considered unacceptable and in conflict with Section 151 responsibilities. That is why CSA, with its focus on the fundamental rather than the routine, and its reliance on self assessment rather than traditional audit trails and coverage is difficult for some auditors, chief finance officers and external auditors to come to terms with.

The Marketing, Media and Tourism participants agreed to disregard 85 of their 172 original issues leaving 87 key issues (27 weaknesses, 16 risks and 44 opportunities) to address, to which they added four fundamental deficiencies in respect of their control environment.

### *Agreeing the action plan*

Even the difficulties of agreeing the residual issues can pale into insignificance compared with endeavouring to agree the action plan. It is not an easy route to get the workshop participants to agree the corrective actions and measures they think should be introduced, over and above the controls and arrangements they already have in place, in order to:

- overcome the weaknesses and risks from the SWOTs
- remedy the deficiencies identified in the control environment
- exploit and manage the opportunities generated by the SWOTs.

The action plan needs to set out the priorities and define how, precisely, the agreed remedies are going to be undertaken. It is not sufficient to agree to bland statements, such as 'The control framework for regulating [the weakness] will be reviewed and improved'. Emphasis must be on how, how and how again and being realistic about it.

The plan of action needs to state precisely who is going to be responsible for making these things happen and when, and these people need to be consulted. Deadlines should be set fairly liberally. They need to be realistic and achievable and they must take into account other workloads and bear in mind that some of the actions may be dependent upon the contribution of others who may not have been part of the CSA process. Additionally, the plan should recognise any costs associated with the remedial action and how these will be funded.

It is debatable whether the action plan should be addressed by all the workshop participants or better left for the facilitator and senior management to sort out. The five participants from the Marketing, Media and Tourism workshop all expressed a wish to contribute to the planning process whereas at a previous CSA exercise at Ashford relating to housing maintenance (see below) where there were eleven workshop participants ranging from the chief officer to clerical assistants, it was not considered practical to discuss the action plan with them all and the action plan was agreed with the liaison officer involved. It is a matter of horses for courses.

## The Real Benefits of CSA – a Working Example

Academics and those selling CSA will speak of the many virtues of CSA. But it is doubtful if theoretical arguments will encourage internal auditors to take the great leap towards developing CSA in their local authorities or convince senior management that they should commit their staff and other resources to the rigours of several workshops in the hope that some tangible benefits might stem from the investment. Hard facts are required. Facts that demonstrate CSA really works and transcends traditional audit methods. Appendix 19.3 therefore provides a summary of the results of a recent CSA exercise undertaken at Ashford on the subject of responsive repairs (jobbing works) to the Council's housing stock, administered by its Managing Agent – the Housing Department's DSO, with annual expenditure of around £1.5m.

A traditional audit carried out on responsive repairs at Ashford would not have covered the wide span of issues that were addressed in the CSA exercise. The wide range of improvements would not have been identified either but even had they been it is unlikely that internal audit would have got the same support for and commitment towards those improvements as was received from the CSA process.

## CONCLUSIONS

Internal auditors in local government can no longer rely on traditional audit techniques to give proper assurances about their local authority's governance or make meaningful contributions towards their local authority's wider business development. Those who believe they can are deluding themselves. The message is a serious one. Internal auditors must 'get real', adapt and go forward, develop and add value, or they will not survive the rigours of change.

The advent of Best Value will require all managers in local government to scrutinise the areas for which they have responsibility and make judgements about costs, standards, quality and performance and how these fit into their organisations' corporate and strategic plans.

Unquestionably, managers will be required to produce Service Delivery Plans for taking their services forward to meet Best Value expectations and they will need the right techniques to achieve this. CSA is an essential part of the Best Value 'toolbag' that managers should use for examination of the principal business objectives, risks and controls that form an integral part of any Service Delivery Plan.

CSA therefore offers a golden opportunity for internal auditors to contribute to service development and enhance the quality of business thinking whilst improving the control environment, widening the awareness of big risks and colouring the appropriateness and effectiveness of the key organisational controls. Careful development of CSA will also enable internal auditors to widen their attention span beyond the normal spectrum of financial administration whilst eventually raising internal audit's profile to corporate and strategic level.

However, the introduction and development of CSA is not easy. It does not happen overnight and it is unlikely to get started and be sustained unless internal auditors provide the initial thrust, energy and enthusiasm and then support it actively thereafter. CSA is unquestionably hard work. It uses up a lot of personal energy, requires perseverance and tact and there is no hiding the fact that it consumes a lot of valuable staff time. It can be a real effort to promote and organise and therefore requires careful planning. But, in the final analysis, the benefits far outweigh the disadvantages and once an auditor is caught by 'the CSA bug' and begins to appreciate the large number and array of fundamental issues that the technique can address, it is unlikely that traditional audit techniques will ever have the same appeal again.

At Ashford Borough Council, CSA is in its infancy but the platform for taking CSA forward as a tool to be operated at corporate and strategic level and contribute to such fundamental issues as Best Value, has been constructed. Important lessons have been learned from the initial pilot schemes and the scene is now set for CSA to become an integral and important part of the internal auditor's work and a major contributor to the governance of the organisation. CSA will never be a complete substitute for traditional audit coverage but it can replace a large part of it.

## APPENDIX 19.1

# Examples of the Questions Posed in the Ashford Control Questionnaire

Participants are asked to answer: Strongly Agree, Agree, Don't Know (where applicable), Disagree or Strongly Disagree.

### *Purpose*

- The purpose of my work has been defined clearly.
- I have sufficient involvement in setting the core values of my work.
- I know what the business risks of my work are.
- I have a clear understanding of the controls associated with my work.

### *Commitment*

- I am committed to high quality work.
- I practise continuous improvement.
- I am often criticised if I do my work poorly.
- I am trusted to do my work well.

### *Capability*

- I have sufficient authority to do my work well.
- I am trained sufficiently to do my work well.
- I have access to all the information I need to do my work well.
- I have an adequate planning process for identifying future work commitments.

### *Learning*

- I measure the work I do.
- I compare my performance regularly with others.
- I comply with the financial controls that regulate my work.
- I have confidence in the operational (non-financial) controls that regulate my work.

## APPENDIX 19.2

# Suggested Wording for an Assurance Statement

To be signed by the Service Manager.

'I (and others) have implemented and maintained effectively, in accordance with the agreed timetable, the key controls, arrangements and development issues identified and acknowledged during the Control Self Assessment exercise in respect of ............................ [the business subject examined] and I am satisfied that there have been no matters of failure or concern of substance that have arisen in respect of the key business risks, systems or other affairs.'

Signed ................................................. Date ................................

Note: In the event of the Service Manager being unable to make this statement, the Assurance Statement will need to make provision for a qualified statement.

## APPENDIX 19.3

# The Real Benefits of CSA – A Worked Example

## Ashford Borough Council: Housing Repairs

Three CSA workshops were held – one full day and two half days – involving eleven representatives from the department and two auditors acting as facilitators.

- Eight main business objectives and twenty-two sub-objectives were identified. The main business objectives were
  - service delivery
  - financial administration
  - integrity
  - staff needs
  - communications
  - the management of contractors
  - compliance with council policy and legislation
  - developing a commercial approach.
- Four fundamental weaknesses in the control environment were recognised.
- The workshop participants agreed on the implementation of twenty-three controls to safeguard against the key financial and operational risks highlighted during the CSA process.
- A further fourteen points of action were agreed to improve procedures, quality and service delivery.

In total, forty-one specific improvements to enhance the governance and service delivery of responsive repairs were acknowledged by the workshop participants. These improvements focused on such issues as

- Improving tenant satisfaction in respect of the quality of repairs and contractor conduct on site.
- Redefining senior management processes.

- Improving the planning of work and use of resources.
- Reviewing approval levels for the ordering of jobbing work and the arrangements for verifying and certifying contractors' invoices.
- Improving the quality of supporting financial controls and developing the accounting system.
- Improving generally the Managing Agent's pre- and post-inspection regime for jobbing works.
- Introducing an inspection regime focusing on compliance with Health and Safety issues for contractors working on sites.
- Introducing a select list of contractors specifically for responsive repairs.
- Enhancing statistical information about contractor performance and quality standards.
- Introducing improved staff training regarding the Council's Standing Orders (relating to contracts) and Financial Regulations.
- Developing Best Value principles.
- Pursuing partnership arrangements.
- Improving communications and liaison between the client and Managing Agent.
- Formalising regular contact between Managing Agent staff to discuss common problems and seek solutions.
- Improve staff briefing sessions given by senior management.

# 20

# Control Self Assessment Techniques

## Integrating Risk Management, Monitoring, Audit and Control

*Mike Dudding*

## INTRODUCTION

This chapter sets out Kent County Council's experience in seeking to maximise the benefits from its departmental and corporate monitoring and control process whilst aiming to identify its exposure to risk. The process the authority has gone through in developing this process is one of gradual evolution mirroring the organisational changes and growing need to improve performance monitoring. It has not been a simple process of applying 'new' techniques but rather one based upon continual learning.

The case study focuses upon the corporate monitoring processes and aims to locate control self assessment in a wider managerial context and identify the learning processes Kent went through and is still going through.

## CONTEXT

Kent County Council (KCC) is a large local authority. Its net budget is in excess of £920m. It employs some 33,000 staff in serving a population of 1.3m. To enable it to provide responsive services it has moved, over the past ten years, from a traditional, centrally managed authority to a highly devolved management structure with managers having budgets and a significant degree of freedom to act within a strategic Corporate Framework. There are currently around 850 units with their own budget managers (including schools).

## CORPORATE FRAMEWORK

The Corporate Framework brings together in one simple document a corporate statement of the ground rules and standards for resource management. It is a matrix of minimum 'must-dos' for all staff across KCC, and is complemented by functional frameworks which expand on the basics and provide guidance and assistance. The fundamental management principle guiding the way KCC works is 'devolution within a clear Corporate Framework'. Managers have the freedom to manage, but also the responsibility for ensuring that resources are used effectively and efficiently to achieve maximum value for money. They have a right to know what is expected of them. The Corporate Framework provides an explicit statement of obligations and a safety net of guidance on good practice and legal requirements. The extract from the framework (shown in Table 20.1) gives an example highlighting where further help and advice can be found.

Taken together with departmentally developed service delivery targets and standards, all managers therefore have a clear statement of what is expected of them. This is a key component in KCC's overall control environment. It provides the basis for the authority's monitoring processes both within departments and corporately. Whilst these frameworks provide a sound platform upon which to judge performance, they were developed during a period of relative stability in local government. Over recent years rising service pressures, increased legislation, tightening finances and growing public expectation have prompted changing working patterns and significant reductions in 'overhead' support activity which inevitably puts the control framework under pressure. There is therefore an increasing need to accept risk in the delivery of services. This reality provided the trigger for seeking an integrated approach to risk, monitoring and control.

## MONITORING ARRANGEMENTS

What are the current arrangements for monitoring?

### *Management's role*

The Corporate Framework clearly identifies the line management responsibility for day-to-day monitoring of both performance and standards. In turn, service chief officers have an explicit responsibility to ensure this happens and secure action where problems arise.

### *Corporate overview*

At a corporate level, the process involves monitoring both the business planning process and associated performance indicators, together with the Corporate Framework standards themselves. The results of this activity are regularly reported to elected members. We will explore later how these

**Table 20.1** Extract from corporate framework

| If my responsibilities include: | What are my 'must-dos'? | Who is there to help me? | Which section of the Management Handbook can give me more information? | What will be monitored each year? | How will it be monitored? |
|---|---|---|---|---|---|
| Finance | Ensure that:<br>■ processes and procedures adopted within the County Council are adequate to provide for the proper control and use of public funds | Departmental Finance Managers | Section 3 Finance and Budgets | The prime responsibility for monitoring rests with Chief Officers and their departments. Corporate monitoring will augment and support this process. | Chief Officer will use existing arrangements or develop appropriate mechanisms to meet departmental needs. Corporate monitoring will operate in partnership with departments to determine the most appropriate method. These could include: |
| | ■ resources are directed only to the purposes for which proper Member authority has been given | Head of Corporate Finance/ Corporate Budget Unit | | | ■ scrutinising reports and agenda items<br>■ Corporate Review Programme studies<br>■ analysis of performance indicators |
| | ■ implementation of and adherence to the Financial Management Action Programme (FMAP) is secured and maintained | Head of Profession | | | |

**Table 20.1** Continued

| If my responsibilities include: | What are my 'must-dos'? | Who is there to help me? | Which section of the Management Handbook can give me more information? | What will be monitored each year? | How will it be monitored? |
|---|---|---|---|---|---|
| Staff | Comply with<br>■ UK and EC<br>■ KCC's Standing Orders<br>■ code of standards for personnel practice<br>■ individual terms and conditions of service<br>■ framework for Health and Safety<br>Ensure that:<br>■ staff are paid correctly in line with KCC policy and practice | Departmental Personnel Managers<br>Head of Corporate Personnel | Section 4 & 5<br>Personnel<br>Health & Safety | An annual programme of key monitoring areas will be agreed within the Corporate Framework and published by the end of April each year.<br>Each year's programme will be decided in consultation with Departments and Members (through appropriate Committee / groups) taking into account:<br>■ the external audit and internal review and audit programmes<br>■ corporate and functional priorities | ■ surveys and documented returns<br>■ liaison meetings and interviews<br>■ business plan reviews<br>■ monitoring forms<br>Where monitoring requires further development/refinement, Corporate Resource Department will work with Departments to set up appropriate mechanisms, using existing 'models' wherever possible. |

processes work in practice. Sitting outside the above, although clearly providing a valuable independent appraisal, is the work of both internal and external audit.

### *Audit context*

Following a joint statement in 1991 on roles and arrangements for improving the way they work together, internal and external audit have evolved a common planning process to facilitate complementary audit coverage. This process has helped to optimise audit resources particularly at a time when internal audit resources are under pressure. As the scope of the audit work is so wide, some form of prioritising is necessary so that audit resources can be directed towards systems where the likelihood or impact of weak control is greatest. Each year, Internal Audit updates its assessment of the Authority's major systems, in excess of 300 of them, in terms of potential risk. This assessment is based on the auditors' knowledge of the Authority, levels of control in the past, problems that may have arisen, the degree of change taking place, current and future issues affecting the Authority and a variety of other information gained from many years of audit experience. This analysis of the risk attached to the Authority's systems forms the backdrop to the annual audit planning cycle. Over time the external auditor has been increasingly able to place reliance on the work of internal audit.

Overall the monitoring arrangements in KCC therefore embrace action at local accountable manager level, departmental level scrutiny and corporate overview together with an independent perspective on the adequacy of the control framework from internal and external audit. However, to what extent has this control framework been rooted in a continuous assessment of risk? Are the controls in place relevant to the key risks confronting the organisation? How are the various components of monitoring coming together to provide a holistic view on organisational health and performance? It was these questions that the integrated approach needed to address.

## THE COMPONENTS

The approach to monitoring has been evolutionary and closely linked to the structural changes. The components of monitoring have each evolved to meet changing needs although no mechanism existed to bring these processes together. So what are the individual elements of monitoring activity that contribute to the management of risk? As we have seen earlier, the prime responsibility for action lies with managers and this is where the

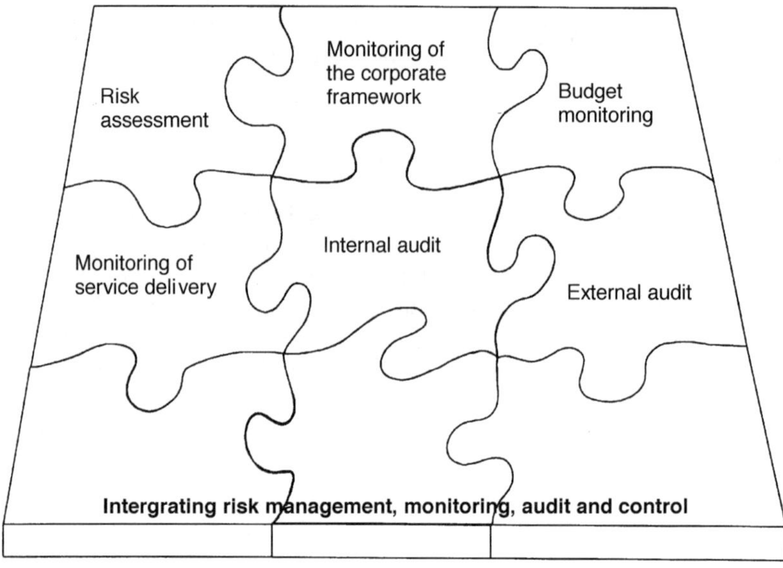


**Figure 20.1** Corporate framework level monitoring.

bulk of monitoring takes place. Corporate-level monitoring is illustrated in Figure 20.1 and these elements are now explored in detail.

## RISK ASSESSMENT

By early 1996 the continued pressure on resources and the implications of the Local Government Review put further strains on the management processes (including monitoring). In a letter to Chief Officers, the Chief Executive said:

> ... It is appropriate, therefore, that we should consider the integrity of our control systems and assess the extent of risk. There is a balance to be struck in seeking to provide the best possible services for the people of Kent and maintaining sound control systems in the management of public funds. An assessment of risk and an approach that seeks to identify how to minimise that risk will greatly assist in achieving an acceptable balance. It will also be a key element in shaping our future management processes.

What followed was a process, handled jointly with the external auditors (Pricewaterhouse Coopers), with the intention of addressing risk in its broadest sense, ie., not just financial but also management, operational and strategic risk.

The objectives of the process were to

1. Provide management with information about risks and support in developing strategies to minimise risk.
2. Build upon the devolved management arrangements to develop managers' ongoing self assessment, and control, of risk.
3. Provide the external auditor with a view on risk assessment in the organisation to support his opinion on the accounts.
4. Develop further Corporate Framework monitoring through a focus on risk.
5. Develop closer working between internal audit, external audit and the central Corporate Framework monitoring.

The approach adopted was in four stages, although the longer-term intention was for the consideration of risk to become part of the ongoing management process.

## *Stage 1*

Test managers' awareness of their responsibilities and their perceptions of significant risks affecting KCC. For this stage a questionnaire was used that sought views on the KCC control environment and understanding of the organisation's values and specifically asked managers to identify five key risks in their part of the organisation and five key risks in their own rôles.

As this was the start of an ongoing risk-assessment process the questionnaire was principally targeted at senior managers in KCC, i.e., all departmental management teams and Chief Officers, together with some limited testing on all levels of management in one department. In order to keep thinking open, the questionnaire did not seek to define risk. A total of 177 managers responded to the questionnaire providing a powerful cross-section of views drawn across the whole Authority.

## *Stage 2*

Following the analysis of Stage 1, the key risks were then explored in depth in a series of proactive workshops facilitated by the use of some powerful decision conferencing software which enabled a very significant amount of data to be handled quickly with all participants being free to contribute. In total 150 of the above managers took part in ten separate workshops. Figure 20.2 shows the workshop process.

Recognising that the pattern of key risks may vary across the organisation, the workshops were organised on departmental lines. The ensuing discussions around risks could then take place within the context of a particular service (eg., Education).

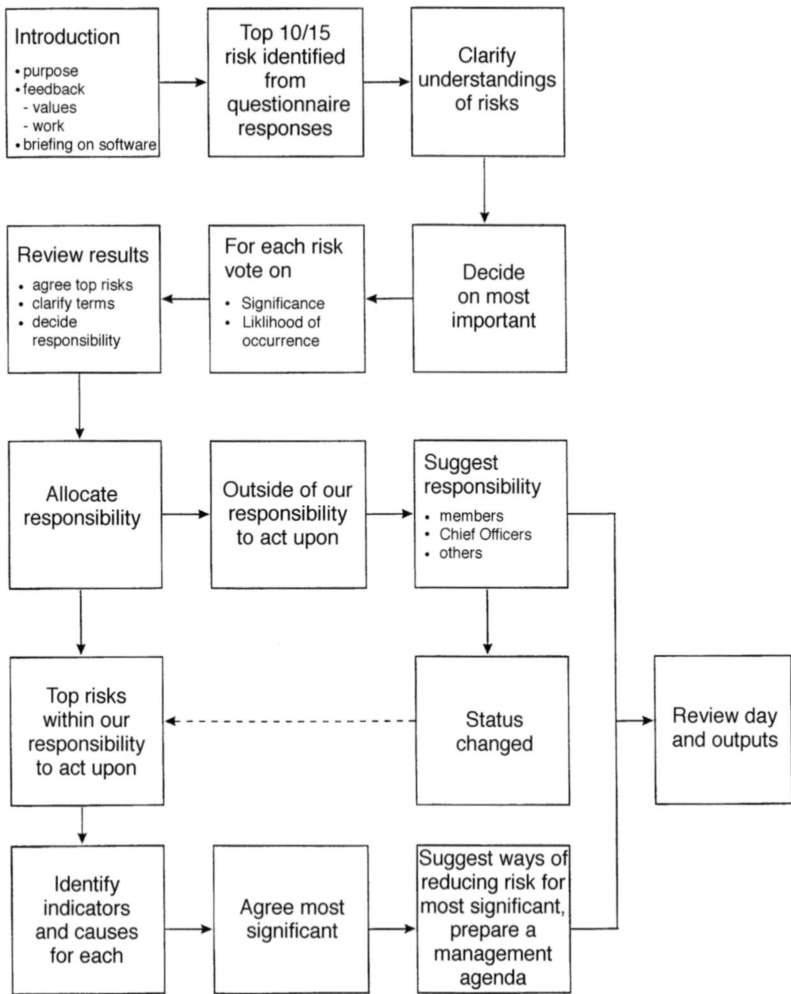


**Figure 20.2** The workshop process.

The aim of each workshop was to provide an opportunity to understand and clarify the key risks, develop an assessment of the potential impact of each risk and the likelihood of the risk occurring. Alongside this assessment each workshop then went on to identify the responsibility for and actions required to minimise the highest risks. As the process developed it became clear that not only were a number of common themes emerging but that the risks could be clustered into four groups:

(a) operational risks: those risks which affect the relationship between the department and their customers

(b) financial: risks which have a financial base

(c) managerial: risk concerned with the day-to-day responsibilities and accountabilities of staff

(d) strategic: major risks which affect KCC with longer-term impacts.

This clustering then provided a pointer to the level at which they needed to be addressed.

The process was unique in that it ensured all concerns and opinions were captured. There was an opportunity to test out understanding of the risks and to clarify and challenge where the responsibility for action lay. It helped identify the personal steps individual managers could take to address agreed key risks.

### *Stage 3*

Build the results into

(a) departmentally focused risk plans

(b) future Corporate Framework monitoring plans

(c) internal and external audit planning processes.

The above three stages form part of the risk management model shown in Figure 20.3.

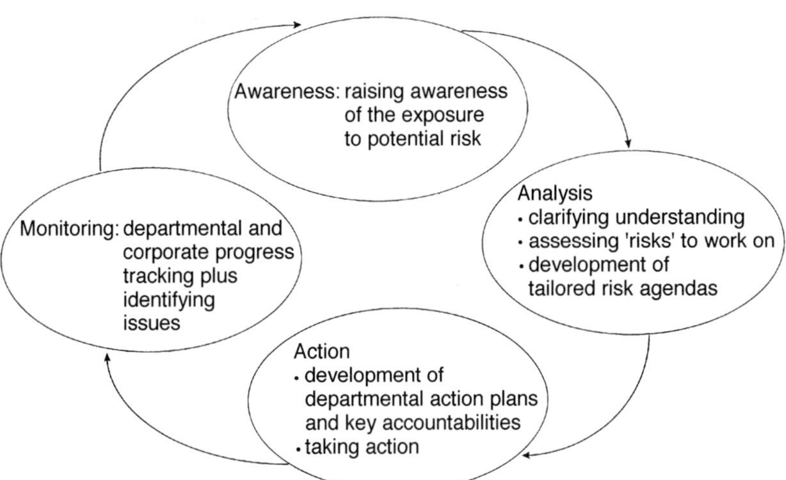


**Figure 20.3** Risk management model.

### *Stage 4*

Take action and confirm results.

From the cycle of workshops (summer/autumn 1996) a table of the top risks and the spread of those risks across departments was developed.

## Key Risks and Actions

Each workshop considered up to 30 risks and voted on these. The top six risks identified from the workshops were:

1. budget reductions/lack of resources
2. impact of decisions of outside agencies
3. lack of investment/adequate information and information systems
4. insufficient staff/low morale
5. not prepared for the Local Government Review changes
6. skills gaps.

Although this analysis provides only a snapshot in time, it has been a useful starting point in identifying risk concerns specific to a department and wider issues cutting across the organisation that call for a corporate response. One such example was 'not prepared for LGR (local government review)'. The corporate response to this has been to develop a resource-by-resource function analysis of the potential risks (grouped into high, medium and low categories) in the form of a checklist to assist individual managers assess their degree of exposure (ie., likelihood of the risk arising and its materiality if it were to occur) and plan action accordingly (see the following tables under the headings high, medium, and low risks).

## *High risks*

| Theme | Risk | Control |
|---|---|---|
| Assets | Details on all assets belonging to KCC not known. Incomplete/ incorrect/inaccurate data, e.g., Asset Register, Terrier, etc., leading to inadequate identification of property. Future KCC assets are transferred to the unitary. | Ensure all inventories/registers are accurate. Increase vigilance on data validation. Ascertain legal title/right to all assets ascertained. |
| | Theft of assets – property, cash, etc., from the workplace. Assets used by staff outside the office not returned when they leave. Future Kent assets are transferred to the unitary. | Asset registers to be correctly and rigorously maintained. Legal title/right to all assets known/ identified. |
| | Inadequate identification of rights/liabilities, e.g., user rights, so that arrangements not in place to support service requirements. | Increased vigour on care and control of documents relating to assets. |
| | On disposal, true value of asset not achieved, e.g., disposal of surplus property. | Increased staff awareness and vigilance. |
| Contracts | Poor/inadequate handling of contractual issues on staff contracts for terms and conditions of service. | Reinforce personnel procedures. |
| | Insecure handling of documents during handover resulting in loss, theft, unauthorised copying, and passing copies to inappropriate people, e.g., contract information, outstanding liabilities not known, etc. | Identification and security of all documents for handover. Guidance issued to staff to increase awareness. |
| | Arrangements for new and existing contracts which straddle/wholly within Medway area not properly dealt with. | Position of all contracts reviewed and required action taken. Increased staff awareness. |

## *Medium risks*

| Theme | Risk | Control |
|---|---|---|
| Staff – deliberate actions | Abuse of security passwords, e.g., staff accessing systems to copy/ obtain unauthorised information. | Reinforce procedures for control, and management of security passwords. |
| | Salary claims, e.g., for work not undertaken, for a person not entitled, at the wrong rate, etc. | Guidance to staff to alert them to the risk. Reinforce process for payroll documentation. |
| | Travel and expenses claims for expenditure not incurred. Relocation costs claimed for expenditure not incurred, or staff not entitled. | Reinforce authorisation process. Increase staff awareness. |
| Staff – errors or over-sights | Errors in payments made to staff from inadequate systems to deal with relocating travel expenses. | Reinforce payments/ authorisation procedures. |
| | Loss arising through inadequate arrangements for severance process for staff. | Reinforce personnel/pensions procedures. |
| | Poor staff morale arising from poor handling of the staff transfer. | Reinforce personnel procedures. |
| | Not chasing returns/credits/ income due to KCC. | Ensure records of all purchases are maintained. |
| Premises/ equipment connected activities | Unauthorised persons have access to KCC premises leading to theft/loss/vandalism of assets, e.g., computer equipment. | Reinforce security procedures with regard to access to premises. |
| | Many office moves leading to breakdown of networks/access to systems/loss of connectivity. | Strengthen plans for contingency action in the event of major systems failures. |
| | Loss of assets at a critical time, e.g., transfer of key equipment to unitary. | Plan for smooth transition of equipment with proper authorised access where required. |

### *Low risks*

| Theme | Risk | Control |
|---|---|---|
| Staff – deliberate actions | Abuse of imprest account, bank account, etc. | Ensure integrity of records. Only authorised staff to access accounts. |
| | Deliberate deletion or corruption of data/systems. | Enforce systems access disciplines |
| Staff – errors and oversights | Errors in payments of enhancements, pension and redundancy payments | Ensure integrity of payroll/ pensions payments procedures. |
| | Failure to meet deadlines, e.g., grant claims leading to lost revenue. | Issue guidance to staff on deadlines. |
| | Cash flow implications of breakdown in normal activities, e.g., debt collection. | Reinforce monitoring procedures. |
| | Loss of reserves, provisions, balances, due to non-optimising accounting treatments. | Staff guidance on correct accounting treatments. |
| | Loss through inappropriate handling of tax transactions. | Reinforce accounting procedures, particularly around vesting day. |
| | Insurance gaps or overlaps, leading to uncertainties over liabilities, claims, etc. | Increase staff awareness. |

## MONITORING OF THE CORPORATE FRAMEWORK

The Corporate Framework and the corporate monitoring process were in place before we embarked on the above risk assessment process. The main aims of the monitoring were to provide a degree of corporate reassurance that managers were complying with the organisation's 'must-dos', to identify and share best practice, and to reveal areas where the framework needed strengthening or updating. Corporate monitoring focuses on 'high-risk' areas and is undertaken by the central departments on a sample basis through a published annual programme. This programme identifies the control

**Table 20.2** Corporate monitoring priorities 1996/7: information systems.

| Area and focus of monitoring | Purpose and reason for selection | All Depts? | Expected output and links |
|---|---|---|---|
| **Control objective:** To plan, develop, implement, operate and support the use of information systems, technology and telecommunications necessary to meet the Authority's business needs and priorities, within the overall IS/IT strategic framework, whilst providing value for money and appropriate security and quality, and ensuring compliance with relevant legislation and the Authority's policies. | | | |
| **Standards review** | | | |
| 1. *Security* (virus protection) Examination of anti-virus procedures and practice and the availability of facilities so as to reduce the risk to the security of information systems and data from computer viruses. | To determine compliance with agreed policy and procedures aimed at ensuring that KCC's IS/IT systems are adequately protected against virus infection. Area identified as requiring attention in conjunction with Internal Audit. This also supports preparation for LGR implementation.<br><br>NB Internal Audit will undertake work in Economic Development, Education and Corporate Resource Departments which will cover this area. | Yes | This information will be used to develop departmental action plans where required, and to determine any amendments required to existing policies and/or procedures. |

| 2. *Asset management* Examination of the arrangements for maintenance of software and hardware inventories in the light of developing new services and facilities, and the associated ability to demonstrate proper acquisition of software licences. | To determine compliance with agreed policy on maintenance of software and hardware inventories aimed at improving the management and security of IS/IT assets. Additionally to assess KCC's ability to prove compliance with software licensing requirements.<br><br>NB Internal Audit will undertake work in Economic Development, Education and Corporate Resource Departments which will cover some of this area.<br><br>Essential information base for the IS LGR project and the new KCC Information Systems Service Desk. Area identified as requiring attention in conjunction with Internal Audit. Also, in preparation for potential supplier and Federation Against Software Theft audits. | Yes | This information will be used to develop departmental action plans where required and to determine any amendments required to existing policies and/or procedures. |
|---|---|---|---|

objective, areas to be focused upon and the reason for selection – as can been seen from the extract from the 1996/7 monitoring plan shown in Table 20.2.

Priorities for monitoring were largely a product of experience gained from past monitoring and consultation within each function. Whilst, through this process of consultation, there was opportunity to reflect the service dimension and through pulling all the mechanisms together to ensure coherence, corporate monitoring was not seen as directly relevant to service managers. The risk-assessment process helped to correct this view and in turn to focus future work so it could be more closely linked to the wider service context.

The above deals with monitoring at a corporate level. However, one of the objectives of the project was to encourage and support monitoring at departmental levels. Knowledge of the corporate priorities coupled with those of each department contributed to the development of a series of departmental plans with lead managers identified to ensure their implementation.

To help managers implement these plans a series of 'tool kits' was developed (one for each function and resource). These working manuals took each of the 'must-dos' and set out:

- what the risks of non-compliance are
- what controls need to be in place to minimise that risk
- what checks need to be carried out to test if that control is in place and working (taking the form of a control self assessment).

For example, the extract in Figure 20.4 is taken from the *Personnel Monitoring Manual.*

The intention was that a collection of the control self assessments could be extracted from the manuals to provide the basis for testing those areas identified in each departmental plan. The overall result is monitoring activity that includes a series of departmental plans tailored to meet each service context, informed by a corporate overview of the key resource risks.

## BUDGET MONITORING

A fundamental principle in the Corporate Framework is each budget manager's personal accountability for their delegated budget. This places on them a clear responsibility to monitor activity against their budget and provide regular feedback through their department to the Corporate Centre highlighting any corrective action that will need to be taken. At the corporate level this data is summarised to provide early warning of potential significant over/under spending. In turn, the key to interpreting these trends is information on service activity and performance.

## MANAGEMENT

Objective: To employ staff in accordance with its statutory duties as an employer, within the employment policies and standards set by Members and KCC regulations.

| **Pay and benefits: deductions**<br>Risks of non-compliance | Key controls |
|---|---|
| Note: Deductions in respect of tax and national insurance are not covered by this test.<br><br>■ Non-authorised deductions are made from pay thereby breaching employment law.<br><br>■ Potential financial loss.<br><br>■ Incorrect amounts are deducted from pay. | ■ Deductions from pay are properly authorised in accordance with local and statutory requirements and conditions of service and are *bona fide*.<br><br>■ Pay and benefits comply with laws, local policies, contract terms and regulations.<br><br>■ Staff are aware of all conditions, allowances, facilities and benefits.<br><br>■ Management are aware of, and can ensure compliance with, relevant employment legislation and regulations. |

| Pay and benefits: deductions | Test performed | Matters arising / action taken | Initials & date |
|---|---|---|---|
| Test check against the system<br><br>Check that correct deductions are made in respect of:<br><br>■ County Court judgments<br>■ leased car<br>■ voluntary contributions, e.g., Help Fund<br>■ private health insurance<br>■ union deductions<br>■ KCC accommodation<br>■ salary overpayments<br>■ industrial action<br><br>Note: Check the authorisation of the deduction (including employee authorisation). | | | |
| Conclusion<br><br>Conclude on the controls around deductions. | | | |

**Figure 20.4** Extract from *Personnel Monitoring Manual.*

## MONITORING SERVICE DELIVERY

Whilst the Corporate Framework monitoring process concentrates upon resource standards, service delivery monitoring focuses upon performance.

The public interface with local government is almost always at the 'front line' at the receipt of services, be they schools, residential homes, roads, or libraries. The quality of local government is thus often measured by public perception. Whilst for the user of those services this may feel very tangible, it is also fair to say that public satisfaction with local government depends very much on their expectations and will almost always be subjective. Local authorities therefore need a package of measures to help monitor service delivery of which one component is the public dimension.

The components are:

- delivering services to meet the public's needs
- delivering services within budget
- delivering services to agreed standards
- delivering services to agreed policy objectives.

In all of the above, local authorities must demonstrate a level of performance in accordance with the public's and Members' wishes and, where possible, demonstrate a process for continual improvement. Crucial in this respect are the commitment and capabilities of employees, and therefore another important component of monitoring service delivery is understanding staff attitudes and needs.

Central to the process for monitoring service delivery is the business planning process. This is fundamental to most organisations and should include all of the items in Table 20.3, to some degree.

The business plan should identify the key service objectives and the resources required to deliver those objectives. It should also identify the key measures against which achievement of those objectives will be tracked.

To obviate the risk of poor or non-performance, the service objectives should have taken account of:

- public expectation and priorities
- staff commitment and abilities
- external pressures and demand
- available or fluctuating resources.

At the start of the year the service business plans are vetted in draft to ensure consistency and harmony with the authority's strategic objectives.

It is almost certainly rare in any local authority for all of the above to be achieved during the business planning processes because resources are seldom

**Table 20.3** The business planning process.

| | | |
|---|---|---|
| (a) | Nature of business | States purpose and (where possible) relationship to strategic objectives. |
| (b) | Pressures, demands and key areas of risk | States outcome of consultation and review processes, highlighting relevant pressures and expectations. |
| (c) | Objectives (see also (i) below) | A clear summary of objectives should be listed at the outset.<br><br>Needs to be specific about:<br><br>■ areas for improvement arising from (b)<br>■ input to strategic objectives<br>■ targets for the year with measurable outcomes expressed in terms of:<br>– changes in efficiency and/or standards<br>– achievement of short-term goals<br>– progress towards longer-term goals. |
| (d) | Performance data (see also (i) below) | Where relevant, plans should incorporate data (and targets) on the authority's Key Performance Indicators (KPIs) and the Audit Commission's Local Authority Performance Indicators.<br><br>Plans should also be specific on measurable outcomes as shown in (c) above.<br><br>Plans should incorporate wherever possible comparative data to demonstrate the unit's business and performance in relation to other local authorities and relevant agencies. It should include benchmarking data particularly in relation to areas viable for market testing. |
| (e) | Resources | Must state resources (money/people/skills/systems) required to achieve (c) above and identify where a lack of resources may have affected standards or the goals in (c). |
| (f) | Priorities | It should be clear which objectives are the more important and identify (or suggest) which objectives may be affected should resources change during the year. |
| (g) | Accountabilities | The plans should identify who has primary accountability for delivery of the primary objectives along with any deadlines where relevant. It should also recognise joint-responsibilities, especially where achievement of an objective is dependent upon other service units. |

**Table 20.3** Continued

| | | |
|---|---|---|
| (h) | Other relevant documents | The plans should not repeat what is already covered in other, perhaps more detailed, plans, e.g., Community Care Plan, Structure Plan, KCC Prospects. It should cross-refer to such plans especially where they identify in more detail any of the above issues. |
| (i) | Monitoring process | Plans should identify the monitoring and reporting process against the plan. To facilitate this the key objectives and performance data in the plans should be formatted in such a way so as to allow easy and consistent reporting of achievement against objectives, perhaps in a tabular form. |

available to undertake the degree of public consultation or meet external demands as authorities would wish. Consequently there is automatically a built-in risk of 'failing' unless authorities are prepared to be realistic about what they can achieve and how resources are going to be targeted. It is important, therefore, that services set sensible targets for achievement. The monitoring process then allows performance to be tracked against those targets, with regular feedback to management teams and to Members. In order that performance can be seen in perspective it is important to keep track of the public's and employees' attitudes.

Although a regular tracking survey of the public's views of local government is useful, it is important that these views are supplemented by more informed views of users against specific services. This allows the authority to gain a much clearer perception of users' or beneficiaries' attitudes and perception of a service, their priorities and their levels of satisfaction, and this enables the service itself to be adjusted accordingly.

The attitude and competencies of staff are critical to an authority's achievement of objectives. Many accepted quality/standard processes such as Investors in People (IIP) focus on the involvement of staff in the planning process and their understanding of aims and objectives. The degree of change in local government has been immense during the last decade and the ability of staff to cope with such change and continue to deliver quality services is fundamental. The Employee Survey has therefore concentrated on a number of factors:

- employees' commitment to their work and their organisation
- employees' level of job satisfaction
- employees' satisfaction with management and change processes
- factors that affect the level and quality of employees work.

In bringing together the threads of the above it can be seen that the corporate monitoring of service delivery needs to integrate the following factors:

- the delivery of services against agreed targets
- the extent to which those targets reflect and subsequently meet public expectation
- the extent to which staff understand those targets and objectives and are supported in meeting them.

A monitoring plan, which maps these issues across services, needs to flag up where the above are most at risk and to identify the consequences. Examples of each could include:

- Demographic fluctuations increase demand upon services for the elderly with the risk of either overspending or reduced service levels.
  - A policy decision needs to be made.
- A change in policy over access to waste disposal sites leaves the public disgruntled and reflects poorly on the image of the council. Yet it results in increased income.
  - The public need to be better informed about the reasons for change and the benefits arising for them.
- Office re-organisation has reduced staff's understanding of their role and thereby reduced commitment. Sickness levels increase but work levels remain the same as staff struggle to maintain standards.
  - Staff support mechanisms need to be in place, but there also needs to be a review of work levels and resources with the view of either revising resources or amending service standards. Both may lead to a policy review.

## INTERNAL AUDIT

The activities described so far are properly part of the overall management process. Audit sits outside this providing an independent appraisal of the control environment. This, as we have seen earlier, is informed by their work on risk and the corporate monitoring activity. Internal audit's work is set out in an annual plan with the results of activity surfacing in individual reports, formal report to Members providing an audit assessment of systems examined and highlighting issues requiring action and an annual summary report. Key to the development of the integrated approach has been internal audit's guidance in shaping the control framework and in the development of the monitoring 'tool kits' (see Corporate Framework) and in promoting control self assessment (CSA) in KCC.

To help make CSA attractive to managers, audit needed to address the ease with which the system could be used, and the time required to perform the assessment. They worked closely with local managers to ensure the format was clear and the questions phrased in familiar terminology. It also became clear early on that managers were keen to use CSA as part of a larger learning experience, not only as a training opportunity, but also as part of performance assessment and quality improvement.

Audit were also concerned that CSA should dovetail with or, better still, replace existing audit activity to ensure that duplication is minimised. One means of doing this is through 'shared audit' where there is a phased replacement of planned Internal Audits by CSA supported by audit staff. Keeping effort to the necessary minimum requires careful tracking of time taken.

Considerable effort was put into designing a simple to use system, both for the assessment itself and for the tracking. Audit opted for a 'compliance' style assessment where managers assess themselves against predetermined standards answering with a simple 'Satisfactory' or 'Action Required'. The size of the assessment package is kept to a minimum so as not to present managers with too daunting a task. The tracking systems should also be kept simple by using summary sheets and reports.

For example, CSA in schools leads to the development of financial control self assessment questionnaires covering:

- imprest accounts
- budget management
- ordering and purchasing of supplies and services
- control and security of equipment and assets
- receipting, banking and security of income
- salary payments and travel and subsistence payments.

## EXTERNAL AUDIT

External audit provides an outside perspective on the overall arrangements for securing value for money as well as discharging their statutory responsibilities to form an opinion on the accounts. The plan for their value for money work is jointly developed each year and the extent of their total audit activity is influenced not only by being able to place reliance upon the work of internal audit but also increasingly upon the other components of the monitoring process.

To support this, regular liaison meetings involving representatives from the corporate monitoring processes have been established. As we shall see in the next section, this in turn feeds into the co-ordinating process.

## BRINGING IT ALL TOGETHER

The individual components described earlier, whilst valuable in themselves, provide a potentially disjointed picture of the overall state of control and exposure to risk in the authority. For example, how are the interrelationships between controls identified? Are there connections between budget monitoring results, staff surveys and service performance? How would this be identified?

The need to address these questions, coinciding as they do with a period of major change and reducing resources, called for a structured response that focused on the key issues. The solution in KCC was initially to map the monitoring components together setting out:

- the components of activity and timescales
- 'touchstones' – key indicators to expose 'how do we know?'
- critical dates throughout the year.

This was used as a working document, updating activity throughout the year, and as a basis for tracking and steering progress. Table 20.4 shows the format.

In practice the 'map' for 1997/98 focused on the two major risk challenges of delivering a balanced budget and a seamless transition through the Local Government Review changes. Given the limited resources available the process was not paper driven but handled through regular meetings of the key players using the map as a prompt to share experiences of the results of monitoring activity to highlight:

- current and potential future problem areas
- harmonise activity
- refocus activity in the light of changing circumstances.

## LEARNING POINTS

These can clustered into two main groups:

- those relating to organisational culture
- those relating to applying KCC's monitoring approach.

**Table 20.4** Map of monitoring components.

| | External audit | | Internal audit | Corporate framework | Budget | Policy and service | Critical dates | Progress |
|---|---|---|---|---|---|---|---|---|
| | Risk assessment | Regularity and VFM | | LGR/future Kent preparation; maintaining probity; managing transition | Delivering 1997/98 and 1998/99 budgets; on-going financial monitoring | Delivery monitoring incl. business planning, consumer monitoring and talkback | Finance Monitoring Group corporate board committees | Assess-ment/issues to be progressed |
| 'Touch-stones' – how do we know? | ■ Informal briefing at liaison meeting<br>■ Manage-ment letter | ■ Strategic audit plan and audit progress charts<br>■ VFM/LGR reporting in year<br>■ LGR project plan<br>■ Dept. LGR service plans<br>■ LGR key decisions schedule<br>■ LGR financial and policy reporting to corporate board<br>■ Heads of function corporate and dept. functional plans | ■ Internal Audit plan<br>■ M&R updates<br>■ Dept. action plans | ■ Head of functions corporate and dept. functional plans<br>■ Framework group report-ing to Head of Corporate Review | ■ Overall position statement of key issues per dept. includes non-financial issues for review 2/3 per year<br>■ That is, (i) identify 'problem' areas (savings clear?, transport, capital) (ii) strengthen link/cross-links between financial and policy monitoring (iii) set early 'indicators' | ■ See financial monitoring opposite<br>■ dept. business plans<br>■ other?<br>■ key perfor-mance indicators<br>■ talkback survey results<br>■ other survey results<br>■ Audit Com-mission Profiles | | |

- Monthly budget monitoring cycle which also informs
- Service committee reports
- Corporate services and overall KCC budget reports
- Key issues report to Finance Director
- The Finance Director's report to Chief Executive/ Corporate Board

## Organisational Culture

Potentially the biggest challenge has been in seeking to establish the management of risk and monitoring of activity and standards as a core component in management.

Specifically:

- raising awareness of 'risk'. Consideration of the key risks is now built into the authority's business planning processes
- helping the organisation to identify and establish appropriate controls to minimise key risks
- establishing a clear set of ground rules – the 'must dos'
- establishing monitoring as an integral part of managing services
- designing tools to help managers self monitor
- keeping the above practical and focused.

## Our Monitoring Approach

1. Strong senior management and Member backing is vital. It is always tempting to reduce monitoring when resources are stretched. That commitment must extend from agreeing to standards and principles into taking action (including accepting risk) when problems arise.
2. Co-ordination of the monitoring components is not easy as there are:
   - different 'cultures'
   - different approaches and techniques
   - widely differing levels of resources.

   As much time and energy went into understanding the differences as went into harmonising processes. The connections are being made but we still have some way to go before we can claim a totally integrated approach.
3. The importance of keeping focused on the key risks must be stressed – monitoring those vital 'must-dos' where the risk of non-compliance *and* materiality are highest.
4. Managers in services need support and help to develop their own skills and in developing self monitoring approaches. Tools need to concentrate on those key risks that line managers can see as relevant to their service responsibilities. Investment here has proved very beneficial both in terms of developing ownership and securing action.

CSA can work well *if* it is user friendly and relevant to the *current* service context. Self selection of the components is advantageous.

5. Be prepared to acknowledge the need to adapt in the light of experience. Being seen to be responsive to management feedback helps secure ownership.
6. It takes time, enthusiasm and energy. You will not get it right first time.

# 21

# In Good Health

## The NHS Experience of Governance, Assurance and Self Assessment

*Tim Crowley*

## BACKGROUND

The National Health Service is at the forefront of good governance in the UK public sector. The recommendations of Cadbury, Nolan and others have not only been accepted but have also been implemented positively and with innovation. Part of that approach has been captured by an initiative launched in the NHS called the Controls Assurance Project (CAP) which has drawn together a range of governance advice and made a coherent link with existing local control systems and practices. Essentially, the Project is founded upon the principle that assurance is built upon systems and cultures that involve people. To that end much of the pilot work and guidance has centred upon techniques to engage wider groups of NHS staff in understanding and reporting upon risk within their areas of responsibility. Also, there has been an emphasis upon ensuring that there is top-down commitment which should be initiated through a Board-level consideration of key risks. The end point of this process is the requirement to produce a statement as from 1999/2000 accompanying the annual report and accounts as confirmation to the general public that the board of directors believes systems of control are operating effectively.

The defining objective of the CAP is: 'With existing resources, used to best effect, what assurance can be gained?' This is supported by the following project principles:

- involving people
- integrating functions
- consolidating and rationalising frameworks.

This chapter sets out how these project principles have been pursued and the part that control self assessment has played within the approaches adopted. In particular, the pilot site work delivered by Mersey Internal Audit Agency is presented to give a practical insight into one route to assurance.

## THE NHS CONTEXT

The history of organisations attempting to achieve cultural or process change is marked more by failure than success. Against this background most organisations, regardless of size or sector, claim that they are unique and often plead that special circumstances apply to prevent initiatives such as self assessment from proceeding. Alternatively, such initiatives are seized by senior management and thrust upon an unprepared workforce with little forethought. The result is inevitable and the excuse is usually that the process was flawed. Therefore, it is all the more remarkable that the NHS has pioneered the requirement for directors to make disclosures and that such disclosures should be supported by systems of self assessment. The following points demonstrate the scale of the task:

- The NHS provides healthcare to the public through over 1.5 million employees nation-wide, possibly the most diverse workforce of any organisation in the UK.
- As such, it is the largest organisation in the UK, employing more staff than the top ten UK companies combined, in providing healthcare to 57 million people.
- As well as providing healthcare through general practitioners, hospitals and emergency services, the NHS delivers long-term care for the elderly and mentally ill and support for the disabled and socially disadvantaged. It is proactive as well as reactive, promoting health education and supporting research, much of which has far-reaching consequences for the future of medical science.
- There have been enormous advances in the treatment of disabilities and diseases that were once untreatable. Not surprisingly, demand has soared, stretching budgets to extremes and making the allocation of resources ever more critical.
- Change is a constant feature in the NHS and the pace is quickening. Advances in medical technology, new thinking on community care, tougher expenditure targets, higher public expectations – all these add up to a complex, dynamic and politically challenging environment.

## THE WIDER ASSURANCE DEBATE

The NHS is not alone in looking at controls assurance. It is taking place throughout the world and in every sector. Indeed, in the UK one of the factors giving rise to the Cadbury report was 'the absence of a clear framework for ensuring that directors kept under review the controls in their business'. Clearly, all organisations require internal control but they meet this requirement with different degrees of formality and success. However, there is general agreement that the greater the size of, and public interest in, an organisation, the more important it becomes for that organisation to match good practice and maintain a formal framework. In many respects the NHS is subject to an unrivalled level of scrutiny from a range of interested parties. The implementation of controls assurance principles will demonstrate to the wider community that a board is not only satisfied that there is an integrated system in place to manage risk and improve healthcare but also that such a system can be clearly and sensibly described.

## BENEFITS OF PUBLIC REPORTING

An assurance statement by itself is of little value. Public reporting on internal control is not necessarily a characteristic of an effective organisation. A trust or authority can have an effective internal control system without making a public statement to that effect. In the end internal control effectiveness is determined by the adequacy of the system not what is said about it. The focus of the Controls Assurance Project is how to improve healthcare through more effective systems with an assurance statement being just one of the outcomes of that process. Nevertheless, there are some important benefits that flow from the journey towards public reporting on risk and assurance:

- The public are 'investors' in the NHS and have a right to full and equal access to enhanced risk reporting.
- The assurance debate raises risk awareness, stimulates a change in culture and supports effective resource prioritisation.
- Accountability is clarified and demonstrated.
- A board is provided with a systematic corporate analysis of its exposure to risk and its controls.
- What gets reported gets managed.
- It should lead to improvements in quality and potential reductions in negligence claims and insurance costs.

## PRINCIPLES OF A COMMON METHODOLOGY

An important principle that has been adopted is that to manage risk sensibly, and move forward to making an assurance statement, with the often bewildering number of professional disciplines and functions that exist within the NHS, a board needs to involve those self-same people in the review process. Virtually all employees perform control procedures or use information present in the internal control system. Such employees should be individually aware of their control responsibilities and be held accountable. They should also be expected to report back on departures from, or weaknesses in, the systems where they have involvement. Clearly, such an objective is laudable but its practical achievement is another matter. Establishing a culture and mechanism that really delivers all-employee involvement in risk awareness and management is a tremendous challenge and is more talked about than accomplished. Control self assessment workshops can be a useful means to secure these outcomes.

Despite the self-evident attractions of the use of a workshop approach it will have little value in the context of controls assurance unless it forms part of an overall strategy. At each of the pilot sites of the NHS Control Assurance Project, workshops are considered as just one element in a wider methodology. Essentially, the use of workshops becomes an available technique to address risk issues alongside a range of other options. The matching of priorities to these options is an iterative process that is driven by a 'top-down' diagnosis at board level. Figure 21.1 illustrates this cycle.

## THE GENERIC PILOT SITE PROCESS

The steps contained within Figure 21.1 are described below.

### *Board assessment of key risks and controls*

If such a process is not already in place a 'top-down' diagnosis of key risks and controls should be conducted. This can be structured in a number of ways depending on the culture of the organisation. An important feature is that results focus on major risks across the full range of the trust's/authority's objectives and that consensus is reached. Also, this stage represents an opportunity to take stock of all existing initiatives and controls to determine where there are gaps and/or overlaps. Another common element of the process is the profiling of risk following debate on potential impact and probability of occurrence. This can then be linked to issues of accountability and monitoring. In overall terms the process establishes an assurance action plan which frames up any future work. All

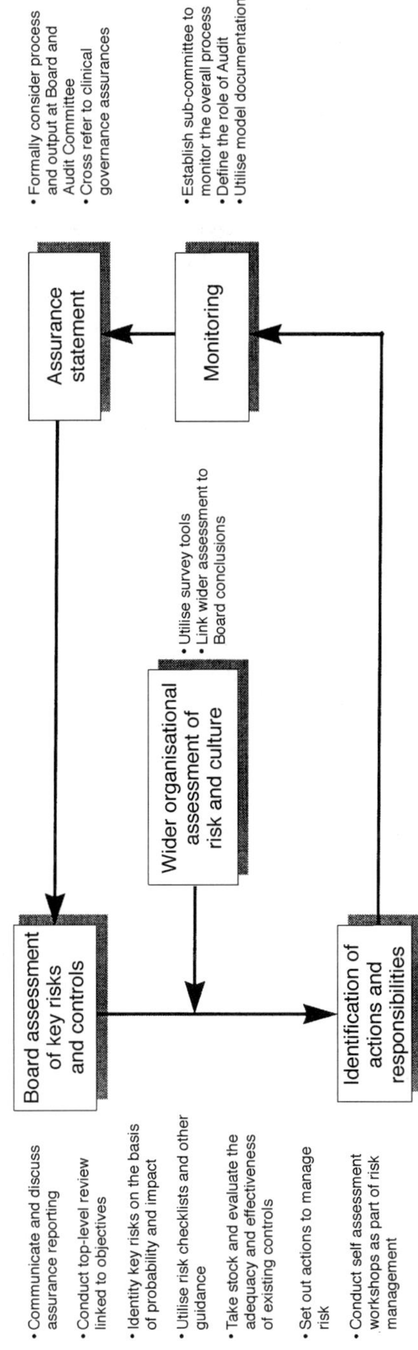


**Figure 21.1** A wider assurance statement: an integrated approach.

these outputs will usually be generated through a facilitated session that may use different emphases to arrive at the same outcome.

### *Wider organisational assessment of risk and culture*

It is often useful to conduct a wider review of risk and attitudes by targeting lower levels within the organisation. In many trusts and authorities there is not always a matching of the board's perception of risks and the opinions of different groups of employees. This lack of congruence can be the root cause of subsequent control failures which go on to take the board by surprise. Also, certain risks in isolation may seem relatively insignificant but when they are attached to individuals who feel very negative about the organisation, perhaps because of poor training or inadequate support, those risks become far more critical. Various tools, primarily survey based, have been developed to collect this information.

### *Identification of actions and responsibilities*

The results of the above establish a sensible and informed point from which to attach action and responsibility to risks that require management attention. Examples from the pilot sites, all with a differing approach, include Optimum Health Services NHS Trust, Hastings and Rother NHS Trust, and United Leeds Teaching Hospitals NHS Trust (see Chapter 10). A range of CSA workshops may well be linked to issues where a multidisciplinary approach is needed and the relevant employees operate in a culture that encourages openness. Not all issues match these circumstances.

### *Monitoring*

Unless a framework is in place to monitor the progress and effectiveness of planned actions then efforts will have been largely wasted.

### *Assurance statement*

This stepped approach will contribute to a trust or authority making an assurance statement based on risk management principles that can be described simply and sensibly to the public. The emphasis is upon reasonable assurance.

Such a process requires some form of underpinning documentation to ensure that a record is maintained of risk and control decisions. If such records are not maintained the process will become unmanageable and will not generate

Department Directorate

Department Directorate

Department Directorate

Key objective

Accountability

| Risk | Control |
|---|---|

Probability and impact assessment

Action

Risk category

Business planning ☐ Environmental ☐ Service management ☐

Corporate strategy ☐ Human resources ☐

| Completed by | Date |
|---|---|

**Figure 21.1** Risk evaluation: example documentation.

sufficient information for the board to conclude on assurance and accountability issues. Any such documentation needs to be practical and fit with existing systems and practices. Example documentation is set out in Figure 21.2.

## THE MERSEY INTERNAL AUDIT AGENCY(MIAA) APPROACH

MIAA is an NHS trading agency providing internal audit and consultancy services. One of the main reasons for MIAA's creation in 1990 was the recognition that individual trusts and authorities were unlikely to be able to sustain viable audit and consultancy teams within their own organisation. An equally important reason was the desire to provide a cost-effective service for the NHS from within the NHS. Audit clients stretch from North Wales through Cheshire and Merseyside to Lancashire. Controls assurance assignments have been delivered across the UK. Indicators of success include the following achievements:

- first public sector internal audit team to gain ISO 9000 quality assurance accreditation (1992)
- first NHS finance team to gain Investors in People (1994)
- winners of the North West Quality Award in the financial sector category (1995).

Since 1994 a significant client has been the NHS Executive. This work has focused upon the shaping of the NHS Corporate Governance Agenda with particular emphasis upon the following:

- pilot site work
- production of guidance
- production of Minimum Financial Control Statements for the 1997/98 annual accounts; (controls assurance statements are being phased in. As a first step the annual reports and accounts of health authorities and trusts for 1997/8 are to include a statement by the board of directors on internal financial controls. A more comprehensive controls assurance statement will become mandatory in the NHS in 1999/2000 embracing all control, whether financial or non-financial.)
- national training and implementation
- supporting organisations in the design and implementation of Controls Assurance strategies.

The MIAA approach follows (and to a considerable extent shaped) the principles set out in the generic process cycle. A range of techniques that can translate the processes described into practical delivery and subsequent action have been developed. However, for the purposes of this chapter, emphasis is being given to the undertaking of top-level self assessment workshops utilising a quality model (The Business Excellence Model) rather than explanation of the more routine processes associated with traditional CSA workshops.

## Top-Level Risk Assessment

An important first element of much of MIAA's Controls Assurance work has been the undertaking of a top-level review. The objective of this exercise is to facilitate senior management in the production of a prioritised risk list which also maps out current processes to mitigate risk. In summary, this is achieved through a workshop that utilises interactive technology. It provides an organisation with a top-down framing up of risk that can act as a platform and focus for subsequent work. A key element of the output is an action plan linking risk to accountability.

The background to developing such an approach has been driven by a range of debates with Chief Executives, Directors and Audit Committees. The consistent message from each of these groups has been that any process to address the assurance agenda must:

- recognise and build upon existing risk management and quality activities
- assess the current position
- be delivered within existing resources
- add value
- not be another initiative.

From that position a process was designed to secure top-level commitment through the conduct of a self assessment exercise with the following characteristics:

- structured quality model approach
- takes stock of existing strengths
- produces consensus over risk profile
- low input/high output.

The decision to use the Business Excellence Model as a focus stemmed from the recognition that the terms risk management, controls assurance and control self assessment were not the common currency of NHS professionals and were unlikely to engage interest. Quality has been a consistent premise for all healthcare workers and support staff. Consequently, the delivery of assurance through self assessment could sensibly be presented as integral to the wider quality agenda. In many respects risk and quality are two sides of the same coin. Quality measures and risk consequences parallel each other but the focus on quality brings the added dimension of continuous improvement. This is a very important point because there is a real concern that self assessment, which is centred upon risk generation and prioritisation, can lead an organisation into risk inertia. Individuals and groups of staff direct their energies to logging and calibrating risk to the exclusion of the very necessary process of seeing and taking opportunities. Quality unlocks the tendency to becoming submerged in the bureaucracy of risk aversion.

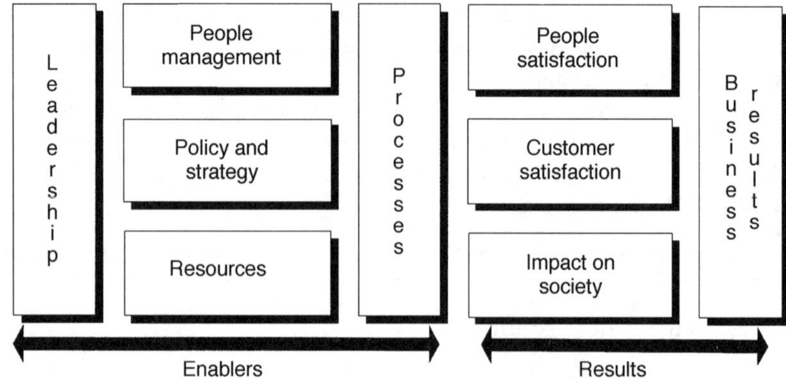


**Figure 21.3** The business excellence model – generic framework adapted for NHS.

## Business Excellence Model

The model forms an ideal framework for assessing any organisation (see Figure 21.3). It consists of nine criteria divided between Enablers (what we do) and Results (what we achieve). The nine criteria of the model are linked by the principle that Customer Satisfaction, People (employee) Satisfaction and Impact on Society are achieved through Leadership driving Policy & Strategy, People Management, Resources and Processes leading ultimately to excellence in Business Results.

## The Process

A top-level workshop is conducted usually with 6–8 Executive Directors and Senior Managers. The Board and Audit Committee are advised of the process but, generally, non-executives do not participate. The workshop takes 4–5 hours and prior to attendance each attendee completes a Controls Assurance Resource Pack. The pack asks a series of questions under each of the Business Excellence Model criteria. An extract from People Management is given in Figure 21.4.Following completion of the questions notes are then made under each section as shown in Figure 21.5. The completed Resource Packs are then individually and anonymously returned to MIAA and a consolidated report is prepared which becomes the agenda for the workshop. The report is structured across each of the Business Excellence criteria and sets out a graphical response of the group to each of the questions and summarises the views on strengths, weaknesses and risks. The facilitator presents the data back to the group and a structured debate

| Questions | Examples of evidence and potential risk |
|---|---|
| A. Are the skills and abilities needed by your Trust known, recorded, regularly updated and aligned to the business needs?<br>0 1 2 3 4 5 | *You keep and regularly review the skills and resources needed to meet your objectives and plans. When changes are made they are measured for effectiveness.*<br>*Undue pressure on management costs.*<br>*Increasingly complex personnel legislation.* |
| B. Are appraisal schemes employed to match the objectives and aspirations of your Trust and the individual?<br>0 1 2 3 4 5 | *Manager/employee reviews or appraisals are a feature of your Trust and are clearly and simply linked to its objectives and plans.*<br>*Inadequate time or funding for training requirements.* |
| C. Do managers coach and support employees through realistically set improvement targets, aligned to the business plan with progress regularly reviewed?<br>0 1 2 3 4 5 | *Managers encourage teamwork, spend time developing individuals, encourage and become involved in improvement activity.* |
| D. Is the full potential of all people being realised to achieve the Trust's strategic direction?<br>0 1 2 3 4 5 | *You are aware of both the skills and aspirations of all your staff and actively seek to utilise these to achieve the Trust's goals.* |
| E. Does the Trust provide sufficient support and protection to employees in relation to violence and other staff health matters?<br>0 1 2 3 4 5 | |
| F. Is the Trust in a position to meet its recruitment needs now and in the future?<br>0 1 2 3 4 5 | *Required numbers of staff, staff with required qualifications and experience, appropriate medical staff. Consider impact upon waiting list initiative targets, delayed treatment, poor quality treatment, costs of locums (with added risk of errors).* |
| G. Is the Trust sufficiently protected from employing an individual who might act fraudulently or negligently resulting in financial or reputation loss?<br>0 1 2 3 4 5 | |
| Key: 0: No – not on any occasion at any level.<br>1:<br>2:<br>3:<br>4:<br>5: Yes – this happens on all occasions at all levels. | |

**Figure 21.4** Extract from business excellence model adapted for the NHS – people management.

| Notes on people management | Strengths identified |
|---|---|
| | |
| Evidence | Risks/opportunities for improvement |
| | |

**Figure 21.5** Business excellence model – narrative matrix.

then ensues around diversity and consensus of attitudes, existence and robustness of evidence, etc.

Because the Excellence Model separates the debate into compartments it helps to focus direction. The facilitator's task is to arrive at an agreed list of key risks and then to vote on probability and impact. Optionfinder technology is used to speed up the voting process. An example of one of the graphs fed back to the workshop is shown in Figure 21.6. The number above the bars represents the number voting and the horizontal axis reflects 0 = poor and 5 = good (this was a workshop with a small number in attendance).

The facilitator would allow the group to explore the reasons for such voting to determine whether risk issues were triggered. Once risks have been defined probability and impact is polled resulting in a graph similar to that in Figure 21.7. Each of the letters represents a risk agreed by the group. In summary this process takes these steps:

- executive briefing
- commitment to proceed

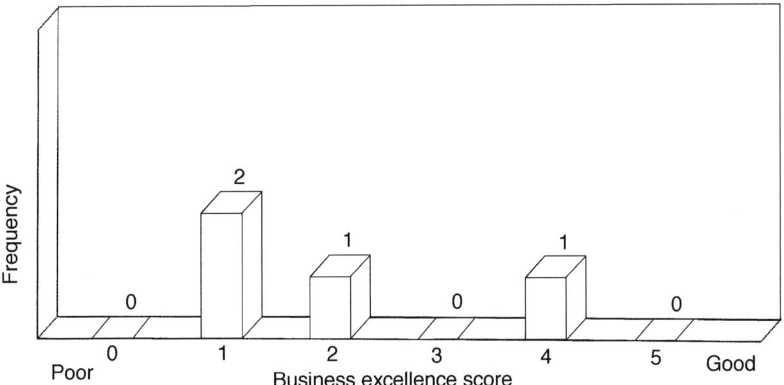


**Figure 21.6** Does the executive team act as a team in taking and communicating decisions?

- completion of controls assurance resource pack
- results collated
- half-day session to review collated results and arrive at consensus
- risk profile report produced.

This leads to

- assessment of overlaps and gaps in control
- consensus on risk profile and related action
- analysis including probability and impact evaluation
- targeted investment of time to reach a sensible view on controls assurance.

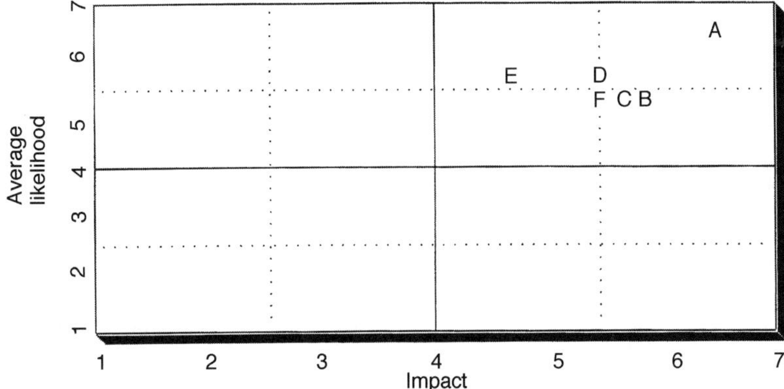


**Figure 21.7** Significance of risks identified.

## CONCLUSION

Once the top-level work has been delivered the results can then inform and direct future assurance strategy. One outcome is that it can target workshops that engage a wider range of staff. Mersey Internal Audit Agency have conducted an extensive range of risk workshops with multidisciplinary groups of staff. These have been selected as a result of the top-level assessment. Examples of the work performed and in progress are: communication at ward level; utilisation of agency/bank nursing; staff mix; payroll; non-pay expenditure. All of this work has engaged front-line staff in considering risks with substantial results. The important distinction from other CSA workshops, however, is that they connect with a Board-led framework and the results can, therefore, be linked to any assurance statements provided by a Board of Directors. If CSA workshops operate in a vacuum, tackling isolated issues, they may well produce worthy results but they will have little value in terms of an assurance agenda or in delivering sustained cultural change.

# 22

# A Workshop Approach to CSA in Housing Associations

*Caroline Greenwood*

## ANGLIA HOUSING GROUP

Anglia Housing Group has a group structure that allows locally based members, in the form of traditional housing associations, local housing companies, foyers and maintenance providers, to operate effectively and efficiently to achieve the Group's commitment to maximising growth and potential in social housing across East Anglia.

Over 10,000 units are owned or managed across the Group by 250 staff with electronic links between locations. Specialist support functions are provided to members by Anglia as the parent to the Group through Service Level Agreements. This arrangement allows members to obtain value for money in essential administrative services so that they can concentrate on their core activity of the meeting of housing need. As an innovator in the housing world Anglia staff and Board members are required frequently to identify and manage risks so that potential benefits to tenants can be achieved.

## INTERNAL AUDIT

In 1996 Anglia appointed a Head of Group Audit and Risk Management. This post reports to the Group Chief Executive and liaises with the Audit Committee. The Head of Audit is supported by an Audit Assistant. The annual audit plan is designed to ensure that systems of internal control are effective but emphasis is placed on developing risk management awareness and skills in all staff.

## WHAT CSA MEANS TO ME

Control self assessment acknowledges that those best placed to identify and control risks are staff who face those risks daily in their work. The process provides education and guidance in the identification, evaluation, documentation and decision making regarding risks so that this ability is promoted at all levels of management.

## CSA ACTION PLAN

First sell the concept to the Board. Use your Audit Committee. Preferably write their report to the Board for them referring to Housing Corporation requirements, best practice, Hampel and emphasise how the development will support the culture of empowerment and personal accountability in a fast-growing business environment. Useful contact points for reference material for housing associations are shown at Appendix 22.1.

Educate the Board. Since the requirement for a statement on internal financial controls was introduced for the financial year from April 1996 you may have already had to do some explanation of control evaluation. Use the opportunity to explain how self assessment by managers and their teams will provide support, together with the work of internal audit, for the Board's confidence in signing the statement. Be prepared to give a short presentation to the Board to demonstrate the CSA process with examples of the output but do not become bogged down in operational detail – the Board should be concerned with strategic risk management. Most Associations have Boards made up of non-executive staff. This is a big plus factor in objective assessment of risk management so make sure they realise their importance in the role and the need for them to understand what risks face their Association so that they can challenge when necessary.

Ensure the Executive team understand risk management and can complete CSA for their own department. It is unlikely that the Executive will be able to devote a whole day to attend the workshop themselves but they should understand the objectives and subject matter if they are to support their teams. Either present a paper at an Executive meeting or arrange to speak to each member of the Executive individually.

Gain written commitment from the Chief Executive and/or Executive team to the involvement of staff in CSA. Provide a paper which will give details of the time required, the content of the proposed workshop, the likely output and examples of the benefits to the Executive in their work. Ask the Executive to suggest staff to attend but have your own list prepared which you can use as guidance – senior managers are often naturally reluctant to suggest key staff 'disappear' for a day and may conveniently forget to nominate them.

Draw up a hierarchy of self-certification to support the Board statement on internal control and use it to support your request for commitment. Be prepared to quote Hampel's conclusion that a sound system of internal control should cover not only financial controls but also operational and compliance controls and risk management when a restriction to internal financial control is promoted to save resources. The Housing Corporation's risk management requirement relates to operational and compliance risks and controls in addition to financial.

Become well versed in your organisation's corporate strategy and plans, core values and mission statement, as applicable. CSA is an aid to the achievement of corporate objectives and must reflect the culture of your organisation. It will be successful only if senior management are prepared to delegate responsibility and authority to their teams and encourage them in turn to use that authority to achieve stated objectives.

Decide whether to run workshops with cross-functional delegates or as a complete work team. The latter approach was promoted in the early days of CSA but I have not yet worked in an organisation that was prepared effectively to shut down a department for a day. Delegates drawn from similar levels of responsibility usually work well together. Combine housing staff with finance, IT, training and personnel to make sure they appreciate that one's opportunity can be a risk to another's objectives and that controls have budgetary implications. CSA should be seen as organisation-wide, albeit that it is broken down into smaller sections for practical purposes.

Arrange a room – one large area for group work and at least one syndicate room. As with most training it will be more effective if you can remove delegates from their normal workplace so that they can concentrate on the topic – ban mobile phones/pagers. Arrange for an overhead projector and flipcharts in the room. Send out joining instructions inviting delegates to bring with them their job descriptions and departmental plans. Prepare your script, visual aids and handouts. Time each session and annotate your text with timings – you will lose track on the day. Run through exercises with volunteers to make sure they produce the expected results.

## WORKSHOP CONTENT

### Introduction

Start the workshop with an exercise to break the ice and to provide information from which you can extract risks and controls. This exercise can be referred to as an illustration of topics to be discussed later. A simple example is to analyse the risks faced in achieving an agreed objective of arriving at the workshop on time (e.g., oversleeping, hangover, etc., the more imaginative the better to start the day), then identify possible controls over those risks and talk through how each delegate decided which controls to implement based on risk, resources and potential impact of the risk materialising. Such an exercise can illustrate every stage of the risk-management process.

## Risk Management Process

Talk through the theory of:

- What is risk management?
- What is the risk management process?
- How do we identify risks?
- Assessing likelihood/consequences/impact
- What could we do with a risk?
- What are controls?
- What is a cost-effective control?
- Risk grid – to assess each risk against its potential impact and likelihood and facilitate decision-making.
- Action Plan.

## Corporate Governance

Give a brief history of current trends in corporate governance and Housing Corporation requirements to set self assessment in context in relation to requirements for Board statements. It is useful to have available the Combined Code, the Hampel Report and relevant Housing Corporation circulars, to illustrate your point. Your Association should already be using a statement on internal financial control in its financial statements, so have this wording available for reference.

## Audit Committee

Explain the role of an Audit Committee in the Association and the importance of non-executive Board members. Your Association should have Terms of Reference for the Audit Committee and perhaps an Audit Charter which you can use to illustrate your points.

## Control Framework

Explain the value of breaking down control and risk assessment into defined sections. The simplest and most widely accepted method of doing so is to adopt the 'COSO' approach. The components of this framework are detailed in Appendix 22.2.

## Control Self Assessment

Give an explanation of CSA and its benefit to an organisation.

## Links with Business Initiatives

Explain the relationship between CSA and corporate strategies and plans, policies, value statements and cultures within your Association. This may be your culture of empowerment, flatter structures, stated policies of team responsibilities or the Housing Corporation's move towards self-certification on annual returns. Examine your own Association's policies and strategy and prepare a file of documents which illustrate your point.

## COSO Assessment

Ask delegates to produce their own approach to the evaluation of their area of responsibility (in groups) using suggested checklists of questions. An example of a checklist approach is given at Appendix 22.2.

## Board Statement

Explain to your delegates that after the workshop, resultant self assessments should provide assurance to the Board in signing the statement on internal financial control in the audited financial statements.

The link between the wording of self-certifications and Board Statements should be discussed at the workshop. Illustrate the wording of proposed or existing forms of self-certification to ensure that delegates will be comfortable with signing the certificates when requested to do so.

## Exercises

Use different, topical exercises to illustrate the stages of risk identification and management. If designed correctly they can be used to take delegates through these stages progressively with the last part demonstrating how they can complete a risk management record for a fictitious enterprise. The case study shown at Appendix 22.3 was based loosely on newspaper reports of the Barings loss which was topical at the time it was first used. One part of the case study illustrates how weaknesses in the Barings management could be applicable to Housing or other organisations to demonstrate the universality of risk management and its value to managers.

## Output

Results of the delegates' COSO assessment are transferred to an example of a template used to document risks and controls provided. An example template is shown in Appendix 22.4.

## Follow-up

Ideally a half-day workshop should be held approximately two weeks later so that delegates have time to carry out their own assessment. This workshop helps them to consolidate their findings and produce a summary self assessment. When this workshop is not possible individual follow-up by internal audit with each delegate or groups of delegates is essential. Emphasis is placed on the manager's ability to demonstrate the basis of their evaluation and on the involvement of their whole team (this can mean further, shorter workshops on a team basis).

## Do's and Don'ts

The following pointers are based on my own, sometimes painful, experience. I make no apologies for the obvious ones – in times of pressure they need to be firmly imprinted in your mind.

### *Do*

- Focus on the key risks facing your Association and demonstrate how these are reflected in the individual objectives of your target group.
- Make sure you are convinced of the benefits of CSA to your organisation or you will have trouble convincing others.
- Get visible support from the Audit Committee and Executive managers in the form of invitations from them to workshop delegates, opening and closing the workshop, attending a workshop themselves.
- Plan how CSA is going to be implemented in your organisation. Involve the Board, through a paper you write for the Audit Committee.
- Make sure the Executive agree to the proposed commitment of time for workshops. I have found it better at the outset to be honest about the time required rather than overrun and find that managers start to resent the time commitment required.
- Carry out research into your workshop delegates so that you can relate

theory to their own area of work. Think of examples for risks and controls in their area – it impresses them with your knowledge and forethought.

- Remember to give feedback to the Executive and Board regularly to keep them interested and committed.
- Use the questioning approach – keep handouts simple with a list of questions which the delegates can ask themselves rather than long narrative.
- Use mnemonics wherever possible as quick checklists.
- Use real-life case studies to illustrate points. This really is effective (but beware ridiculing other Associations or departments to delegates as stated below). Many real-life control weaknesses sound very amusing when described in a matter-of-fact way. When the laughing has finished ask: 'could this happen in your area of responsibility?' You may be surprised by the answers.
- Before the workshops ask colleagues to think of every possible argument against or question about CSA and to fire them at you so that you can prepare your responses should they arise for real.
- Bring some humour into the workshop if at all possible. Look for comic articles and cartoons which illustrate risk and control to get delegates in a relaxed mood.
- Base some exercises on topical or light-hearted subjects – it really does help to demonstrate the process in a more interesting way.
- Talk about your own operational experiences, especially if you have had any control failures. It helps to show you know what it's like at the sharp end, even if the experience is outside the housing world.
- Illustrate the workshop objective by doing you own brief CSA of internal audit as an example and a chance to gain the delegates' views.
- Cut out and display around the workshop newspaper cuttings or quotations which illustrate your points. These will normally be failures in risk management because that is what makes the headlines. You can use these as the basis of discussion about how the delegates would have assessed and managed the risk.
- Encourage interaction between delegates; ask them to challenge each other's assessment of risk management in their area in a friendly way to bring some action into the workshop.
- Make sure you plan the day to include the delegates moving around at least every hour to keep attention, have separate rooms for syndicate exercises, for example.

- Admit it if you do not know the answer and make sure you let the delegate know when you have found the information requested – they will be impressed.
- Make definite arrangements for the follow-up action with each delegate before they leave the workshop or you will never tie them down. Make every effort to stick to these arrangements.
- Be enthusiastic – it may not be expected of auditors so will take your delegates by surprise and make them realise CSA can be fun.
- Again, focus on the key risks facing your Association's objectives and the benefits self assessment will bring to the achievement of those objectives. This is the point of the activity.

### *Don't*

- Ever be heard to talk of self assessment as a project – people will see it as a one-off form filling exercise.
- Have just one facilitator all day if at all possible – it's very dull for the delegates to hear only one voice.
- Talk in audit jargon – we may find the classification of controls fascinating but operational managers want to know what it all means to them in practice.
- Delay follow-up to the workshop – you will lose impetus and undermine the credibility of the work.
- Relate tales of control weakness, however great, which you have found during an audit which apply to any of the delegates – 'naming and shaming' will not gain commitment and co-operation.
- Be hung up on filling in the forms perfectly – it's the thought processes and what the delegates will remember in their daily work which will ultimately benefit your organisation.
- Refer to CSA as an audit requirement. Even if it is a Housing Corporation regulatory requirement, focus on the ongoing benefits or it will lose its credibility with delegates.

## APPENDIX 22.1

# References/Guidance Relevant to CSA

## HOUSING CORPORATION

### *Circulars*

R2 – 11/94 *Internal Controls in Registered Housing Associations.*
R2 – 02/95 *Code of Audit Practice for Registered Housing Associations.*
R2 – 18/96 *Internal Financial Control and Financial Reporting.*
R2 – 18/98 *Risk Management.*

### *Publications*

*Risk Management for Registered Social Landlords* (Executive Summary and Detailed Guidance) March 1997.

Code of Audit Practice January 1995.

Contact: Housing Corporation, 149 Tottenham Court Road, London W1P 0BN. Tel: 0171 393 2000; fax: 0171 393 2111; web site – http://www.open.gov.uk/hcorp

## HOUSING ASSOCIATION INTERNAL AUDIT FORUM

- Best Practice Guides issued by practising auditors in the Housing field.
- Benchmarking research carried out and published.
- Regular meetings, training and interest groups arranged.

Contact: Jane Bloodworth (Chair), Hanover Housing Association, Hanover House, 1 Bridge Close, Staines TW18 4TB.

## APPENDIX 22.2

# Sample Checklist for Assessing Control

## COSO: RISKS AND CONTROLS

### Control Environment

What are we supposed to be achieving? Do we have:

- an organisation chart
- job descriptions
- key targets and performance indicators
- written business plans and objectives
- corporate values and policies
- ISO 9000 registration
- visible support from senior managers
- written authority levels
- staff with qualifications appropriate to their responsibilities
- knowledge of regulatory requirements.

Are we involved in:

- preparation on business plans
- review of performance against plan
- consideration of business expansion and development.

### Identification and Evaluation of Risks

What could go wrong? In relation to our objectives have we:

- identified what must go right and could go wrong in our operation?
- considered the likelihood and consequences of things going wrong?
- done something to make sure our businesses will continue even if things should go wrong?

- used our resources/staff to limit our exposure to failure/make sure things go right?

## Information and Communication

How do we know what is going on? Do we use:

- management information systems
- performance indicators
- reports of transactions/events out of the ordinary
- system prompts related to authority/transaction levels.

Do we know:

- how our team/area is performing against plans?
- how plans for the future will affect our work and training requirements?
- performance measures in time to make necessary adjustments before next assessment?
- results of how we are performing against our individual objectives?

Does information go to the person with the responsibility for the outcome as soon as possible after the events?

Can we request reports with a range of specifications to satisfy particular business demands at any time?

## Control Procedures

How do we make sure that everything is OK? Do we take action:

- to ensure that everything we produce is
  - valid
  - accurate
  - complete
  - correctly timed
- to make sure that one person does not have sole control from start to finish of any transaction/project?
- to assign appropriate authority levels to staff and transactions?
- to protect assets physically and logically?

## Monitoring and Corrective Action

How do 'they' know how we are doing? Do we:

- act on reported information (performance indicators, etc.) to amend business plans
- revise job descriptions and key targets when plans alter
- respond to internal/external audits
- examine accounts and investigate variances monthly
- respond to Housing Corporation reviews
- report to the board as required.

## APPENDIX 22.3

# Example Case Study

This is the tale of the collapse of a supposedly booming business – you are asked to read the information provided and note what you think went wrong.

You have ten minutes for this part of the exercise.

### GRABINS FINANCE PLC

Grabins: a long-established financial institution dealing with conventional banking and investment services.

A decision was made to expand operations into the sale of time-share options in Australia which looked to be a growing market. This function was to be autonomous on a day-to-day basis with a local man as Manager. Ultimate control rested with the London office.

ORGANISATION CHART

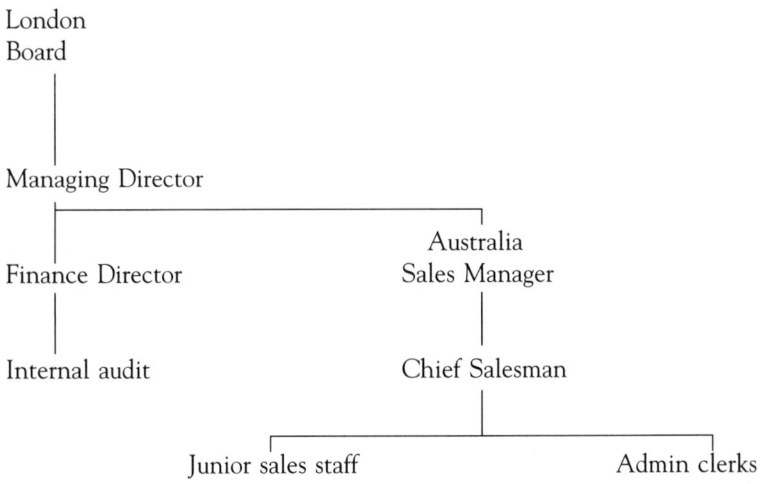

## Case Notes

### *Managing director*

A remote, cautious banker of the old school. Believed everyone knew their job and their place in the pecking order and should be satisfied within their social lot in which advancement would be based on hard work and structured career progress. Proud of Grabins' reputation and his personal royal connection for which he expected official honours soon.

### *Finance director*

Relatively new to the organisation, Anxious to make a good impression on the MD. Grasp of budgeting seen as poor by his staff but was convinced by the MD's assertion that clerks would sort out the figures as long as the FD reviewed the overall accounts. No overseas trading experience.

### *Internal audit*

Reported to the Finance Director. Seen as rather a necessary evil and hindrance to real work. No direct reporting line to the Board. No strong characters – all in the department for years and saw their futures tied to Grabins. No previous experience of auditing overseas trade but sound accounting knowledge.

### *Sales manager*

Australian so knew the territory. New to Grabins. Happy to let his direct report handle deals whilst he concentrated on corporate hospitality aspects of promotion of the organisation. Impressed with the energy and helpful approach of his direct report. Disliked long-haul travel and modern communications – liked to think he was king of the Australian empire and avoided interference from London.

### *Chief salesman*

Promoted twelve months ago after joining as a clerk in administration two years previously. Had dealt with all aspects of administration office in turn, covering purchases of properties, sales of time-share options, receipts and payments and accounts. Very personable with excellent sales skills. Quiet and reliable. Promotion to Chief Salesman followed secondment to a project team which uncovered wrong-doing by a group of clients. His fellow team members were high-flyers and consultants (he was there to provide administrative details of the process) with whom he enjoyed a fine lifestyle for the six months of the case. Negotiated and finalised all deals for property purchase and time-share allocations. Passed paperwork and accounting instructions to administration clerks whom he supervised.

### *Back office*

Recorded all receipts and payments (authorised by their manager or the Sales Manager). Produced accounting reports and advised manager of discrepancies. Looked after property deeds and time-share certificates as passed to them when the deals were finalised.

### *Background*

Time share deals were carried out in different currencies and converted to sterling for the final accounts. Property sales in Australia were loosely governed and there had been cases elsewhere of title deeds being used for more than one 'sale' of the same property. One clerk had recently received a payment of £20,000 which he could not match with a customer account. He had advised his manager and was a little concerned that he seemed to have forgotten about it. No one queried it further, however, and as he had posted it to the suspense account number 44444 in accordance with their accounting instructions he felt he had done all he could. Printed reports of all accounts, including suspense, were passed monthly to the Sales Manager and Chief Salesman. The latter considered these to be an accounting matter and the concern of the London staff.

### *Prior to 'collapse'*

The Chief Salesman started to arrange deals in selling time-shares, on properties not yet built, at discounted prices to purchasers (and promises of future benefits) and using their deposits to invest funds on behalf of Grabins until stage payments were required by the property developers. His manager saw the investment returns and wished he had thought of this idea himself to impress the Board. His protégé thrived on his new responsibilities and performance bonuses, bought a luxury home and moved into quite an exotic lifestyle – well – he was young and free of responsibilities and good company too. He worked hard, rarely took more than a few days off at a time and could cope with not only the selling but with sorting out the administration office too, an invaluable all-rounder.

The clerks relied on him for guidance and all agreed that the report from the London Internal Auditors was nothing but nit-picking. They were pleased that the Finance Director had accepted their Sales Manager's assurance (after consultation with the Chief Salesman who was the system expert) that the audit recommendation to carry out a 'one-for-one' reconciliation of property deeds and time-share certificates would be an unnecessary waste of resources.

After this incident business flourished and London received unbelievably handsome returns from the investment deals but the Chief Salesman started to look tired and drawn and was uncharacteristically irritable with staff. He was quite snappy when they asked for help as the first properties under the new scheme started to be completed and there appeared to be double-bookings of the time-share options which had to be sorted out. He did, however, use his sales skills to smooth ruffled feathers amongst staff and clients.

A month later the Finance Director arrived from London unannounced to say that Grabins had decided to sell selected properties for which he would require both the title deeds and the relevant time-share certificates.

Within three days they realised that some properties on which options had been sold did not even exist, options had been double booked and, worse still, funds collected in option payments were not in Grabins' accounts. The resultant debt put them into bankruptcy.

## Lessons to be Learned: Could it Happen to us in Housing Associations?

Distribute at end to illustrate how lessons are transferable.

1. Profits (surpluses) are great news – unless you don't understand how you achieved them. If performance results are 'unbelievable' maybe that's just how they should be treated *(business plans, forecasts)*.
2. Know what you are expecting and question variances *(budgets, financial monitoring, costcentre control)*.
3. New opportunities can be rewarding but be aware of the new risks they present which need to be managed *(Group structures, PFI)*.
4. Concentrate on cash movements – cash is real, entries in accounting systems can be misleading *(bank statements)*.
5. Reconcile, reconcile and reconcile again – especially suspense accounts and material assets *(control accounts, certificates, deeds, equipment, properties)*.
6. Information Technology may have reduced the global trading world to a computer screen but physical remoteness requires close operational management. How do you know what is happening if you're not actually there in a decentralised organisation? *(sheltered schemes, partnership arrangements, development projects)*.

7. Specialist activity requires specialist knowledge in operation and in monitoring *(diversification, LHCs)*.
8. A function in which one man is an island is at the mercy of that man's skill and integrity *(tendering, purchasing, project management)*.
9. People who rarely take annual leave may be dedicated to your organisation's objectives. They may also be dedicated to their own ends; make rules apply to everyone *(personnel policies)*.
10. People do inherit fortunes and win the lottery but are you sure this is the source of their new wealth? (SENSITIVE).
11. If you employ experts in risk management and controls take note of what they say and make them as independent as possible *(Audit Committee, reporting line for Internal Audit/external agents)*.

## Grabins: Risk Management Weaknesses

Distribute for comparison with delegates' results:

1. No acknowldgment of need for special attention to manage increased risk in activity outside field of experience.
2. Historical, customary procedures applicable to traditional business transferred unmodified to new, fast-moving activity.
3. No questioning of unexpected results.
4. Failure to appreciate the lack of external regulation and insist upon self-regulation.
5. Poor internal communication and co-operation.
6. Distance between accountants and day-to-day administration.
7. Poor financial reporting and monitoring system.
8. Lack of imagination/insular view of senior managers.
9. No segregation of duties between dealing and administration.
10. Internal Audit not valued or heeded.
11. No independent avenue by which Internal Audit could pursue concerns.
12. No check of assets.
13. No monitoring of suspense account.
14. No monitoring of errors and complaints to establish cause, frequency or common link.
15. No consideration of life-style and personality of staff – or changes.

## Next Stage of Exercise

Assume the role of consultant adviser to the Grabins Board and record your observations of what went wrong and recommended action on the record sheet provided which already has functional headings added. (To save time you can number your points and show number only in 'what went wrong' column.)

You have ten minutes to complete this part of the exercise.

**WHAT GROUNDED GRABINS?**

| AREA OF ACTIVITY (BUSINESS RISK AREA) | WHAT WENT WRONG? (SPECIFIC RISK) | WHAT COULD BE DONE ABOUT IT? (CONTROL: how, who, when?) | HOW COULD BOARD MAKE SURE IT HAD BEEN DONE? (MONITORING: how, who, when?) |
|---|---|---|---|
| FINANCIAL | 7 | Access to financial systems from London/ regular specified reports. | Appoint Office Manager in Australia, reporting to FD, independent of Sales team. |
| (FINANCIAL) | 12 | Periodic check of title deeds – documented. | FD monthly reviews/report to Board. Review of checks by FD/annual audit. |
| | 13 | Monthly reconciliations by Office Manager – documented. | FD review of reconciliations. |
| REGULATORY (COMPLIANCE) | 4 | Setting of performance standards – based on similar regulations. | Compliance reports (audit) to Board regularly. |
| ORGANISATIONAL | 5 | Use Office Manager as liaison between Australia and London. | Visits by FD/MD. |
| (OPERATIONAL) | 9 | Split functions in back office/sales. | Audits/Office Manager's job description. |
| | 10 | Appointment of Head of Audit from o/s Grabins. Professional approach. | Professional standards required/appoint Audit Committee. |
| | 11 | Reporting line to Audit Committee (Board). | Audit Committee reports to full Board, at least annually. |

**WHAT GROUNDED GRABINS?**

| AREA OF ACTIVITY (BUSINESS RISK AREA) | WHAT WENT WRONG? (SPECIFIC RISK) | WHAT COULD BE DONE ABOUT IT? (CONTROL: how, who, when?) | HOW COULD BOARD MAKE SURE IT HAD BEEN DONE? (MONITORING: how, who, when?) |
|---|---|---|---|
| EMPOWERMENT | 8 | Education in fraud alerts – by external experts. | Training/feedback reports/reliance on senior managers 'MBWA'. |
| (OPERATIONAL) | 15 | As above | As above |
| OPERATIONAL | 2 | Project team/brainstorming approach to new initiatives. | Summary of project work before Board approval given. |
| (OPERATIONAL) | 6 | Office Manager appointment reporting to FD. | Reports from FD/reliance on staff. |
| DIVERSIFICATION | 1 | As for item 2 – plus risk management education and documentation. | As for item 2. |
| (OPERATIONAL) | | | |
| MONITORING/VERIFICATION | 3 | Pre-determined performance results – documented explanation of variances. | Review of performance actual vs. projected. |
| (FINANCIAL) | 14 | Procedure to document complaints and outcome – by Office Manager. | Report to MD – quarterly summary. |

YOU HAVE JUST COMPLETED A RISK MANAGEMENT RECORD!

## APPENDIX 22.4

# Risk Management Record

| TEAM FUNCTION/JOB TITLE:<br>OBJECTIVE: | | | | | | | OPERATIONAL<br>FINANCIAL<br>COMPLIANCE | | |
|---|---|---|---|---|---|---|---|---|---|
| BUSINESS FUNCTION/ RISK AREA | SPECIFIC RISK | CURRENT CONTROL | O.K.? | ACTION | | | MONITORING | | |
| | | | | WHAT | WHO | WHEN | HOW | WHO | WHEN |
| | | | | | | | | | |

# Part 5

## The Way Forward

# 23

# Winning Hearts and Minds

*Steven Barlow*

## INTRODUCTION

The management culture of the late 1990s demands a fresh approach to assessing controls and risks. Leading organisations are now beginning to implement Control Self Assessment (CSA) frameworks to meet this demand and ingrain a control consciousness into their people and processes. The objectives of this chapter are to:

- provide a definition of CSA
- explain why the demand for CSA has grown
- emphasise the importance of an integrated approach to business risk management
- consider critical success factors and practical tips for the successful implementation and adoption of CSA
- review how internal audit can be involved in, and benefit from, CSA
- suggest how CSA is likely to evolve in the future.

## DEFINITION OF CSA

CSA is an all-encompassing phrase that can be defined in many different ways. The key objectives are to identify and, to the extent possible, measure business risks and improve related controls and business processes to help strengthen business performance. CSA provides a means to achieve these objectives by having a formal procedure for extracting knowledge from business stakeholders and developing action plans to help manage and control risks. Companies that implement CSA should be able to gain competitive advantage through the improvement in business performance arising from their ability to manage business risks more efficiently.

The components of CSA depend upon the desired outcome. A comprehensive approach would be to utilise the tools and techniques described below to self assess the strategy of a business; the risks to the organisation in achieving its strategic objectives; the controls in place to mitigate the risks; and the processes operating, to identify performance gaps and opportunities for business improvement by reference to best practices.

CSA can use two broad categories of tools, facilitated workshops and/or surveys and questionnaires.

### *Facilitated workshops*

These involve:

- preliminary work and planning for either single sessions or a series of connected meetings
- a facilitator guiding the meeting of the 'process owners'; management who are involved with the issues being considered and are critical to the implementation of controls in the area
- an agenda used by the facilitator to help ensure the session examines the processes, risks and controls in a structured manner
- use of a framework or model to cover all issues which could focus on controls, risks or specific issues developed for that project; optionally
    - a recorder to record the issues
    - an expert on the area to ensure the session brings out key issues (for example an industry or information technology specialist)
    - electronic voting software to help analyse and prioritise issues
    - reporting and development of action plans.

The British Standards Institution provides a good example of how this type of CSA can be successfully implemented. The output of the workshops helps to drive audit plans by assessing the business processes related to each risk and using this to help identify projects to be carried out. In addition, the board of the British Standards Institution is using CSA as an integral part of its strategic planning process to help ensure that business risks throughout the organisation are being appropriately identified and addressed.

### *Surveys and questionnaires*

These involve management completing questionnaires on risks and key controls in paper or electronic form. This can be supplemented by interviews and attest work by internal audit (to avoid 'cheating'). ASDA plc provides a good example of the implementation of electronic self assessment (for further details of how this operates see Chapter 15).

Both types of tool emphasise that the system of internal control is not the responsibility of internal audit or simply of senior management but a *shared* responsibility among all employees in the organisation. Therefore the place to start is to *ask the people* who work within the process for *their* assessment of the risks and controls in *their* process. This assessment covers both those managing the process and the employees who work in it.

## DEMAND FOR CSA

CSA is still in its infancy both in terms of thinking on the process and the application of the tool. This helps to explain why only a small number of organisations around the world have adopted a comprehensive CSA approach out of the many which are implementing elements of CSA by bolting them onto existing procedures.

The idea for CSA came from the recognition that the best way to get management to own the system of internal control is to empower them to assess the elements of it themselves. Human nature is such that if you come up with an idea yourself, you are more likely to want to own it.

Internal audit has been a catalyst in the development of CSA as part of its evolution from compliance auditing, with internal audit carrying out reviews from its 'ivory tower', to a more enlightened approach which covers operational and business issues and related risks.

The need for better risk identification and management is a key driver of the development of CSA. An Economist Intelligence Unit survey (*Managing Business Risks – an integrated approach* Economist Intelligence Unit 1995) of the Chief Executives of nearly 3,000 of the largest companies in the world highlighted that less than 50% have 'high confidence' in their business risk management systems.

There is accordingly need for better risk identification and management in its broadest sense, not only covering financial but also commercial and operational areas. This demand has been fuelled by:

- highly publicised business control breakdowns such as those at Barings, BCCI, and Polly Peck
- companies empowering their staff which is leading to individuals having higher and greater authority levels
- organisational downsizing, flattening, restructuring and re-engineering which is removing middle management who used to provide important checks and balances and enable adequate segregation of duties
- the Cadbury and Hampel Committee reports, and the Combined Code, which have increased the focus on the importance of effective internal

controls and endorsed the move towards a wider definition of controls to cover operational and commercial as well as financial areas

- the desire of non-executive directors and members of audit committees to have more extensive and structured information presented to them on the quality of the control environment and the extent to which executive management are identifying and managing the business risks in respect of the companies they serve
- increasingly global and competitive marketplaces resulting in a greater need to identify risks and take appropriate remedial action on a timely basis
- management incentive schemes which are creating greater pressure to perform and potentially take shortcuts.

Traditionally, responsibility for the identification and management of business risks has not been defined and a number of functions have been involved in the process: treasury, financial control, internal audit, external audit, IT security, credit control, production control, physical security, etc. The need is for a more integrated approach to business risk management whereby there is a common understanding of what constitutes risk across the organisation, and information on these risks is shared within a framework and related processes which enable them to be effectively managed and controlled.

## ADOPTION ISSUES – EVALUATING THE FEASIBILITY OF CSA AND CRITICAL SUCCESS FACTORS

### Importance of Culture and Environment

In order to have confidence to proceed with the implementation of a CSA framework, it is important to be sure that the ideas will work in the organisation. Companies that seem best suited to CSA are likely to be those that have an open corporate culture and are willing to discuss control and risk issues.

Understanding the culture of an organisation is vital to the successful launch of CSA. In some organisations the need for complete honesty and frankness could be seen as a threat and gaining buy-in and acceptance of the process could become an issue. Resistance could be met in respect of companies where the culture is not 'open' and employees are encouraged to focus on their own jobs rather than the bigger picture. This is likely to be made worse where there is downsizing and staff are more concerned about protecting their jobs. CSA can sometimes be seen as a threat. People naturally feel threatened by something new. The candour and honesty required by CSA can exacerbate this, particularly if there is a fear that problems identified may be held against the people who have helped to identify them.

By recognising cultural and environmental factors at the outset, the CSA approach can be tailored to take advantage of each organisation's strengths using an appropriate mix of workshop sessions, paper questionnaires, individual interviews and on-line questionnaires. Broadly speaking, the following types of organisation may tend to be more suited to implementing CSA based on surveys and questionnaires – those which have:

- hierarchical structures
- staff with defined responsibilities and close supervision
- limited employee participation and training
- a tendency to be run by policies and procedures
- a number of locations with largely uniform systems and procedures.

Organisations which allow their employees more empowerment and accountability and have more of a continuous improvement culture will tend to be more suited to CSA using facilitated workshops.

Although research has shown that there is little correlation between industry and the use of CSA, two exceptions appear to be the oil and gas industry, where the concept originated, and the financial services industry where there has historically been more focus on control and risk awareness. It may be that these types of companies operate in a stringent regulatory environment and so are more likely to benefit from CSA more quickly.

## Role of Top Management and Importance of their Support

Organisations with top management who have realised that control and risk management are integral to their long-term success will be well suited to CSA, but the implementation takes ongoing management commitment. All too often management have a number of demands on their time and the prospect of yet another initiative may sometimes be overwhelming, especially if the organisation has a small management team. There must be commitment, particularly throughout the implementation phase, to invest the time necessary to train staff and undertake the assessment process. Support from top management is crucial to the success of any CSA launch. Accordingly, it is important to:

- get an enthusiastic CSA sponsor; one member of top management committed to influencing other members of management and supporting

key decisions relating to the CSA program – this will normally be the Director of Finance and/or Chief Executive
- obtain the support of the audit committee and board, and subsequently the top management of all businesses within the organisation.

Management support can be improved if the objectives, expectations and deliverables of the CSA initiative are clearly specified at the outset and in respect of each project within it. To facilitate winning this support throughout the organisation, consideration should be given to:

- encouraging the management team to send out a communication to relevant employees endorsing the initiative and explaining how it will be rolled out
- asking the most senior manager at each workshop to introduce it to demonstrate the commitment to CSA.

## Establishing a Risk Management Process, Committee and Risk Register

The formal establishment of a risk management process creates a framework for risk assessment and ongoing monitoring. Giving a director formal responsibility for risk management and setting up a risk management committee as a subcommittee of the board which regularly reports to the latter are useful ways of creating a central focus for risk management.

The use of a risk management action plan or risk register to record all risks identified and monitor progress in managing them is a tool which helps promote accountability and ownership of risk management initiatives. This should record each key risk, the person responsible for managing the risk and the status of action taken in relation to the latter. It should be regularly reviewed by management to monitor the implementation of agreed actions and periodically updated by the CSA process.

## Importance of a Risk Identification Framework

In relation to workshops, establish a risk identification framework which is capable of operating at either the strategic, entity or process level and which has two main components.

1. A clear understanding of business strategies and objectives.
2. A common risk language.

The definition of business risk, namely something that might adversely affect an organisation's ability to achieve its business objectives, confirms that it is vitally important that business objectives are understood before risks can be identified. It is therefore important that whoever is undertaking any identification of risks becomes fully conversant with the organisation's business objectives and its individual strengths, weaknesses, opportunities and threats.

Without a common language to describe risks, any effort to identify them will have no clear structure, and communication, categorisation and aggregation of them will be difficult. Many forms of language exist to describe frameworks. Figure 23.1 sets out the Arthur Andersen Business Risk Model™. This model can be used to simulate ideas about risks which might not be readily apparent to the organisation. Systematically utilising a framework is the best way to help ensure that all possible risks have been identified. It also allows risks to be categorised and understood in a consistent way.

## Importance of Quick Reports and Feedback

It is critical for all types of CSA to ensure that the information gathered as a result of the process is fed back to the relevant managers in a coherent, timely and meaningful way. In relation to workshops, this means producing a formal report of the results of the session incorporating management's action plans to address issues identified. It is important to ensure that responsibilities for each action are allocated and there is a regular follow up mechanism so that progress on implementation is monitored. The output may include:

- a record of discussion comments and survey votes recorded as the meeting progressed
- two-dimensional risk and control matrices of voting results showing the significance and likelihood of risks occurring
- feedback based on a post-meeting analysis of the information gathered during the meeting.

The following are two examples of the types of report which can be generated:

1. A first-stage vote to prioritise risks on the basis of their significance and likelihood enables the risk map or matrix in Figure 23.2 to be produced. Risks in the top right corner are risks which would have a significant impact and are considered likely to happen.
2. A further vote on the risks in the top right-hand corner can help to prioritise risks and develop a risk management action plan. The matrix in

**ENVIRONMENT RISK**

| | | | |
|---|---|---|---|
| Competitor | Sensitivity | Shareholder relations | Capital availability |
| Catastrophic loss | Sovereign/political | Legal Regulatory | Financial markets |

**PROCESS RISK**

**Operations risk**

Customer satisfaction
Human resources
Product development
Efficiency
Capacity
Performance gap
Cycle time
Sourcing
Obsolescence/shrinkage
Compliance
Business interruption
Product/service failure
Environmental
Health and Safety
Trademark/brand name erosion

**Empowerment risk**

Leadership
Authority/limit
Outsourcing
Performance incentives
Change readiness
Communications

**Information processing/technology risk**

Relevance
Integrity
Access
Availability
Infrastructure

**Integrity risk**

Management fraud
Employee fraud
Illegal acts
Unauthorised
Reputation

**Financial risk**

*Price*
Interest rate
Currency
Equity
Commodity
Financial instrument
*Liquidity*
Cash flow
Opportunity cost
Concentration
*Credit*
Default
Concentration
Settlement
Collateral

**INFORMATION FOR DECISION-MAKING RISK**

**Operational**

Pricing
Contract commitment
Performance measurement
Alignment
Regulatory reporting

**Financial**

Budget planning
Accounting information
Financial reporting evaluation
Taxation
Pension fund
Investment evaluation
Regulatory reporting

**Strategic**

Environmental scan
Business portfolio
Valuation
Performance measurement
Organisation structure
Resource allocation
Planning
Life cycle

**Figure 23.1** Arthur Andersen business risk model.

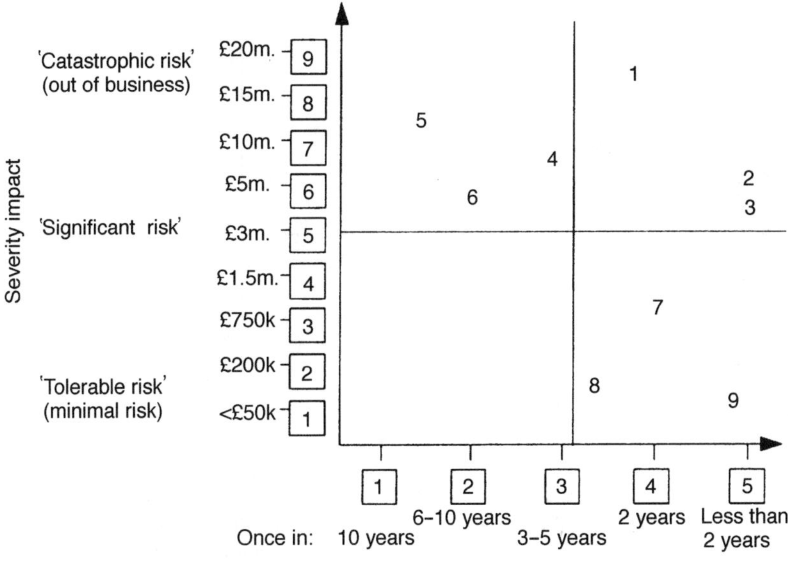


Key.
1. New products replace our product
2. Consumer confidence
3. Housing market/demand
4. Brand image of UK plc
5. Disaster recovery
6. Takeover by competitor
7. Tax/VAT rule changes
8. EEC labour rules
9. Consumer credit restrictions

**Figure 23.2** Expected frequency and impact of risks.

Figure 23.3 indicates the level of opportunity to improve risk management and the timescale within which the actions should be achieved.

## Practical Tips for Successful Implementation

Useful tips include:

*Treat the launch as a formal project*
The launch should have:

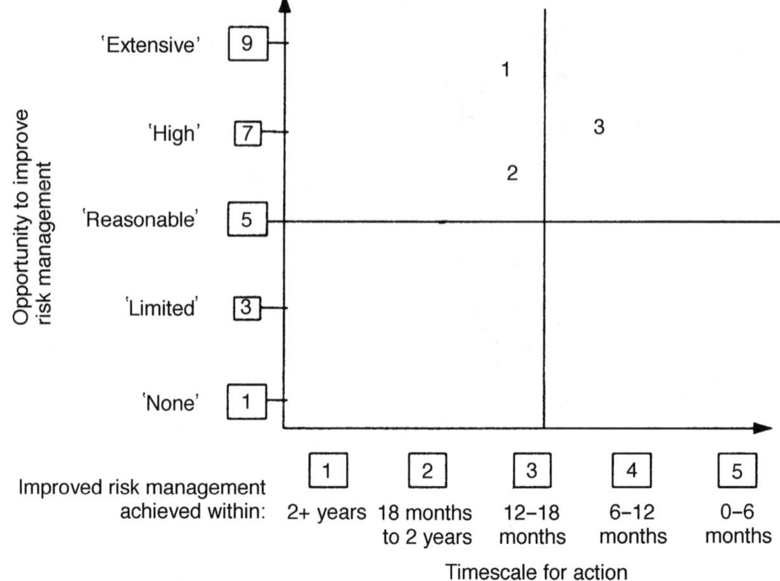


**Figure 23.3** Opportunity to improve risk management and timescale for action.

- a project sponsor
- a project manager
- justification, objectives and deliverables
- a timetable and plan
- a budget
- a steering committee
- monitoring and reporting back on progress.

*Use a pilot to 'trial' the CSA approach*
Select a business that is well known and with which a good relationship has been developed. This can be useful in identifying whether the fit is in fact correct and provide a valuable learning experience to fine-tune the approach before the programme is implemented more widely.

*Create a 'risk free' environment*

When issues are identified give management the chance to implement actions and to address them without criticising the staff concerned. Escalate issues to top management only if action plans are not being implemented within agreed timescales.

*Ensure there are tangible deliverables*

Reports on workshop sessions should include an action plan to address the risks identified and results of surveys and questionnaires should be fed back to the management who have contributed to them on a timely basis.

*Avoid major pitfalls*

- Having the wrong attendees at workshops: ensure that there is an appropriate mix of skills and experience for the objective of the session.
- The selection of the wrong facilitator: either people who are not good facilitators, or who do not believe in the value in the process.
- Too narrow a focus on controls: internal auditors have been trained to take a financial view but when it comes to CSA a wider perspective is required to ensure that all relevant business risks and controls are considered and to enable the maximum value to be added to the organisation.
- Underestimating the investment: learning or planning is necessary to mount a successful CSA launch.
- Not being aware of the limitations of CSA: in relation to workshops, the potential difficulty in identifying 'actionable' results and having a lack of evidence to support recommended actions. In relation to surveys, the risk that the audit universe of risks is not identified and the fact that reliance is effectively placed on the integrity, and potentially view, of only the person who completes the questionnaire. It can also tend to identify 'obvious' problems and symptoms.
- The danger of more bureaucracy: management can tend to see survey-based CSA as yet another questionnaire from head office to be filled in. It can be perceived as bureaucratic and become a mechanical form-filling 'exercise' which management completes without an objective consideration of risks and controls. The actual assessment process also takes time, especially in the first year, in attending workshops, completing questionnaires, etc. The danger can be countered if management are given something back, for example, information on how they have assessed themselves versus other business units or access to best control practices in respect of operational as well as financial controls. ASDA plc's on-line self assessment tool is a good example of how this can work successfully in practice. This produces quarterly information so that

management can see progress on improvements. Line management can therefore see the benefits and accordingly support compliance.

*Focus on good practice*

- Ensure that time is effectively used during a workshop. Planning for each session should be at a very detailed level to assess how long each section will take. This needs to be done to ensure that the session remains on track. The tendency will invariably be for each section to take longer and the facilitator therefore needs to ensure that the detailed agenda is closely followed if all elements are to be covered.
- Keep the CSA approach fresh and simple. Once management's buy-in has been obtained it is vitally important to ensure that the momentum and interest is maintained. This can be achieved by demonstrating that process improvements are actually delivered as a result of CSA. This can also be achieved by highlighting key outputs, for example, maximising the use of colour in the reports and 'keeping it simple', for instance, any grading of risks and controls should not be made overly complex.
- Focus on business improvement opportunities as well as risks. Ensure that the risks associated with not identifying and implementing business improvement opportunities are identified as part of the CSA process.

## ROLE OF INTERNAL AUDIT IN CSA

A strong and well respected internal audit group is ideally placed to facilitate and manage the implementation of CSA. Internal audit could have a major role in initiating the idea of introducing CSA, evaluating which tools should be used to implement it (workshops and/or surveys) and planning and executing the subsequent implementation. CSA is generally more likely to be implemented by organisations which have larger internal audit departments because of the skills required over and above the normal audit competencies, for example, the facilitation skills necessary to run a workshop.

At the more detailed practical level, in respect of workshops, internal audit could:

- provide the facilitator, recorder and voting software for each session
- agree the programme of workshops to be carried out with top management
- before each workshop meet with the most senior manager amongst attendees to agree the session objectives and the parameters to be used for voting in relation to the significance and likelihood of risks

- send a communication before the session to attendees to explain the objectives
- facilitate the meeting and then report the results.

In respect of surveys, internal audit could:

- determine whether the surveys are to be electronic or paper based
- populate the survey with key control questions
- disseminate the surveys
- review and summarise responses
- carry out attest work on responses to ensure that there is no manipulation of the results.

## ADVANTAGES TO INTERNAL AUDIT OF CSA

In recent years 'traditional' financial audits have been criticised for:

- the perception that they do not add value
- lack of focus on needs of the auditees and the 'real issues'
- slow turnaround time to provide reports
- too 'backward' facing and reactive
- lack of identification or focus on risk areas.

CSA can help address a number of these criticisms and thereby significantly improve the effectiveness and perception of internal audit's value to the business. CSA has the following main potential benefits which all, either directly or indirectly, benefit internal audit.

*Management takes more responsibility for the maintenance of the control environment and auditees understand the purpose of controls and risk management.* This leads to process and control improvement opportunities being identified and action plans being developed to implement them.

*Auditors accomplish control assessment.* CSA improves internal audit's efficiency and effectiveness and increases coverage through:

- creating a more streamlined audit approach with less time for auditors and auditees
- the ability to customise the workshop to focus on the department, group or process being audited

- helping internal audit to focus on risks and understand the business
- increasing internal audit's ability to track and report on improvements in controls over time
- reducing the time taken to identify and prioritise risks and controls, due to the group inputting their views once rather than having a series of interviews
- assisting internal audit to address more difficult areas to evaluate such as 'soft' controls (control environment, and awareness, degree of accountability for controls, etc.) and areas not traditionally included in the scope of audits such as customer satisfaction, research and development activity and quality issues.

CSA *helps to position internal audit as a business partner and consultant involved in operational process improvement.* It provides internal audit with the opportunity to reposition itself by delivering a new service, which it can, for example, evidence by generating new reports for the board and management, on the results of workshops and surveys. These:

- increase the quantity and quality of information on the state of control and risk available to them
- increase the motivation and capability of work units to design, build and maintain effective control and risk management systems
- decrease the amount of inspection work required on control systems.

CSA *improves the morale of the internal audit team.* The CSA approach requires different skills to be learnt which tends to lead to an improvement in morale, providing a broader base of experience. This in turn assists internal audit to attract and retain good-quality staff.

## WHERE IS CSA GOING?

CSA currently tends to be a tool which is introduced by internal audit across an organisation. However, as the benefits of CSA become more widely recognised, management is likely to take over ownership of the CSA process, for example, running the workshops, reporting the results, and developing and implementing risk management action plans. CSA will then become a technique driven by management to help manage and control the strategic direction of the business.

BG plc (formerly British Gas plc) is a good example of where this has happened. CSA has enabled BG plc to identify and manage risks in a more systematic way. Internal audit's role has become one where it reviews CSA as a key business process in the way that it reviews other business processes, evaluating the controls in the process and identifying improvement opportunities. In this situation internal audit will check the validity of responses to control questionnaires and use the output of CSA as a key input to the development of its audit plans, but it will not own the CSA process.

The focus on corporate governance will continue to fuel the demand for CSA because top management will need to gain the additional level of assurance on their systems and controls which CSA can produce.

Other future developments in CSA are foreshadowed by a major FTSE 100 company which has had a significant amount of experience of CSA. It is recognising that it can become an integral part of its management information systems and is accordingly considering moving to a monthly CSA reporting framework and linking the CSA results to its key performance indicators and managers' annual performance reviews and even possibly their remuneration. There are clearly dangers with developing CSA in this way but it emphasises that CSA has the potential to become an integral part of management's information and control systems.

The embedding of CSA as a business management tool is at an embryonic stage. It is likely that the future focus will be upon further increasing the level of accountability and ownership of the recommendations at the end of the CSA process and the follow-up procedures for evaluating the implementation of change.

The old adage that 'if it cannot be measured it should not be done' is likely to increase the focus on measuring the benefits of CSA. In respect of workshops, the benefits can be readily measured at the end of the workshop by using the interactive software to get the participants to vote on the session's perceived value. Similarly customer satisfaction questionnaires can be used for each type of CSA to ask contributors various questions aimed at evaluating the impact and usefulness of CSA.

A trend towards process rather than entity-level CSA will encourage managers to think in terms of process risks. This will be facilitated by the use of electronic documentation of processes, quality control manuals and CSA evaluations. This should help CSA to become integral to an organisation's creation of a continuous improvement philosophy and total quality culture in which all employees own and are empowered to help improve its systems and controls. If this happens, staff at all levels will become the main evaluators of the adequacy, efficiency and effectiveness of their controls and quality will be built in, not on, control and risk management systems. In so doing, CSA should continue to strengthen its role in:

- generating reliable information on the status of controls and risks
- optimising control designs and thereby reducing the likelihood of risks occurring

- clarifying and reinforcing management's ownership and accountability for control and risk management.

Accordingly companies that successfully implement CSA will be able to manage their risks more efficiently and effectively and this in turn will give them a competitive advantage.

# 24

# CSA Risk Management and Internal Audit

## The Future

*Andy Wynne*

### INTRODUCTION

CSA techniques are now well into the second decade of their development. They have been implemented in a variety of organisations across the world as described in the preceding chapters of this book. In general, what has been the main thrust of the development of this technique and what have been the main benefits of its implementation to the organisation and internal audit itself? What can we learn from this in terms of the likely future development of the technique?

The claimed benefits of CSA are numerous, they include, for example:

- improved internal auditing processes
- broader role for internal audit
- improved internal audit and other staff morale
- enhancing the prestige and image of internal audit
- greater audit coverage with the same resources
- better understanding of risks and controls
- better communication across the organisation
- establishment of management responsibility for process controls
- helping meet external controls assurance and corporate governance requirements.

CSA has been marketed at many conferences and seminars and advocated by a range of consultants. Despite this, the take-up has not been enormous. Most of the contributors to this book have only been using CSA type techniques for up to two or three years. In a survey the ICAEW found that internal auditors spent only 4% of their time on CSA ('Internal Audit and

Its Value' – Institute of Chartered Accountants in England and Wales 1996). As Dave Gammon says (Chapter 8) 'There have been lots of quitters ... amongst whom are numbered pharmaceutical companies, banks, insurers and oil companies'. There has even been some suggestion that in the organisation generally credited as the birth place of CSA, Gulf Canada, there has been at least some restriction in the use of the CSA technique. As would be expected, few people are actually prepared to publicise the failures of CSA, so Neil Cowan's contribution (Chapter 18) is particularly important in registering this aspect of CSA's development.

## WHY IS CSA NOT MORE WIDELY ADOPTED?

There have been a variety of reasons for organisations or their internal audit section not using CSA or for it being dropped, once introduced. These have included:

- the culture of the organisation not being appropriate
- the fear internal auditors have of introducing new techniques in public
- the cost of computer technology that many consultants suggest is essential for CSA
- CSA is a technique with many benefits that are not easily repeatable after the first workshop
- CSA has not become part of the normal business process
- CSA has been a consultant's dream that often dies when they leave the organisation.

Control self assessment is dependent upon the managers and staff involved having trust in the organisation and an expectation that the results of the exercise will be implemented. CSA will not work in traditional organisations with a hierarchical and dictatorial management structure where managers are blamed for their mistakes. CSA requires its participants to be empowered to take risks and also to implement the changes that are necessary to manage these risks effectively. Few organisations live up to these ideals.

Internal auditors, like all people, have a fear of failure. CSA by its very nature has to be carried out publicly. This has put off all but the most adventurous audit managers. In addition, for many internal auditors the introduction of CSA would mark a huge change in their role and their relationship with the organisation's other managers. Many internal auditors are distrustful of change because of the disrupting effects this can have on the control environment. The view that CSA requires state-of-the-art computer equipment has provided the excuse, for many internal auditors, for not implementing the technique. Few organisations have been prepared to invest tens of thousands of pounds in a technique for a back-room function like internal audit.

A major advantage of CSA is the introduction of improved control and risk awareness across the organisation. However, this is largely a one-off gain from the first workshop that particular managers attend. In addition, the first workshop in any particular area should identify the major weaknesses or risks. If suitable action is taken to address these, then the outcome from a second workshop is likely to be less significant. CSA requires active audience participation. This will not continue unless the problems identified in the last workshop have been clearly acted on and removed. For these reasons, and because of the lack of novelty value of the second workshop, it is much less likely to be considered a success by its participants. All these factors make it more likely that CSA workshops will be one-off events in any particular area of an organisation.

CSA needs to be part of, and embedded within, a corporate risk management strategy. This is recognised by almost all the contributors to this book. Without this framework, it is difficult to ensure that appropriate action will be carried out to address poor controls and significant risks across the organisation. CSA can be a useful tool within an organisation's corporate risk management framework. However, in many ways it has been oversold. It is not a stand-alone technique that will revolutionise the quality of internal control across an organisation. It is little more than managers coming together to identify and analyse the risks that they face, although this can be an essential stage in effective risk management.

CSA is a new technique often based on impressive state-of-the-art computer technology with its own jargon and mystique. It can be a useful experience once in a while, but its selling point is its difference. As such it has been a bonus for consultants who can market a novel product and thus command different rates of pay. One indication of this is that four of the big five accountancy firms have provided chapters for this book. Another is that several other contributors to this book gained their knowledge of CSA direct from Makowsz or Leech, the original two 'gurus' of CSA.

It could be argued that CSA has depended upon charismatic individuals for its introduction and has ceased to be used when their influence is no longer available. However, although many organisations have been willing to pay quite heavily for consultants to introduce the technique they have not been willing or able to pay for continued consultant participation. This could be necessary to ensure that the technique is tailored to the particular organisation and fits in with the existing management processes. Without this internalisation any new technique will not survive. It has to be adapted to the particular environment and culture of the organisation.

CSA must be changed to fit the working habits of the organisation. Managers cannot be expected to alter significantly the way they work to fit in with CSA.

Not all CSA programmes have involved high technology and high consultant fees. Many attempts have been lower-key, simple and effective nevertheless. An example of this is described by David King (Chapter 19). But again, some have faltered when the prime mover, often the chief internal auditor, has moved on or some other pressing issue has assumed priority.

Despite the relatively low uptake for CSA it has still been around for over a decade; several books continue to be written about it and the attendance at CSA conferences continues to increase. What have been the major lasting benefits to CSA and what will the future bring?

## LONG-TERM BENEFITS OF CSA

It seems to me that there have been two major advantages from the development of CSA.

1. It is a useful tool in corporate risk management.
2. It is a stimulus for the development of internal audit becoming a more participatory experience for managers.

## CSA AND CORPORATE RISK MANAGEMENT

Corporate risk management as a structured analysis and review of the major risks that an organisation faces has now been accepted as a fundamental aspect of any effective internal control system. All organisations all required or encouraged to identify, analyse and manage the risks that they face in the achievement of their objectives. CSA type techniques are useful tools in this process. There has been a move from the more traditional CSA type approaches (for example the BT experience – Chapter 13) where workshops are used to consider the effectiveness of controls to using CSA as an integral part of a corporate risk management strategy (for example at Kent County Council – Chapter 20).

Workshops can be particularly useful at two stages of the risk management cycle. These are identifying the risks and identifying which of these risks is the most significant. CSA workshops can be effective vehicles for a brainstorming exercise to ensure that the full range of risks that the organisation faces are identified. Risks may be identified individually by relevant managers, but the process is likely to be more effective if the managers and their staff are brought together. This should allow them to feed off each other's ideas and comments and ensure that all significant risks are identified. It may also help identify risk causes and not just their effects.

The assessment of the significance of each risk and each of its aspects is a subjective judgement. This assessment may be made more accurately within a workshop setting. The views of each member of the workshop can either be averaged or the differing views may be discussed and a consensus reached. This discussion of the risks and their relative significance should have the bonus of ensuring a deeper understanding of these risks and the extent that the significance of a risk may vary between or across departments. Once the risks have been identified and assessed, then the individual managers can take responsibility for developing action plans to manage the most significant of these risks. It is generally accepted that there are four types of action that may be taken to deal with the risks that have been identified. They may be accepted, reduced, transferred or avoided.

Risks may be accepted if they have a low impact or are not likely to occur in the near future. Risk with a high impact but low likelihood may be accepted, but plans should be developed to ensure the smooth running of the organisation if they do actually happen. Risks may be reduced by improving the quality of internal control over the relevant process.

Taking out insurance is the usual way of transferring risks away from the organisation. This is especially so for risks with a high potential impact that would have a major effect on the organisation if they were actually to happen and as a result should not just be accepted. If a risk is too great for the organisation to bear and it is not practical to reduce the risk, then the risk should be avoided. For example, it may be better for a college to avoid the risk of establishing a completely new course if the demand cannot be readily and accurately assessed and the teaching skills required are not already available within the college.

This approach to risk management will be more successful in organisations with more open management styles. In these organisations problems or risks tend to be solved collectively and managers and staff are not blamed for their errors or mistakes. Risk management will also be more successful if it is undertaken as an intrinsic aspect of the organisation's business planning and reporting process. Managers are usually busy people. They may accept novel and inventive procedures in the short term, but these are unlikely to be adopted permanently unless they can be integrated into the core business processes and are seen to be ensuring that the business achieves its objectives more efficiently as a result.

Risk identification and analysis should occur as part of and be integrated within the business planning process. It may be seen as a development of the traditional business planning tool, the SWOT analysis. And indeed this tool has been used as part of a CSA approach as David King has described (Chapter 19).

Each dimension of the SWOT analysis may include risks to the business:

- strengths will be a risk if they are not nurtured and used to develop the business
- weaknesses are clearly risks that need to be addressed, where possible
- opportunities may become a source of risk if they are not clearly identified and exploited
- threats to the business are another source of risk that must be overcome to ensure success.

Once identified, risks and how they will be managed should then become part of the corporate and departmental business plans. Managers should be required to report the extent that they have managed the significant risks within their area of responsibility when they report on their financial and operational successes.

## CSA AND INTERNAL AUDIT

The origins of internal audit are as an internal check on the accuracy and validity of all payments made by an organisation. No payments could be made without them first being reviewed and stamped for payment by the internal audit section. The echoes of this role can still unfortunately be seen in many internal audit sections. Normally, invoices are not now authorised by internal audit, but internal auditors in some organisations will still review all final account payments on major capital contracts.

Most modern internal audit sections have moved on from this original role, although current practice now forms a spectrum. At one end we have internal audit in a narrow role as part of the control framework, acting as an internal check on financial transactions. At the other extreme we have fully fledged CSA where internal audit merely facilitates managers' self assessment of the adequacy of their internal control systems. Several intermediate stages can be identified in this spectrum. These stages can be viewed as the gradual transfer of responsibility for internal control from internal auditors to operational managers.

The first stage is where internal audit no longer checks all payments, but restricts its activities to a significant sample of these transactions. Managers have been given some responsibilities to check and authorise payments, although they cannot be fully trusted in this role. Internal audit is there to police this system, to identify mistakes and act as a deterrent to potential fraudsters. Internal audit's main objective is to find errors and omissions and to ensure that these individual findings are corrected.

Regrettably, this is a reasonably common role for internal audit and is the perception of internal audit that many managers still hold. Many internal auditors consider that it is appropriate for them to check a week's or even a month's transactions each year. External auditors are sometimes still encouraging internal auditors to maintain this role. They are prepared to see internal audit's main role as undertaking checks on large samples of financial transactions to help provide evidence for the external auditor's annual opinion on the accuracy of the financial statements.

The development of interrogation software has given a new lease of life to this role. Internal audit can again review all financial transactions and identify suspect items for further investigation. Computer software has made the original role of internal audit more efficient and made auditors more effective at identifying errors, mistakes and possible fraud. However, this type of internal auditing prevents managers from accepting full responsibility for internal control. For example, managers do not have to worry too much about undertaking comprehensive checks before they authorise (or rubber stamp) payments. Internal audit can be relied upon to identify or detect any problems.

The next stage is systems audit. Here auditors review the adequacy of systems of control and make comments on these rather than solely on the accuracy or validity of the actual outputs from the system. Systems audit is considered the best approach and, for instance, the Further Education Funding Council's (FEFC) Code of Audit Practice recommends that at least 75% of internal audit work in UK FE colleges should consist of this approach. The systems approach does not necessarily mean the direct substantive testing of transactions (i.e., system output) is abandoned. However, *The Government Internal Audit Manual* (HMSO 1996), for example, states that substantive testing is 'usually uneconomic' and 'has a limited role to play in systems auditing'. Some internal audit functions have reduced direct transaction testing to a minimum, and this worries some people. CSA can be yet one further stage removed from the direct examination of performance.

Within systems audit a number of different dimensions can be identified. These include the extent that managers are actively consulted on internal audit reviews before, during and after the review. The degree that internal audit reviews non-financial systems is also very variable. Finally, there are currently two possibly contradictory objectives for internal audit: providing assurance to senior management and the board on the quality of the internal control system; and working to improve the quality of that system.

As Phil Tarling identifies (Chapter 3), there is considerable variability in the extent that internal auditors discuss with managers before, during and after an internal audit. For some internal auditors there is very little discussion with managers about the system, its risks, any problems and possible improvements. For example, a leading internal auditor has suggested that the internal auditor's role during a review is first to ascertain the system.

At this stage 'the auditor should listen attentively to the responses' to the questions that they have put. It is only at the wash-up meeting, at the end of the field work 'that the management and audit team have the opportunity to work together on the best way forward to achieve the objectives of the business unit'. (Marion Lower *Internal Audit*, Financial Times Pitman Publishing, 1998).

At the other extreme managers are actively involved throughout the audit process. Their views are an important consideration of which systems or areas of the organisation should be reviewed by internal audit. At the start of each review the relevant managers are asked to indicate areas that internal audit should pay particular concern, any problems are identified and the internal auditors are asked to suggest suitable controls to address risks that the managers have identified. During the review at each interview with managers and staff their views are actively sought on alternative ways of achieving their objectives and the significance of any risks that are identified and the practicality of introducing controls to manage these risks.

Some people, for example Phil Tarling (Chapter 3), say that 'the essence of systems based auditing [is] involving the customer in the process and producing ownership of the internal audit report'. Other people, for example Gus Cottell (Chapter 9), consider that this type of internal audit is actually CSA. Whatever the case may be, the introduction of CSA should encourage a more participatory form of auditing. Whether internal auditors adopt this form of auditing as their approach to systems auditing or whether it is introduced under the banner of CSA does not really matter. A more participatory form of auditing should be more effective. All the weaknesses within the system are more likely to be identified and any recommendations made are more likely to be realistic and adopted by managers if they have had a significant input into their development and consideration of their practicality.

Many internal audit sections restrict their reviews to the main financial systems. Even those internal auditors that consider themselves to have a comprehensive scope across their organisations are often actually only reviewing the financial aspects of departments and locations outside the narrow confines of the finance department. The introduction of CSA or even just the consideration of the technique or listening to expositions of the technique should help to ensure that more internal auditors consider reviewing systems other than merely the financial ones that their external auditors will be interested in.

If serious consideration is given to the full range of risks that any organisation faces it should be obvious that these do not always have a financial aspect. Many organisations claim that their most important assets are their staff. If this is the case then human resource management will also be a vital area for review by internal audit. For many organisations health and safety and marketing will be significant risk areas. Again, it is these areas and not just the financial aspects of the organisation that should be reviewed by internal audit. The introduction of risk management and the use of CSA techniques within this process can be an important step in ensuring that internal audit is used effectively to review the controls that are in place to manage all the significant risks that the organisation faces. CSA can be an important method of overcoming possible prejudice from non-financial managers that as internal auditors we have little of value to bring to their management function.

The extent that internal audit is directly involved in risk management is subject to considerable debate. Steven Barlow (Chapter 23) says that 'internal audit could have a key role initiating ... CSA ... and executing the subsequent implementation.' Leech and McCuaig (Chapter 2) also refer to (and so appear to support) the integration of audit and risk management functions. In contrast the Housing Corporation in their guidance on risk management state that 'it is ... unlikely that the objectives of internal audit could be met if it were to form part of the risk management strategy [of a housing association]'. A prime objective of CSA is transferring responsibilities (including those for risk) to where they properly belong – with line management.

The range of current internal audit practice also includes a lack of clarity of internal audit's fundamental objectives, should internal auditors be police or advisors? The two extreme positions are first that the objective of internal audit is to provide assurance on the internal control system to the board of the organisation and secondly that internal audit's role is to improve the risk management process across the organisation and ensure that appropriate controls are introduced where necessary to mitigate all the significant risks that the organisation faces.

Within the UK public sector an influential source of guidance on internal audit is the *Government Internal Audit Manual*. This states very clearly that 'The prime objective of internal audit ... is to provide ... assurance on the internal control system', and defines internal audit as 'an independent appraisal within an organisation which operates as a service to management by measuring and evaluating the effectiveness of the internal control system'. CSA has been used as part of the process of providing an overall opinion of an organisation's internal control system as indicated by Duncan Stephenson (Chapter 15). However, usually CSA places more emphasis on identifying improvements in the organisaton's internal control system rather than merely commenting on it. Thus one of the impacts of the development of CSA should be to move internal audit further along the line to actually contributing to improving their organisation's internal control system rather than just reporting on it.

It is only through facilitating improvements to the management of the risks that the organisation faces that internal audit adds value by improving the effectiveness of the organisation. However, many internal auditors worry about the consultancy aspects of their work and believe that this may undermine their independence. One way of overcoming this dilemma is to analyse the role that internal audit plays into Keith Wade's four 'As':

- Assure
- Alert
- Advise
- Assist.

It is only through ensuring that each of these roles is adequately undertaken that internal audit can provide a comprehensive and effective service to their organisation.

## CONCLUSIONS

Many commentators and consultants may have exaggerated the possible benefits of introducing CSA. In almost all organisations its introduction will not have a revolutionary effect on the way that internal controls are reviewed or the way that the organisation manages its risks. However, it can be a useful tool to be used as part of risk management and corporate governance; and CSA can have a beneficial effect on the approach that is adopted for internal audit. As more organisations are encouraged, cajoled or forced into adopting a formal risk management procedure then CSA can be a useful tool for identifying and analysing the risks that the organisation faces.

Whether CSA is formally adopted or not by any particular organisation it has had, and will continue to have, a beneficial effect on the practice of internal audit by encouraging a more participatory approach to internal audit; by stimulating audit to review all significant systems across the organisation, and not just their financial aspects; and by ensuring that internal auditors see their role as improving their organisation's internal control systems rather then merely commenting on them.

CSA-type approaches and techniques should be seriously considered by all internal auditors and senior managers and, once the consultant hype is avoided, can be a useful tool in helping to effectively manage modern organisations.

# Part 6

## Appendices

APPENDIX A

# UK Guidance on Internal Financial Control

(*Internal control and Financial Reporting: Guidance for directors of listed companies registered in the UK* December 1994, ICAEW Technical Department)



In considering the effectiveness of internal financial control, directors should have regard to the criteria set out below, recognising that these criteria should be interpreted in accordance with the statement of principles. The framework for these criteria is similar to that set out in *Internal control – integrated framework*, a report published in the USA by the Committee of Sponsoring Organisations of the Treadway Commission (COSO).

## 1. CONTROL ENVIRONMENT

- A commitment by directors, management and employees to competence and integrity (e.g., leadership by example, employment criteria).
- Communication of ethical values and control consciousness to managers and employees (e.g., through written codes of conduct, formal standards of discipline, performance appraisal).
- An appropriate organisational structure within which business can be planned, executed, controlled and monitored to achieve the company's/group's objectives.
- Appropriate delegation of authority with accountability which has regard to acceptable levels of risk.
- A professional approach to financial reporting which complies with generally accepted accounting practice.

## 2. IDENTIFICATION AND EVALUATION OF RISKS AND CONTROL OBJECTIVES

- Identification of key business risks in a timely manner.
- Consideration of the likelihood of risks crystallising and the significance of the consequent financial impact on the business.
- Establishment of priorities for the allocation of resources available for control and the setting and communicating of clear control objectives.

## 3. INFORMATION AND COMMUNICATION

- Performance indicators which allow management to monitor the key business and financial activities and risks, and the progress towards financial objectives, and to identify developments which require intervention (e.g., forecasts and budgets).
- Information systems which provide ongoing identification and capture of relevant, reliable and up-to-date financial and other information from internal and external sources (e.g., monthly management accounts, including earnings, cashflow and balance sheet reporting).
- Systems which communicate relevant information to the right people at the right frequency and time in a format which exposes significant variances from the budgets and forecasts and allows prompt response.

## 4. CONTROL PROCEDURES

- Procedures to ensure complete and accurate accounting for financial transactions.
- Appropriate authorisation limits for transactions that reasonably limit the company's /group's exposures.
- Procedures to ensure the reliability of data processing and information reports generated.
- Controls that limit exposure to loss of assets/records or to fraud (e.g., physical controls, segregation of duties).
- Routine and surprise checks which provide effective supervision of the control activities.
- Procedures to ensure compliance with laws and regulations that have significant financial implications.

## 5. MONITORING AND CORRECTIVE ACTION

- A monitoring process which provides reasonable assurance to the board that there are appropriate control procedures in place for all the company's/group's financially significant business activities and that these procedures are being followed (e.g., consideration by the board or board committee of reports from management, from an internal audit function or from independent accountants).
- Identification of change in the business and its environment which may require changes to the system of internal financial control.
- Formal procedures for reporting weaknesses and for ensuring appropriate corrective action.
- The provision of adequate support for public statements by the directors on internal control or internal financial control.

APPENDIX B

# The Criteria from the CoCo Report

(*Guidance on Control* November 1995 CA) ISBN 0-88800-436-1.



## Purpose

A1 Objectives should be established and communicated.

A2 The significant internal and external risks faced by an organisation in the achievement of its objectives should be identified and assessed.

A3 Policies designed to support the achievement of an organisation's objectives and the management of its risks should be established, communicated and practised so that people understand what is expected of them and the scope of their freedom to act.

A4 Plans to guide efforts in achieving the organisation's objectives should be established and communicated.

A5 Objectives and related plans should include measurable performance targets and indicators.

## Commitment

B1 Shared ethical values, including integrity, should be established, communicated and practised throughout the organisation.

B2 Human resource policies and practices should be consistent with an organisation's ethical values and with the achievement of its objectives.

B3 Authority, responsibility and accountability should be clearly defined and consistent with an organisation's objectives so that decisions and actions are taken by the appropriate people.

B4 An atmosphere of mutual trust should be fostered to support the flow of information between people and the effective performance toward achieving the organisation's objectives.

## Capability

C1 People should have the necessary knowledge, skills and tools to support the achievement of the organisation's objectives.

C2 Communication processes should support the organisation's values and the achievement of its objectives.

C3 Sufficient and relevant information should be identified and communicated in a timely manner to enable people to perform their assigned responsibilities.

C4 The decisions and actions of different parts of the organisation should be co-ordinated.

C5 Control activities should be designed as an integral part of the organisation, taking into consideration its objectives, the risks to their achievement, and the interrelatedness of control elements.

## Monitoring and Learning

D1 External and internal environments should be monitored to obtain information that may signal a need to re-evaluate the organisation's objectives or control.

D2 Performance should be monitored against the targets and indicators identified in the organisation's objectives and plans.

D3 The assumptions behind an organisation's objectives should be periodically challenged.

D4 Information needs and related information systems should be reassessed as objectives change or as reporting deficiencies are identified.

D5 Follow-up procedures should be established and performed to ensure appropriate change or action occurs.

D6 Management should periodically assess the effectiveness of control in its organisation and communicate the results to those to whom it is accountable.

APPENDIX C

# Sample Assessment Questions from the CoCo Report

(*Guidance on Control* November 1995 CA) ISBN 0-88800-436-1.



## Sample Assessment Questions

To assess the effectiveness of control, an organisation may find it helpful to express the criteria as questions tailored to its circumstances. The following is a simple example of questions a group might use to conduct a self-assessment. They have been tailored by drawing on some of the explanatory material in this guidance. In each case, the answer to the question would be followed up by 'How do we know' to trigger identification and discussion of the control processes.

## Purpose

- Do we clearly understand the mission and vision of the organisation?
- Do we understand our objectives, as a group, and how they fit with other objectives in the organisation?
- Does the information available to us enable us to identify risk and assess risk?
- Do we understand the risk we need to control and the degree of residual risk acceptable to those to whom we are accountable for control?
- Do we understand the policies that affect our actions?
- Are our plans responsive and adequate to achieve control?
- Do we have manageable performance targets?

## Commitment

- Are our principles of integrity and ethical values shared and practised?
- Are people rewarded fairly according to the organisation's objectives and values?
- Do we clearly understand what we are accountable for, and do we have a clear definition of our authority and responsibilities?
- Are critical decisions made by people with the necessary expertise, knowledge and authority?
- Are levels of trust sufficient to support the open flow of information and effective performance?

## Capability

- Do we have the right people, skills, tools and resources?
- Is there prompt communication of mistakes, bad news and other information to people who need to know, without fear of reprisal?
- Is there adequate information to allow us to perform our tasks?
- Are our actions co-ordinated with the rest of the organisation?
- Do we have the procedures and the processes to help ensure achievement of our objectives?

## Monitoring and Learning

- Do we review the internal and external environment to see whether changes are required to objectives or control?
- Do we monitor performance against relevant targets and indicators?
- Do we challenge the assumptions behind our objectives?
- Do we receive and provide information that is necessary and relevant to decision making?
- Are our information systems up to date?
- Do we learn from the results of monitoring and make continuous improvements to control?
- Do we periodically assess the effectiveness of control?

Appendix D

# Control Assurance Statements in the NHS

The following shows the minimum control standards to be adopted by organisations within the NHS. It is an extract from the NHS Executive circular EL(97)55 with the additions detailed in HSC 1998/070. It is reproduced with the kind permission of the NHS Executive.

## 1 THE CONTROL ENVIRONMENT

### Minimum Control Standards

### *1.1 Standing Orders are in place*

Some points to consider:

- Have Standing Orders been produced, approved by the Board and issued to all staff?
- Do the Standing Orders include all areas as set out in the NHS Executive model?
- Do they set out the procedure for overriding Standing Orders?

### *1.2 Standing Financial Instructions are in place*

Some points to consider:

- Have Standing Financial Instructions been produced, approved by the Board and issued to all staff?
- Have the Standing Financial Instructions been prepared from one of the NHS Executive's model sets?
- Is their approval minuted in the Board minutes?
- Do they include a statement on private use of the organisation's assets or benefiting from contracts with the organisation's suppliers?
- Do they set out management's responsibility for internal control?

- Do they set out the procedures for overriding the Standing Financial Instructions?
- Do they set out responsibility for accounting policies?
- Do they set out the requirement for reports from the Director of Finance to the Board?
- Do they include statements on the management of the treasury function and is the Director of Finance required to report this function's performance to the Board?
- Do they include statements on the organisation's financial reporting which set out the procedures to be followed when issues emerge that affect the current reporting process?
- Do they include a statement on the acceptance of gifts?

## 1.3 *There is a Fraud and Corruption Policy and Response Plan in place*

Some points to consider:

- Has a Fraud and Corruption Policy and Response Plan been produced, approved by the Board and issued to all staff (possibly in an abridged format)?
- Does the plan/policy define what staff should do if they suspect or are aware of improper behaviour?

## 1.4 *There is an Audit Committee in place*

Some points to consider:

- Has an Audit committee been established with appropriate terms of reference and have these been properly approved?
- Are the terms of reference in line with and do they include all aspects of the Audit committee handbook?
- Is the Committee required to meet at least three times per year?
- Does the Committee's remit include the review of the adequacy of internal controls?

## 1.5 *There is a Remuneration Committee in place*

Some points to consider:

- Have terms of reference for the Committee been established and approved by the Board?

- Is the remuneration of the Executive Directors considered by the Committee?
- Does the Committee review the remuneration of Executive Directors at other similar organisations in setting the remuneration of their directors?

## 1.6 *There is an adequate Internal Audit function*

Some points to consider:

- Have Internal Audit produced a report on internal controls as required by Section 3.4.17 of the NHS Internal Audit Standards?
- Is Internal Audit adequately resourced?
- Does the Internal Audit function operate under terms of reference approved by the Board?
- Is the function independent of operational management?
- Does the Chief Internal Auditor have access to the Audit Committee, Chairman and Chief Executive?
- Have appropriate strategic and operational audit plans been produced and agreed by the Audit Committee?
- How is Internal Audit's scope of work approved?
- How is it ensured that Internal Audit are sufficiently qualified, trained and experienced?
- How is the quality of Internal Audit's work monitored?
- How does Internal Audit monitor the implementation of agreed actions emanating from reports?

## 1.7 *There is a mechanism in place to facilitate control over the acquisition, use, disposal and safeguarding of assets*

Some points to consider:

- Has an asset register been established and maintained?
- Is responsibility for the management of assets devolved to budget holders?
- Is there a process for identifying asset purchases?
- Is there a process for identifying asset movements?
- Is there a mechanism for identifying asset disposals, condemnations and losses?
- Are asset lists regularly disseminated to budget holders to confirm the accuracy of the register contents?

### 1.8 *There is a budgetary control system in place*

Some points to consider:

- Have clear reporting and responsibility lines been established?
- Have budgets been established which will meet key statutory financial targets?
- Are budget reports received by budget holders on a timely basis?
- Are budget variances acted upon?
- Are budget reports subject to independent review?

## Other Possible Controls

### 1.9 *Standards of Business Conduct have been produced, approved by the Board and issued to all staff*

Some points to consider:

- Do they set out policies on acceptance of gifts/hospitality?
- Do they set out policies regarding conflicts on interest?
- Do they include policies regarding the establishment and maintenance of a register of interests?
- Does the plan/policy define what staff should do if they suspect or are aware of improper behaviour?

### 1.10 *A scheme of reservation and delegation has been produced, approved by the Board and issued to all staff*

Some points to consider:

- Are levels of authority defined?
- Are they sufficient but not excessive for the purpose?

### 1.11 *A staff appraisal system has been established for all staff with financial responsibility which ensures that individual objectives flow from Trust objectives*

Some points to consider:

- Does the appraisal system allow for the Board to review the performance of senior staff?
- Does the system allow for the definition and communication of responsibilities/objectives? (including such things as job specifications, objectives, etc.).

- Are quality and performance standards built into objectives?
- Does the procedure allow for the identification of poor quality work and for relevant discipline?
- Do policies in relation to Finance staff encompass the principles of 'Building on Framework for the Future'?
- Does it set out the technical and professional attributes required for each position?
- Have all staff been appraised against the required attributes?
- Have personal development plans been produced for all staff setting out training required to meet set standards?
- Are the appraisals formally based with documented outcomes?

## 2 IDENTIFICATION AND EVALUATION OF BUSINESS RISKS

### Minimum Control Standards

### *2.1 There is an annually produced Business Plan (or equivalent in the case of Health Authorities)*

Some points to consider:

- Does the Business Plan set out performance standards?
- Does the production of the Business Plan incorporate a review of the appropriateness of the organisation's structure?
- Is the Business Plan distributed to staff at all levels?
- Does the Business Plan explicitly link the organisation's structure to control priorities and monitoring procedures?
- Are changes identified in the Business Plan assessed in terms of both cost and quality?
- Have Business Plans been produced for individual departments and for the organisation as a whole?
- Are departments required to produce annual Business Plans?
- How are departmental Business Plans linked to the overall Business Plan?
- Are those who are expected to implement plans involved in their development?
- Have plans allocated resources in line with organisation-wide objectives?

- Is there a timetable for the planning process and is this monitored?
- How are plans and budgets communicated to those responsible for their management?

### 2.2 *A plan has been prepared for the implementation of a Risk Management Strategy in 1998/99*

Some points to consider:

- Has a system been set up to identify business risks?
- At what level is this undertaken and by whom?
- Have risks been prioritised and controlled?
- How are risks prioritised?
- Are the resources necessary to implement controls identified?
- Have resources been aimed at high-priority risks, and,
- Does the procedure allow for consideration of cross departmental risks/ controls and for the subsequent revision of objectives?
- Are all staff involved in the identification of risks?
- Has implementation of controls been monitored?
- Do the management team regularly assess progress towards the implementation of agreed controls?
- What procedures exist for dealing with issues that have not been addressed?

## 3 INFORMATION AND COMMUNICATION

### Minimum Control Standards

### 3.1 *There are systems in place which produce reliable financial information and proper accounting records*

Some points to consider:

- Are users canvassed on the adequacy of information supplied?
- Are timetables in place for the production and distribution of reports?
- Are procedures in place to reconcile reports transcribed from the ledger to their source?

### 3.2 *There are controls in place concerning the security of financial systems and data*

Some points to consider:

- Has an IM&T strategy and policy been prepared and has this been approved by the Board?
- Is there a director with IT responsibility on the Board?
- When was the strategy last reviewed and how often is this done?
- Does the strategy assess the size and quality of the IT function?
- Does the strategy include policies on security of systems and data? (Are they in line with BS7799 and the NHS Code of Connection?)
- Does the strategy state a policy on the Data Protection Act? (Is the registration up to date?)
- Does the policy make mention of the use of software and licences? (Is there a system for assessing the legitimacy of all software and licences?)
- Does the strategy include arrangements for contingency operation?
- Does the strategy include procedures for the implementation of new systems?
- Does the strategy include the control of access to systems and ownership of data?
- Does the strategy include the monitoring of crashes/errors/breakdowns, etc?

### 3.3 *The 'Millennium' impact on the organisation's significant and fundamental financial systems has been assessed and, where required, appropriate contingency plans have been prepared*

## Other Possible Controls

### 3.4 *All stakeholders are involved in the implementation of new systems*

- Have project teams been set up for the introduction of new systems?
- Do these teams include representatives from all parties involved?

## 4 CONTROL PROCESSES

### Minimum Control Standards

#### *4.1 Procedure notes are in place for all financial systems*

Some points to consider; do the procedure notes cover

- financial reporting and budgetary control
- financial ledger
- treasury management
- contracting & PAS
- income
- payroll
- non-pay expenditure
- stores
- assets
- capital.

#### *4.2 Financial systems are subject to Internal Audit coverage*

- Have the areas above been subject to Internal Audit review in line with the objectives set out within the NHS *Internal Audit Manual*?

#### *4.3 There has been adherence to the mandatory requirements contained within the current NHS Executive costing guidance*

### Other Possible Controls

#### *4.4 Is there evidence of Standard Orders not having been applied?*

- Where this is the case has the appropriate action as set out in Standing Orders been applied to waive their necessity?

#### *4.5 Is there evidence of Standing Financial Instructions not having been applied?*

- Where this is the case has the appropriate action as set out in Standing Financial Instructions been applied to waive their necessity?

### *4.6 Is there evidence of the Scheme of Reservation/Delegation not having been applied?*

### *4.7 Is the competence and performance of staff appraised and is training undertaking where appropriate?*

Some points to consider:

- Have the technical and professional attributes required by all positions with financial responsibilities been profiled?
- Have staff been appraised against the profiling?
- Have development plans been produced detailing necessary training where appropriate?

## 5 MONITORING

### Minimum Control Standards

### *5.1 The Audit Committee reviews and monitors internal financial control and the implementation of agreed control improvements*

Some points to consider:

- Has an Audit Committee comprised of Non-Executive Directors been established?
- Has the Committee been established in line with the Audit Committee Handbook?
- Does its remit cover all areas within the handbook?
- In assessing internal control does the Committee consider
  - the control environment (commitment to truth and fair dealing, leadership by example, communication of ethical values, appropriateness of organisational structures, independence, integrity and openness, delegation of authority and accountability and professionalism in financial reporting);
  - identification of risks, control priorities and objectives;
  - information and communication; and,
  - control activities (accountability for performance, financial statements, minimisation of fraud, assessment of control procedures, follow up of internal and external audit recommendations, timeliness of monitoring procedures and providing evidence of appropriate monitoring)?

### 5.2 *The Board regularly receive and review financial and performance reports*

Some points to consider:

- Are the reports adequate to enable the Board to make decisions to support their business plan objectives?
- How often are reports produced and presented to the Board?
- Are variances reported along with explanations and remedial action necessary?
- Is the information provided to the Board consistent with the information provided externally?

## Other Possible Controls

### 5.3 *Staff are required to assess the adequacy of internal financial controls regularly*

Some points to consider:

- Who is involved in the process?
- How often is it undertaken?

### 5.4 *Has a process for the continuous improvement of control procedures been established?*

APPENDIX E

# Introducing Control Self Assessment to the Inland Revenue

*Norman Buckley*

(Reproduced from Volume 1, issue 5 of *Internal Control* with the kind permission of Accountancy Books)

Control self assessment (CSA) first came to the attention of the Inland Revenue Department in 1992. It was rejected on the grounds that it appeared to be a continuation of, and was in many ways very similar to, Total Quality Management. As an audit technique it was considered to have limited use. In 1994, the Controller of Internal Audit had the opportunity to visit Canada and to exchange best practice with a number of companies and organisations.

## THE GULF CANADA EXPERIENCE

One of these was Gulf Canada who by then had been using this technique for six years. Their experience was interesting not least in that auditors facilitated meetings with the practitioners who represented a business operation as a vertical slice, from top to bottom. The participants voted anonymously in response to questions so as to identify the business operation's strengths and weaknesses, and most important, the actions needed to overcome these problems.

Surprisingly, Gulf Canada was similar in many respects to the Inland Revenue – albeit the size, nature and culture of the organisation were very different. They had gone through a period of decentralisation, empowerment and downsizing, and had used CSA to identify available monetary savings. Internal Audit in the Inland Revenue was already in the following position:

- internal auditors were already working closely with practitioners;
- they intended to produce demonstrable savings from their audits;
- they had identified potential growth in demand for their services;

- they needed to reduce the time scales of their existing techniques in order to accommodate this increased demand.

In principle this tried and tested technique of CSA appeared to offer considerable benefits for an organisation like the Inland Revenue. It also appeared to have considerable potential for the customer in using the facilitation approach to roll out major changes in quality and delayering in the various business operations within the Inland Revenue.

## FEASIBILITY APPRAISAL

There was a need to test the feasibility of this approach to CSA from both the perspective of the auditor, and the customers who would represent the business operations.

An introductory course was being run by Gulf Canada and the Inland Revenue were offered places on this one-week course. An audit manager was selected, who was experienced in the ways and culture of the Inland Revenue – a person with a questioning mind as well as being an experienced auditor and qualified accountant.

To test customer perception, one of the major tax regions of the UK was selected to trial this technique. This was a region with a dynamic Regional Controller and one with which Internal Audit had particularly good relations. In turn, this Regional Controller selected his Deputy, and also the Quality Manager, to attend the week's training course with the audit manager in Calgary.

Their impressions were favourable. They judged there to be scope and potential to use this approach to CSA within the Inland Revenue.

## THE TECHNIQUE OF CSA

This approach to CSA is a combination of psychology, control and technology.

With respect to psychology, the approach is grounded on the principle that people are the most important control factor. They can make a poor system work well; and they may cause a good system to fail. This approach to CSA uses the practitioners as experts to help the auditor.

With respect to control, the control model which is used is derived from the criteria of the Control Committee of the Canadian Institute of Chartered Accountants (CoCo).[1,2] It has four components:

- Purpose – knowing what to do
- Commitment – wanting to do it

- Capability – being able to do it
- Learning – to do it better

The technology aids the participating practitioners to identify the strength and weaknesses of their systems and operations as well as any action which is required to correct the deficiencies. It allows them to vote anonymously on a series of questions posed by the auditor and displays the results immediately in graphical format.

## THE BUSINESS OPERATION TO BE 'AUDITED'

The Inland Revenue's internal auditors chose a major customer of theirs, and one with which they had good relations, on which to trial the technique. They needed to think very carefully along with the customer about their choice of locations which would be used for the trials, and in particular the operation to be reviewed using this technique. They chose one which was fundamental to the business: 'the assessment of personal tax'. They conducted CSA workshops in seven Tax Districts which were equally responsible for this work and each workshop included the Officer-in-Charge as well as a vertical cross-section of members within the team of staff who dealt with this type of work. They used anonymous voting technology and and software for each workshop as well as for a rather similar workshop with the Regional Headquarters' team who were responsible overall for the quality control of this work.

## OBJECTIVES

These objectives were set for the trial:

- to evaluate the facilitation technique;
- to achieve savings in audit time;
- to improve the final product;
- to add value to the customer, and
- to identify a wider application of the technique.

## THE WORKSHOPS AND TRIALS

The workshops consisted of about 10 to 12 people who were a mixture of those staff involved in the particular operation which had been selected. The Officer-in-Charge was included and also often the lower grade members within the office. Two facilitators managed the workshops supported by the external consultants and there were observers present. These observers were both senior management of Internal Audit and staff from the regional headquarters. The observers were present to assess the approach itself and its wider application.

The workshops commenced with an introduction to control, and to the control model. The importance of people in systems and operations was endorsed. The participants were introduced to the anonymous voting technology and used it to identify the current major problems in their working environment as well as their team's strengths and weaknesses.

For each component of the control model, questions were asked and the facilitators obtained votes which were obtained anonymously through the OptionFinder technology and displayed immediately in graphic format. Discussion identified the concerns, strengths and action required, and this information was all captured.

At the conclusion of a workshop participants were allowed to give their views of the technique and within 24 hours the auditors produced a report back to the staff who had participated, summarising the results of the workshop. These reports reproduced the graphs, the strengths and concerns which had been identified and the agreed action to be taken. Initial response from the participants was very positive.

The graphs for all the workshops were summarised into a comprehensive report for the Regional Controller. They showed a marked correlation across all of the eight workshops.

Presentations of the findings were made to senior Internal Audit management, to the Regional Controller and to the Officers-in-Charge as a regional senior management team.

## THE CORPORATE GOVERNANCE PROGRAMME

CSA and the Canadian control model were found to have worked successfully on a major operational system, and to have satisfied one customer group. Internal audit considered they needed another trial to confirm these positive reactions. This time a major business 'unit' was selected to review corporate governance. Corporate governance was defined as:

> The management of management. It is concerned with the roles, responsibilities and accountability of top managers as individuals and collectively as members of management boards.

A workshop was staged for the Senior Management Team of this major business unit, again using the CoCo control model and the CSA technique. Again there was a very positive response.

## THE 1996–97 AUDIT PLAN

When this was drawn up it contained the following programme of reviews using CSA:

- the Departmental Senior Management Board; and
- the Senior Management Teams of 12 business units.

The meaning of control and corporate governance, and the CSA technique, were explained to senior management and board members through a series of papers and presentations. A control self-appraisal workshop was held on the Senior Management Board in 1996 and the programme of reviews on the Senior Management Teams of the 12 business units were completed. The results of the reviews of the Senior Management Teams of the 12 business units were used to support the interim findings from the review on the corporate framework of control of the Senior Management Board.

## RISKS

There appear to be a number of risks:

- Workshops are conducted in a spirit of trust: no documentary evidence is produced to support the strengths and weaknesses which are identified. As such this is not in line with traditional, professional auditing standards and the requirements to gather evidence from which auditors can provide an opinion.
- The use of the technology considerably enhances the workshops and the presentation of the findings; but if the technology fails then credibility can suffer.
- The facilitators can make or break the success of the discussion. Equally the participants may not wish to talk.

## CONCLUSION

CoCo as a control model works well. Coupled with CSA it concentrates on people, the most important factor of control. The concept and importance of control is now acknowledged at the highest levels of the Inland Revenue Department, and is seen as an integral part of achieving business excellence. Our results to date show a very good framework of control of the top levels of the organisation. This has reassured management and stakeholders. Aligning the control model with CSA has been beneficial to participants and auditors. And it has been fun!

## NOTES

1 'Guidance on Internal Control', Control and Governance – Number 1 (Toronto: The Canadian Institute of Chartered Accountants, November 1995), 32 pps. These four components are given elsewhere in this issue in the article entitled 'CoCo's sample assessment questions'.

2 'Guidance for Directors – Governance Processes for Control', Control and Governance – Number 2 (Toronto: The Canadian Institute of Chartered Accountants, December 1995), 18 pps.

# Further Sources of Information

## Books

*Business Risk Management* (Chapman and Hall) Bob Ritchie and David Marshall 1993.

More of a textbook – some useful information and theories but more geared to the business school user than a practical guide.

*Business Risk Management* – Technical Focus Number 10 (January 1997) ICAEW 0171 920 8486.

The most comprehensive introduction to corporate risk management.

*CoCo Report – Guidance on Control* (The Canadian Institute of Chartered Accountants) ISBN 0-88800-436-1. November 1995

An alternative control framework usually considered more accessible and useful for assessment than the COSO framework.

*Committee on Corporate Governance: Final Report* (Hampel Report) (Gee) ISBN 1-86089-034-2. January 1998.
*Committee on Corporate Governance – The Combined Code* (Gee) ISBN 1-86089-036-9. June 1998.

Recommendations on corporate governance for companies quoted on the London Stock Exchange

*Complete Guide to Business Risk Management* Sadgrove, K. Gower (1996) ISBN 0-566-07551-2.

An introduction to the identification and management of the range of financial and non-financial risks that all organisations face.

*Control Model Implementation: Best Practices* Roth, J., IIA-USA (1997) ISBN 0-89413-390-X.

Case studies on procedures for the practical implementation of the COSO framework.

*Control Self Assessment and Internal Audit* (IIA-UK) Professional Briefing Note 7 1995. Replaced by Professional Briefing Note 14: *Control and Risk Self Assessment* 1999.

CSA is designed as a useful supplement to independent assessments performed through conventional internal audit activity.

*Control Self-Assessment: Making the Choice* (IIA-USA) Glenda S. Jordan ISBN 0-89413-337-3 June 1995.

Anecdotal first-hand experience from internal auditors (mainly in the USA) who have found CSA to be an effective management tool.

*Control Self-Assessment: Workshop Facilitators Guide* (IIA-USA) ISBN 0-89413-391-8 August 1997.

The World Bank's guide to workshop facilitation

*Controls Assurance Project* – NHS Executive November 1996.

An introduction to the Controls Assurance Project aimed at introducing public reporting of the effectiveness of the control systems in NHS Trusts.

*CSA Experience, Current Thinking & Best Practice* (IIA-USA) Richard P. Tritter and Daniel S. Zittnan ISBN 0-89413-370-5 1996.

Research on the adoption, implementation and continuous improvement in CSA in a variety of organisations mainly in the USA, but also in the UK.

*Facilitated Self-Assessment* (Management Control Concepts) David & Fran McNamee December 1995.

Six methods of CSA are described.

*The Financial Aspects of Corporate Governance* (The Cadbury Report) (Gee) ISBN 0-85258-915-8 December 1992.

The classical report on corporate governance in UK companies quoted on the London Stock Exchange.

*Internal Control and Financial Reporting – Guidance for Directors* (ICAEW) December 1994.

Guidance for the implementation of the Cadbury Report recommendation for directors to report on the effectiveness of the internal control system for their company.

*Internal Control-Integrated Framework (The COSO Report)* (Committee of Sponsoring Organisations of the Treasury Commission) September 1992.

The classical control framework. Difficult to apply, but provides a suitable framework for reporting on internal control. Adopted and adapted by several organisations in the UK for reporting on internal control e.g., Stock Exchange Listing Requirements, NHS Executive.

*Managing Business Risk – an integrated approach* Economist Intelligence Unit ISBN 0-85058-850-2 (1995).

A major study into the corporate risk management strategies of major international companies.

*Managing Risk* (IIA-UK) 1998.

Introduction to a risk-oriented approach to management; its implications for internal audit and how such an approach can be applied within internal audit.

*Risk: Analysis, Perception and Management* (The Royal Society) 1992

Report of a Royal Society Study Group.

*Risk Management for Registered Social Landlords*; detailed guidance and executive summary. Housing Corporation 0171 393 2228. (1997).

Guidance developed for the introduction of risk management to housing association.

## Magazine Articles

'A Question of Ownership' Robert Outram *Internal Auditing*, November 1997.

'Auditing, assurance & CSA' Bruce McCuaig *Internal Auditor*, June 1998

'COSO-Based Auditing' Mark R. Simmon *Internal Auditor*, December 1997.

'Managing Risk Down Under' David McNamee *Internal Auditing*, April 1998.

'Risk–Based Auditing' David McNamee *Internal Auditor*, August 1997.

'Using CSA to Implement COSO' Kyleen W. Hawkins and Bill Huckaby *Internal Auditor*, June 1998.

'Control Self Assessment' *Internal Auditing*, February 1999.

## Miscellaneous

Further information on CSA is available from the big five accountancy bodies and other consultants, for example:

Oxley Fitzpatrick & Associates Ltd, The Wic, Glapthorne Road, Oundle, Peterborough PE8 4JQ. Tel: 01832 274350 Fax: 01832 274846.

CATS International, 105 Chevening Road, Chipstead, Sevenoaks, Kent TN13 2SA. Tel: 01732 451223 Fax: 01732 741482.

Information on computer applications for CSA is available from:

Option Technologies Ltd, Toad Hall, Odiham Road, Winchfield, Hook, Hampshire RG27 8BU. Tel: 01252 844720 Fax: 01252 844051.

Ventana (UK) Ltd, 16 Copperfields, Beaconsfield, Bucks HP9 2NS. Tel: 01494 680650 Fax: 01494 677840 Web Site: www.ventana.co.uk

**Internet Site:** http.//www.open.org/soc/csalinks.htm
This is designed to support people who want to learn more about CSA and to interact with other internal audit professionals who are implementing CSA. There are links to other CSA resources on the Internet and current CSA events and publications.

**UK CSA User Group**, c/o IIA-UK, 13 Abbeville Mews, 88 Clapham Park Road, London SW4 7BX. Tel: 0171 498 0101 Fax: 0171 978 2492 e-mail: iia@easynet.co.uk

# Index